THE PSYCHOLO

THE PSYCHOLOGY OF HUMAN MOVEMENT

EDITED BY

Mary M. Smyth

Department of Psychology
University of Lancaster
Lancaster, England

Alan M. Wing

Medical Research Council
Applied Psychology Unit
Cambridge, England

ACADEMIC PRESS

Harcourt Brace Jovanovich, Publishers

London San Diego New York Berkeley
Boston Sydney Tokyo Toronto

ACADEMIC PRESS LIMITED
24-28 Oval Road,
London NW1 7DX

Second printing 1989

United States Edition published by
ACADEMIC PRESS, INC.
San Diego, CA 92101

British Library Cataloguing in Publication Data

Main entry under title:

The psychology of human movement.

Bibliography: p.
Includes index.
1. Movement, Psychology of. 2. Perceptual-motor
processes. 3. Perceptual-motor learning. I. Smyth,
Mary. II. Wing, Allan
BF295.M675   1984   152.3   84-14561
ISBN 0–12–653020–3
ISBN 0–12–653022–X (pbk.)

Printed in Great Britain by
T. J. Press (Padstow) Ltd, Padstow, Cornwall.

Contents

Chapter 5 Perception and Action
Mary M. Smyth

Chapter 6 The Sequencing of Movements
Gerard van Galen and Alan M. Wing

Chapter 7 Doing Two Things at Once: Process Limitations and Interactions
Herbert Heuer and Alan M. Wing

Chapter 8 The Acquisition of Skill
Peter Johnson

Chapter 9 **The Development of Movement Control**
Laurette Hay

Chapter 10 **Disorders of Movement**
Alan M. Wing

Afterword

Contributors

Kerry Greer, Department of Psychology, University College London, London WC1E 6BT, England

Laurette Hay, Institut de Neurophysiologie et de Psychophysiologie, Centre National de la Recherche Scientifique, 13277 Marseille Cedex 9, France

Herbert Heuer, Abteilung fur Experimentelle und Angewandte Psychologie, Universitat Bielefeld, 4800 Bielefeld 1, Federal Republic of Germany

Peter Johnson, Ergonomics Unit, University College London, London WC1H OAP, England

Martin Sheridan, Department of Psychology, University of Hull, Hull HU6 7RX, England

Mary M. Smyth, Department of Psychology, University of Lancaster, Lancaster LA1 4YF, England

Gerard van Galen, Psychologisch Laboratorium, Katholieke Universiteit, 6500 HE Nijmegen, The Netherlands

Alan M. Wing, Medical Research Council, Applied Psychology Unit, Cambridge CB2 2EF, England

Foreword

A few years ago a well-known investigator in the area of motor learning visited the University of Oregon, and in the course of his lecture he lamented on the decline of research in motor learning. After some thought, I decided that he was partly right but also partly wrong. The part about which he was wrong was more important. True, little current research concerned how to practice—for instance, whether spaced practice was better then massed practice, or whether knowledge of results affected learning speed. However, it was not true that less research was being conducted on motor control. What had happened was that over the years the focus of research had shifted from an emphasis on procedures of learning to one describing the processes that underlie motor control. This was all part of a larger revolution in psychology from a dominance of behaviorism to information processing. While behaviorism is concerned only with the end product, skilled behavior, information processing is concerned with describing the processes involved in achieving that skill.

While the well-known researcher was partly correct in that less research was being conducted on motor learning than in the past, he was largely wrong in that the new approach has great relevance for learning. The best way to promote improvement in motor performance is to understand in a fundamental way the underlying processes of motor skill. From such knowledge emerges ideas on how to improve performance. Such knowledge suggests not only improvements in training technique but also ways to change the task itself (which is a major aspect of the field of ergonomics) and better ways to select more appropriate people for some tasks. Thus, the information-processing approach to skill provided a unifying theme for the applied fields of learning, ergonomics, and personnel selection. The approach may ultimately yield other applications, as in the diagnosis and treatment of neurological disorders.

There are many textbooks on motor learning, but most of those fail to reflect satisfactorily this information-processing approach. Only a few textbooks accurately reflect a modern approach to understanding motor skill that puts primary emphasis on the processes of movement and action. Smyth and Wing's book is a welcome addition to the few suitable texts for instructing undergraduates or beginning graduate students in motor control, and it will be an excellent text for students of psychology and of physical education at both levels of training. The book does an admirable job in teaching not only basic concepts but also in giving a dynamic view of research in the motor area.

Another notable change in the motor area over the years concerns its increasingly interdisciplinary character. A student who is seriously interested in motor control must learn much about the physiology of the motor system, neurological disorders of movement (e.g., those occurring with Parkinson's disease or cerebellar damage), and the course of motor control development from infancy to adulthood. Although we appreciate the need for an interdisciplinary approach, it is difficult for one person to be really proficient with such diverse areas. A strength of this book is that it draws on experts in each of the necessary sub-disciplines, and yet by use of the information-processing theme it keeps the chapters well integrated. The chapter authors are all expert in one area while familiar enough with others to provide effective integration. Kerry Greer writes on the physiology of motor control, and Laurette Hay on motor development. Alan Wing, whose specialty is the psychology of motor control, has also worked with neuropsychological patients and hence is an excellent person to write about neurological disorders. The other chapter authors—Smyth, Sheridan, van Galen, Heuer, and Johnson—are all specialists in the areas about which they write.

I have always felt that on the whole the best teachers are those who have a first-hand effort in the research enterprise. It is doubly useful when the research of such teachers is at the leading edge of the discipline. Such teachers are up to date and best express the enthusiasm for their field. The editors of this book, Mary Smyth and Alan Wing, are active researchers at the forefront of the field. Their work has been important for basic conceptions of motor control. The other chapter authors are also active researchers in their specialties. The result is a progressive text on movement, action and skill, a book modern in its concepts and incisive in its focus.

Steven W. Keele
Department of Psychology
University of Oregon

Preface

This book is an introduction to the study of human goal-directed movement. It provides a comprehensive survey of experimental work that crosses several disciplines, including psychology, kinesiology, physical education, and neurophysiology. In the main, the framework for the many and varied research findings covered in this book comes from psychology and brings to the fore the information processing that underlies purposive movement. The approach taken emphasises the higher-order, organizational processes that contribute to coordinated goal-directed movement. However, the need to take account of constraints on voluntary movement arising in the movement apparatus of muscles and joints is not forgotten.

The book is written for undergraduate students who may have little or no prior knowledge of studying movement and, therefore, care is devoted to the definition of specialised terms. In this respect, the provision of a glossary should also help the reader. Liberal use is made of figures, as a good pictorial representation of the subject matter can greatly help the student assimilate new material. Although primarily intended for undergraduate students, particularly those studying psychology and motor behaviour, some of the material included would provide a good starting point for more advanced, graduate seminars on human movement. To this end, there is a thorough bibliography.

The book may be viewed in two parts. The first part, comprising Chapters 2 to 7, develops major theoretical ideas within motor neurophysiology, voluntary control of simple aiming movements, memory for movement, perception and action, sequencing of movements, and the demands made by movement on information-processing resources. The subject matter has important interrelations with topics in areas such as psychology, neurophysiology, and kinesiology. Chapters 8, 9 and 10 in the second part treat changes that can occur in the organisation and execution of movement through training, in development, or as a result of damage to the central nervous system. This reflects our conviction that any approach to movement, action and skill should draw on a wide range of sources of data and not be confined to a narrow empirical base founded in studies of 'normal' adult subjects. While the student in psychology or kinesiology will appreciate this broadened perspective, it also makes this book very relevant to the needs of students in physical education and the therapy professions.

Due to the co-authored nature of this book, assistance and advice in its production has come from sources too numerous to list in full. We particularly appreciate the detailed comments received from Karl Newell on an earlier version of the complete manuscript. For their opinions on individual chapters we are grateful to Franco Denes, Andrew Ellis, Jonathan Grudin, Philip Levy, David Margolin. We thank Alan Copeman and Derek Simmons for their photographic assistance and Marge Eldridge for typing the references. Chapters 4 and 5 were prepared while the author was supported by grant No HR6780/2 from the SSRC.

THE PSYCHOLOGY OF HUMAN MOVEMENT

1

Movement, Action and Skill

Mary M. Smyth
Alan M. Wing

INTRODUCTION

People move. Indeed, all animals move, and it is movement that allows them to respond adaptively to the environment. We often ignore the basic movements that an animal or a person makes because we are interested in the effect that the movements have on the environment, particularly in relation to intentions that movements help fulfil. This means that we are often more concerned with the actions we perform than with the actual movements of which they are composed. It does not matter whether we use the right hand or the left hand to drink a glass of water when thirsty, and we could describe many different movements as "drinking a glass of water" because that description relates to the action being performed, not to the particular groups of muscles that are performing it. Nevertheless, if we want to understand people as effective operators on the world in which they live, then we have to consider not only the decision about the action that they have taken, but the way in which they implement such decisions and produce particular sets of movements.

1

DESCRIBING AND UNDERSTANDING MOVEMENT

If we are going to understand movement, the first thing we have to do is to describe it. This may seem simple, but the ordinary observer who reports that someone drank a glass of water is not actually describing the movement, only the end result. To understand how people reach for things, pick them up, and use them, we need to describe many aspects of the movement, such as where it begins, its speed, where and when the speed changes, the way in which the hand is shaped to grasp, and where the grasp begins. This description would take us to the point at which the object is contacted, then force has to be exerted to lift it, the lift may be smooth or jerky, and it may be watched continuously or checked occasionally. A description of an arm movement may have to include eye movements and movements of the whole body when balance is altered. Our description will obviously be affected by what we think is important about studying movement, and it will probably leave out some things that we consider to be unimportant. Even the most complex descriptions of human movement cannot deal with all the available detail, and what is selected will relate to the purpose for which the movements are being described.

For most everyday purposes we want to know what someone did, not exactly how they did it. However, if the movements were part of a dance and we wanted someone who had not seen the dance to be able to repeat it then we would need a very detailed description. An anthropologist who is trying to understand the role of ritual dance in a particular culture may need to record movements very accurately and to compare them on more than one occasion. A choreographer who wishes to make a permanent score so that others who have not seen a dance can reproduce it, may also wish to record each movement in detail. The difficulties experienced in devising systems for notating movement illustrate the complexity of movement itself.

The main difficulty in devising a written notation for dance is that there are so many simultaneous positions of the body parts to be recorded as well as many possible movements through space linking the positions (Knust, 1979). Two of the best known of the modern systems for recording dance are *Labanotation,* first devised by Rudolf Laban, and *Benesh notation.* Both of these systems use a set of parallel time lines (a staff) to record units of movement in the sequence in which they occur. Labanotation uses a staff with three vertical lines, the centre line representing the centre of the body. Parts of the columns created by the lines represent the means used for support (usually steps), leg gestures that do not carry weight, the body (chest, pelvic girdle, and torso), the arms, the hands, and the head. So, the staff is organised to provide information about which part of the body moves.

In Labanotation many other components of movement are recognised, including the direction and the level at which the movement takes place. An example of the notation can be found in Figure 1. The position on the staff indicates the part that moves and time increases from the bottom of the staff to the top, so that movements written side by side occur at the same time. There are extra markings for step length, for contact with the floor, for relative positions of the feet, for the degree to which the arm or the leg is bent, and for all the major joints of the body, so that the score quickly becomes extremely complex.

Benesh notation is less detailed than Labanotation and can be used more easily to describe dance as it takes place. The path of the movement is traced between salient positions so that intermediate positions are shown only when they are changed in order to eliminate redundancy (Benesh & Benesh, 1977). Another system of notation, the *Eshkol–Wachman system*, is similar to Benesh notation in that it records initial and final position and the trajectory between them (Eshkol & Wachman, 1958). Unlike the Benesh system however, Eshkol–Wachman notation describes different kinds of trajectory that may occur between the initial and final position. This system has been used in describing movement in several experimental studies (e.g., Golani, Wolgin, & Teitelbaum, 1979).

The difficulties experienced by choreographers and dancers in developing a notation for movement, and the complexities of the systems that have evolved make it clear that it is not easy to describe the movements of the human body. Yet, even the complex and detailed descriptions provided by these notation systems do not capture the full variety and complexity of human movement control. The score for a dance, like the score for playing a piece of music, is a framework that a performer elaborates, not a complete transcription of the event itself.

Of course, the development of video recording and the use of film have made it possible to produce a record of movement that can be seen again and again, and which can be slowed down to allow details to be picked up. The film is not itself a description of movement but it does allow a more accurate description to be produced. Early film of people and animals walking and running allowed the actual events that took place in locomotion to be made clear for the first time. Muybridge (1899) showed that, contrary to popular belief, all four feet of a trotting horse leave the ground (or at least do not support weight) at some stages in a stride (see Figure 2). Muybridge was very critical of the artistic represen-

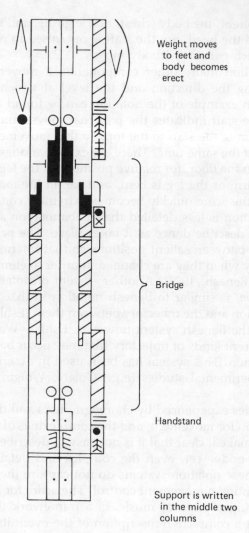

Weight moves
to feet and
body becomes
erect

Bridge

Handstand

Support is written
in the middle two
columns

Figure 1. An example of Labanotation. This is the notation for a walkover, in which there is first a change from standing upright into a handstand (the central columns indicate weight is taken by the hands), then there is a change into a bridge, the feet are placed together on the floor and weight is shifted to the feet as the body lifts to return to an upright position. From *A dictionary of Kinetography Laban (Labanotation)*, by Knust, A. (1979). Plymouth, England, MacDonald and Evans. Reprinted with permission.

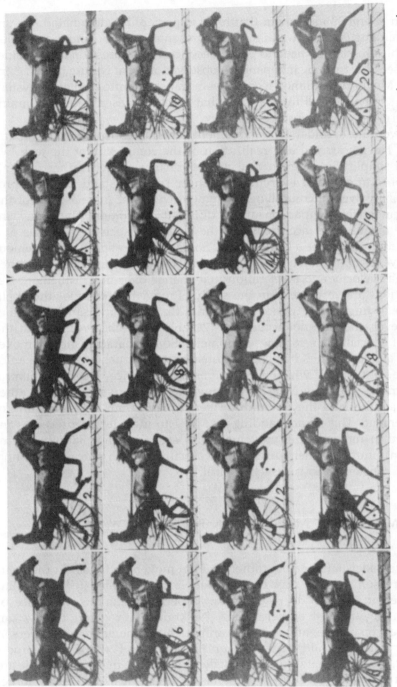

Figure 2. Muybridge's photographic sequence of a horse trotting, printed in 1879. A complete cycle taking .44 seconds encompassed 18 frames.

tation of animal movement that has "imperceptibly dominated our understanding (so that) we think the representation to be unimpeachable" and he stressed the need to put "preconceived impression on one side, and seek the truth by independent observation from Nature herself." (p. 164). Muybridge's filmed records were translated into a notation system with symbols for all four feet, so that he could describe the locomotor patterns as well as observe them.

If we want to understand movement, a good description is only a first step. Having arrived at a realization of the complexity of the task, we often simplify in order to deal with particular aspects rather than attempt to understand everything at once. To understand the basic processes involved in controlling movement we select some aspects of the movement for comparison under different conditions. These may include overall time, accuracy, and the elements, such as the angle of a joint, that change as a body moves. Some of these aspects of movement involve the provision of *kinematic information,* which describes quantities such as velocity and acceleration that change over time. Kinematic descriptions are very useful in the study of movement because they help us to distinguish between movements that have the same outcome. However, they are not accurately available to an observer without the aid of specialised recording equipment. Some characteristics of movement are determined by physical considerations, such as the mechanics of the joint around which the movement takes place. These mechanical constraints may determine why a movement appears in one form rather than another and they should not be ignored in our understanding of movement. This understanding also has to include the processes involved in remembering movements, in selecting and planning them, and in controlling them during their execution. Such processes are normally considered to be psychological.

MOVEMENT AND SKILL IN PSYCHOLOGY

Psychologists have not studied human movement much in the past. One reason for this may be that people have tended to become interested in, and to do research on, aspects of human experience of which they themselves were aware. We know that we read, that we can tell tea from coffee, and that we can remember the name of the person who taught our undergraduate course in statistics. Perhaps more importantly, we know that we make mistakes in reading, that some people are poor readers, that we can confuse tastes, and that we can easily forget the names of people whom we know quite well. These failings readily suggest topics for research. However, in everyday activities, most of the movements that we make do not lead to obvious errors. We reach for and grasp objects, catch projectiles, and walk from place to place without apparent error so that we tend not to be aware of the elements of which our actions are comprised. For many people, however, there are situations in which they do make movement errors. These usually occur in the context of skill. We know that another person can make smooth efficient movements that we cannot match, and it is in the effort to become skilled, to change our movements, that we meet with the experience of error. We make mistakes when we first try to drive a car, or to do a dance step or to type a page, so we become aware of the problems of controlling movement. If psychologists do tend to investigate areas in which they are aware of problems, areas in which they make errors, then it is not surprising that the work on movement that has been done in psychology in the past 100 years has tended to emphasize the learning of new movements and the errors that occur in such learning.

The everyday use of the word skill suggests that if we cannot remember learning to do something, and if everyone can do it, it is not skillful. Yet we can all pick up an egg without breaking it, a task that is very difficult for a robot, and we can reach for and pick up a glass and drink the contents without spilling any, something a young child finds very difficult. The very young baby cannot grasp an object and bring it to its mouth. The infant does not have the appropriate structures in its nervous system to allow it to organise muscles to carry out the intention to grasp. Some of the structures that allow this to occur have yet to mature, and some will depend on practice. The infant has to become a skilled perceiver and a skilled actor.

Perceptual-motor skill is the term most often used to describe the area covered by research in human performance in which movement is an important part. Perceptual-motor skill emphasizes the relationship between input from the environment and the selection and control of movement, and the name makes it clear that movement does not occur in isolation from perception. Such skill is quite different from that shown by experienced chess players who are clearly skilled but who do not make movements different from those made by inexperienced players. Both the skilled and unskilled player can show the same degree of perceptual-motor skill, but the difference lies in skill that is specific to chess. Bartlett (1958) felt that thinking could be considered a skill, and it is clearly a nonmotor skill of this sort that is the main component of expert chess playing. Generally accepted perceptual-motor skills, such as typing, driving, and learning a new sport have been studied by psychologists together with laboratory tasks that have some aspects of skilled tasks in industry. However, the main focus of interest is not on the skills themselves, but on nature of the changes in control and organisation that occur as skill is learned. While skill may be present in situations in which it is not normally recognised such as drinking a cup of tea, this does not mean that there is no difference between skill and movement. As movements are practised changes take place in the way in which they are organised, in the detection and use of relevant perceptual information, and in the efficiency with which the activity of the motor system is coordinated.

One possible starting point for a history of the study of skill is the work of Bryan and Harter (1897). They studied Morse code operators and the improvement in speed and accuracy that took place with training. They found that improvement did not occur gradually but that learners moved from being able to receive individual letters to whole words to small phrases. As learners become more proficient they move from lower to higher units in the hierarchy. The concept of hierarchy in skill is also appropriate for the understanding of many kinds of movement. Other American functionalists at the turn of the century also made observations or did experiments on perceptual motor skills. James (1890) described the difference between the automatic control of movement, such as normal walking, and the attentive control necessary when walking along a narrow beam. Issues raised by James about the automatic control of action are still important in current work on attention and simultaneous performance of more than one task.

Woodworth (1899) was perhaps the first psychologist to show an interest in movement itself, rather than in learning or attention. He described a two-phase unit of movement in which there was a preliminary fast phase, an initial impulse, and a second phase in which corrections were made. This may be observed if you hold your right hand out to one side and then quickly bring your right index finger to touch the tip of your nose. You may be aware of a slowing down or hesitancy just before your finger contacts your nose. Woodworth's description of movement has provided a starting point for a great deal of work on the processes involved in the control of simple movements aimed at targets.

During the behaviourist period in the United States movement and skill were studied relatively little. Psychologists were interested in how often a rat or a pigeon responded, not in the nature of the response itself. When the Second World War led to a renewed interest in human skill the prevailing emphasis on learning was reflected in the kind of research that was carried out. Studies were concerned with the number of practice trials required, the way in which practice was massed together or spaced over time, the amount of information about success or failure that was provided, and the different ways in which such information could be given (Bilodeau & Bilodeau, 1969). Experimenters tended to avoid theorising about the processes involved in making the movements underlying the skill. It was practice that was of interest rather than the nature of movement itself.

In Britain, the research that was motivated by the Second World War used a slightly different approach. In 1947, Craik described the human operator as an *intermittent servomechanism*. This description referred to the way in which people seem to allow error, that is, a discrepancy between the intended or required movement and actual movement, to build up to a measurable level before a correction is initiated to bring the movement back on course. This contrasts with the continuous regulation of error afforded by many physical control systems. The use of terms from information theory and from control theory became an important part of descriptions of skill. The study of various kinds of perceptual-motor skill in tracking moving targets allowed emphasis to be placed on changes in perceptual skill and on the control processes involved in being able to predict more of the track or to use preview of the track to plan movements in advance (Poulton, 1957).

The processes underlying skilled behaviour were divided into three major groups by Welford (1968). These were input processes concerned with understanding and interpretation of information from the environment, decision processes that related incoming perceptual information to possible actions, and output processes that controlled the movements themselves. Subsequent study of skill often emphasized the choice of responses, and researchers investigated factors such as the number of signal and response alternatives, the compatibility of the signal and response alternatives, and the repetition of particular signals or particular responses (Rabbitt, 1981). Such an approach is part of an information-processing psychology of decision and choice in which the analysis of the response goes as far as response selection (press this button with the right index finger), but ignores response execution.

The study of the processes involved in movement itself has become more important in the 1970s and 1980s, due in part to input from physical education and kinesiology that has enriched the psychologists' account. In 1971, Adams put forward an influential account of motor learning and control that dealt with movement per se. He suggested that there were two states of memory, a memory trace and a perceptual trace. The *memory trace* is a stored set of instructions to the muscles capable of initiating a movement (a motor program) and the *perceptual trace* is a stored representation of the perceptual information fed back from the movement as it is made. The subject uses this perceptual trace to correct error in slow movements while they are being made. This theory, which was intended only to apply to slow linear-positioning tasks, is not currently accepted as a full account of how movement is learned, remembered, and controlled. However, it resulted in a large number of studies on simple aimed movements in which the processes involved in making the movement were of central importance.

MOVEMENT, ACTION
AND INFORMATION PROCESSING

An information processing account of movement views people as adaptive systems that pick up and process information from the world and respond appropriately to it. Such a view allows us to ask questions about action that arise from the short history of studies of skilled movement we have just outlined. These questions stimulate the research that is reported in later chapters of this book. The main emphasis is not on information processing at the level of perception or choice, although these are clearly relevant to many of the issues raised. Our approach is to investigate the processes involved in the acquisition, generation, storage, selection, correction, and control of movements in goal-directed actions.

Action differs from movement in some of the same ways that perception differs from sensation. When we describe ourselves and our movements we say "I picked up the pencil", not "I moved my hand through this trajectory", or "I contracted these muscles in this order". That is, when we think of action, defined in terms of a goal, we do not think of the particular movements by which it is mediated. The use of the term *action* implies a higher-level description of what we do. Some interesting questions in the study of action derive from the difference between the description of what was done and the understanding of how it was done. In order to explain how people act we have to consider the relationships between different executions of the same act and to understand how one set of environmental circumstances causes an act to be performed using one movement, while a different set of circumstances leads to a different movement being made to carry out the same act. This concern with the relationship between action and movement leads to some interesting issues that must be addressed by any theory of movement control. The issues relate to the equivalence of movements, their consistency over different situations, and their ability to be modified and adapted to fit new situations.

The first issue is that of the *constancy of action* or *motor equivalence*. We can repeat the same action, such as picking up a pencil, making a tennis stroke, or writing a signature, but the movements will not start in the same place, finish in the same place, or go through the same path, and the muscle groups involved may be different each time. We can write our names on a piece of paper or write them on the blackboard. In the first case the movement will be chiefly from the fingers and the wrist while in the second case the whole forearm is moved by the elbow and shoulder. The signatures will be recognizably the same, but the same actions clearly involve different movements. It is, of course, possible to try to use exactly the same movement, to write the signature in exactly the same way, or to make exactly the same tennis stroke. In spite of this, there is always variation even when someone attempts to make exactly the same movement, that is, there is a second issue relating to the *uniqueness* of movement. Variation may reflect the fact that the state of readiness in the muscles is different before action begins and the demands of the environment may be different too. Each tennis volley will be different from every other tennis volley, because each will be produced from a different initial configuration of the body and will require different adjustments to deal with the input from the flight of the approaching ball. Constancy and uniqueness are two aspects of the same phenomenon—the amazing flexibility and variety shown in the movements that people produce.

Although different muscle groups, and indeed limbs, can be used to produce the same action, and no two repetitions of the same movement will be exactly the same, there are remarkable consistencies in the way in which a skilled act, like writing one's name, is performed. That is, the spatial and temporal structure of an action as it is produced remain consistent on different occasions. If two people write the word "movement" on two separate occasions, each person will produce a pattern of marks on paper due to a pattern of forces exerted over time that is individual and consistent; this raises the question of the central representation of action. In handwriting, as in any activity that we call skilled, the most obvious feature is not variation, but consistency and stability (see Figure 3). Consistency of action has to be offset, somewhat paradoxically, by its *modifiability*, which is the final issue in the relationship between action and movement. Changes in information from the environment can lead to adjustments so that optimal performance is obtained in different circumstances.

These issues in the control of movement are clearly interrelated. They lead us to consider the way in which we use perceptual information in selecting and controlling movements, to investigate the nature of the

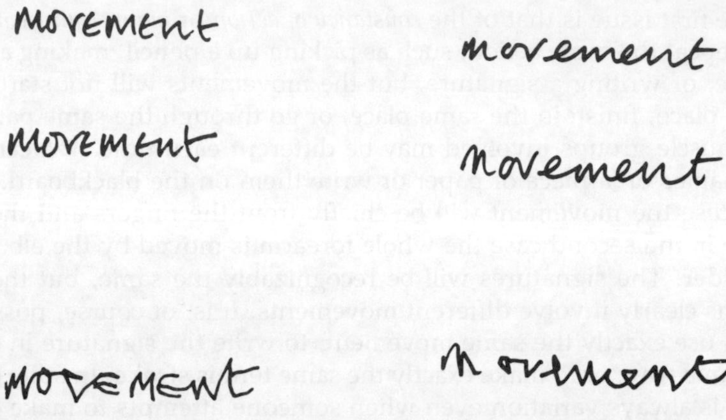

MOVEMENT   movement

MOVEMENT   movement

MOVEMENT   movement

Figure 3. Motor consistency and constancy. The writing on the left is by MS and on the right by AW. The first two lines were written with the dominant right hand, the third line with the left hand. The first two lines show consistency of style within individuals, both in the forms of the individual letters and in the way the letters are joined. Even though there is a deterioration in line quality with left-handed writing, style is preserved, that is, constancy is demonstrated.

central code for movement which can be expressed in so many different ways, to look closely at the time course of individual movements and the way in which different parameters such as acceleration are varied or maintained over repeated trials, and to think of the ways in which the different levels of a system of action and movements could be organized. These areas of investigation make up much of the content of the chapters that follow.

THE REST OF THIS BOOK

To provide a structural basis for developing argument and discussion on the nature of movement control we have to consider the basic physiology of the motor system of the body. This is not a suggestion that all questions about action and movement will eventually be solved at the physiological level, but rather it emphasizes the continuity in understanding that will have to be achieved. Ultimately, any action is expressed by activity of the nervous system. Some classes of explanation relate to organization at a higher level in a hierarchy of control, but the units that are controlled at the lowest level presumably have some effects on the kind of control that can be exerted, and these units must involve the contraction of muscle. Chapter 2 describes the current state of knowledge of the physiology of the motor system, emphasizing the many levels at which control is organised.

In Chapter 3, issues related to equivalence and consistency are viewed in the context of the control of simple movements, many of which are made to a target. Starting from a consideration of the simple task of drinking a cup of tea, the account returns to the work of Woodworth (1899) to introduce the distinction between ballistic and controlled movements and the relationship between time and accuracy in making movements. Two sources of control for movement are discussed. One is central and reflects advance planning and programming and the other is peripheral, related to the sensory consequences of the movement that are fed back as it is made. The notion of *motor programming* leads to a discussion of how a programmed movement is actually organized— what sort of instructions are sent to muscle?—while that of *feedback* leads to a discussion of how corrections are used to make accurate aiming movements, the nature of the sensory input on which they are based and the type of corrections that can actually be made. The chapter concludes with an account of central representations for movement, called *schemas*, which deal with many aspects of equivalence, consistency, and modifiability.

Chapter 4 is concerned with memory for movement. Much of the work that followed from Adams' (1971) paper on learning and memory has dealt with questions of how movements are represented using short-term memory for simple linear movements of the hand from one position to another, or for movements through a particular distance. Memory for movement is different if the person moving is in full control of the movement or if there is some degree of guidance. This implies that in remembering movement, the sensory consequences of our movements, the instructions that produced the movement, and also the plan of action that we were attempting to carry out are all important. Memory is an active rather than a passive process and even in remembering simple movements people are able to generate strategies that enable them to code movement information accurately.

Movement occurs against a background of incoming information from the environment in which it takes place. In Chapter 5 the nature of the perceptual information that is used in the planning and control of action is considered. This perceptual information is obtained via the eyes, ears, the skin, and even the nose, and it can be used to tell us about objects and events in the world, about our spatial relationship to these, and even about our own movements. Information coming back from the body and limbs, which also tells us about the course of our movements, has traditionally been called *proprioception*, and some of the issues dealt with in this chapter are concerned with the relationship between pro-prioception, vision, and other sensory systems. Vision plays an ex-tremely important part in the control of movement, probably more so than we normally realize. It allows for advance planning in response to environmental events, and allows for the monitoring of both the move-ment itself and of its consequences in relation to the environment. The chapter also deals with some of the questions that arise in considering perceptual processing and perceptual learning and concludes by return-ing to the schema concept but, this time, applies it to perception.

Many "real-world" skills, such as handwriting or playing a musical instrument, contain a complex sequence of elements that could appear in any order but which have to be produced in particular orders for the intention to be carried out. A sequence at the level of musical notes has to be transformed into a sequence of finger movements if the pianist is to play, and the finger movements have to be in the appropriate order if the pianist is to play correctly. Programming is clearly an important concept in dealing with organization and Chapter 6 considers different levels of programming, using as evidence details of timing within se-quences and the nature of errors.

When we move, we do so in order to carry out an action, and it is possible to try to carry out more than one action at a time. If we seem to exert little conscious control over one action, if it is automatic, it may seem relatively easy to do another at the same time. Questions about the nature of attention, of automaticity, and of the processes involved in the simultaneous execution of more than one task, have been of interest to psychologists since before the time of James. Our ability to do more than one task at the same time is limited. This is taken up in Chapter 7, where the interactions between particular movements, such as simultaneous movements of both arms and legs, are also considered. Interference may occur at different levels in a hierarchy of movement control and some of the problems in the area relate to the difficulty of deciding what it means to be doing more than one thing at a time. There are many situations in which two movements may be integrated into a single unit of action, rather than performed separately and simultaneously.

When we combine movements together to produce new sequences we may be learning a new skill. One of the most common elements in the learning of new skills is the restructuring and reorganization of movements that can already be made. The acquisition of skill is no longer an easy topic to write about. When number, type, and distribu-tion of practice trials were the main focus of research interest it was possible to give advice to teachers and trainers on how skill learning should be structured. We are still trying to understand the processes involved in learning and the nature of the changes that take place in organization and control of action. In Chapter 8 the issues involved in this area are presented. If we can understand the changes that take place with practice, the development of hierarchies of control and the development of schemas that are consistent and stable, yet modifiable, then advice should follow from the understanding. The changes in approaches to skill learning that have taken place in the last 15 years are leading us towards this understanding and we hope that the reader will be able to apply the results of many of the areas of research presented in other chapters to the real-world problem of developing skill in a task.

As we said earlier, even simple movements can be skilled because they depend on learning and practice that occurs in childhood. In Chapter 9, we go back to the beginning of movement in the young child and consider the differences between reflexive and voluntary movements and the relationship between these. Concepts that have been developed in earlier chapters on reaching to a target are applied to the control of reach and grasp as it develops from infancy to the teenage years.

Chapter 10 takes the processes that earlier chapters have shown to be involved in the control of movement and action and looks at how disorder of the central nervous system affects them. There are two purposes for such a chapter. One is to attempt to understand the nature of the disorders themselves, and the other is to try to extend our knowledge of normal processing by considering what happens when the system is disrupted. Damage to the brain can lead to problems with intentions and plans as well as with execution and control. The more we know about the processes involved in normal movement the more likely we are to be able to understand disorders.

Movement, action, and skill are parts of the overall cognitive functioning of the human being. This is why we feel it is worthwhile to produce this book. Representations of knowledge have to be transferred into action and to do this we have to use other kinds of knowledge, which must also be represented. This means that cognition needs action and that action itself is part of cognition. We hope that our treatment of some of the issues involved in movement, action and skill will help to elucidate some of these relationships.

2

Physiology of Motor Control

Kerry Greer

INTRODUCTION

The majority of our movements are the result of an extremely complex interaction between orders to the musculature to move and preceding, concomitant, and predicted sensory information from the external world and our bodies. The complexity of even a simple movement serves to make the repertoire of human skills more impressive. Apart from the range of motor activities one of the most striking aspects of human behavior is its sheer flexibility. We are able to use very different effector systems to achieve the same end result. Thus, we can write using our hands, our feet, and even our mouths to hold the pencil. We can adapt a coordinated sequence of movement to fit a variety of environmental demands, some of which impose quite different constraints on our musculature e.g., walking in a Force-10 gale as opposed to a summer breeze. We can alter spatiotemporal aspects of some skills seemingly at will (e.g., dancing the waltz to different tempos).

The neural mechanisms underlying such diversity and flexibility have attracted much investigation over the past century and we now know that the functional unit fundamental to all our motor behaviour is a cell, the neuron. Neurons differ from other cells in the body in that they can

THE PSYCHOLOGY OF HUMAN MOVEMENT

communicate with each other, via electrical signals, sometimes over great distances. It is the properties of neurons, and the way in which they communicate with each other that underly any movement, be it a simple reflex such as the knee jerk, or a detailed voluntary motor skill.

BUILDING BLOCKS OF THE NERVOUS SYSTEM

Neurons

Although neurons vary considerably in size and shape (it has been estimated that there are at least 1000 types), most conform to the schematised structure shown in Figure 1. Each neuron consists of a cell body that gives rise to two processes: an *axon* that transmits signals to other neurons or specialised cells such as muscle fibres, and a *dendritic tree* that

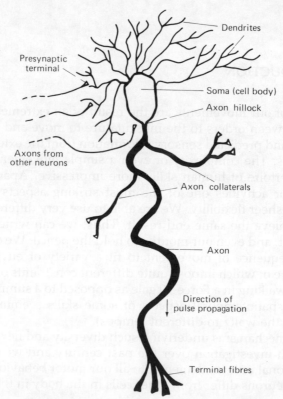

Figure 1.   The schematic structure of a neuron.

receives incoming signals. Nerve cells exert two types of influence on each other, both of which are achieved as a result of changes in the electrical voltages of the cells receiving the signals. A neuron is said to exert an *excitatory influence* if it causes increased activity in other cells and an *inhibitory influence* if it causes decreased activity.

A single neuron can influence the activity of up to 1000 nerve cells and can itself be influenced by anything in the region of 1000 to 10,000 inputs, some of which will be excitatory and some inhibitory. A process of integration takes place within the neuron such that its own output reflects the more dominant influence. Axons carry along their length discrete electrical signals, in the form of pulses, that are produced at the part of the neuron called the axon hillock. A pulse is triggered on the axon as a function of the spatial and temporal distribution of pulses impinging on the cell body and its dendritic tree. The further away from the axon hillock, the less weight or influence a given input signal has. This is called spatial weighting. Temporal weighting is a function of primacy. The earlier a signal occurs relative to other signals the more weight it has. Thus, the neuron arrives at a voltage sum taken over all its inputs. If this sum is greater than its threshold voltage, then the axon hillock triggers a pulse, in which case the cell is said to fire. If the sum is less than threshold, then the neuron does not fire. We see then that the output of a neuron is determined in a complex fashion. The neuron is much more than just a means of conducting electrical signals through the body.

The velocity of information transmission is of great importance. If an animal is to respond effectively to noxious stimuli in its environment, then sensory information about the stimuli and resultant orders to the musculature must be conducted along the nerves with the minimum of delay. There are two independent means in the CNS for increasing transmission velocity along the nerves. One depends on the size of the axon. Axons of larger diameter conduct the signal more rapidly. The other method involves partial insulation of the axon with a fatty substance called myelin, punctuated at regularly spaced points known as nodes of Ranvier.

Synapses

The term *synapse* was coined by Sherrington (1906) to refer to those sites within the nervous system at which information is passed from one cell to another. At a synapse, neuronal extrusions come close together but do not make contact physically. Axons split towards their endpoints to form many terminal branches called presynaptic terminals. These terminals are in close proximity with the receptive surfaces of other postsynaptic cells. The intercellular gap between the presynaptic and postsynaptic cells is called the *synaptic junction*. Electrical activity in the presynaptic cell is transmitted across synapses either by direct spread of current (*electrical transmission*), or, more commonly, via the action of a chemical mediator (*chemical transmission*).

Electrical transmission can only occur if the synaptic junction is extremely small, of the order of a few nanometers. Most synaptic junctions are of the order of several angstroms, which precludes direct electrical transmission. At these synapses, activity in the presynaptic cell liberates a specific chemical transmitter that diffuses across the intercellular gap and influences the excitability of the postsynaptic cell membrane. Several chemicals have been identified as neurotransmitters. An example of a neurotransmitter, important to motor function, is acetylocholine (ACh). Dale, Feldberg and Vogt (1936) established that ACh was released when the motor nerves innervating skeletal muscles were stimulated. This discovery became more exciting when it was found that ACh, if injected into the arteries supplying muscles, caused the fibres to contract. In other words, ACh was the link mediating between the electrical activity in nerves and the contraction of muscle. At these neuromuscular synapses the transmitter substance is always ACh, and its effect on the postsynaptic muscle membrane is always excitatory. However, at synapses within the central nervous system (CNS) the situation is more complex.

Dale and his colleagues originally proposed that because a given neuron releases the same chemical transmitter at all of its synapses, whether the effect is excitatory or inhibitory, its effect it will be the same throughout. However, as Eccles (1957) demonstrated, this is not the case and the effect of a given transmitter on a postsynaptic cell may be excitatory or inhibitory or, in some cases, both. Apparently, it is the interaction of the chemical transmitter and the receptor that determines whether a synapse will be excitatory or inhibitory. So, for example, in the case of ACh release at synapses within the brain, the effect of this substance is to excite some synapses and inhibit others. The effects of the transmitter are not a function of the chemical per se, but of its interaction with the receptor cells. Furthermore, postsynaptic cells can be receptive to more than one transmitter agent.

Skeletal Muscle

A single skeletal muscle is largely composed of bundles of elongated cells known as *extrafusal fibres*, joined together by connective tissue.

Neurons innervating muscle are called *motoneurons*. In general, several muscle fibres are innervated by a given motoneuron. A presynaptic impulse in the motoneuron causes local depolarization postsynaptically on each of the muscle fibres it innervates. A voltage spike then propagates along each fibre allowing a flow of calcium ions into the fibres. These ions activate a special protein structure that results in a twitchlike contraction. A single motoneuron impulse arriving at a given muscle fibre will result in a single twitch. The duration of the twitch, that is, the time taken for a complete cycle of contraction and relaxation, is of the order of half of one second but depends on the type of muscle. If a series of motoneuron action potentials occur sufficiently close together, the muscle-fibre twitches fuse into a sustained contraction known as tetanus.

It is usual to categorise skeletal muscle fibres into two types: fast and slow. *Fast fibres* are characterised by short relaxation and contraction times. They fatigue easily and tend to be pale in colour. *Slow fibres* are red, resistant to fatigue, and have longer contraction and relaxation times. Most muscles contain unequal proportions of slow and fast fibres, such that one type predominates. Thus, for example, the leg extensor muscles contain a majority of red fibres and are ideal for postural maintenance, which requires sustained background contraction (*tonic activity*) without fatiguing. Changes in limb position movements tend to be produced by bursts of activity (*phasic activity*) in the more rapidly acting, fast muscles. The properties of the pale muscle fibres are more suited to these movements.

There are two modes of muscle contraction, isometric and isotonic. The prefix iso means equal; metric and tonic refer to muscle length and tension, respectively. In *isometric contraction*, the fibres build up tension, but do not actually shorten. Most postural muscle activity is isometric. For example, in standing the muscles of the trunk and legs act against the forces of gravity in such a way that the isometric tensions developed are equal and opposite. If, however, these muscles are to produce movement, then *isotonic contraction* is required. In this case the muscle tension must be greater than the opposing forces, enabling the muscle to shorten. In fact, all isotonic contraction incorporates an isometric phase; shortening can only occur if the muscle tension is greater than the resisting force. The muscle first develops isometric tension equal to the load it is to lift; when the tension equals the load, then the muscle starts to shorten. As tension exceeds the load, then more-rapid movement takes place. Thus, isometric contraction causes muscle to develop force without a change in muscle length so no apparent movement results. Conversely, isotonic contraction results in muscle length changes or movement. This terminology, that is, of loads and forces, might seem a bit strange, but all organisms are constantly operating against loads both external such as gravity or weights, and internal such as the load of the muscles themselves. Furthermore, these loads are usually variable and we later describe how spinal reflexes are able to compensate automatically for load fluctuations.

SPINAL MECHANISMS

The question of how neurons control muscular movement is best answered by looking at a simple neuron network, such as the neural circuits that connect each muscle with the spinal cord. Sherrington (1906) called these spinal circuits the final common path because it is through these paths that the CNS actually controls the muscles. The movements we make, no matter how complex, are the result of CNS commands causing muscles to contract. An individual muscle exerts an

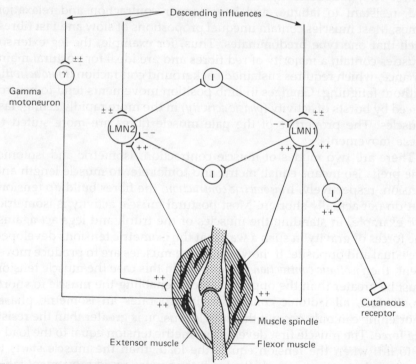

Figure 2. Schematic representation of the neural circuitry underlying spinal reflexes. The direction of information flow in the neurons is from the circle toward the bifurcation. The type of influence on the postsynaptic membrane may be excitatory (+ +) or inhibitory (− −).

unidirectional force. The jointed limb system of vertebrates compensates for the limitations inherent in only being able to exert unidirectional force by arranging muscles in opposing pairs. When a pair of muscles oppose in action they are said to be *antagonistic*. If a group of muscles act to stabilise a joint, their action is said to be *synergistic*. A schematic diagram of a typical joint with its associated neural circuitry is outlined in Figure 2. One muscle acts by contraction to open the joint and is called an *extensor*; the other muscle acts to close the joint (again by contraction) and is called the *flexor*.

Alpha Motoneurons

The muscle pair illustrated in Figure 2 is linked by a network of neurons with cell bodies in the spinal cord. The convention followed in the figure is that the cell body and dendrites are represented by a circle and the axon is represented by the long Y. The direction of information flow is thus from the circle toward the open arms of the Y. There are two kinds of motoneurons innervating the muscles, *alpha* and *gamma*. The principal neurons in the circuit are the large alpha motoneurons. Spinal motoneurons are commonly referred to as *lower motoneurons* or LMNs. The qualifier lower is to contrast these neurons with *upper motoneurons* connecting the cerebral motor cortex with the spinal cord. In Figure 2 flexor-muscle fibres are innervated by LMN1, and muscle fibres in the opposing extensor by LMN2. A network of interneurons (I) is shown between LMN1 and LMN2. These crossconnections result in inhibition of LMN2 if LMN1 is active so that the flexor action is not rendered ineffective by antagonistic activity in the extensor and vice versa. Such reciprocal inhibition is an important feature of spinal networks, operating automatically unless overridden by commands from higher centres.

Some LMNs innervate many fibres within a muscle, whereas others cause contraction in a single muscle fibre. A motoneuron plus the fibres that it innervates is called a *motor unit*. Fine control of muscle usually occurs when the motor unit is small (i.e., the motoneuron innervates a small number of muscle fibres). For example, the muscles of the fingers that subserve precise manipulative functions have small motor units with far fewer fibres than muscles of the shoulder that produce gross arm movements.

As stated earlier, muscle fibres vary in their contraction time. Pale muscle fibres contract very rapidly, whereas red muscle fibres have a relatively slow contraction time. In a complementary fashion motoneurons differ in their ability to start firing quickly, and it happens that

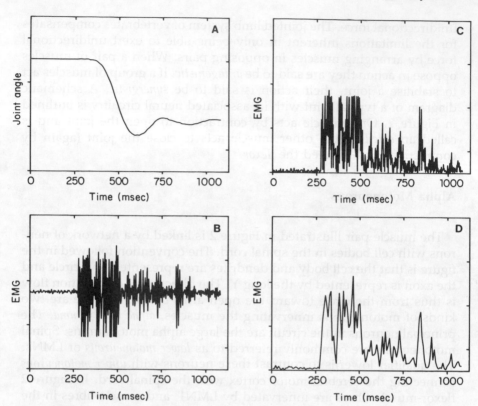

Figure 3. Electromyography (EMG). During elbow flexion, surface electrodes over the belly of the biceps pick up the high-frequency AC voltage pattern shown in (B) associated with the change in joint angle shown in (A). Rectification of the signal (C) followed by smoothing gives a clear picture of muscle electrical activity as seen in (D).

rapidly firing motoneurons usually innervate the pale muscle fibres. The properties of the motor units thus enable the CNS to grade the force developed by muscle. The CNS can do this in two ways. The first is by recruitment, that is, by selecting a suitable number of motor units; the larger the force required, the more units recruited. This process operates on a size principle, with neurons that have fibres of small diameters and lower thresholds firing before neurons with larger diameter fibres. The second method by which force can be graded is by adjusting the firing rate of the motoneurons; the greater the firing rate, the greater the force developed.

Recall that each muscle-fibre twitch results from a voltage spike sweeping over the surface of the fibre. If the force developed by a given muscle is to be increased, more voltage spikes will be generated over all the individual fibres and an appreciable voltage will be developed between the muscle and the surrounding tissue. Given suitable conducting electrodes and sufficient amplification, as the force developed by a muscle is varied voltage fluctuations may be observed at the skin over the body of the muscle, (see Figure 3). The technique of using electrical signals to observe the activity of a muscle is known as electromyography (EMG). In the present context there are three major points to note. The first is that EMG can be useful for deciding which muscles are active in a given movement. However, a surface electrode may pick up activity from more than one muscle because many muscles are in close proximity to each other. Thus, for this type of work it is normal to use fine wire electrodes inserted into the muscle. The second point is that surface electrodes are good for giving information about the relative timing of activity in muscles that are anatomically (and therefore electrically) well spaced. An example would be flexor and extensor muscles acting on opposite sides of a joint. The third point relates to a difficulty in the interpretation of EMG records. The EMG voltage level depends critically on electrode placement; absolute voltage levels should not be compared over different muscles. Even comparisons of absolute voltage levels over the same muscle on different occasions are suspect if the electrodes have to be reapplied.

Reflexes and Gamma Motoneurons

The simplest functional sequence involving the circuitry in Figure 2 is a spinal reflex in which sensory input from a cutaneous receptor is relayed via an interneuron to LMN1. The resulting activity in the flexor moves the limb. If this withdraws the limb from the source of stimulation, sensory input to LMN1 will be terminated and hence activity in the flexor will be arrested. Another example of a simple spinal reflex involves a receptor in the tendon of the muscle, the Golgi tendon organ. Suppose muscle contraction occurs as a result of activity in LMN1. If the load to be moved is so great that the tension developed in the muscle is likely to cause damage, the Golgi tendon organ provides an inhibitory signal to LMN1 through an interneuron.

We now consider the role of the gamma motoneurons that innervate special structures within the muscle called *spindles* that have both sensory and motor functions. The *monosynaptic stretch reflex* is a reflex that can provide automatic compensation for unexpected changes in the load acting on a muscle. Consider what happens when a load is placed on a person's outstretched arm. Holding the arm up against gravity requires a certain degree of activity in the alpha motoneurons that innervate the elbow flexors. If a weight is placed in the hand, the forearm will begin to move down; the load imposes a stretch on the flexor muscles. Spindles are responsive to this and increase their firing rate. The afferent fibres from the spindles synapse on the alpha motoneurons, and their firing rate increases in turn. This serves to increase the contraction of the main, extrafusal muscle fibres. (The time from the loading to the first detectable change in extrafusal activity is of the order of only 30 msec— spinal reflexes are very fast). As the extrafusal muscle fibres contract, the stretch on the muscle spindles is reduced causing a decrease in the rate of spindle afferent firing. This means that the alpha-motoneuron firing rate can drop back to its original level. This, then, is an example of a *negative-feedback loop* that tends to maintain the desired position of the arm.

The muscle spindles are sensory receptors for stretch, but they also have contractile properties. The spindle contractile fibres are referred to as *intrafusal* fibres to distinguish them from the prime contractile component of muscle, the extrafusal fibres innervated by the alpha motoneurons. Activity in the gamma motoneurons (see Figure 2) causes the muscle spindles to contract. This contraction of intrafusal muscle fibres increases the stretch on the sensory component of the spindle, thereby increasing the spindle-afferent firing rate. This will then stimulate the alpha motoneurons and the extrafusal muscle fibres will contract. The activity in the spindle afferents will maintain this contraction until the extrafusal contraction removes the stretch on the spindle.

The gamma motor system is thus capable of providing indirect control over muscle contraction. But why should movement be controlled in this fashion rather than directly via the alpha motoneurons? One explanation for the indirectness is that it allows the system to operate as a follow-up servomechanism (Marsden, Merton, & Morton, 1972). For muscle contraction to be controlled by the gamma route, the intended degree of muscle contraction must be signalled by the length of the intrafusal fibres. Should the muscle contract further than required, for example, because of an unexpected reduction in load on the muscle, then the spindles would become unloaded. This would depress spindle activity, and the extrafusal muscle fibres would stop contracting until the spindles began to fire again. Thus, the extrafusal fibre follows the degree of contraction of the intrafusal fibre.

The experiments cited by Marsden, Merton, and Morton (1976) in support of the follow-up servomechanism hypothesis involved EMG recordings. Figure 4 illustrates average data from two subjects both of whom were required to produce flexion movements (angular displace-

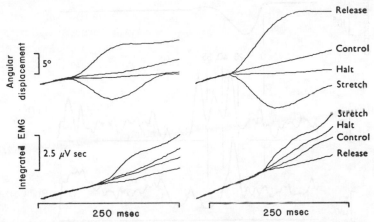

Figure 4. Perturbation of slow thumb movements. Angular position of the thumb (upper traces) and integrated EMG (lower traces) showing the response on halt, stretch, release, and control trials for two different subjects (left and right). Each trace is the average of 16 trials taken in random order. From "Servo action in the human thumb" by Marsden, C. D., Merton, P. A., Morton, H. B. (1976). *Journal of Physiology*, 257, 1–44. Reprinted with permission.

ments) of the thumb. The movements were made against a manipulandum which both registered angular displacement of the thumb and enabled the experimenter to introduce sudden changes in resistance to the subject's movement. On each trial the subject was required to flex the thumb at a relatively slow, constant rate. On a quarter of the trials the resistance to movement was abruptly reduced, and the thumb would briefly accelerate. However, the EMG records show that, at about 50 msec there was a compensatory decrease in muscle activity as compared to control trials on which there was no perturbation to movement. Two other conditions, one in which movement of the thumb was halted or even reversed, are also consistent with the theory. In both cases, changes may be seen in the EMG at about 50 msec. Under the proposed theory, these EMG changes are the result of the tension put on the spindles because of the discrepancy in length between the intrafusal fibres (providing a reference) and the extrafusal fibres (attempting to follow-up the reference).

We saw earlier that the monosynaptic stretch reflex is involved in changes of resistance or load. However, if a subject is asked to maintain a position against a constant load and a mechanical perturbation is then applied, careful study of the EMG records indicates there are several components to the resulting activity in the muscle. Figure 5 shows averaged responses to a fast, brief stretch of the long flexor of the thumb of each hand in a patient with proprioceptive losses in the right arm result-

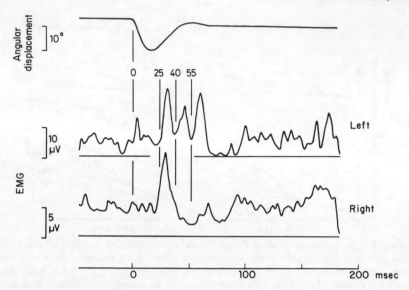

Figure 5. Response to a fast brief stretch of the long thumb flexor. The upper trace shows the angular displacement of the (left) thumb. The middle and lower traces are the rectified EMG records (averaged over 24 trials) for the left and right thumb respectively. No long-latency components of the response are seen for the right thumb. From "The effect of lesions of the central nervous system on long-latency stretch reflexes in the human thumb", by Marsden *et al.* (1978). In Desmedt, J. E. (Ed.), *Cerebral motor control in man: Long loop mechanisms. Progress in clinical neurophysiology,* Vol 4. Basel: Karger. Reprinted with permission.

ing from a brainstem stroke. The upper trace shows the angular position of the thumb. The middle trace shows the EMG record for the left thumb. Three components may be seen: M1, the monosynaptic spinal reflex, M2 with an onset latency of around 40 msec, and M3 with a latency of about 55 msec. M2 and M3 are affected by suprasegmental lesions (i.e., lesions at levels in the CNS above the final common path segment), as can be seen in the response to perturbation of the right thumb shown in the bottom trace. On the basis of these data Marsden, Merton, Morton, and Adam (1978) argued that M2 and M3 reflect reflex loops that take in pathways to and from the brain.

A major assumption of the follow-up servomechanism hypothesis is that the gamma motoneuron is activated prior to the alpha motoneuron, (see Figure 6a). Vallbo (1971) tested this assumption of the servo theory by inserting fine wire electrodes into his own peripheral nerves. He found that contraction of the muscle as shown by its electrical activity always preceded activity of the spindle afferent. According to the servo

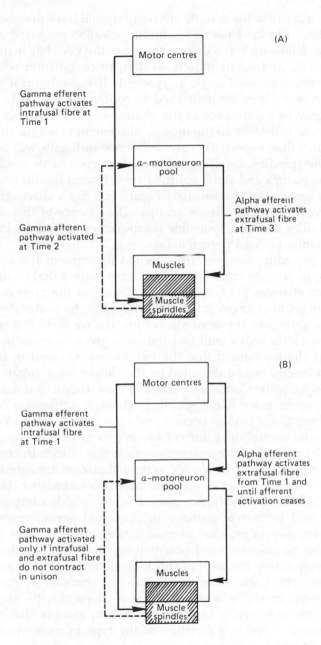

Figure 6. Operation of (A) the follow-up servomechanism and (B) the alpha–gamma coactivation theories of voluntary movement control.

hypothesis, activity in the spindle afferents should have preceded muscle contraction. On the basis of his findings Vallbo proposed an alternative to the follow-up servo theory. Suppose the CNS has instructed a certain LMN to contract its muscle so that, in conjunction with other muscles, a specified joint angle is reached. If the intrafusal and the extrafusal muscle fibres are instructed to contract to the same degree, there will only be a difference in the change of length achieved if, for example, some resistance to the muscle movement exists (or there was less resistance than expected). Any difference in length will be transduced by the spindles, resulting in corrective action. This mechanism, whereby the gamma and alpha neurons are activated simultaneously, is called *alpha–gamma coactivation,* (see Figure 6b). Such coactivation has been observed in several muscle groups. The essence of this theory is that the spindles are not responsible for movement initiation, but assist in compensating for load perturbations.

The two preceding theories are couched in terms of the control of muscle length. Nichols and Houk (1976) have argued that what is controlled is not changes in muscle length alone, but the ratio of muscle tension changes to changes in length. This ratio, termed *stiffness,* emphasizes the springlike characteristics of muscle; we think of a spring as stiff if it requires a heavy pull to produce a given increase in length. Nichols and Houk assumed that the two factors involved in stiffness, tension and length, can be signalled by the Golgi tendon organ and the spindles, respectively. Consistent with this view, they found that a muscle behaves much more like a spring of constant stiffness if feedback pathways from Golgi tendon organs and spindles are intact. What advantages would control of stiffness have over control of muscle length? Stiffness is a property or parameter of muscle that reflects the resistance offered to external disturbance. A system that can regulate stiffness would enable muscle to act as an adjustable shock absorber (Harvey & Greer, 1982). Mechanical shocks caused by the sudden imposition of load could lead to muscle damage or disrupted performance. If the spinal circuitry assists muscles in maintaining stiffness, then much of the shock can be absorbed and potential negative effects reduced in a manner appropriate to the level of shocks likely to be encountered in the environment. The issue over what muscle parameter is controlled, length, tension, or stiffness is yet to be resolved. In the absence of evidence to the contrary, it is probably wise to assume that the controlled property varies as a function of the type of movement (Stein, 1982).

So far, we have discussed the role of muscle spindles in terms of reflex compensatory mechanisms. But they are also capable of providing sensory information to the CNS about the movements of the muscles, and perhaps provide us with an awareness of the disposition of our limbs. The Golgi tendon organs providing information about muscle tension may also contribute to our perception of limb movement. There are also sensory receptors situated inside the joints. These joint receptors provide the CNS with information about pressure on the joint (Matthews, 1972) and some authors believe that they also provide information about joint angle and rate of change of joint angle (Skoglund, 1973).

SUPRASPINAL MECHANISMS

We have described the functioning of spinal networks primarily in terms of what happens at a particular level in the spinal cord. There are other networks operating at different levels of the spinal cord, consisting of divergent muscle groups linked together by spinal interneurons. Some of these networks underly quite complex motor behaviours, such as locomotion or scratching, so that these behaviours may be seen in animals with CNS lesions that leave them without any pathways for descending commands from the brain. We will return to these spinal behaviours in more detail later but first we consider motor centres in the brain and the way in which they are organised.

The brain is composed of an enormous number of neurons arranged together in a highly organised fashion. The neuron cell bodies clump together to form what are called *nucleii*. A major subdivision of the brain is into areas of *white matter* comprising myelinated axons and *grey matter* that is made up of cell bodies and unmyelinated axons. Where these nucleii are collected together in a convoluted sheet the term *cortex* is used. Cortex is found over the surfaces of the cerebellum and the cerebrum. Other areas of grey matter are seated deep in the brain (e.g., the basal ganglia and the thalamus). Axons of myelinated neurons (white matter) are often collected together in cablelike tracts. It is via these tracts that the various areas of grey matter in the brain communicate with each other and with the segmental circuits of the spinal cord. There are literally thousands of such nuclei within the brain but we only consider those involved in the motor systems. Figure 7 shows a cut-away diagram of the major brain components involved in the control of movement. Anatomically, the cerebral cortex is at the highest level and the spinal cord at the lowest level. Situated in between are a variety of motor structures including the cerebellum, the basal ganglia, and the thalamus. Early observations on the anatomical layout of the motor system originally led theorists to believe that its operation was of a simple linear

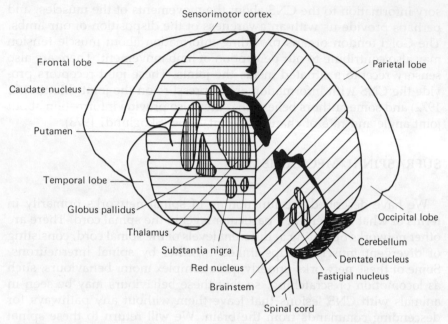

Figure 7. The brain with a 90-degree pie-shaped slice removed to show the anatomical arrangement of subcortical structures involved in motor control.

nature. Thus, it was believed that the motor system components formed a command chain with instructions simply relayed unaltered from the highest to the lowest levels.

Figure 8 is a simplified summary of current knowledge about the major efferent and afferent pathways between the motor components. The discovery of feedback (and feedforward) loops both within and between levels indicates the inadequacy of models based on a linear chain of command, or even of branching, hierarchical models. We show in the following sections that the motor-system components probably operate in a heterarchical fashion: each level can both influence and be influenced by other levels.

The Motor Cortex

There are two main pathways that originate in supraspinal sources to exert descending influence on the spinal circuits. One issues from the brainstem, the other arises directly from the cerebral motor cortex. The latter pathway, the *pyramidal tract* or *corticospinal pathway*, consists of

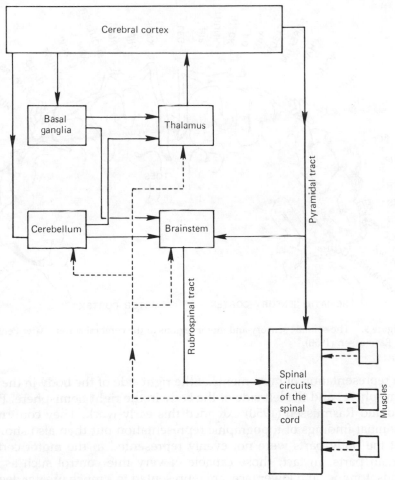

Figure 8. Schematic representation of the motor-system pathways. The arrows indicate the direction of information flow. Afferent input is shown with dashed lines.

over 1 million axons. The giant Betz or pyramidal cells of the motor cortex are the source of tens of thousands of these axons. The rest stem from neurons lying in the premotor and sensorimotor areas of the cortex.

The motor cortex is topographically organised. In other words, certain parts of the motor cortex are responsible for the movements of specific parts of the body. Fritsch and Hitzig (1870) established that electrical stimulation of the motor cortex of one cerebral hemisphere elicited movement on the opposite or contralateral side of the body. Thus, there

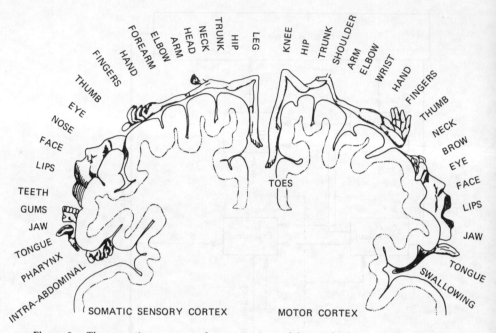

Figure 9.   The somatic sensory and motor regions of the cerebral cortex. After Penfield and Rasmussen (1950).

is a representation of movements of the right side of the body in the left hemisphere, and the left side of the body in the right hemisphere. Penfield and Rasmussen (1950) extended this early work. They confirmed the initial findings of topographic representation but then also showed that the body parts were not evenly represented in the motor cortex. Certain parts, in fact, those capable of very fine control such as the hands, tongue, and lower face, are represented to a much greater degree than the torso (see Figure 9).

Penfield used stimulation of the surface of the cortex to produce his topographic maps of the cortex. Asanuma and Sakata (1967) devised a new microstimulation technique whereby smaller and more controllable electrical stimuli could be delivered to different depths of the cortex. Using this technique, and also by recording from single cells within the motor cortex of experimental animals, Asanuma showed that motor cortex is organised into a set of columns running perpendicular to the surface. He called these columns *cortical efferent zones*. If a zone is stimulated near the surface it tends to elicit movements produced by a group of muscles, if it is stimulated at deeper levels these elicited contractions become more and more discrete, involving just one extensor or flexor muscle. Just as in the spinal circuits, where there is a topographical relationship between a given muscle and its sensory input, Asanuma found a corresponding relationship in the cortical efferent zone responsible for a given muscle. For example, neurons in the cortical efferent zone that controls finger flexion muscles receive peripheral input (afferent feedback) from sensory receptors in the skin and muscles stimulated by the movement.

Thus, a feedback loop appears to exist between the motor cortex and individual muscles, which could enable the system to make rapid adjustments in compensation to unexpected load changes. This loop may relate to the long-latency components of the response-to-movement perturbations observed by Marsden *et al.* (1972). Recently Marsden *et al.* (1978) made observations on the consequences of lesions to the sensory and motor cortex that resulted in weakness and loss of sensation in the contralateral arm. In general it was found that no long-latency responses could be elicited in the muscles of the thumb in the affected arm, though more or less normal responses were observed in the other arm, (see Figure 10). One patient was studied during the recovery period following removal of a small tumour. Motor function recovered before sensory function; in the response to perturbation a 55-msec component returned followed by a depressed earlier 40-msec component. These observations are consistent with the idea that the long-latency components reflect transit time for a loop that includes the cerebral cortex.

In our discussion of spinal mechanisms of motor control the controversy over which muscle parameter is regulated was mentioned. Is it muscle length, tension, or stiffness? The possibility exists of addressing a related issue by asking about the relation between activity at higher levels in the brain, perhaps at the motor cortex and the parameters of movement. This approach was taken by Evarts and Tanji (1976) using monkeys as subjects. They found that certain pyramidal neurons are active prior to movement, starting to fire approximately 20–50 msec before the onset of muscle contraction. The activity of some of these neurons was correlated with the direction of the intended movement. (The correlation is with intended movement because no movement is taking place). In other pyramidal neurons, the recorded activity reflected changes in the magnitude of force exerted over time. Other work on this topic led Humphrey (1972) to suggest that not only force, but its time derivatives (e.g., how quickly should the applied force be changed) are regulated. It is possible that the brain can select various movement parameters to control, according to the task requirement.

What is the relationship between activity of the pyramidal neurons in the motor cortex and the reflex mechanisms we have already described

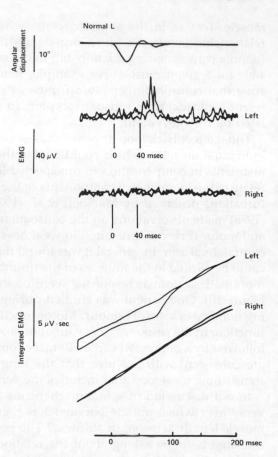

Figure 10. Responses to a fast brief stretch of the long thumb flexor in a patient who had had a small tumour excised from the hand area of the left sensorimotor cortex. The upper traces show the angular position of the thumb on stretch and control trials. The middle traces show the rectified EMG, the lower traces show the rectified and integrated EMG for control trials and perturbation trials superimposed. The data are averaged over 24 trials. On the right side there is no evidence of a long-latency response. From "The effect of lesions of the central nervous system on long-latency stretch reflexes: the human thumb", by Marsden *et al.* (1978). In Desmedt, J. E. (ed.): *Cerebral motor control in man: Long loop mechanisms. Progress in clinical neurophysiology,* Vol 4. Basel: Karger. Reprinted with permission.

as operating at the spinal level? Evarts and Tanjii (1976) trained monkeys to either push or pull a lever as a function of two visual instruction signals. One indicated the animal would be required to pull the lever whereas the other indicated a push would be required. On each trial, after one of the instruction signals had been presented, the response limb was physically jerked. This served as a command to begin the instructed movement. Evarts and Tanjii recorded from the pyramidal tract neurons of the contralateral motor cortex. They found the neuronal firing pattern was a function of both the visual instruction signal and the command to move provided by the jerk. Thus, for example, a pyramidal tract neuron that showed only a burst of responding to a signal calling for preparation of flexion, showed continuous rapid discharge following the signal that extension should be prepared. These discharges were also related to the intended movement. When the responding limb was jerked as a command to move, the pyramidal tract neurons showed two quite distinct patterns of discharge. There was an initial, short-latency burst reflecting spindle-afferent activity as a result of the applied muscle stretch. This did not change as a function of the instructed direction for movement. This supports the idea raised earlier that the motor cortex is involved in a long-latency reflex loop. About 50 msec later a discharge pattern occurred that was a function of the original visual instruction. It suggests there are neural mechanisms that can gate or switch on or off the pathways between the spinal cord and motor cortex.

The long, monosynaptic pathways of the pyramidal tracts are relatively easily seen in examination of the CNS. Thus, they were described by neuroanatomists long before the more complex, polysynaptic pathways involving the other major components of the motor system, the cerebellum, and the basal ganglia. The latter were given the rather dismissive term *extrapyramidal system* (i.e., other than pyramidal) and typically assigned a minor, supportive role. One of the problems for this view is that normal, voluntary movement has been seen to return in a patient who had a surgical lesion in one pyramidal tract (Bucy, Keplinger, & Siqueira, 1964). In the following two sections we first consider the cerebellum then turn to a discussion of the basal ganglia.

The Cerebellum

The cerebellum is tucked below the occipital lobes of the cerebral hemispheres. It lies behind the brainstem to which it is connected by three bundles of white matter, the *cerebellar peduncles*. There are two symmetrial halves separated at the midline by a strip called the *vermis*. The cerebellum consists of an outer cortex, internal white matter and, deep within, three pairs of nucleii called the *dentate*, the *interpositus*, and the *fastigial*. There are two broad classes of input to the cerebellum. Proprioceptive information is received (ipsilaterally) from receptors in the muscles and joints and from the vestibular apparatus, and there are projections from the cerebral cortex. The vestibular- and spinal-afferent information projects to the phylogenetically older flocculonodular and anterior lobes of the cerebellum. If there is cerebellar damage confined to these lobes, balance and gait are likely to be seriously affected, while individual voluntary movements of the extremities may be normal. This is observed in a condition known as late cortical cerebellar atrophy, which occurs mostly in chronic alcoholics (Mauritz, Dichgans, & Hufschmidt, 1979). The input to the posterior portion of the cerebellum (the neocerebellum), which comprises the predominant part of the cerebellar cortex in higher mammals, is exclusively from the cerebral cortex.

The major output of the cerebellum passes via the deep nuclei and projects primarily to bilateral structures called the red nuclei in the brainstem and to the ventrolateral nuclei of the thalami in the midbrain. The projections are to the contralateral red nucleus and thalamus. Although the cerebellum has no direct pathways to the spinal cord comparable to the pyramidal tract from the motor cortex, it can influence motor activity through connections between the thalamus and the motor cortex and through synapses with neurons whose axons run from the red nucleus to the spinal cord (the rubrospinal tract). It should be noted that, by virtue of the decussation (crossing over) of the corticospinal pathways, each cerebellar hemisphere has ipsilateral (same side) influence on the musculature.

The cerebellum has a very regular anatomical structure that has been the subject of intensive study with much speculation about its possible mode of operation (for a recent review see Llinas, 1981). The most precise behavioural data on the contribution of the cerebellum to movement control comes from research using monkeys by Thach (1978) and by Vilis and his colleagues (1977). Recordings taken from microelectrodes inserted into the dentate and interpositus nuclei showed activity beginning upto 85 msec before EMG changes accompanying wrist flexion or extension movements (Thach, 1978). In this study it was observed that dentate activity tended to precede activity in the interpositus and this may indicate the two nuclei serve different roles. Differentiation of function of these nuclei is also suggested by some other results. Thach (1978) found that if, prior to voluntary movement, the monkey is required to maintain arm position against loads of different values, the interpositus neurons are much more sensitive to change in load than neurons in the dentate. This suggests the interpositus may serve more of a postural function than the dentate. To explore the role of the dentate nucleus in movement initiation, Vilis, Hore, Meyer-Lohmann, and Brooks (1976) made reversible lesions using local cooling procedures. They trained their monkeys in a choice-task similar to that used by Evarts and Tanji and recorded the activity of pyramidal-tract neurons. Vilis *et al.* found that cooling the dentate depressed the intention-related component of the response occurring some 50 msec after perturbation. On the basis of these and other findings, Brooks (1979) concludes that the cerebellum is important in adapting intended movements to changing conditions. Through past experience, it permits smooth rapid movements to be made by setting up programs that anticipate, and thus render corrections to achieve a target unecessary.

In people clinical observations have shown that damage to the neo-cerebellum results in disorders of voluntary limb movements. The symptoms displayed by the patient will include disorders in the range, speed, and trajectory of aimed movements of the limbs, generally de-

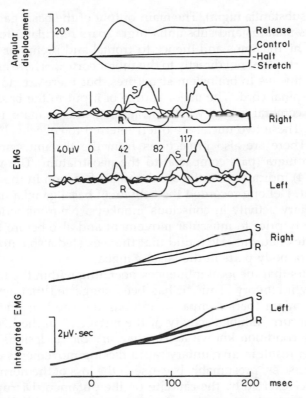

Figure 11. Responses to sustained stretch, halt, or release of the long thumb flexor in a patient with unilateral left ataxia. The upper trace shows the angular position of the (right) thumb. The middle pair of traces show the rectified EMG records; the integrated EMG is shown in the bottom pair of traces. The long-latency reponse of the left thumb is abnormal. From "The effect of lesions of the central nervous system on long-latency stretch reflexes: the human thumb", by Marsden *et al.* (1978). In Desmedt, J. E. (ed.): *Cerebral motor control in man: Long loop mechanisms. Progress in clinical neurophysiology,* Vol 4. Basel: Karger. Reprinted with permission.

scribed as *ataxia* (Holmes, 1922). Marsden *et al.* (1978) studied the effects of lesions of the cerebellum on the EMG response to unexpected perturbations to movements of the thumb. In patients with cerebellar ataxia affecting one side, they found the long-latency components delayed or reduced on that side, (see Figure 11). These findings with patients thus seem to parallel the experiments with monkeys.

The Basal Ganglia

The basal ganglia consist of a number of bilaterally symmetrical subcortical nuclei (caudate nucleus, putamen, subthalamic nucleus, globus pallidus, substantia nigra). The main output of the basal ganglia is from the globus pallidus and substantia nigra (pars reticulata) to the ventral nuclei of the thalamus and thence to frontal and premotor areas of the cerebral cortex (but not directly to the motor cortex). There are also some output pathways to brainstem structures, but there are no direct links with the spinal cord. The major source of input to the basal ganglia is from the cerebral cortex which projects to the caudate nucleus and putamen. These two nuclei are often referred to collectively as the *neostriatum*. There are also projections from the thalamus and from the substantia nigra (pars compacta) to the neostriatum. The work of De-Long (1974) indicates that the basal ganglia function in the initiation of movement. DeLong recorded the activity of basal ganglia neurons during voluntary activity in conscious monkeys. Neurons tended to alter their activity prior to muscular movement and also before the relevant motor cortex neurons. He found that there existed a somatotopic representation of body parts in the basal ganglia.

It appears that the local influences operating within the basal ganglia are largely inhibitory. Thus, it has been suggested that activity in the substantia nigra (pars compacta) inhibits the caudate nucleus whose activity, in turn, inhibits activity of the putamen. In the hereditary degenerative condition known as *Huntington's chorea*, lesions of the caudate nuclei result in involuntary rapid flicking movements of the limbs or facial muscles, presumably because of the loss of the normal inhibitory influence exerted by the caudate on the putamen. Disruption of the pathways projecting from the substantia nigra to the caudate nuclei can result in overinhibition by the caudate of the putamen as seen in the symptoms of slowness in the initiation of movement (*akinesia*) or execution of movement (*bradykinesia*) often associated with Parkinson's disease.

Parkinson's disease is a degenerative disease in which there is a deficiency in the amount of the neurotransmitter dopamine in pathways linking the substantia nigra (pars compacta) with the caudate nucleus. A common symptom is tremor of, for example, the hand when it is held motionless. The tremor usually disappears on the initiation of voluntary movement. This form of tremor is usually conceived of as due to release from an inhibitory effect that would normally have been provided by the substantia nigra. In some parkinsonian patients, a primary symptom is bradykinesia. Administration of the drug L-dopa, a metabolic precursor of dopamine, can provide some relief, albeit for only a few hours at a time. Drugs that potentiate dopamine action worsen chorea in, for example, Huntington's patients and this supports the hypothesised inhibitory links between substantia nigra, caudate, and putamen referred to above.

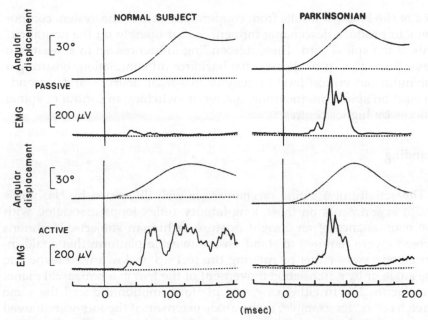

Figure 12. Averaged responses to sudden extensor displacements of the wrist in a parkinsonian patient and a normal control subject. The upper trace of each pair shows the position of the handle, the lower trace shows the rectified EMG from the wrist flexors. The upper pairs of traces show the response to passive wrist displacement, the lower pairs of traces were recorded from the subjects instructed to actively oppose passive displacement. From "Long loop reflexes in man: Clinical applications." In Desmedt, J. E. (Ed.), *Cerebral motor control in man: Long loop mechanism. Progress in clinical neurophysiology*, Vol 4. Basel: Karger. Reprinted with permission.

A third clinical symptom of Parkinson's disease can be an excessive resistance of muscles to passive stretch, known as *rigidity*. Lee and Tatton (1978) examined the response of parkinsonian patients to limb perturbation, (see Figure 12). They found that the monosynaptic reflex was normal whereas the long-latency components were elevated. This may underlie the patients' rigidity.

INTERACTIONS BETWEEN COMPONENTS OF THE MOTOR SYSTEM

This brief overview of the main motor-system structures and their connections has of necessity been superficial. Nevertheless, it should now be apparent that each component can interact with a number of other structures. Motor behavior therefore cannot be localised to one area of the brain, it results from cooperation among the system components to produce descending influences that operate on the neural circuits of the spinal cord. These descending influences act in at least two ways. First, they provide essential background stimulation, ensuring a minimum but critical level of activity in spinal neurons and, second, they act on spinal interneurons, gating or switching in control of spinal reflexes by higher centres.

Standing

The activity of a gating mechanism is well illustrated by Nashner's (1976) experiments on those long-latency reflex loops associated with the maintenance of an upright posture in human subjects. Nashner's subjects were required to stand on a moveable platform that could induce body sway either by rotating the feet up or down with respect to the ankle or by a translation movement of the feet in a horizontal plane, (see Figure 13). In either case, the platform motion induced the same stretch reflex, for example, in the ankle extensors if the toes were moved upward or if the translation moved the feet backwards. The clever part of this method is that the biomechanical consequences on body equilibrium are quite different and in one case the reflex in the ankle extensors is inappropriate. When the platform is shifted backwards, the stretch reflex in the calf muscles would tend to bring the body back to an

A   B

Figure 13. Platform movements inducing: (A) forward sway of the body, (B) pure ankle rotation. From "Adapting reflexes controlling the human posture", by Nashner, L. M. (1976), *Experimental Brain Research, 26,* 59–72. Reprinted with permission.

Figure 14. EMG records showing adaptive changes in response to forward sway (A) and ankle rotation (B) on four successive trials. From "Adapting reflexes controlling the human posture", by Nashner, L. M. (1976), *Experimental Brain Research, 26,* 59–72. Reprinted with permission.

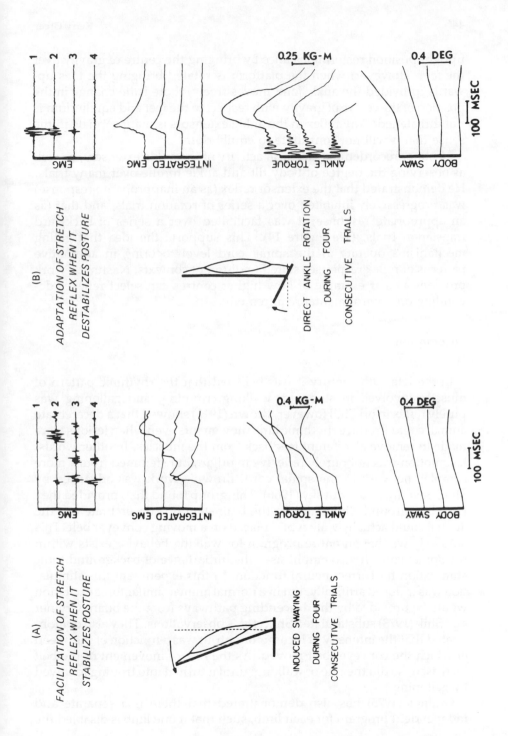

(A) FACILITATION OF STRETCH REFLEX WHEN IT STABILIZES POSTURE

INDUCED SWAYING DURING FOUR CONSECUTIVE TRIALS

EMG

INTEGRATED EMG

ANKLE TORQUE   0.4 KG-M

BODY SWAY   0.4 DEG

100 MSEC

1
2
3
4

(B) ADAPTATION OF STRETCH REFLEX WHEN IT DESTABILIZES POSTURE

DIRECT ANKLE ROTATION DURING FOUR CONSECUTIVE TRIALS

EMG

INTEGRATED EMG

ANKLE TORQUE   0.25 KG-M

BODY SWAY   0.4 DEG

100 MSEC

1
2
3
4

upright position restoring balance by bringing the centre of gravity over the feet. However, when the platform is rotated bringing the toes upwards, provided the ankle joint moves freely, there is no change in the position of the centre of gravity with respect to the feet and equilibrium is not threatened. Any reflex in the ankle extensors is inappropriate in the sense that it will not contribute to equilibrium.

Nashner recorded the electrical activity of the ankle extensors, as well as observing the degree of body tilt and ankle torque over many trials. He demonstrated that the extensor reflex (as an inappropriate response) was progressively inhibited over a series of rotation trials, and that (as an appropriate response) it was facilitated over a series of backward translation trials, (see Figure 14). This supports the idea that gating mechanisms operate at the spinal cord level to bring in alternative patterns of reflex responses suited to different contexts. Nashner's work provides a clear example of how higher centres can select reflexes depending on environmental requirements.

Locomotion

In the late 19th century it was believed that the rhythmic pattern of muscles involved in stepping, walking, running, and galloping was purely reflex in origin. However, Brown (1911) showed that a decerebrate animal could produce rhythmic limb movements even when lesions were made to remove all afferent feedback from the muscles. In other words, locomotion was not purely reflexive in origin, but stemmed from a more complex network in the spinal cord. Brown's work was advanced by Shik, Severin, and Orlovsky (1966). This group found that, provided they gave background stimulation to the brainstem of a decerebrate cat, the animal could actually walk when placed on a moving conveyer belt. This study shows that an entire program for walking behavior exists within the spinal cord. It also emphasises the importance of background tonic stimulation for correct neural function. In this experiment this stimulation was induced artifically, but in a normal animal similar tonic excitation would be provided by the descending pathways from the brain. Grillner and Shik (1973) substantiated Shik *et al.*'s observations. They also demonstrated that the intensity of locomotor output was a function of the speed at which the conveyer belt moved. As the rate of movement of the belt increased, so did the rate of walking, until it turned into trotting followed by galloping.

Grillner (1975) has also demonstrated that there is a separate and independent program for each limb, such that if one limb is disabled the others produce intact rhythmic motions. However, if all limbs are unimpaired, these programs couple or gate together such that the outcome of one influences the others. A single-step cycle in a normal walking movement consists of two stages: the *swing phase* in which the limb is swinging forward through the air, and a *stance phase* in which the foot is on the ground. At critical points of these stages, afferent input from the stretch receptors causes a switch to the other phase. Although these experiments demonstrated that the intricate spatial and temporal patterns of muscular contraction expressed in locomotion result from a spinal motor program, this does not mean that such behaviours cannot be modified by peripheral events. Visual, auditory, or integrated feedback can affect locomotive behaviour via the descending supraspinal influences we have discussed.

Arshavsky, Berkinblitt, Gel'fand, Orlovsky, and Fukson (1972a,b), recorded the activity of afferent neurons in the spinocerebellar tract during locomotion. They found that these neurons showed bursts of activity rather than continuous background firing during the movement. Broadly speaking, the tract can be divided into dorsal (afferent) cerebellar axons and ventral efferent axons. Arshavsky *et al.* cut both types of fibre and looked at the effect of this on the activity of the cerebellar neurons. The dorsal afferent spinocerebellar neurons ceased to show bursts of activity during locomotion. The ventral efferent spinocerebellar neurons, however, continued to show bursts of activity with the locomotor activity. Arshavsky's results are strongly supportive of the notion that efferent copies of motor commands are sent to the cerebellum, not just from supraspinal structures, but also from the spinal circuitry.

CONCLUSION

The overall picture emerging from physiological studies of motor control is as yet just a sketch. But the outline of that sketch is fairly clear. The motor systems of the brain and spinal cord can be envisaged as a series of interlocking feedback loops, ultimately converging on the lower motoneurons connecting each muscle with the spinal cord. At different levels of the system there are representations of what is going on at other levels. For example, the cerebellum, because of its connections with other motor-system structures, receives representations from several levels of the system. These representations need not be isomorphic copies of the output of other structures; they could reflect the potential output of the structures. The answer to the question of why this might be the case is that such a system would be capable of an enormous degree of flexibility. It would enable anticipation of the output of spinal circuits and allow movement patterns to be manipulated in an abstract form so that their suitability to environmental demands could be assessed prior to actual activity.

The level of explanation of motor control used in this chapter is different from the level used to deal with movement and action in the remainder of this book. However, there are similarities between some of the topics raised here and elsewhere, and some of the ideas presented here constrain our selection of psychological accounts of movement control. Physiology gives us some of the building blocks in the control of movement, such as the organisation of muscle about a joint and the parameters of muscle that might be controlled. Having a feel for these blocks, we are now in a position to select from them in order to generate plausible models of how movements are controlled. The next chapter treats the way in which movements aimed at clearly defined targets are planned and executed. Consideration of processes that occur prior to movement will turn our attention to reaction time, that is, the time taken to initiate voluntary movement. Discussion of factors affecting the speed and accuracy of execution of aimed movement will lead to further development of the topic of feedback.

One of the topics addressed in this chapter was the question of what property or parameter of movement is controlled by the brain. What does the brain represent about movement? A different way of dealing with this topic is taken up in Chapter 4 on memory for movement. In asking why certain types of movement are reproduced more accurately than others we will be led to consider the ability to manipulate movement information in an abstract form and the ways in which that information can be strategically controlled. The treatment of motor physiology in this chapter has also emphasised the idea that there are a number of different levels of control in the nervous system and that these have to exist in some kind of balance. Development of this balance as the organism matures and the types of disruption that can occur if the CNS is damaged are topics that make up the closing chapters of the book.

3

Planning and Controlling Simple Movements

Martin R. Sheridan

INTRODUCTION

In a sense, the use of the term *simple movements* in the title of this chapter belies the complexity of operation of the human motor system. Relative to more complex skills, such as driving a car, playing a game of tennis, or playing the piano, simple movements such as raising a cup of tea to one's lips or picking up a pen from a tabletop may appear straightforward perhaps even trivial. This illusion of simplicity is due in part to the apparent lack of attention devoted to the task. While moving a cup of tea to the lips is relatively easy for an adult to accomplish, this is not true for the young child. Clearly, learning has improved and stabilized performance. In line with many theories of skill acquisition, one consequence of motor learning is to move from conscious performance to more automatic control, thereby freeing information-processing capacity for other activities (see Chapter 8). The task thus seems, and indeed is, easier in the sense that it is less demanding of attention. For practiced tasks, until one experiences a certain amount of difficulty there is no need to attend to components of the task, and indeed, as James (1890) recognised, it can be positively disadvantageous to do so, leading to a deterioration in performance. In order to move a limb from one position to another,

Copyright © 1984 by Academic Press.
All rights of reproduction in any form reserved.
ISBN 0-12-653020-3 (hardbound)
0-12-653022-X (paperback)

however, the motor system still has to overcome some problems that are common, regardless of the extent to which control is automatic.

Bartlett (1932) illustrated the complexity of motor behaviour by reference to the high-level skill of a tennis player, but let us consider a much simpler example, that of holding a cup of tea at a particular position and then moving it towards one's lips. To achieve this one must be able to hold the cup at a particular location in space (the start position) and with a particular orientation (to avoid spilling the tea). It is then necessary to move the cup towards the target, in this case the mouth, in order to make contact.

The position of a static object can be described completely in terms of six dimensions of movement, the three Cartesian coordinates of its location in space, and the three angular coordinates of its orientation at that location. It is necessary to control these six dimensions to place an object, in this case the cup, in a particular position. To avoid spilling the tea it is clear that some degree of precision is required, particularly when one begins to move the cup. Within the arm there are three pivoted points about the wrist, elbow, and shoulder joints, if to simplify we ignore the flexibility of the hand and the ability to move the complete shoulder girdle. Including rotations about the wrist and shoulder the three joints provide us with a total of seven degrees of freedom of movement. This is one degree of freedom more than is necessary to control the position of our cup. Since each of the joint angles is continuously variable, there are an infinite number of ways in which we might accomplish the same final cup position. The different joints can be moved varying amounts to achieve the same end position of the hand. In two different movements bringing the hand to the same final position, the individual muscles of the arm could finish at different lengths with the joints at different angles. This can be illustrated more easily by considering movement between two points in a single plane limited to only two dimensions instead of the six in our cup example. This can be conceived of as moving the arm over the top of a table positioned at shoulder level. In this example, three degrees of freedom of movement are provided by the joints as compared with seven in an unconstrained situation. Figure 1 illustrates a few of the movement options in this more limited situation.

While we may not use all of the movement options open to us, we do use more than one. Indeed, the fact that we can achieve the same end result in a number of different ways, provides us with flexibility in dealing with the environment. If, in the example illustrated in Figure 1, our elbow was jammed against a wall, we could not make the movement using method C, but either A or B would suffice. It is clear that the patterns of innervation to the limb muscles must be different in the three

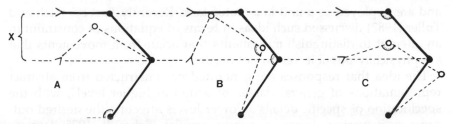

Figure 1. With three continuously variable joints there are an infinite number of ways of moving the hand a distance X towards the body. In (A) the elbow and wrist move anticlockwise, (B) the shoulder and wrist both move anticlockwise, (C) the shoulder moves clockwise and the elbow anticlockwise. Although the three movements are different in form, they start and finish at the same point.

movements illustrated in Figure 1. Thus, even an ostensibly simple movement taking the hand between two positions in space requires specification of the innervation patterns for many muscles and must be selected from a wide range of possibilities.

How then do we plan, construct, and execute the movements? Do we perhaps store in the brain the patterns of innervation for each of the vast array of possible movements? While this is possible, such a system would be highly inefficient in terms of storage and would create further difficulties related to accessing and retrieving the patterns from memory. The complete storage of all movement patterns is most unlikely, and it would seem desirable to postulate mechanisms that do not require this level of storage. More complete storage of movement patterns may occur in limited instances, for example, in repetitive or highly practiced situations. In general, however, it may be more efficient to use a generative process, whereby responses are constructed according to sets of rules or principles appropriate to particular classes of action. By storing a limited set of rules and tailoring the construction process to specific movement conditions (e.g., speed of movement, force against which we are moving, accuracy required, etc.) we can generate a vast array of movements. The concept of a generative process is one component of the schema theory of movement control that will be described later. The array of movements may, however, have constraints placed on the possible relations between movement at different joints, and hence limit the choice of movements generated. The concept of synergy was proposed in the last century by Ferrier (1886) and later elaborated by Bernstein (1967). It relates to the idea that motor coordination involves a reduction in the number of degrees of freedom of the sensory-motor system by functional groupings of muscles constrained to act as a single unit. Thus, *functional synergies* (coordinative structures) are collections of muscles that share a common pool of afferent and/or efferent information and are deployed as a unit in a motor task. Recently Turvey, Fitch and Tuller (1982) discussed such ideas in terms of equations of constraint in an attempt to distinguish movements that occur from movements that are physically possible yet do not occur.

The idea that responses are generated or constructed from abstract representations of general classes of action at higher levels, with the specification of specific details at lower levels affecting the desired outcome is, in various forms, currently popular (Schmidt, 1975; Turvey, 1977). If one views the motor system in hierarchical terms, then by implication our ability to perform simple actions necessarily underlies more complex behaviour. Studying simple movements can then be seen to have relevance to more global actions. Understanding simple movements can provide insight into the basic processes operating in a system capable of producing a wide variety of behavioural responses, and the view has even been advanced that, "If we are to build a science of skilled behaviour we should begin with simple motor movements . . ." (Adams, 1971, p. 113). The hierarchical view does not mean, however, that higher levels necessarily control lower levels. In attempting to understand executive ordering and plans for action, Lashley (1951) discussed the integration of levels and the transfer of control between them. The concept of transfer of control is important because, as Broadbent (1977) points out, it avoids a rigid view of levels and hierarchies. Rather than higher levels necessarily incorporating and controlling lower levels, it becomes necessary to understand the influence of one level on another, and to recognise that control can shift between levels. Control may even appear to reside at several levels of complexity simultaneously, with processes occurring in parallel at different levels. This has been termed by some as a *heterarchical view* (McCulloch, 1945).

CATEGORIES OF MOVEMENT

Simple movements of the arm to effect a change in hand position may have varying restraints placed upon their execution. They range from situations in which all movement dimensions are under the control of the subject, through moderately restricted situations, such as moving a slider along a predefined linear track, to completely constrained situations involving movement of a single joint in one plane, as in a movement about the elbow joint. Accuracy of the more unrestricted movements tends to be recorded in terms of distance from the target, while more restricted movements tend to be recorded in terms of degrees of rotation about the joint. Another important way of characterising simple movements is in terms of movement time (MT).

Probably the most fundamental conceptual distinction in the field of motor control is between ballistic and controlled movements. *Ballistic* movements are basically conceived of as fast movements which it is argued, do not allow the amendment of an internally-specified set of commands that will produce the required pattern of muscle activity (a *motor program*). The movement thus runs its course without correction, rather like the flight of a shell from a gun after it has left the barrel, or as in the downward movement of hammering a nail. The muscle commands are necessarily prepared in advance (*preprogrammed*), and speed of movement and final accuracy are a direct function of the initial motor program. Feedback information is not used during the current movement, although various sources of information may be used to amend the next response. If one has hit one's thumb the first time, some effort will be made not to do this a second time! *Controlled* movements, on the other hand, are performed at a slow or moderate speed, and allow the possibility of amendment during movement. This could be likened to a guided missile capable of correcting its flight path to home in on a target once it has been launched, or, for example, to a person using visual feedback to guide a key into a lock. In the latter case, the initial preprogrammed movement is unlikely to get the key into the lock, but it can be made to approach the target, if available feedback about the relative positions of key and lock are used.

Woodworth (1899) was one of the first to investigate this distinction between fast and slow movements. To the beat of a metronome his subjects, using a pencil, drew back and forth between mechanical stops or between ruled lines (acting as targets) on kymograph paper that moved past them. Woodworth could thus compare how accurately the hand could move to the targets at different speeds. In slower movements he distinguished two phases of movement, an initial impulse which he argued was programmed in advance, rather like ballistic movement, and a subsequent period of current control during which secondary adjustments were made to obtain the required degree of accuracy (i.e., guide the pencil onto the target). In a sense, therefore, slower movements can be seen to have both a ballistic and control phase. The period of current control was lengthened in relation to the degree of difficulty in attaining the target, and because current control slowed the movement, an inverse relation was observed between speed and accuracy. The greater the speed, the less the accuracy (see Figure 2), a relation that has been investigated and developed many times up to the present day.

Woodworth also observed, as may be seen in Figure 2, that the movement ". . . governed by the eye is much the most accurate at low speeds, and that the movements with eyes shut (are) less accurate than this . . . But though this is true at low speeds; it is less and less true as

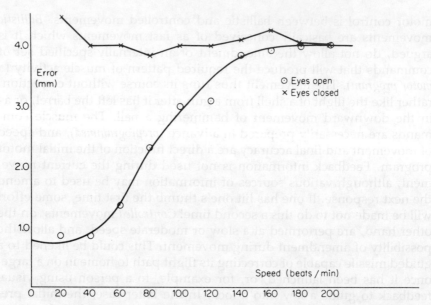

Figure 2. Woodworth's (1899) demonstration of the inverse relation between accuracy and speed. Subjects had to draw lines between two targets at a rate set by a metronome. From "Discrete movements", by Howarth, C. I., Beggs, W. D. A. (1981). In Holding, D. H., (Ed.), *Human skills*. New York: Wiley. Reprinted with permission.

speed is increased" (1899, p. 65). At fast rates (on the order of 140/min) the secondary adjustments disappeared, and the accuracy of the movements reflected simply the accuracy of the initial impulses. The disappearance of the period of current control suggested that insufficient time was available for feedback to be used to control movement in these fast responses. Vince (1949) determined that in the course of rapid movements there is a period of acceleration followed by an approximately similar period of deceleration. If the distance travelled is plotted against time, the curve resembles a normal ogive (S-shaped), with the first phase (half) of the movement and the second phase (half) of the movement being approximately equal (see Figure 3a). Welford (1968) suggested that these types of rapid movement appear to be made for a given extent with no final adjustment into the target; that is, the movements are ballistic. Vince also distinguished movements aimed precisely at a target, and showed that these contained a prolonged final deceleration, with the second phase being longer than the first. The prolonged deceleration has been argued to represent a homing in on the target rather than merely bringing the movement to a halt, and a number of studies (e.g., Annett, Golby, & Kay, 1958) have shown that a large proportion of

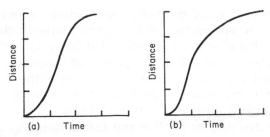

Figure 3. Trajectories of aimed movements: (a) symmetrical, (b) extended homing-in phase.

time taken in accurate movement is related to the last part of the travel (see Figure 3b). Welford (1968) following Woodworth, also recognised that in these controlled movements there is a fast distance-covering phase and a slower phase of homing on to the target. Welford argued that it seemed reasonable to regard the former as similar in speed to that of a ballistic movement and the latter as implying an additional process of visual control.

The psychological distinction made between fast ballistic and slow controlled movements may have a neurophysiological basis in that the different movement types may be directed from different regions of the brain. In this regard, the motor cortex is seen as having no preferential status because it is involved in both fast and slow movements. Aiming movements having a ballistic and control phase may in the course of movement be innervated from different centres, the basal ganglia and the cerebellum. If this is indeed the case then more detailed analysis of the components of movement can be seen to be important in relating brain structure to function. Care is necessary in detailing which centre may be involved in which type of movement because some studies (Kornhuber, 1971) indicate that the cerebellum controls fast movements and the basal ganglia control feedback-dependent slow movements, while evidence from other sources (Flowers, 1976) suggests that the reverse is the case. As yet we are clearly some way from understanding the involvement of these systems in movement.

In order to coordinate movement, muscles driving the movement (agonists) must be activated in the proper temporal sequence and to the required degree, while an appropriate amount of inhibition has to be directed at the muscles opposing the motor act (antagonists). Wacholder and Altenburger (1926) discovered that the EMG activity of agonist and antagonist depends on whether the movement was performed slowly or rapidly. In slow movements agonist activity was observed throughout, whereas in rapid movements the activity in the two muscles was *tri-*

phasic. There was an initial burst of agonist activity with the antagonist inactive, then a second phase consisting of a marked reduction in agonist activity with a clear burst of antagonist firing and a third phase in which there was a resumption of agonist and antagonist activity. In rapid movement, if initially there is tonic activity of the antagonist muscle *before* the first phase, this is inhibited prior to the first burst of agonist activity (Hallett, Shahani, & Young, 1975a,b).

While these descriptions of slow and fast movements are fairly well accepted in the literature, they are task dependent. A laboratory task involving a slow or fast flexion movement of the elbow, say with a 60 ° displacement, would produce the types of movement patterns described. However, other types of slow or fast movement are available. For example, Richer (1895) (cited in Brooks, 1979), who appears to have been the first to use the term ballistic movement, investigated the quadriceps muscle during the act of kicking. By photographing the leg during motion, he noticed that it was flung by this muscle, which then ceased activity long before the leg completed the movement. Stopping of such a ballistic movement is normally achieved, in part, by the inertia of the ball. Many everyday ballistic movements are not actually stopped at a specific location by the antagonists, but are stopped externally, for example, by contact with a nail when hammering, or are carried through the point of contact as in kicking a ball, throwing a ball or dart, or playing a golf, tennis, squash, or cricket stroke. Indeed, emphasis is laid on following through with the shot (sometimes to the natural extension of the system) rather than attempting to halt it. Furthermore, slow tension movements may be made, in which antagonists contract against agonists in an attempt to avoid or reduce the effects of external perturbations on the limb, such as a weight being placed on the limb while moving. Clearly, task demands can affect the pattern of movement in a more complicated way than a simple fast–slow dichotomy would suggest. The context in which the response occurs is intricately linked to the structure of the movement.

FITTS'S LAW

It has long been recognised that when movement distance increases or when greater accuracy of movement is required, then the MT of the limb usually increases. Fitts (1954) attempted to produce a description of the motor system's capacity to control movement in terms of its information-processing capacity, and to classify tasks according to their difficulty in terms of informational demands. He argued that the degree of precision required in any movement is a function of the number of alternative movements which could have been made. That is, precision can be specified as the amount of information required to select an appropriate movement from the total range of possible movements. Fitts suggested that *tolerance* (W, target width) and *amplitude* (A, movement distance) specified the *index of difficulty* (ID) of movement, according to the formula:

$$ID = \log_2(2A/W) \text{ bits/response}$$

In this formula, to increase the amplitude of movement or to decrease the tolerance allowed is to increase the difficulty of the movement in terms of Fitts' interpretation of information theory. The equation weights distance and target width equally, so that in terms of task difficulty, doubling the amplitude is equivalent to halving the tolerance. It is also clear that tasks with different movement distances and tolerances can have the same ID provided that the ratio of amplitude to tolerance remains the same. Fitts reasoned that the speed with which movements are made is limited by the information-processing capacity of the motor system. Thus, the information-transmission rate of a specified limb system can be calculated for a given person and task. Given Fitts' argument of relative constancy in the rate of information processing of the human motor system, a linear relationship is predicted between ID and movement time (see Figure 4). This relationship is commonly referred to as Fitts' Law, and is given by the equation:

$$MT = a + b \log_2(2A/W)$$

where *a* and *b* are empirically determined constants: Constant *a* represents the intercept of the straight-line function, while constant *b* represents its slope. Fitts and Peterson (1964) indicated that constant *a* had a value of about −70 msec, while constant *b* averaged +74 msec (see Figure 4).

Fitts obtained his data from a variety of different tasks. One still commonly used in research today is his reciprocal tapping task. This involves tapping back and forth with a metal-tipped stylus between two rectangular target plates of varying sizes and varying distances apart, placed to the right and left of the midline of the body. Instructions are to move as fast as possible while making as few errors as possible. Errors are recorded if the stylus fails to strike the target area. Fitts and Peterson (1964) developed a useful variant of the original approach. Subjects start a trial with the stylus centred on the midline of the body and then make a single, discrete movement at a target either to the right or left, as

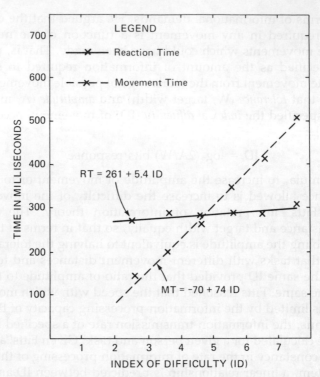

Figure 4. Relation of RT and MT to the index of task difficulty for a task involving discrete movements. After Fitts and Peterson (1964).

indicated by the experimenter (see Figure 5). Tasks currently used to investigate simple movements are typically discrete. The reason for this is that in continuous tasks it is often difficult to determine when one movement finishes and the next commences. For example, in continuous tasks, preparing to make the next movement can affect performance of the current movement. Because movements are separated in time, it is argued that this does not occur in discrete tasks. Moreover, feedback used to control movement can clearly be seen as directly relating to one specific movement.

Fitts' (1954) paper has stimulated a very large body of research, and Fitts' Law appears to receive support from numerous studies involving a diversity of tasks (for a review see Keele, 1981). Moreover, it is often reported that the linear relationship accounts for a large proportion of the variance in mean MTs. Some inadequacies have, however, been noted with Fitts' approach (Welford, 1968) and a breakdown in Fitts' Law for short movements has been detected (Klapp, 1975). Fitts' view

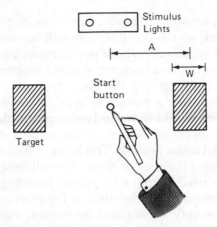

Figure 5. Apparatus used by Fitts and Peterson (1964) to determine the effects of movement difficulty on reaction time and movement time.

that the logarithmic relation results from information transmission characteristics is not now generally accepted, and other models have been developed that lead to Fitts' Law. One such model is that of Crossman and Goodeve (1963) in which it is assumed that a visually controlled movement consists of an initial impulse plus a number of corrections to converge on the target. The corrections are seen as being based on visual feedback and it may be that the relation between speed and accuracy for these controlled movements is different from that for ballistic movements (Sheridan, 1979). That is, Fitts' Law may, in general, be more applicable to controlled movements.

One problem with Fitts' description is that it says nothing about how a movement is controlled. Movements may have equal ID values, but their preparation and execution may be different. For this reason more recent work has concerned itself with the processes involved in movement. Although a number of problems have been identified, Fitts (1954) provided a lead with his realization that, when studying the motor system, it is critically important to consider the nature and complexity of the task, and with his attempt to provide a taxonomy of motor skills based on task difficulty.

SOURCES OF INFORMATION IN THE CONTROL OF MOVEMENT

Before we can consider theories of the control of movement we need to be aware of the sources of information about movement that are available to the performer. These sources have been detailed in the preceding chapters, so the account here will be more of an overview. The availability of information about performance has been argued to be essential for the control and learning of motor responses. Clearly, if one had *no* information concerning the correctness of movement, or even what it felt like to make a particular type of movement (kinaesthetic feedback), then one would have no basis upon which to judge performance in order to improve. Miller, (1953) made a distinction between *learning feedback* and *action feedback.* The latter, which will later be important in distinguishing theories of motor control, refers to feedback that arrives and can be used during a response. Learning feedback refers to information available after completion of the response, such that it can only be used to modify subsequent responses. Figure 6 represents a schematic representation of the various sources of information potentially available.

Two main types of information can be identified. First, information that indicates whether the movement is being carried out as planned. Second, information that relates to the correctness of the original plan. The learning-feedback pathway of Figure 6 relates to the correctness of the original plan, that is, was the action successful in achieving the desired result? If I made the movement which I intended and yet failed, for example, to get my key into the door lock, then the type of movement I originally decided to make may have to be altered. The plan itself may have to be revised, and I will have to make the movement in a different way. If, for example, I was under the influence of alcohol, my normal method of unlocking the door may not work too well, because of disruption to the sensory-motor system. It may be necessary to revise my plan, and perhaps place my other hand around the keyhole to provide a bigger target in which I can jiggle the key until it enters the lock.

The action feedback and central-information pathways, on the other hand, provide information about whether the movement is being performed as intended, and if sufficient time is available the information can be used to correct the movement, if necessary, returning it to the planned path. Sources of such information are both *proprioceptive* (from the muscles, joints, skin and inner ear), and *exteroceptive* (from vision and audition). While the importance of these sources of information is in little doubt, more controversy surrounds the issue of central information. Feedback from the periphery (*afference*) is not the only means of obtaining information about performance, or influencing it. Information from the outgoing commands (*efference*) could also be used.

One way in which outgoing commands could be used is to compare signals commanding the movement with a reference model for correct

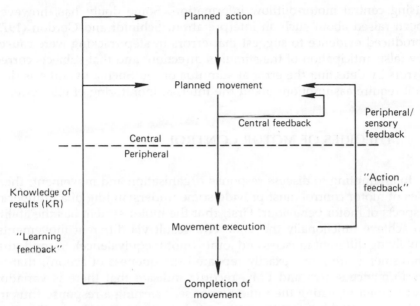

Figure 6. Sources of feedback in movement control.

movement, to determine if the correct set of commands has been sent to the musculature. This is done without use of peripheral feedback and is a mechanism by which we can check internally if we are attempting to move as originally planned (Festinger & Canon, 1965; Jones, 1974b). Evidence supporting the proposition that subjects can regulate responses at some central level based only on motor-outflow information comes from studies showing that error correction is faster with self-generated error than with target-induced error (Rabbitt, 1966), and is faster than kinaesthetic reaction time (Higgins & Angel, 1970). In the Higgins and Angel study, movement errors made by subjects when attempting to superimpose a cursor on a rapidly moving visual target were measured. Any response in which the initial acceleration of the subjects' movement caused the cursor to move away from the target was defined as a tracking error. The interval between the onset of the movement and the onset of deceleration was defined as the error-correction time. Comparisons revealed that mean error-correction times (range 83–122 msec) were in all cases less than mean kinaesthetic reaction times (range 108–169 msec). Kinaesthetic reaction time is the time required for movement to be amended on the basis of feedback information from the joints and musculature. This suggests that subjects were able to amend errors without using kinaesthetic feedback, and by implication were using central motor-outflow information. Some doubt has, however, been raised about such an interpretation. Schmidt and Gordon (1977) produced evidence to suggest that errors in step tracking were caused by false anticipation of the stimulus direction, and that subjects correct errors by detecting the error at stimulus onset. Such a hypothesis does not require assumptions about the internal monitoring of efference.

THEORIES OF MOTOR CONTROL

In attempting to discuss response organisation and movement, theories of motor control must provide some understanding of a number of aspects of motor behaviour. First, that the motor system has the ability to achieve functionally the same end result via different movements, involving different muscles and joints (motor equivalence). Second, that movements are never exactly repeated (uniqueness of action), that is, performance scores and EMG records indicate that there is variation even when repeating the same response. Learning a response thus involves repeated attempts to achieve the desired result, but without exactly repeating the same movement, and without getting the same feedback. This has led Whiting (1980) to observe that acquiring a skill in these terms "does not mean to repeat and consolidate, but to invent, to progress" (p. 543). Third, that despite the apparent uniqueness of each movement, the most obvious feature of skilled performance is the consistency and stability of both temporal and spatial structure (stability and consistency of action). Fourth, that not only is skilled action consistent and stable, but it is also capable of amendment as a consequence of changes in information available to the performer (modifiability of action).

Historically, there have been two major attempts to deal with these issues, one is predominantly peripheral in nature while the other stresses central factors. Although this dichotomy has led some authors to an either/or discussion concerning the control of movement, the positions are not mutually exclusive. An integrated view of the theories can be taken, particularly for movements of moderate speed, although a distinction arises for fast ballistic movements. Basically, the peripheral control position emphasises the role of sensory information in movement, and the way in which such feedback is used to guide movement. This is referred to as *closed-loop theory*. The central control position, on the other hand, argues that movements can be successfully completed without recourse to feedback, and is known as *open-loop theory*. Open-loop theory does not deny the importance of feedback for modifying the response after the movement has been completed and before the next movement is made, but deemphasises its importance in the current (or in computer jargon, real-time) control of movement.

MOTOR PROGRAMS

While feedback is the key element in closed-loop theory, the motor program is the fundamental concept in an open-loop description of movement. Centralists have invoked the motor program to account for movements apparently made in the absence of feedback, as in the ballistic movements we have already mentioned. Lashley (1917) was one of the first to characterize humans as controlling movements with central motor programs. Lashley described the movements of a patient suffering from complete anaesthesia of the lower limbs, resulting from a gunshot wound to the back. Although the patient could move his leg, if deprived of visual feedback, he was unaware that his limb had actually moved. So while the efferent pathways remained intact, the afferent pathways had been effectively severed. Lashley reported that, when blindfolded, the patient was still able to control the extent of his movements with almost normal accuracy, to vary the speed and extent of movement independently, and to make rhythmic alterations of flexion and extension. This suggests that accurate movement is possible in the absence of afferent kinaesthetic feedback although it does not define the relative importance of such information when it is available as a source of control. Kinaesthetic feedback appears at least necessary for efficient adaptation to changing conditions during movement. Lashley found that, in reproducing a movement, the patient was unable to compensate for the addition of spring loading during recall. Having no means of detecting it, he could not compensate for it.

In probably the most influential statement of motor programming theory, Keele (1968) defined the motor program as, "a set of muscle commands that are structured before a movement sequence begins, and that allows the entire sequence to be carried out uninfluenced by peripheral feedback" (p. 387). This has generally been taken to represent a strict interpretation of motor programming, with all the details specified in the program such that once initiated it will run its full course without sensory intervention. Lashley (1951) used the concept of the motor program to account for fast movements, arguing that such ballistic movements could not possibly be regulated by feedback because there was insufficient time for the feedback to have any effect.

Lashley's statement stimulated a line of research concerned with investigating (in the intact organism) the time required for movement to be modified on the basis of feedback. The time for visual feedback to be effective in modifying movement has been estimated by Keele and Posner (1968) to be between 190 and 260 msec. Their task involved moving a stylus from a home position to contact a quarter-inch diameter target six inches away. Subjects were trained to complete this movement in four different times, 150, 250, 350, and 450 msec, and then were required to produce these durations, in blocks, during a testing session. The subjects were instructed to make their movements as accurately as possible and to keep within ± 10% of the intended MT. On half of the trials the light illuminating the task was turned off immediately when the stylus left the home position and the movement was completed in the dark. The time to modify movement on the basis of visual feedback was estimated to be the shortest MT in which target accuracy increased when the light was left on as opposed to switched off. It was found that the visual feedback did not facilitate accuracy when the movement time was 190 msec (subjects' actual MT in the 150 msec condition), but did improve accuracy when the speed of movement was on the order of 260 msec (250 msec condition). Latency of the visuomotor feedback loop was thus estimated to be between 190 and 260 msec. A figure in this range was also obtained by Gibb (1965). However, Hick (1949) in an experiment which tricked subjects into executing an incorrect movement, estimated the time before movement was amended to be a minimum of 300 msec on average. Christina (1970) has suggested that the average minimum time to modify movement on the basis of visual feedback is 190–260 msec, but that when the subject is surprised about the error and left in a "psychological refractory state", on average 300 msec is required to modify the response. Recent work, using delayed visual feedback (Smith & Bowen, 1980), suggests that visual correction may operate as quickly as 150 or even 100 msec. Moreover, Carlton (1981) reports apparent discrete corrections of aiming movements after visual feedback had been available for only 135 msec. These data suggest minimum visual correction times that are much less than traditionally reported. Although at the present time the interpretation of such findings is open to debate, it would seem unreasonable to think that one could detect some absolute visual-feedback processing time that is independent of task demands, such as the context in which the movement occurs, the task difficulty, the movement time, the desired outcome, and the expectations of the performer.

This need not imply that responses faster than about 260 msec (adopting the conservative figure) are ballistic and hence controlled by a motor program because kinaesthetic feedback is potentially available. Chernikoff and Taylor (1952) estimated kinaesthetic reaction time to be on the order of 120 msec. The subject's arm was supported in a horizontal position and the stimulus to respond was the release of the arm, which started the reaction time. Subjects were to stop the downward movement of their arm as soon as possible, which was recorded using an accelerometer, and the first indication of deceleration was taken as the completion of the reaction time. Higgins and Angel (1970) using the technique described earlier estimated kinaesthetic reaction time to be about 136 msec. Even movements faster than 120 msec may not be ballistic according to Lashley's (1951) definition of the term. Fast-acting (30–50 msec) muscle spindle initiated feedback loops have been discovered in both animals (Evarts, 1973) and humans (Marsden, Merton, & Morton, 1972). Saccadic eye movements have been argued to be under central control. The duration of a saccade varies with amplitude, but for a 1° saccade duration is about 10–20 msec, while a 20° saccade takes about 60–70 msec, (Yarbus, 1967). The weight of evidence suggests that saccadic movements of the eyes are under central control, however, Fuchs and Kornhuber (1969) report a 10-msec cortical feedback loop to the eye muscle in the cat, so there may be an element of peripheral control even here. Findings such as these have led to a less-strict interpretation of ballistic movement in the literature. It has been suggested that in ballistic movements the motor program, to paraphrase Schmidt (1975), once initiated, carries itself out as planned, correcting for deviations from the intended path of movement, but that if a new movement is required by an occurrence in the environment, then the performer cannot accomplish any such changes until the program has run its course for one reaction time (approximately 200 msec). In general terms this has come to mean that ballistic movements are movements which cannot be modified by current exteroceptive feedback. According to Rosenbaum (1980), Keele's definition of a motor program, in fact, always allowed the possibility of modification by peripheral feedback. Although a programmed sequence can be unaffected by feedback from the periphery, it need not be. A motor program viewed in this way could be regarded as a more general plan for movement (Keele & Summers, 1976).

One approach to demonstrating the existence of motor programs has been to show that movement can be organised and controlled in the absence of any peripheral feedback. Many studies of deafferentation (cutting peripheral nerve input to the spinal cord) in nonhuman species have been carried out, ranging from locusts (Wilson, 1961) to monkeys (Bizzi, 1980), with the recent work on monkeys proving particularly insightful. Without going into detail, a massive body of data has been obtained from deafferentation studies, the vast majority of which supports the concept of the motor program. Animals can certainly move in the absence of feedback, although a good deal of the finer control is lost. Because experimental surgical deafferentation is not possible in human subjects, the technique of the temporary nerve-compression block has been used. Laszlo (1967) attempted to eliminate kinaesthetic feedback by applying a nerve-compression block (an inflated cuff that occludes blood flow) to the upper arm. As described in Chapter 4, she did not find complete loss of control. The technique is, however, not without problems of interpretation, because the blocking of all kinaesthetic and tactile cues must be completely effective, and there is some doubt whether this is true in practice (Glencross & Oldfield, 1975).

Taken together, the evidence would seem to be weighted in favour of the existence of some variety of motor program, even though a number of sources of evidence are potentially flawed. Because there are inherent difficulties in showing, either that feedback is present but not used, or in removing feedback and demonstrating that movement can still occur, an alternative approach is to consider the process of planning the response before any movement takes place, and thus before the possibility of feedback guiding the response arises.

Response Programming and Reaction Time

If one accepts the existence of motor programs, then it becomes possible that movement can be preprogrammed, that is, preselection and construction of the motor program can occur before the movement is made. It is possible to time the interval between the stimulus to respond and the start of the movement. What processes are involved in the reaction time (RT) interval? Briefly, they can be classified as response selection and response preparation, often together thought of as programming. The response selection stage involves the selection of a generalized program (or schema), after stimulus processing has taken place. In response preparation, the specific motor control parameters are computed and elaborated. As such speculation implies, RT is currently thought to vary with the complexity of the response program, more complex movements requiring greater programming time, thereby producing longer RTs. Using a computer programming analogy, the organization of the elements of a movement can be likened to writing a computer program. As the complexity and length of the computer program increases, so does the time required to write it and compile it, that is, to turn it into usable machine instructions. Similarly, as the complexity of the prospective movement increases, so does the time needed to select and assemble (write) the elements of the motor program and possibly, to turn these instructions into muscle-usable form (compile).

Study of the relationship between movement parameters and RT has a chequered history, which seems to owe more to theoretical considerations dominant at the time, than to the available empirical evidence. Certainly, clear-cut patterns of results have remained elusive. Evidence from the early 1900s (see Woodworth, 1938), indicated that RT could vary with motor task demands, and research up to the 1950s suggested that adding complexity to movement (e.g., an aiming response), produced longer RTs than simply generating movement (e.g., pressing or lifting one's finger from a telegraph key). Evidence for increased levels of complexity increasing RT was somewhat less clear. This is perhaps not surprising, when a classification of complexity was not, and still is not, agreed upon.

The view that motor-task demands influence RT coalesced in Henry and Rogers' (1960) memory-drum theory. The original statement of the theory led to some confusion in the literature concerning its exact nature, although recently, Henry (1980) has clarified his position. The basic proposition of the theory is that the time to initiate a movement varies directly with the complexity of the movement, more complex movements producing longer reaction time. Complexity was not originally defined, but Henry (1980) makes it clear that complex movements were considered to be movements which were made up of a number of connected parts. The three movement types used in the 1960 study, and labeled A, B, and C, illustrate this. An auditory stimulus to respond was used in all the movements. Movement A required the subject to lift a finger from a reaction key. Movement B required the subject to make a forward and upward thrust of the arm to grasp a tennis ball suspended by a string. Movement C involved the subject striking a suspended tennis ball and then pressing a button before executing movement B. Time to initiate movement C took longer than movement B (about 7%), and time to initiate movement B took longer than movement A (about 20%).

Interestingly, at the time, Henry and Rogers' work was not accorded great interest. The view favoured in the literature was that the processes involved in the selection of movement were independent of the processes involved in the execution of movement (Welford, 1968). Such a view seems to have stemmed from a study by Brown and Slater-Hammel (1949), which reported finding no relationship between RT and direction or length of movement. Other studies of this period were used to support this position, concluding that little relationship could be detected between RT and task parameters (Fitts & Peterson, 1964), and reporting low correlations between RT and MT (Henry, 1952). As Kerr (1978) points out, however, a failure to find high correlations between RT and MT is not surprising and need not imply that initiation and execution stages incorporate independent processes. Moreover, Fitts and Peterson (1964) did, in fact, detect a small, but statistically significant trend in the data, with RT increasing with task difficulty [as specified by Fitts' (1954) index of difficulty (ID)]. This finding was probably obscured at the time by the more noticeable large changes in MT observed with alterations in motor-task demands.

Because there was only one allowable response to the stimulus, Henry and Rogers investigated their theory using simple RT. Using simple RT measures, differences in RT observed to movements of different complexity have been attributed to the time required to load an already constructed program into a temporary output memory state or response-output buffer (compile or key in the program) (Henry & Rogers, 1960), to make final adjustments to the motor program (Rosenbaum & Patashnik, 1980), or to search the response-output buffer for the section of loaded program containing the initial instructions (Sternberg, Monsell, Knoll, & Wright, 1978). While simple RT may provide understanding of how already-constructed programs are executed, choice RT (where two or more responses are possible) would seem to provide greater insight into the construction of motor programs. The merits of using choice-RT procedures to investigate response programming have been well-aired in the literature (e.g., Klapp, 1980).

Recently, numerous studies have reported changes in RT contingent upon motor-task demands, and this indeed is the current finding, although it is by no means totally consistent (Kerr, 1978). A typical, and perhaps the best known, more recent study is reported by Klapp (1975). He used a discrete aiming task (see Figure 5), and adopted a similar experimental procedure to the one devised by Fitts and Peterson (1964). At the start of each trial the subject placed the response stylus on a central resting position. Identical targets (same tolerance and amplitude) were set up to the right and left of the central position and in response to a light either to the right or left of this central position the subject moved to hit the appropriate circular target. The target tolerances used were, 2, 4, 8, 16, 32, and 64 mm, and the amplitudes from the rest position to the edge of the target were 2, 11, 70, and 336 mm. From an analysis of his data, Klapp concluded that there was no main effect of amplitude, that RT increased as tolerance decreased and that there was an interaction between tolerance and amplitude. The significance of the interaction was argued to reflect the finding that the smaller the amplitude, the more RT increased with decreasing tolerance.

In many experiments investigating the relationship between RT and movement parameters, prior to responding, subjects have been able to preview the parameters of the movements they are required to make. That is, they could examine the spatial and, by implication, the temporal constraints of the impending movement. Clearly, visual analysis is a critical element in this process. In such a situation the subject can select and prepare the movement (or alternative movements) before entering the RT period. This reduces the programming required in the RT period, and makes it more difficult to detect a consistent relationship between RT and motor-task demands, thereby contributing to confusion in the literature. A study by Sheridan (1981) attempted to eliminate preview by not allowing subjects to view the parameters of the movement (target tolerance and movement amplitude) before entering the RT interval (no-preview mode). Subjects sat facing a cathode ray tube (akin to a television screen), on which was a spot of light (the cursor). Subjects controlled the position of the cursor by moving a lever. Forward movement of the lever produced a corresponding vertical movement of the cursor on the CRT screen. The resting position of the lever placed the cursor at the bottom of the CRT. The subjects' basic task with each discrete movement was to wait until a target appeared on the cathode ray tube (a pair of horizontal lines), and then to move the lever forward in order to move the cursor from its resting position into the target area. Movement amplitude and target tolerance were varied, and before the appearance of the target the subjects did not know which movement they were going to be required to make.

The results of this experiment showed that, for small tolerance targets, there was a significant and consistent decrease in RT between amplitudes of about 19 to 150 mm. That is, short-extent movements had longer RTs than long-extent movements. This effect was much less marked in an equivalent preview condition when subjects could see the movement parameters before entering the RT period. Thus, preview, by allowing subjects to prepare the movement before entering the RT period, makes it more difficult to detect a consistent relationship between RT and task parameters. On the other hand, in the no-preview situation more of the preprogramming has necessarily to be shifted into the RT interval, thus making the detected changes in RT a more complete reflection of response programming time. A difficulty with the interpretation of the RT data from this study was that the changes in RT related to task parameters may have stemmed from theoretically rather less interesting changes in motor RT; that is, the changes may have been related to peripheral factors, such as the rate of tension development in the muscle. Indeed, Anson (1982) has recently indicated that Henry and Rogers' (1960) findings may be attributable to motor effects. It is, therefore, necessary to determine if premotor RT varies with motor task demands. Premotor RT is defined as the time from the imperative stimulus until the first detected changes in EMG, and is argued to reflect central processes. Recording premotor RTs, Sheridan (1984) confirmed the findings of his earlier study.

Klapp (1975) has argued that programming effects on RT are only obtained for short-extent, ballistic movements. The movement times he obtained in his work were, however, sufficiently long to permit feedback control. Data from his second experiment actually suggest that short movements showing changes in RT were visually controlled to some extent, as errors were significantly greater without vision than with vision. Movements in Sheridan's studies took sufficient time to allow visual control (upward of about 350 msec), and yet RT was still affected. As the first phase of even controlled movements is presumably programmed in advance, until a point at which visual control can exert influence, there is no reason to believe that programming effects on RT are limited to short movements. Indeed, in some models it is argued that where greater accuracy is required the average velocity of the entire movement is reduced to bring the final visual correction nearer to the target (Beggs & Howarth, 1972). Detection of a consistent relationship may, however, require some design akin to the no-preview procedure.

The reason shorter movements considerably affect RT may actually derive from increased difficulty in programming low-velocity responses. Newell and colleagues (e.g., Newell, Carlton, Carlton & Halbert, 1980) have advocated average velocity as an important kinematic factor in the initiation and control of discrete-timing movements, with control breaking down for low-velocity movements. Data from Sheridan's experiments accord well with this position. In the 1984 study, for velocities greater than about 15 cm/sec, a strong negative-linear relationship (e.g., $r = -.94$) was detected between the average velocity and premotor RT, while for velocities below 15 cm/sec a curvilinear relationship was obtained. Slow movements also appear to be more difficult to remember and reproduce (Carlton, 1978), and there is also some evidence that movements of longer duration have longer RTs (Klapp & Erwin, 1976). It may be that some combination of duration and velocity is important in determining programming difficulty. Although Newell et al. argue that average velocity is a key kinematic factor in the initiation of movement, they are cautious about suggesting that velocity is a feature of the response program. The impulse-timing and mass-spring models (see next section) suggest other characteristics more fundamentally linked to the program.

Program Structure

Having introduced the concept of the motor program, one might reasonably ask what is actually specified in advance by the program. Current interest has, for simple movements, centred around two possibilities, which have been described in terms of an *impulse-timing* model and a *mass-spring* model. Basically, the impulse-timing view assumes that embedded within the program is some derivative of the direction and distance to be moved, while the mass-spring model views end location (final position of the movement) as being specified without reference to distance.

Impulse-Timing Model

In making a movement from one position to another, there is an initial acceleration toward the target, which is then turned off, and followed by a period of deceleration as the limb approaches the target. The motor program is argued to produce the impulses (forces applied over time, or force-time integral) that accelerate and decelerate the limb. The size of the impulses (both amplitude and duration) determine where the limb will eventually stop, how rapidly it will travel there, and the spatial trajectory of the movement. Clearly, variability in the impulses will produce variability in the movement trajectory and/or in the movement endpoint.

Schmidt and colleagues (e.g., Schmidt, Zelaznik, Hawkins, Frank, & Quinn, 1979) have pointed out that for aiming movements, where the muscular impulse for deceleration is only part of the force acting to stop the limb (the remainder being associated with the deceleration forces imparted by contact with the target), increasing the movement distance increases the force, which in turn increases force variability and leads to increased variability in the movement endpoint. The proposition that the magnitude of error in producing a force increases in proportion to the magnitude of the force produced is intuitively plausible. For a fixed distance, increasing MT allows lower forces to be used and this might be expected to produce less endpoint variability. However, increasing MT also increases time variability by increasing the period between the onset of the accelerative and decelerative forces, and this could lead to more endpoint variability. Two opposing factors are therefore at work. Consideration of these factors led Schmidt, Zelaznik and Frank (1978) to propose a relationship between movement amplitude (A) and movement time (MT) as they jointly affect the movement accuracy. Movement accuracy is measured in terms of the effective target width, W_e, which is the standard deviation of the movement endpoints about their own mean. The relationship is expressed in the equation:

$$W_e = a + b(A/MT)$$

As can be seen, the model proposes that variation in movement endpoints is linearly related to the distance of movement (A) divided by the MT.

The model assumes that no feedback corrections are taking place within the MT, and is based only on the relationship between force and its variability, and time and its variability. In such fast unidirectional ballistic movements the final location of the limb is thus argued to be determined by the timing (and the forces) provided by the motor program. The impulse-timing model deals with the same factors as Fitts' Law, but has a different form. For rapid responses, Schmidt et al. (1978, 1979) have found that the equation fits the data very well. Newell, Carlton, and Carlton (1982) have confirmed that impulse variability increases as the size of the impulse generated increases, either through moving at a faster velocity and/or moving a system of heavier mass, but suggest that the increase in impulse variability occurs at a decreasing rate with gains in impulse size. They argue that while impulse size is related to movement timing error, it is, as yet, premature to argue that impulse variability is a causal agent in timing error. Recently, Meyer, Smith, and Wright (1982) have pointed out a number of flaws in Schmidt et al.'s model of rapid movements. Meyer et al. account for the observed linear trade-off in terms of the result of the concatenation of a sequence of overlapping accelerative and decelerative force impulses. They assume that the force-impulse pairs are preprogrammed and that successive impulses overlap. Meyer et al. further proposed that Fitts' Law might be accounted for in these terms, with visual feedback being important only in the final corrective phase.

Relating Schmidt's work to our discussion of response programming we can construct a tentative picture. Following Schmidt's work, slower movements are more accurate, because slower movements require smaller starting and stopping forces, and these are less variable. However, when movements are slower, the interval of the time between the onset of the accelerative and decelerative forces is increased, resulting in increased difficulty in timing. This involves greater programming time, which is reflected in the observed increases in reaction time. The impulse-timing model is, however, not the only means by which a limb might move from one position to another.

Mass-Spring Model

The mass-spring model holds that final limb position is specified in advance of movement in terms of an equilibrium point between the torques in the agonist and antagonist muscles, with limb movement being produced by the purely mechanical properties of the muscles. Thus, what is programmed by the system is a new equilibrium point based on the length-tension relationship of the agonist and antagonist muscle groups at the new position. Where the opposing torques about the joint are equal, the limb is in a state of equilibrium and remains static. Changing the level of innervation to one or both of the muscle groups changes the slope of the length-tension relationship, and the limb moves to the new point such that the torques are again equal. The movement is caused by the springlike physical properties of the muscles acting on the mass of the limb, hence the term mass-spring model. It should be noted that according to this model the desired ending location can be achieved independent of starting location, or knowledge about starting location.

Asatryan and Fel'dman (1965) were among the first to introduce the mass-spring view as an analogy for voluntary movement control. More recently it has been revived by Bizzi and his colleagues (e.g., Bizzi, Polit, & Morasso, 1976), in an attempt to explain how a limb can achieve a new location independent of starting position, after unexpected changes in mass, after brief perturbations, and under deafferented conditions. The predictions of the impulse-timing model and mass-spring model can be compared in these situations (see Schmidt & McGown, 1980). Where the initial position of a limb is unexpectedly changed just prior to movement, the impulse-timing model predicts that the program would produce the impulses to the muscles as originally planned, and that the movement endpoint would be shifted by about the same amount as the initial position was. Using deafferented monkeys Bizzi and colleagues found, however, that in spite of shifting the initial position, movement was made to the originally intended target, as predicted by the mass-spring model. Moreover, Kelso (1977b) found that in humans, location was reproduced better than distance, even though different start positions were used. In these experiments subjects are not allowed to view the limb otherwise they would use vision to control movement. If the moving limb is suddenly loaded inertially either by increasing the mass to be moved or by perturbing movement momentarily with a torque motor, then the impulse-timing model predicts a shorter distance movement of normal time because the timing of the accelerative and decelerative forces would not be altered, but the forces would be too small to carry the increased mass the intended distance. On the other hand, the mass-spring model predicts a slower movement, but one which finishes at the intended location. Studies using deafferented monkeys (Bizzi, 1980), using anaesthetised finger movement in humans (Kelso & Holt, 1980), and rapid arm movements in humans (Schmidt & McGown, 1980), all support the mass-spring model over the impulse-timing model, at least for the discrete unidirectional movements investigated. However, recent data (Bizzi, Accornero, Chapple, & Hogan, 1982) suggest that the representation of movements solely in terms of their terminal muscular states may only apply to a somewhat restricted class of responses.

Cooke (1980) has produced a model of human arm extension and flexion with the muscles considered as an agonist–antagonist pair of damped springs. Limb movement occurs by a step increase in the stiffness of the agonist, with the speed of movement being determined by the initial stiffness (tension) at the starting point. The model predicts that peak velocity is a linear function of distance moved and occurs about midway through the movement, as observed in humans. However, because error in producing stiffness is likely to be proportional to the stiffness, there will be greater error for faster movements. Programming location could then be seen to produce the observed speed–accuracy trade-off of visually uncorrected movements. Movement by location programming has the distinct advantage that the same end result can be achieved in a number of different ways by effectively the same program. This might appear to provide a simple solution to the problem of motor constancy. Because it is final position that is programmed, starting position is of little importance. The situation is not, however, so straightforward, and in any event location programming has, as yet, only been shown to be viable for a limited range of simple movements.

As we noted in the section on the categories of movement, the patterns of EMG activity for fast and slow movements are very different, in that agonist activity is observed throughout slow movements, while fast movements are characterized by three phases. In the first phase is an initial burst of agonist activity with the antagonist silent. In the second phase agonist activity is markedly reduced with a clear burst of antagonist firing. In the final phase there is a resumption of agonist and antagonist activity. This triphasic pattern may represent a centrally directed program rather than a reflex pattern, since Hallett *et al.* (1975) observed the pattern in a patient with complete sensory loss due to lesions of the peripheral sensory pathways. Their data showing temporal patterning rather than balancing of opposing activity levels in agonist and antagonist suggest that rapid movement to a target may involve more than simply resetting the stiffness of the opposing muscle pairs.

It would seem that slow and fast movements are made in different ways. Keele (1981) suggests that movements made relatively slowly and smoothly may be carried out primarily as described by the mass-spring model, involving the programming of locations, while he considers that fast movements may best be described by a hybrid of the impulse-timing and mass-spring models. The first phase of fast movement is argued to be best described by the impulse-timing model, with the final or fixation phase involving programming of intended location as described by the mass-spring model. This is very similar to the suggestion that movement need only be planned in general, and that lower levels in the system then rapidly tune the response (Arbib, 1972). It has been suggested that the general response might involve a system of alpha–gamma coactivation, while the fine tuning might operate according to the principles of follow-up servo theory as discussed in Chapter 2, or as now suggested by the mass-spring model, according to the physical properties of the muscles. Movement of this type has come to be known as a ballpark response; the initial movement gets you into the general area of the target (the ballpark), while tuning in the periphery actually guides the movement to the target. It is not clear how general the first phase of the movement could be and yet still allow tuning of the response, because in short rapid movements the opportunity for tuning would seem limited. Of course, in many varieties of movement, if vision is present and if sufficient time is available, feedback can be used to make the final adjustment. It is this process of feedback control we will now consider.

FEEDBACK CONTROL

The peripheral position is also referred to as a closed-loop theory, in the sense that feedback closes the loop between the performer and the ongoing consequences of the movement. Information about the output of the system is fed back into the system and used to modify the current output. Feedback is compared against the reference for a correct response, and if there is error the movement is amended. Error is thought of as the difference between the current position and the desired position. The reduction of error is the essence of negative feedback systems.

Two main factors limit the precision of movement. First, there is inherent variability in the motor system, as discussed in the previous section. Second, the accuracy with which the perceptual system can translate the distance to be moved or the location to be achieved into actual movement is limited. When the requirement for movement accuracy (e.g., threading a needle) exceeds the inherent accuracy of the visual translation or the inherent variability in the motor system, then corrections based on visual feedback must be made as the target is approached. As we noted earlier these visual corrections take time (approximately 260 msec), and hence MT increases. This slowing of the movement can also have the effect of reducing the variability in the motor system, as we discussed previously. By slowing the movement the performer can thus respond with greater accuracy. We can now consider attempts that have been made to explain the processes underlying Fitts' Law.

Multiple-Correction Model

The idea that movement to a target consists of a series of submovements, has been proposed by both Crossman and Goodeve (1963) and Keele (1968). The submovements were considered to be successive attempts to reduce the distance to the target (thought of as error) as indicated by visual feedback, and each was considered to have the same MT and relative accuracy. For a movement without vision, mean absolute error has been estimated to be between about 7–10% of the size of the movement (Vince, 1948). So, the first submovement would leave an error of about 10% of the size of the movement, the next would on average correct 90% of this error, leaving an error of 1% of the size of the original movement. For greater accuracy further submovements would be required. Using Vince's accuracy estimate of about 7% and Keele and Posner's (1968) estimate of 260 msec as the time required for movement to be modified on the basis of visual feedback, then the value obtained for constant b in Fitts' Law is very close to that obtained empirically by Fitts and Peterson (1964).

There are, however, problems with the multiple-correction model. It is only viable if sufficient time is available during movement for a number of visually based corrections. Clearly, movements faster than about 500 msec would only allow one correction if we base our estimate of time for visual correction on Keele and Posner's figure. However, as

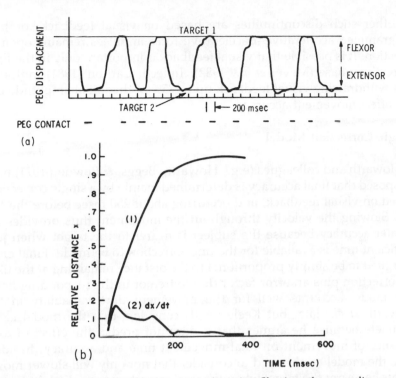

Figure 7. Discontinuities in movement trajectories. Slowing, then speeding up near the end of movements to a target are clearly seen in the traces (a), giving an average movement pattern shown in (b). From "An investigation of Fitts' Law using a wide range of movement amplitudes", by Langolf, G. D., Chaffin, D. B., Foulke, J. A. (1976). *Journal of Motor Behavior, 8,* 113–128. Reprinted with permission.

was indicated in our discussion of motor programs, there is evidence to suggest that the minimum time for visually based correction of movement may be considerably less than Keele and Posner's original estimate. A second problem is the assumption that the initial movement component is independent of the required accuracy. Langolf, Chaffin, and Foulke (1976) have shown that the entire course of movement is slowed as required accuracy increases, rather than simply the final section. Langolf *et al.* also noted that usually only one clear correction could be seen in the movement trajectories (see Figure 7). Multiple discontinuities have, however, been observed in movement trajectories, and these have been inferred to represent discrete corrections (Carlton, 1980). Studies using wrist-rotation movements have been advocated because they have relatively low inertia and make any changes in muscular control more readily apparent in the observed movement trajectories.

Whether such discontinuities are based on visual feedback, or pre-programmed accelerative–decelerative force impulses remains open to question. It is possible that visual feedback is important only in the final corrective phase (Meyer *et al.*, 1982). Indeed, Carlton (1981) indicated that withdrawing visual feedback up to 75% of the initial amplitude did not affect movement accuracy.

Single-Correction Model

Howarth and colleagues (e.g., Howarth, Beggs, & Bowden 1971) have proposed that final accuracy is determined mainly by a single correction, based on visual feedback, and occurring about 250 msec before the target. Slowing the velocity throughout the movement thus provides for greater accuracy because the subject is nearer to the target when just sufficient time is available for the one correction to be made. Final error is argued to be simply proportional to the distance remaining at the time of correction plus an error factor due to tremor in the responding limb. The model accounts well for the movement time variability in the Howarth *et al.* data, but Keele (1981) considers that the model is incomplete because he argues that it does not predict the effect of total distance of movement on total movement time and accuracy. In addition, the model might need to consider that not only will slower movements be nearer the target when the final correction is applied, but as we noted in the previous section, slower movements are also less variable, so that less or no visual correction might be necessary. In any event, greater accuracy is often achieved by reducing the velocity of the movement.

It is important to bear in mind that the transmission of feedback information through the CNS, the processing of that information, and the modification of movement, introduce a lag into the system. As a consequence, movement control on the basis of feedback may be intermittent as suggested by Craik (1947). Feedback always provides information about events that have already occurred. At the time corrections are applied to the motor output, the movement has already progressed from the point of feedback detected error. Presumably, in applying corrections some compensation is made for the current position or current parameters of the movement (e.g., force, velocity). This would seem to involve predicting, at the point of error detection, the consequences of the error for a time in the future, and correcting for that. While we have discussed the various forms of discrete feedback correction, rather little detail is known at the present time about the processes involved in these predictive corrections.

MOVEMENT VARIATION AND SCHEMA THEORY

Having discussed specific models of motor control some consideration will now be given to a more general approach, in an attempt to place the study of simple movements in a wider context. While the specific models we have considered so far indicate how discrete movements may be produced and executed they make little attempt to consider how performance is modified by experience. It was suggested in the introduction that planning and controlling even apparently simple movements must involve a generative process. That is, each movement in a given class is created from the rules governing movements of that class, in the light of the current situation—the position of the limbs, balance, and so on. The rules are produced from an abstract representation of the movement class called a schema. A definition of a *schema* has been proposed by Evans (1967): "A schema is a characteristic of some population of objects (movements) and consists of a set of rules serving as instructions for producing a population prototype" (p. 87).

When individuals make a movement that attempts to satisfy some goal, Schmidt (1975) considers that they store four things:

1. The initial conditions (information about the preresponse state of their muscular system and the environment in which they are to move);
2. the response specification for the motor program (specification of elements such as speed of movement, forces involved, etc.);
3. the sensory consequences of the response produced (an exact copy of interoceptive and exteroceptive information); and
4. the outcome of the movement (the success of the response in relation to the outcome originally intended).

Schmidt argues that the four sources of information are stored together after movement and when a number of such movements have been made, the subject begins to abstract information about the relationship among these four sources of information. The strength of the relationship among the four stored elements is postulated to increase with each successive movement of the same general type and to increase with increased accuracy of feedback information from the response outcome. This relationship is the schema for the movement type under consideration.

When an individual is required to make a response of a type for which a schema has already been developed, Schmidt believes that there are two inputs to the schema: the desired outcome for the movement, and the initial conditions. From the relationship between past outcomes and response specifications (the recall schema), the subject determines what set of specifications will achieve the desired outcome, selects the schema for the general type of movement, and then sets the response specification for that particular movement, thereby generating the appropriate motor program. Because the specifications may never have been used in exactly the same way before, the resulting program may be novel, and strictly speaking, the movement may never have been executed before (uniqueness of action). At the same time the recall schema is used to generate the response specifications, the subject generates the expected sensory consequences of the movement, both interoceptive and exteroceptive, using the recognition schema. Then during and/or after the movement, depending on the speed of execution, each of these expected sensory consequences is compared with the respective inflow of sensory information. Any mismatch produces error that is fed back, providing information as to the outcome of the response. Figure 8 is a schematic representation of Schmidt's theory in which the recall schema and recognition schema have been combined under the heading of motor response schema.

Evidence supporting Schmidt's schema theory comes from a number of sources, Glencross (1973) found in handwheel cranking, a task similar to turning an old-fashioned grindstone, that the movements were very similar in terms of the onsets of force application even when resistance was added and the radius was changed. Glencross labeled this phenomenon *gradation of effort* and it appears as if there was a schema for cranking and that changing the quality of the cranking (e.g., less force, more speed, etc.) provided a situation in which the subject used the same schema, but with a different set of response specifications. Glencross (1975, 1977) produced further evidence that one schema can apparently be used to effect an appropriate response even though there may be a number of changes in the task conditions. He did not discuss his results in terms of schemata, but independently proposed a two-stage model of motor control to account for them. At one level the motor program operates in an open-loop fashion. At another level an executive control system integrates all the feedback arising from the task and controls the motor program. The executive might very loosely be considered to represent the response schema in Schmidt's terms, or at least represent a combination of initial conditions, desired outcome and response schema in Figure 8.

A major prediction derived from Schmidt's schema theory is that increasing variability of practice on a given task will result in increased (positive) transfer to a novel task of the same movement class. Ten years

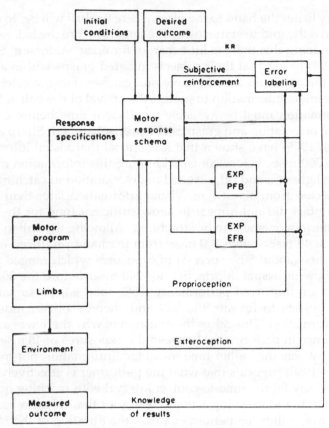

Figure 8. Schema theory. Abbreviations: KR = knowledge of results, (EXP)PFB = expected proprioceptive feedback, (EXP)EFB = expected exteroceptive feedback. From "The schema as a solution to some persistent problems in motor learning theory", by Schmidt, R. A. (1976). In Stelmach, G. E. (Ed.), *Motor control: Issues and trends*. London: Academic Press, Reprinted with permission.

earlier Holding (1965) had similarly observed, when discussing transfer of training, that one tendency was toward better transfer from tasks which give wider experience. The basis on which one decides whether movements are in the same class or not, is unspecified by Schmidt. Commonsense notions have been used to classify movements, although clearly this is highly unsatisfactory because failure to support the hypothesis could, in a circular fashion, be ascribed to movements not being sufficiently similar. Chapter 8 deals with schema learning in more detail.

Catching and hitting a ball can be considered comparatively simple actions that are different each time they are produced. They require remarkably precise predictive visual information. To catch a ball it is necessary to get the hand to the place where the ball will be, to orient the hand correctly, and to start closing the fingers before the ball reaches the hand. In doing this there is little margin for error. Alderson, Sully, and Sully (1974) found that their subjects initiated grasps within about ±14 msec of the optimum time in successful catches. For the catcher to use time-to-contact information to predict the arrival of the ball at the hand, this information must be available a sufficient time before contact, so that hand orientation and grasp can be precisely timed. Sharp and Whiting (1974, 1975) have shown that it is critical that visual information is available 300 msec before contact. Limiting this information by turning the room lights on and off, resulted in deterioration in catching a tennis ball projected from about 7 m. Visual information later than 300 msec before contact did not appear to allow sufficient time for the reaching and grasping movement to be structured. Allowing the ball to be visible for at least 40 msec when 300 msec from the hand produced equivalent performance (about 50% success) to exposures which ranged up to 160 msec. Allowing visual information for 240 msec before the 300 msec to contact point improved performance (85% success), presumably by allowing subjects to foveate the ball and thereby obtain more precise visual information. This raises the question of why there was apparently no difference in performance between the exposures of 40 msec and 160 msec. Why was the earlier time-to-contact information not more effective? Lee (1980) suggests that what the performer is effectively trying to do is precisely fill the time-to-contact interval with reaching out, orienting the hand, and grasping action. He argues that this can be achieved in two ways, either the performer varies the duration of the movement or keeps duration constant and manipulates the time at which the movement is initiated. Evidence from similar studies suggests that performers attempt to maintain a constant movement duration and that this tendency increases with practice, at least for these predictive type responses (Schmidt, 1969; Schmidt and McCabe, 1976). In this case, starting the catching movement earlier would only result in greater error. A similar emphasis on constant timing seems to be present when hitting a ball. In studies of the swing of baseball batters (Hubbard & Seng, 1954), and the forehand drive of experienced table-tennis players (Tyldesley & Whiting, 1975), constant stroke duration seems to be present. In the case of the table-tennis players the shots were consistent to within about ± 4 msec.

In many sports involving hitting, kicking, and catching, it would seem necessary to develop two components; the ability to produce the movement in a sequenced temporal order over a stabilised movement duration, and the ability to integrate the initiation of the sequence with environmental contingencies. The two components may be thought of as *technique* and *experience*. In a varying environment, practiced and stabilised technique will not produce good performance without the experience obtained when learning to tailor performance to varying environmental demands (e.g., angle, speed, and spin of the ball). It is possible that basic technique for a particular shot, in this sense, could be thought of as the schema or prototype movement, into which are fed the desired consequences and the initial conditions, determining such things as the release of the shot. While the relative timing of the components of the response is maintained, initiation of the response is varied to meet environmental demands. Experience with a variety of demands could strengthen the schema, although in this case it may not be the movement itself which is altered, but its time of initiation. In Glencross' terms, the motor program may be maintained while the executive controls its time of initiation. The definition of "movement class" remains, however, a problem for research in this area.

It would seem necessary that the schema provide information about the spatiotemporal organisation of both the microstructure and macrostructure of movement (Glencross, 1975). What is meant by *microstructure* is the temporal organisation of the components of movement, which it appears the performer may attempt to stabilise across any variations in performance which occur in a relatively stable environment (i.e., one which does not involve anticipating environmental change). *Macrostructure* refers to the structuring of movement in relation to varied environmental demands. Where such demands vary the performer appears to attempt to maintain the temporal microstructure of movement (e.g., timing of the grasp element in catching), while tailoring the temporal macrostructure to the specific environmental demands (in the catching example, when to initiate the response). The schema would seem to operate at different levels, determining both the microstructure and macrostructure.

CONCLUSION

We have seen that even a simple movement of the arm to effect a change in hand position is not as straightforward as it might appear. The limb system has a number of degrees of freedom, allowing many different movements that are functionally equivalent. The availability of such a range of movements provides us with flexibility in dealing with the environment. Even though functional synergies constrain the available patterns of movement, it is unlikely that, in general, the brain stores the patterns of innervation for the vast array of possible movements. Rather, movement would seem to involve a generative process, whereby responses are constructed according to sets of rules or principles appropriate to particular classes of action, and tailored to specific movement conditions.

Movement requires advance organisation, and, where the requirement for movement accuracy exceeds the inherent accuracy of visual translation or the inherent variability in the motor system, a process of concurrent control. This concurrent guidance is typically based on visual feedback and in Chapter 5 we will return to consider the organisation of feedback in further detail. One method of investigating advance organisation has been to use RT measures. Reaction time is currently thought to vary with the complexity of the response program, more complex movements requiring greater programming time, thereby producing longer RTs. Average velocity seems implicated as an important kinematic factor in response programming, with slower movements appearing to require greater programming time. This may relate to the problem of programming the timing of the accelerative and decelerative forces involved in slower movements. Where concurrent guidance is necessary to attain the required degree of accuracy, then often the entire course of the movement is slowed down, with discrete correction, based on visual feedback, being applied. In Chapter 6 the concept of a program will be extended and complexity will be discussed in terms of the number of components involved in a sequence of movement and the relationship between the components.

This chapter has treated the organisation and execution of movement aimed at clearly defined targets. The next chapter focusses on factors affecting the accuracy of movement to a remembered target or, to be more specific, to a target defined in terms of a movement made earlier in time. This will take us into a consideration, not only of the way a movement to be remembered is held in memory, but also how it is initially encoded prior to storage. Although the methods used in studying memory for movement are designed to minimise, or at least control for, the factors involved in execution discussed in this chapter, a strong link between the two chapters will be seen in that movements are better remembered if they have involved advance planning.

Memory for Movements

Mary M. Smyth

INTRODUCTION

When we make movements we can feel and see our limbs and we can see and hear, and sometimes feel, the consequences of the movements. This proprioceptive, visual, and auditory information can be put into memory, or *encoded*, stored for a period of time, and then recalled to enable us to repeat the movement. In addition to perceptual input we have information about the movement we intended to make, which may include a verbal label (such as the name of a particular position in dance or yoga), and the instructions to the motor system that implemented the movement. This information too may be encoded, kept in a memory store, and retrieved for later use. The study of memory for movement is concerned with how information from all these sources is utilised when movements are put into memory, with the nature and efficiency of the memory store or stores that are involved, and with the presence or absence of the appropriate cues to the correct movement when we come to retrieve it.

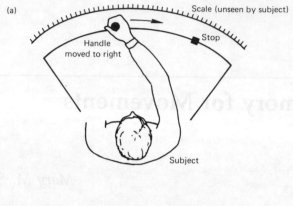

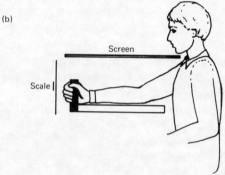

Figure 1. The linear positioning task used by Laabs (1973). (a) view from the top with screen removed, (b) view from the side.

THE SHORT-TERM MOTOR-MEMORY PARADIGM

The majority of the studies of memory for movement have dealt with recall of movement after a short interval, and have used a task known as *linear positioning*. This task involves moving the hand and arm in a straight line or curve and then trying to make another movement that may be of the same length or to the same final position. The movements are typically slow enough for modifications to be made by the subject during movement execution. The equipment used by Laabs (1973), which is shown in Figure 1, allowed subjects to make movements of the whole arm from the shoulder. The subject moved a bar until it touched a stop, the experimenter moved the bar to another starting position and the subject tried to repeat the movement, either to the same final position or for the same distance. In this case, and in many others, the subjects' first movement is an active one. In other studies the experimenter moves the subject's arm, while the subject remains passive. In some studies there is a delay between the first and second movement which may be empty, occupied by another movement task, or occupied by a nonmovement task.

In these linear-positioning studies we often speak of criterion and reproduction movements. The *criterion* is the movement that is to be remembered and the *reproduction* is the subject's attempt to recall it. If the criterion distance and final position are selected by the experimenter and the subject moves to a stop, or if the movement is passive, then it could be argued that the criterion is not produced by the subject and so the trial in which memory is tested does not involve movement reproduction. However, when retention after active and passive presentation of the criterion is of interest in the same study, then it is simpler to refer to all test trials in the same way, that is, to call them all reproduction trials.

When movements are presented to subjects they are passive or active movements, depending on whether the subject's arm is moved by the experimenter or not. In addition, the subject may be allowed to choose the position at which the movement will terminate, that is, to *self-select* it. In an active self-selected movement the subject initiates, executes, and terminates the movement. In a passive self-selected movement the experimenter initiates and executes the movement by moving the subject's arm, but the subject tells the experimenter when to stop the movement, so that termination is under control. If the terminal position of the criterion movement is not under subject control then it is *constrained* in some way by the experimenter. This may be done by putting a stop in the track, although it would be possible to tell the subject to stop moving, or to use some other cue such as a visual or auditory signal. In an *active* constrained movement the subject initiates and executes the limb movement, but does not terminate it, and in a *passive* constrained movement the limb movement is initiated, executed, and terminated by the experimenter. In most cases the reproduction trial is an active self-selected movement in which the subject controls all three aspects of the movement.

Controlling Visual and Verbal Cues

Direct sight of the hand and of the track along which movements are made is prevented in many studies. This is because subjects may use visual markers from the environment rather than try to remember the characteristics of the movement itself. If a movement stopped in line with a mark on the table top then its end position could be recalled accurately. Even when sight of the equipment and surrounding area is not allowed subjects can use spatial reference points to help them code movement in a way which the experimenter may not be expecting. The midline of the body provides a location that can be remembered and used to generate a new movement to the same position. "Just past the mid-line" could be used in the same way as a visually mediated label.

Remembering what we have done and what has happened to us is often concerned with words, both the words we use to describe things to ourselves and so code them into memory, and the words that we use to describe our memories to other people. When presented with new movement information we may re-cast it verbally into a form which is easier to use. One way to do this is to count while making the criterion movement, remember the final number, and count again when repeating the movement. This means that both the rate of movement and the speed of counting have to be controlled accurately, which may be just as difficult as remembering the movement in another form. Some experimenters have attempted to prevent subjects from using counting because they want to isolate other factors such as the role of proprioceptive information. In other cases, experimenters have recognised that the strategies that subjects use to make sense of information and to help them code and retrieve it, are of interest in themselves.

Counting is not the only way in which a verbal label can be used to make coding and retrieval more efficient. It is also possible to label a distance as a number of centimetres or inches and then to use that number to reproduce a movement that feels or looks as if it is of that length. As with counting, error can occur when the movement is encoded as a certain number of inches, when that number is retrieved, or when the movement is actually produced.

Very few studies of short-term memory for movement have been concerned with patterns of movement, or with memory for movements of different types. Some studies have looked at memory for drawing or tracing simple figures so that pattern is important as well as distance and position. However, the majority of the experiments reported in this chapter deal with linear positioning and are concerned with perceptual effects in encoding and retrieval, memory for distance and position, relations between perceptual modalities, the role of subject choice and control, and the nature of the strategies that subjects use to help them deal with simple movement information.

MEASURING MEMORY FOR SIMPLE MOVEMENTS

In many of the experiments on short-term motor memory (STMM) a
subject is presented with several criterion movements during an experimental session. Each criterion is presented several times and is reproduced following each presentation. In some cases a criterion is presented once and then is reproduced several times in succession. It is also
possible to have each criterion movement presented once and reproduced once.

Absolute, Constant, and Variable Error

In the first two types of experiments described above there are several
reproductions of each criterion movement and the amount by which
they differ from the criterion is used to calculate an error score for each
subject. There are three ways in which such a score can be calculated.
The first way is to take the size of each error (the difference between the
criterion and production), regardless of sign, and average over the
number of reproduction trials. This gives a measure of *absolute error*
(AE). The second way is to retain the sign of each error when the
average is calculated to produce an arithmetic mean error, or a *constant
error* score (CE). The effect of using these two methods is shown in
Figure 2. If a subject sometimes moves too far, and sometimes not far
enough, some errors will be positive and some negative. When CE is
calculated these errors may cancel out so that CE approaches zero. AE
could, however, be quite large. If all errors are overshoots or undershoots then the size of CE and AE will be the same.

The third way in which accuracy of repeated reproduction is measured relates to the consistency with which the movement is reproduced
and is termed *variable error* (VE). This has been calculated as either the
variance around the mean CE score for each individual, or as the square
root of the variance (the standard deviation).

In general, the measures of accurate performance used in a study will
relate to the theoretical issues being investigated. If the experiment is
concerned with perceptual factors that may lead to a directional bias, or
with the way in which reproduction is affected if a movement of a
different size occurs between criterion and reproduction, then CE will be
used, because it provides a measure of directional error. Variable error
on the other hand, is a measure of the strength of the memory for

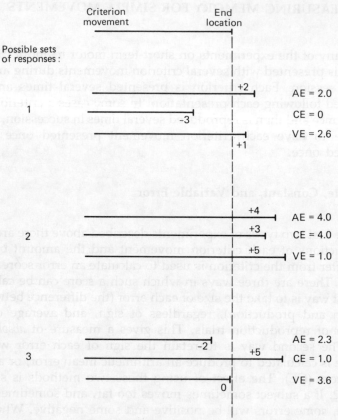

Figure 2. Absolute, constant, and variable error for three sets of reproductions of a criterion movement. In the first set the responses bracket the target so that CE is zero while AE and VE are similar to each other. In the second set all responses are overshoots so that AE and CE are the same while VE is small. In the third set, the three measures give different results.

movement in that it is concerned with reliable, consistent reproduction. Consistency in reproduction need not, however, relate to the accuracy with which the criterion was encoded. Seashore and Bavelas (1941) showed that subjects who repeated a movement without any idea of whether they were correct or not, and without any standard to compare with, became more consistent over trials. They were able to develop a movement plan, without reference to a criterion, which allowed them to maintain a low variable error score. Consistency may increase over trials if an experimental session is long. Laabs and Simmons (1981) have argued that VE is the appropriate measure when the storage characteristics of motor memory are being studied. However, if there are many ways in which a movement can be encoded, particularly if the subject can plan the criterion movement, this could also lead to greater consistency in reproduction.

AE has been criticised by some researchers (e.g., Schutz & Roy, 1973) because it confounds VE and CE. AE is a function of the other two measures. When CE is equal to zero, that is, when the subject overshoots and undershoots the target distance by the same amount, VE and AE provide the same information, which is a measure of the spread of the scores round zero. If CE is very much different from zero (as when all attempts are either overshoots or undershoots), then AE and CE provide the same information. However, if CE is not zero but some test movements are longer and some shorter than the criterion, then AE reflects a combination of CE and VE that may not be known. This has led Henry (1974) to suggest a composite measure of error which is given by the sum of the CE squared and the VE squared. Schutz (1977) has suggested that AE should not be used at all, that CE should be used as a measure of individual bias and VE as a measure of an individual's consistency in performance. However, there may be cases in which there are no theoretical reasons to expect alterations in direction of error, or its consistency. If it is possible to argue that AE is more relevant to the question being asked, then it may be possible to use AE. In a practical context it may be more useful to know how far out the response is, rather than the direction of the error or its consistency. In many studies all three types of error are reported.

As we have suggested, the question of how to measure error is not one that can be answered independently of the processes that are thought to be involved in memory, but the answer does affect the way in which an experiment is carried out. Consistency in reproduction may relate to the strength and clarity of the representation in memory, or the accuracy with which the representation can be implemented at reproduction, but estimating consistency does require repetition of either the criterion and the reproduction, or of the reproduction only. If there is no repetition of the reproduction then VE can not be used and, if no bias is expected, the use of the unsigned error for each subject is appropriate.

Repetition Effects

When the same criterion is presented to a subject several times, the reproductions of the movement may change over testing because the subject is using information from all the previous trials as well as the current one. Thus, repetition effects may be confounded with the effects of the variables being investigated (Gentile, 1974).

When an experiment uses a small set of criterion movements of different sizes and a subject is asked to reproduce each of them several times a *range effect* or central-tendency bias can be found. This means that short movements tend to be made longer, while long movements tend to be made shorter. Poulton (1981) has suggested that only the first trial in a series is uncontaminated by bias of this type because every subsequent trial is affected by the previous ones. However, even the first movement is affected by bias as a subject has some idea of the possible range of movements that can be presented. In addition to this, the experimental situation in which subjects are placed may be new to them, and the task they are asked to do is also a strange one. People are not accustomed to making simple arm movements without being able to see the arm and hand and without a goal other than the execution of the movement itself. Normal movements are part of an intentional sequence of actions and may be coded as such, so trying to remember the distance the hand has moved, or the position to which it moved may not be as simple as it seems. The first of such movements will be an uncertain one and differences due to experimental conditions may be obscured. Using one trial per subject requires very large numbers of subjects, but this should not be taken as the chief reason for deciding against this experimental approach.

Range effects do not always occur in the same way, even when movements are repeated. Different ways of presenting movements to the subject produce different types of error over a range of movement extents. Subjects can be asked to move actively and select the terminal position, or the movement may be constrained by the insertion of a stop so that the terminal position cannot be selected, or the subject's arm may be moved passively by the experimenter. If interactions between these experimental manipulations and the range of movements are found it may be that the extent of bias differs in these conditions (Martenuik, 1977).

MEMORY FOR CONSTRAINED MOVEMENTS

When movements are imposed on a subject their perceptual characteristics determine what the subject is able to encode into memory. The information available may be mediated by sight or feeling, it may be based on the end location or on the actual distance moved, and the subject may attempt to structure the input into a more accessible form. In the interval before a movement is reproduced the subject may be able to rehearse some of the information in memory, so that reproduction can be accurate provided no other task interrupts the rehearsal. This is similar to the way in which we can remember a recently heard telephone number for a short period provided no one asks us a question during the period. If we do not rehearse, then performance is better if we recall the number immediately than it is after a delay.

The interference that prevents rehearsal may not have to be movement information; a verbal task, such as counting backwards in threes from a large number, can be used. A study by Posner (1967) asked subjects to reproduce a movement immediately, after an unfilled interval, or after an interval filled with a digit-classification task. He found that visual memory for movement was as accurate after an unfilled interval as it was immediately but was less accurate after a filled interval. For kinaesthetic information, however, performance became less accurate after an interval whether it was filled or not. These results suggested that visual information could be rehearsed but that kinaesthetic information could not. Following this work one approach to memory for movement has been to investigate which movement cues are coded into memory in a form which can be rehearsed and which will become less useful over time whether rehearsal is possible or not.

Location and Distance

One of the most obvious questions to be asked about encoding linear movement is whether people remember the distance they moved through, or the position at which they ended up. Normally, both cues are available and they both give the correct terminal position if the starting position remains the same, but the fact that cues are available does not mean that they are used, or that they are equally helpful. If a criterion movement from point A to point B is 10 cm long then a reproduction movement that has a new starting point C, and is required to terminate at B measures *location accuracy;* a reproduction movement that also starts at C but which has to be 10 cm long, measures *distance accuracy.* In most studies on STMM the reproduction movement begins in a different place from the start of the criterion movement and subjects are told that this is the case when they are asked to reproduce the criterion distance or terminal position.

Posner (1967) suggested that nonvisual cues for movement could not be rehearsed. Subsequent studies separated these into location and dis-

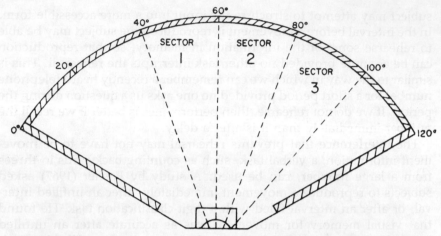

Figure 3. The size of movements and the sectors in which they ended in Laabs' (1973) experiment. Sixty degrees is straight ahead of the subject. From "Retention characteristics of different reproduction cues in motor short-term memory", by Laabs, G. J. (1973). *Journal of Experimental Psychology*, *100*, 168–177. Reprinted with permission.

tance cues. Laabs (1973) asked subjects to reproduce either location or distance, either immediately after the criterion movement or after a delay. He used a curvilinear track on which subjects made criterion movements by moving a handle to a stop set by the experimenter. Neither the stop nor the track could be seen. The arc of the track was divided into three 20° sectors in which final locations could occur. Subjects moved from left to right, so that a 60° movement from 0° would end up straight ahead of the subject between sectors 1 and 2 (see Figure 3).

Each reproduction movement commenced from a position which was different from the start of the criterion movement. Subjects in one condition reproduced distance and in the other condition they reproduced location. The reproduction movements in each group were matched for length and final location, so that accuracy could be compared across groups. This means that if a subject in the distance condition was required to move 20° and the movement started 40° along the track then a subject in the location condition would be required to move to 60° and would start at 40° along the track. When distance and location movements are matched like this any error which results from the particular movement lengths and end positions which are used is found equally in both conditions, so differences between the conditions are more likely to be due to the experimental manipulations.

Laabs used the VE score made by each subject in each sector under the two delay conditions and found that there was a much greater increase in VE when distance information was recalled after an interval than there was for location information. This is interpreted as meaning that distance information decays over an empty retention interval while location information does not. If people tend to have a clear idea of the movements they are making, then their errors will not vary a great deal, but if their memory is poor, then some movements will be much too long and some much too short, so the VE score is greater. After an unfilled interval it seems that memory for distance is very uncertain while that for location is no worse than it is immediately after presentation. If the interval is occupied by an activity like counting backwards in threes then location is also reproduced less consistently.

There have been many other studies which support the claim that location is a more accurate cue for movement reproduction than distance (e.g., Roy, 1977) and in general it would appear that for simple movements of this sort a spatial location is retained over a short interval more accurately than an extent. This may be because a spatial location is not only specified by proprioceptive inflow but can be located within a spatial coordinate system in a more abstract way. Wallace (1977) asked subjects to make a movement to a target location with one hand and in one direction and then to reproduce the location with the same hand or with the other hand, by moving in the same direction or the opposite direction. He found that switching limbs and moving in the opposite direction led to considerable error while switching limbs and moving in the same direction did not; that is, specific information about the felt position of the limb is not required if the end position can be coded into a spatial framework in which direction of movement is held constant. If the location code involves a relationship between the position of a limb and the surrounding context, as well as perceptual information about the felt position of the limb, then the maintenance of consistent reproduction of end location may be due to this elaboration of the perceptual input. Distance, on the other hand, may not be coded in as many ways so there are fewer cues for recall after an interval.

Each criterion movement provides both distance and location information, and although each may have different memory characteristics this does not mean that it is possible to use one type of information independently of the other. If it is possible to select out and remember only location cues, moving the starting position for a reproduction closer to the subject (the criterion having started on the subject's left side) should not lead to consistent overshooting or undershooting of the end position. However, because the distance involved in such a reproduction would be shorter than that in the criterion, systematic overshooting would indicate that distance cues had also been picked up and that location information could not be isolated.

A study by Walsh, Russell, Imanaka, and James (1979) investigated

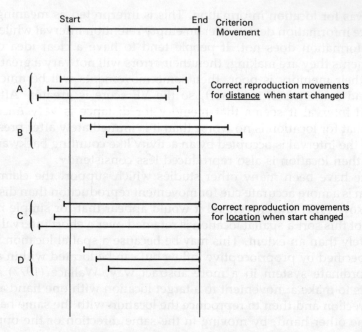

Figure 4. Prediction of error direction in the reproduction of distance and location when the start of the reproduction movement is varied to the right and left of the start of the criterion movement. Errors towards the end location of the criterion in A will be overshoots, in B will be undershoots. Errors towards the criterion distance in C will be undershoots, in D will be overshoots.

the independence of location and distance cues. Subjects were asked to make long and short movements to a stop and the starting position for reproduction was varied to both right and left of the criterion start (see Figure 4). This means that half of the distance reproductions moved beyond the criterion terminal location and half did not, while half the location reproductions were longer than the criterion distance and half were not. Walsh *et al.* predicted that distance reproductions would err in the direction of the terminal position of the criterion movement but that location reproduction would not err in the direction of the criterion distance.

In this experiment CE is the appropriate measure of performance because directional bias is expected. The analysis of CE showed that the reproduction of both distance and location erred in the direction of the other cue (see Figure 5). Subjects were unable to prevent the information that was not required from influencing their reproduction movement. Two conclusions follow from this finding. One is that CE differences that are found between location and distance conditions may be artifacts

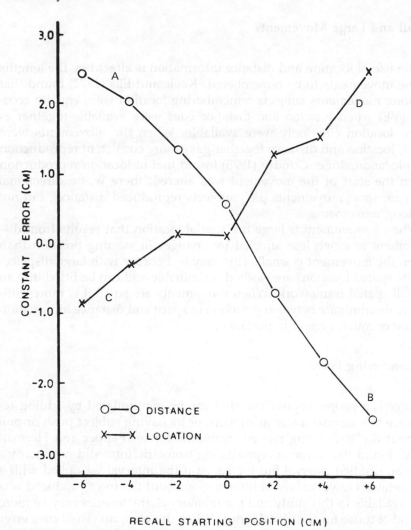

Figure 5. CE for the reproduction of distance or location as a function of the starting position of the reproduced movement. A, B, C, and D refer to the categories of error shown in Figure 4. From "Memory for constrained and preselected movement location and distance: Effects of starting position and length", by Walsh, W. D., Russell, D. G., Imanaka, K., James, B. (1979). *Journal of Motor Behavior, 11*, 201–214.

of the experimental design if the starting position for reproduction is moved in one direction only. The second conclusion, which is more interesting in terms of the memory processes involved, is that memory for movement to a stop cannot be accounted for in terms of only one of the two types of information available.

Small and Large Movements

The use of location and distance information is affectd by the lengths of the movements to be remembered. Keele and Ells (1972) found that for long movements subjects remembering location were equally accurate (VE) when location and distance cues were available together as when location cues only were available. When the movements were short, location and distance together gave more consistent reproduction than location alone. Gundry (1975) found that in location reproduction when the start of the movement was altered, there was a directional error for short movements (i.e., subjects reproduced distance), but not for long movements.

When a movement is large the spatial location that results from displacement is much less affected by changes in starting position than when the movement is small. This may be because with large displacements spatial locations are easily discriminable and can be fitted into an overall spatial framework. When movements are small it is more difficult to discriminate between positions in space and distance information can be of much greater importance.

Remembering Force

Force is a proprioceptive cue that can be manipulated by adding resistance to a normal linear movement or by having subject push or pull without the limb being moved (isometric force). Pepper and Herman (1970) found that error in reproducing isometric force did not increase over an unfilled interval but increased if the interval was filled with a verbal task. However, visual information about the force produced was also available in this study and the memory characteristics may be more typical of those for the visual input. When there are no visual cues error in reproduction of force increases over time (Fowler & Notterman, 1975).

The difficulties in force and distance reproduction over time suggest that both are normally coded in terms of the proprioceptive input while location can be translated into spatial coordinates and maintained more easily.

INTERFERENCE IN MEMORY

Memory is not static. Items that are memorised today will be affected by items memorised yesterday and will affect items that are memorised tomorrow. This may happen because previous items alter the processes used to remember future ones by changing the framework we use to remember things. It may also happen because similarities between items lead them to be coded and recalled in similar ways so that error and confusion can occur when we try to recall items which are not sufficiently differentiated.

The difference between remembering movements at the beginning of learning a sport or other skill and remembering them after skill has developed reflects the first kind of change in memory processes, changes due to the development of new mental structures that allow coding to take place differently. Most STMM studies do not provide enough experience for this kind of reorganisation to take place. However, the interference between different items when we try to recall one of them has been used to investigate the kinds of coding in STMM. If it can be shown that one movement or type of movement interferes with the recall or recognition of another, then the movements either share some attributes or involve the same processes.

In some motor-memory studies a distinction has been made between capacity and structural interference (Kahneman 1973). *Capacity interference* is taken to relate to the operation of a general purpose central processor that is used for many tasks and cannot be shared over two tasks with high demands. *Structural interference,* on the other hand, occurs when two tasks require the use of the same processes. If two tasks require visual processing, interference may occur because they cannot both occupy the same processes simultaneously, while two tasks such as looking at pictures and playing the piano may not interfere because they do not share the same processes (see Chapter 7).

These kinds of interference are more easily understood when tasks are being performed simultaneously than they are when they involve the use of sequential items in memory. However, there are some differences in memory that relate to whether an interfering task prevents the elaboration of encoding which would allow the remembered item to be retained accurately, or to whether the interfering task produces memory codes which are similar to those produced in the first task so that recall is confused.

In Laabs' (1973) experiment, which was discussed earlier, subjects who were asked to count backwards in threes before they reproduced a movement had greater error (VE) in reproducing location than they did after an unfilled interval. Distance was inaccurate after an unfilled interval and this did not alter if the interval was filled. Laabs concluded that kinaesthetically presented location coding can be maintained provided rehearsal is possible, but that kinaesthetic distance coding deteriorated over time whether rehearsal was possible or not. Because counting backwards uses quite different resources from remembering a movement this capacity interference may also be understood as preventing the elaboration of location coding which takes place over an unfilled interval and allows for more cues to be useful for reproduction.

When different movements are interpolated between criterion and reproduction the errors that occur may be due to the generation of similar movement codes which prevent accurate retrieval of the first movement, that is, both movements may be specified in memory in similar ways. Alternatively, if the second movement follows the first very quickly it is possible that the elaboration of encoding that occurs once the perceptual information is available treats the two movements as one.

Diewert (1975) found that a distance-judgement task led to greater error in reproducing distance than visual interference or a delay but that a visual distance judgement and a kinaesthetic judgement led to greater error in reproducing location. This suggests that spatial coding uses some of the same processes as a visual task. The felt location is in a different perceptual mode to the visual input so that the interference occurs at a more abstract spatial level. Johnson (1982) has shown that watching visual spatial cues while imagining making a movement of a length specified by the visual cues also results in interference.

If a movement can be coded in many ways its retention after an interpolation will be affected by the similarity of the cues available in the interpolated movement. That is, if location cues are confused with subsequent location cues, rather than with distance, then errors should be greater when there is a different end location for the interpolated movement than they are when it is a different distance (Laabs 1974). Hagman (1978) used interpolated movements in which distance was repeated and location varied, distance varied and location repeated, both distance and location varied, and both remaining the same. He found that recall was not affected by an unfilled retention interval for either location or distance but that interpolation led to greater errors when the aspect of the movement which the subject was attempting to remember was varied. So, for distance recall there were large errors when distance was different in the interpolated movement, whether location was altered or not, and for location recall it was the presence of a different location in the interpolated movements which led to most error, again whether distance was altered or not.

Hagman concluded that location and distance can be coded quite separately, although some experimental situations will encourage the use of multiple cues for any movement. Because Walsh et al. (1979) have indicated that distance does affect location and vice versa, there is clearly a need to discover why these two aspects are separated in some studies but not in others. Apart from the use of interpolation, Hagman's procedure differed in one important way from other studies. His subjects reproduced the criterion immediately, then experienced the interpolated movements, and then reproduced the criterion again. This means that they had already attempted to reproduce distance or location from a new starting position before the interpolated movements were presented. The interpolated movements were actually affecting the memory for a self-selected reproduction movement which was chosen for either its length or its terminal location. In this situation the effects of interpolated distance and location can be expected to be different from those found when a movement is constrained and only perceptual cues to distance and end location are available.

When subjects are allowed to define their criterion movements and make a constrained movement before reproducing the criterion, interference effects are different from those found when the criterion is constrained by the experimenter. This was shown by Patrick (1981) who concluded that the magnitude of the interpolated response relative to the criterion affected the reproduction of constrained movements but not of subject controlled movements. Distance and location cues were not separated in this study but the result does suggest that the findings in studies of constrained movement in which only the perceptual consequences of movement are available may not generalise to memory for movements which are made under the subject's control.

ACTIVE, PASSIVE
AND SELF-SELECTED MOVEMENTS

When a subject does not have control of all aspects of a criterion movement the number of cues available for encoding and retrieval is decreased. If the movement is constrained the subject has to use proprioceptive information about terminal position although the rate of movement can be controlled. The control of rate may occur when there are repeated trials in an experiment so that the subject knows what the movement is likely to be, can learn to move at a steady rate and try to move at the same rate when reproducing distance. If the criterion movement is passive then all information about it comes from inflow, and in most experimental situations this means proprioception only.

When we make normal voluntary movements many more cues are available, as they are when a subject in an experiment is allowed to control all aspects of the criterion movement. Movements that the subject controls differ in three major ways from those that are made passively; the subject has a plan for the movement, knows how the movement was executed and is expecting the sensory consequences of the movement, and we can investigate the contribution of each one of these to the coding and retention of movement. These three aspects can be broken down further. The plan for the movement may be coded verbally, in visual imagery, in nonvisual imagery, or in a motor-specific code which is not very accessible to the subject.

The execution of the movement allows the subject to monitor efference, that is, to check and store the actual outflow pattern for the movement. The efferent information may also be used to signal that sensory input related to the movement is expected. This is often called *corollary discharge* (Teuber, 1974) and it may indicate that movement has occurred, or it may give specific information about the nature of the movement and therefore of the sensory input to be expected. The first of these two meanings of corollary discharge is similar to the concept of efference copy that has been used to account for the stability of the visual field in voluntary eye movements (Helmholtz, 1866). The copy of the efferent commands that is retained as a movement is made could be used to signal that movement had occurred or to assess the input from a movement in terms of its match to the stored efferent copy. Some confusion about these terms exists in the literature. We will use *corollary discharge* to refer to advance knowledge of sensory input and *efference copy* for stored information about the efference itself.

Efference Copy

Efference copy was suggested to be crucial for accurate reproduction of movement by Jones (1974a). He found that the accuracy of reproduction of distance was not affected by varying the starting point of the reproduction if criterion movements were produced actively by the subject. This finding, and the general improvement in recall of movements that are made actively led Jones to suggest that efferent commands for the movement were stored as efference copy and could be used to reproduce the movement without any contribution from peripheral feedback. This view was in sharp contrast to that of Adams (1971), in which the control and retention of movement was seen as dependent on peripheral feedback, which could be matched with a copy of the correct feedback to produce an accurate reproduction. The growing evidence that active movements are more accurately recalled than passive ones suggests that there is more to memory for movement than matching peripheral feedback.

Jones' hypothesis was that the efferent commands that were sent out and stored as efference copy would be in terms of distance as they would specify rate and duration of muscle contraction. This means that active selection of a terminal location should not lead to accurate reproduction if the reproduction movement starts from a different place so that distance does not remain the same. An experiment by Stelmach, Kelso, and Wallace (1975) showed that this was not the case. They found that self-selected location was reproduced with greater accuracy than self-selected distance. However, because Stelmach *et al.* also showed that self-selected location was reproduced more accurately than constrained or passive location it cannot be concluded that proprioceptive cues alone are allowing self-selected location to be reproduced more accurately than self-selected distance.

Encoding Strategies

Because active, subject-controlled movement is recalled more accurately and consistently than passive or constrained movement, and this is not chiefly a function of distance coding, some other aspect of the choice of movement must be important in storing and recalling the movement accurately. It has been suggested by Roy and Diewert (1975) that subjects who choose their own movements have a superior encoding strategy. This means that they have more information about the movement available to them and they can encode it more accurately. Roy and Diewert allowed subjects to move a slider to the end of a track and back, before they produced a criterion movement. Subjects who could select their movement were then asked to make a criterion movement which was half the length of the slider. Each subject in a second group was matched to a subject in the selection condition and moved to a stop placed at the end of that subject's criterion movement. Subjects in the constrained group were told that their criterion movement was half the length of the original movement along the track. So, in both the self-selection and constrained groups subjects knew how long the criterion movement was in relation to the first movement, and criterion distances were matched between the groups. AEs were reported and no differences in recall of the criterion movement were found between the two conditions.

The findings of Roy and Diewert indicate that advance knowledge of the type of movement may be the important component in the reproduction of self-selected movements. These findings have been extended by Roy (1978), who included a third experimental group. His subjects could select and produce the criterion, move to a stop with advance knowledge of the movement distance, or move to a stop without this knowledge. The procedure was similar to that of Roy and Diewert except that the third group did not have a preliminary movement along the track and did not know that the criterion was half that length. In addition, recall was either immediate, after a 20-second unfilled interval or after a 20-second interval in which the subject counted backward in threes to prevent rehearsal. The results were analysed in terms of VE, CE, and AE, but CE showed no effects (i.e., there were no consistent directional differences). For AE and VE the uninformed constrained group performed less accurately than the other two groups which were equally accurate. This was true for immediate reproduction and after the unfilled interval but after a filled interval all groups made equally large errors.

Planning and Efference

So, knowing something in advance about how long a distance will be allows that distance to be remembered as well as one that is self-selected. Advance information that may be part of the intention or plan may be one of the most important components in memory for simple movements. However, this position has been disputed by Kelso (1977a), who argues that it is actually making the movement that counts, not just advance information. He asked subjects to choose a movement but did not allow them to make it. Instead, the arm was moved passively by the experimenter until the subject said "stop". In this case the advance information exists, but not the efference itself, and subjects were trained not to allow any muscle activity in the arm while it was being moved so that it was completely passive and only incoming information about its position was available. In this situation active self-selection was found to lead to more accurate reproduction than passive self-selection, which was no better than active or passive constrained movement (see Figure 6). That is, knowing where to end a movement is not enough to code it accurately if the movement is not made actively.

In Kelso's first experiment subjects reproduced the criterion actively, as they do in the vast majority of motor memory experiments. However, in a second experiment subjects were asked to reproduce the criterion by saying when their passively moved limbs had reached the correct distance and position. In passive recall all groups made equally large er-

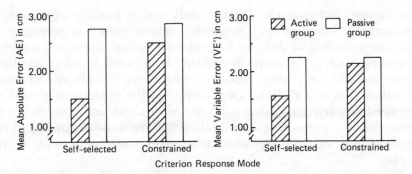

Figure 6.   AE and VE in reproduction of actively and passively produced criterion movements that were either subject-selected or constrained. From "Planning and efferent components in the coding of movement", by Kelso, J. A. S. (1977a). *Journal of Motor Behavior 9*, 33–47. Reprinted with permission.

rors, although for the self-selected condition these were much larger than the active recall error score. The advantage found for the retention of selected, active movements only occurs if the reproduction movement is also made actively, and even for constrained movements there is some increase in VE with passive recall. This means that the memory for either the selected location or the proprioceptive input from the movement is coded best when efference is present, but the circumstances of the criterion trial must be repeated for accurate recall to occur.

Actually making the movement seems to be important to accurate memory, possibly because the kinaesthetic information is coded more efficiently when the movement is actively produced. However, Roy (1978) in a second experiment, found that there was no difference between reproduction of an active, informed, constrained movement and reproduction of a passive, informed, constrained movement. As he had already found that active informed constraint did not differ from active selection, he concluded that it is advance information that is most important, not active or passive execution. He also showed that for an uninformed constrained movement active production of the criterion led to more active reproduction than passive production. Thus, when a subject knows how far a movement is likely to be it does not matter whether efference is present or not, but if the subject does not know this then the presence of efference is important for coding and retaining the movement.

In an attempt to evaluate the contribution of efference and planning in the consolidation of a movement memory Summers, Levey, and Wrigley (1981) found that for reproduction of selected location active or passive practice of the criterion led to more accurate subsequent reproduction, but that for distance only active practice improved reproduction. Summers *et al.* suggested that efference is necessary for accurate encoding of distance but not for location, for which a plan or encoding strategy is more important. If selected location coding is strengthened by expected sensory consequences that are also locational in nature (Kelso & Wallace, 1978) control of the movement itself is not required. For selected distance, on the other hand, active control of the execution of a movement allows rate and force to be controlled so that more accurate distance reproduction requires active movement, not just a plan.

This position is in opposition to that of Roy (1978) and Roy and Diewert (1978), but these authors allow verbal labeling of the movements which Kelso (1977a) and Summers *et al.* (1981) do not. If Kelso's subjects had also had a label for the criterion movement (e.g., "half the length of the slider—about 5 inches") the effects of efference might have been obscured. It seems that one important factor is the number of sources of information available. If there is a good plan or a functional verbal code, then efference is not so necessary, but selection without extra help in coding the plan, forces subjects to use the efference to code a movement that can not be accurately recognised when proprioceptive input occurs without that efference. However, if the plan relates to distance or location in an abstract code while efference coding relates to the specific details of the movement produced then the independence of planning and efference can be shown.

Planning and Feedback

Selection is more than active production of a movement, and it affects the input of proprioceptive information. Both the planning component and the relationship of active movement to its sensory consequences are important topics in our attempts to understand how movements are remembered, and both require that we consider another source of movement related information and a possible component of a plan—vision. The role of vision in the formation of plans and the execution of movements will be considered in the next section and we will end this section by considering a finding which suggests that it may be possible for subjects to maintain a plan for a movement separately from other components.

Kelso and Wallace (1978) report that when subjects are asked to select a terminal position and tell an experimenter where a stop should be placed, they can reproduce the movement accurately. However, if the stop is not placed in the selected position and the subject is asked to reproduce the movement actually made, this movement will err in the direction of the plan. If the stop is placed closer to the subject than the plan indicated, then the reproduction of the movement will be an overshoot. This suggests that the plan interacts with the actual sensory consequences of the movement made to produce a biased memory, part plan, part sensory consequences. However, when subjects tried to reproduce the planned movement there was no bias from the sensory consequences of the actual movement made. The plan, however specified, may remain in memory although the movement was not carried out correctly. This would make sense in situations where external environmental factors cause a planned movement to go wrong. If the original plan can be maintained it can be corrected to deal with the prevailing conditions, or executed again when conditions have changed. When plan and execution agree there may be no way of showing that the components can be coded separately if necessary. If such a disagreement is unlikely to occur there would be no reason for subjects to separate out components of movement, particularly as it seems that accurate reproduction occurs when all the information available in criterion production is also available for reproduction.

Another attempt to separate the image or plan from the actual movement made and stored in memory was made by Laszlo and Ward (1978). They asked subjects to draw a triangle and then to repeat the same triangle. They found that when subjects had no proprioceptive or visual feedback they produced criterion movements which were not triangular but added loops or curves or omitted angles (see Figure 7). Repetitions of these movements without feedback were accurate and they also contained the nontriangular components. So, peripheral input was not necessary for the reproduction of a correct sequence of movements when the subject was trying to implement a well-formed plan, but the execution, which could be repeated by using the same central mechanism, was not a good attempt at the plan itself as it could not be monitored and corrected.

Plan is not being used in the same way when it is referring to such different entities as a well-formed concept of triangularity providing a general schema for movement and an attempt to move a short distance along a slider. The subject performing the second task is not able to plan at a high level, so movement plans may be closer to efferent programs for the actual movements produced. The use of movements that have meaning for people would require changes in the concepts and terminology of motor memory and until this occurs words like plan can only be understood with reference to the experimental circumstances in which they are implemented.

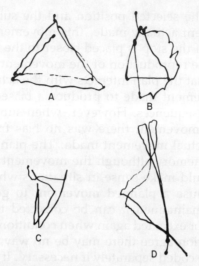

Figure 7. Subjects' performance traces of first and recall triangle: (A) active control with vision, (B) passive vibration, no vision, (C) passive ischaemic block with vision, (D) active ischaemic block, no vision. From "Vision, proprioception and corollary discharge in a movement recall test", by Laszlo, J. I., Ward, G. R. (1978). *Acta Psychologica*, 42, 477–493. Reprinted with permission.

SIGHT AND FEEL IN MEMORY FOR MOVEMENT

It is possible to watch someone else make a movement and then to make it oneself. It is also possible to watch someone else make a movement and then to recognise the feel of the movement if one is moved through it. The first of these abilities is an obvious one, learning would be difficult in many tasks if the sight of someone else moving could not be used as a pattern for movement, but it does imply that there are close relationships between visual input and the choice of movement. The ability to recognise that one type of input comes from the same movement as another type of input suggests that there is a common system for perception of movement-related information. One input may be translated into another, or each could be translated into a neutral code and matched in that.

Verbal labeling seems one obvious method of translating one type of input into a central code. If a seen movement is called "5 inches" and a felt movement is also called "5 inches" then they would be recognised as being of the same extent. However, because preverbal children can match felt and seen movements (Bryant, Jones, Claxton, & Perkins, 1972), and so can some apes (Davenport & Rogers, 1970), it is unlikely that verbal labeling is the only way in which visual and kinaesthetic information can be matched or integrated.

Connolly and Jones (1970) suggested that vision and (nonvisual) kinaesthesis are held in different short-term memory stores and that if a subject was asked to match a seen movement with a felt movement the visual information would be translated into a kinaesthetic code and stored in that form. As they believed that kinaesthetic information decayed over unfilled intervals while visual information did not, this meant that matching vision to kineasthesis would be less accurate than matching kinaesthesis to vision (K–V match) because the kinaesthetic input in the second case would be translated into a visual representation and so maintained by rehearsal. Connolly and Jones proposed that the translation between the modalities was based on an internal representation of the relationship between visual and kinaesthetic input but they do not specify what this representation is, and they do not consider that some aspects of perception may be amodal, others may depend on a categorisation system which allows labeling, and others may give more weight to the input from one sensory modality.

The asymmetry in cross-modal matching found by Connolly and Jones disappears when visual cues in the experimental apparatus are controlled for, (Martenuik & Rodney, 1979), and changing the time at which subjects know that the reproduction trial will require vision or kinaesthesis does not make any difference to the accuracy, either crossmodally, or intra-modally (Newell, Shapiro, & Carlton, 1979). In addition, Connolly and Jones allowed both location and distance cues to be used but it has been shown that crossmodal matches in which location cues are unreliable produce very large errors (Newell et al., 1979), which suggests that the relationship between vision and kinaesthesis may be a function of the type of information that is being conveyed.

When distance and location cues are separated for presentation and test it was found that intramodal matching (V–V and K–K) was more accurate than cross-modal (V–K or K–V) for location, but that for distance K–K matching was no more accurate than the cross-modal matching (Salmoni & Sullivan, 1976). Visual distance information is more accurately retained and recognised than kinaesthetic distance.

In real-world movements vision provides information about the relationships between body parts and the environment directly. So, a hand position can be marked by environmental objects and easily repeated. Distance presented visually is normally simultaneous, the complete extent of a movement can be taken in all at once, but kinaesthetic distance is presented sequentially. This can lead to greater errors in coding because the early parts of the movement may have to be maintained in

TABLE 1. Mean Recognition Errors by 4- and 5-Year-Olds under
Visual–Visual (V–V), Kinaesthetic–Kinaesthetic (K–K), Visual–Kinaesthetic
(V–K), and Kinaesthetic–Visual (K–V) Modality Conditions for Simple
and Complex Patterns[a,b]

Age	Input pattern	Intramodal		Cross-modal	
		V–V	K–K	V–K	K–V
4	Simple	2.42	3.50	3.33	3.67
	Complex	3.33	3.92	3.83	3.58
	Mean	2.88	3.71	3.58	3.63
5	Simple	1.92	2.08	2.58	2.75
	Complex	3.17	3.33	3.83	3.67
	Mean	2.55	2.71	3.21	3.21

[a]Four-year-olds make more errors with kinaesthetic input, both within and
across modalities, but complexity does not make crossmodal matching more
difficult than intramodal matching.
[b]From Millar (1975a).

memory while the later parts are carried out. One way to investigate the
superiority of vision apart from the possibility of unitary perception, is
to present visual movement which is sequential. Bairstow and Laszlo
(1979) have shown that watching a dot of light moving through a pattern
leads to greater error in recognising the pattern later than does seeing
the complete pattern. For young children Rudel and Teuber (1964)
found that when visual patterns were presented sequentially they were
more difficult to match.

If the ability to relate input from one modality to that from another
requires a translation into a neutral code this would have to be acquired
by children as they developed. Millar (1975a) has argued that this would
mean that more errors would occur cross-modally with younger children, and that more complicated patterns would lead to more errors as
more translation would be required. She used sequential visual and
kinaesthetic input and found that overall difficulty did not affect cross
modal matching, that 5- and 10-year-olds made more cross-modal errors
than intramodal errors, but that 4-year-olds had great difficulty whenever kinaesthetic input was involved, either in presentation or test (see
Table 1). This does not support the view that a special translation system
operates. Because the order in which simple and complicated trials were
presented to the subjects made a considerable difference to their performance, it is possible that the subjects use strategies for matching which

are affected by the type of task. That is, subjects do not have to use a visual code, a verbal code, or search for a feature to match between the two inputs, but all of these may be available, and any could be used if the task required it.

Cross-modal matching may not be carried out in any one way that can be specified independently of the task involved. However, the use of kinaesthetic information is affected by the availability of visual coding strategies. Blind children, without any visual experience, make more errors in a spatial-memory task than sighted children do, even although no visual information about the task is available to the sighted children (Millar 1975b). Millar found that the blind children could not repeat a simple series of movements backwards, while sighted children could remember the movements backwards as well as forwards. The kinaesthetic information used by the blind children could not be manipulated in memory and decayed over time, but the sighted children formed an image of the movements which could be scanned in either direction and did not decay. Further evidence for the importance of past visual experience in the coding of movements comes from Hermelin and O'Connor (1975) who found that blind children had greater difficulty with extent cues than with location ones. They suggest that a visual reference system is necessary for the accurate coding of movement extent. Taken together with Millar's findings from a more complicated task this indicates that memory for movements presented kinaesthetically uses stored visual experience, particularly when the movement needs to be manipulated as an image or concerns only distance cues.

Many of the cross-modal studies mentioned here have used simple movements like those in other STMM studies. This leads to a distinction between distance and location. Millar (1975b) has shown that when the pattern of a movement and a position in that pattern is important, past visual experience is necessary for accurate coding. Perhaps more concentration on patterns of movement rather than on extent and location will help to show how important a visual reference system is in the coding of movement.

Interference in motor memory and cross-modal matching both help us to understand the nature of the encoding available for spatial location and the difficulties in retaining distance information. Distance, which is input sequentially, is difficult to encode and retain yet is more accurate after some visual experience than after no visual experience at all. This suggests that distance is not remembered purely in terms of the perception of proprioceptive input but uses a spatial system with visual components although it does so less accurately than location.

VISION AND SUBJECT CONTROL

The dominance of vision over other modalities can be altered by changing the task requirements, but in most cases the default strategy is to give most weight to visual input. Stored relationships between visual and proprioceptive input are also important for remembering movements presented kinaesthetically, although again task demands can affect the accuracy of recall and recognition, particularly with simple linear movements.

When a planned movement is executed, feedback from it can be used to determine whether the movement has been executed correctly or not, and that input may also be used to remember the movement. Stored spatial relationships between vision and proprioception are important for movement planning and the relationships between these modalities may also contribute to the assessment of correctness of a movement and to the memory trace for that movement. The experiment by Laszlo and Ward (1978) mentioned earlier allows a distinction to be made between the role of feedback in control and its role in memory. If the pattern for a movement, such as a triangle, does not include all the instructions for producing a triangle unless feedback is available, then there are clearly some situations in which people do not plan a movement completely in advance in the sense that they do not totally predetermine all aspects of it. If the plan is not a complete one, then it may be stored separately from the actual movement made and its perceptual consequences.

Although Kelso and Wallace (1978) believe that this separation of plan from feedback in memory is possible, Kelso and Frekany (1978) have suggested that when subjects can plan and execute their own movements the presence of visual information can be ignored so that what is planned is executed, stored, and repeated, without influence from vision. The movements used in Kelso and Frekany's study were simple linear ones and it is possible that feedback was not necessary for execution of the planned movement, so the roles of feedback, particularly vision, in control and memory cannot be separated. If the planned movement does not give rise to the expected perceptual consequences, however, the movement *is* changed during execution.

When the visual feedback from a simple linear movement is not what the subjects expect, they alter the course of a self-selected movement as it is made. Smyth (1980) has shown that subjects who saw a display movement that was larger than the movement they were actually making terminated the movement earlier than they did when the display and the movement were the same size. This occurred even though subjects knew that the visual display could be a different size from the movement and that vision would not be present in reproduction. The perceptual consequences of the movement were perceived as incorrect because the erroneous visual information dominated the kinaesthetic information and so the planned movement was altered. When subjects were unable to select their movements but watched a visual display while they made them, the reproductions erred in the direction of the seen size (i.e., the memory for the movement was biased in the direction of the distorted visual information). For self-selection this was not the case, that is, the reproduction was not biased in the direction of the visual size, although the criterion movement itself had been affected by the visual feedback. Selection allowed a central plan to be maintained and repeated although the planned movement was not actually executed.

Vision plays a very important part in memory for movement. It gives accurate position information when the surrounding environment can be seen and accurate distance information when the environment is not visible. Visual experience allows the development of visuospatial codes for movement which are used even when there is no visual input when the movements are made. Vision prevents attention being paid to kinaesthesis when both are available and it can bias memory for movements. It is also very important as a source of feedback about movements and is used to ensure that movements are executed as planned. However, it seems likely that plans can be maintained in memory and repeated without being influenced by the visual feedback which is provided as they are executed.

STRATEGIES

Remembering distances and reproducing them, in isolation from all other movement related activity, is a task to which subjects are not accustomed. They may try to develop ways of coping with the situation which lead to different ways of coding the available information. These strategies have been manipulated by Diewert and Roy (1978), who showed that subjects count and use movement time to remember extent, or they use location cues for the same purpose. When location cues were made less reliable, counting increased. When subjects were encouraged to count they produced very consistent movements that did not differ for immediate reproduction and reproduction after filled and unfilled intervals. When subjects were encouraged to use a location strategy they became less consistent after a filled interval, that is, they needed to rehearse the coding and could not do so.

When subjects are encouraged to encode distance actively they can reproduce movements accurately and the coding can be rehearsed. Few studies have encouraged subjects to be constructive in their movement coding but have emphasised one aspect of the movement and the results from such studies have led to a belief that there is only one type of code for one type of movement, or for one aspect of a movement. It is not always possible to find out what strategy is being used simply by asking subjects, as strategies are not always available to consciousness. Although subjects can be encouraged to use elaborated encoding, the question of whether normal memory is constrained by the nature of the information available, or by the ways in which subjects approach the task, is not easy to answer. Motor-memory studies have not tended to be concerned with individual variation in strategic allocation of resources.

The use of words to code movement has already been discussed in the context of mediation between visual and nonvisual memory codes and whether meaningful movements such as dance steps could be chiefly verbally coded. With simple linear movements verbal labels can be used as aids for both encoding and retrieval. Whitaker and Trumbo (1976) asked subjects to estimate the length (in inches) of passive constrained or active constrained movements, or to produce a movement of a required length which was specified in inches. They found that estimates and productions increased as criterion length increased in all of the conditions. Females tended to overestimate while males tended to underestimate, and females were more variable in their estimations. The reasons for these differences are not clear but they do suggest that individual differences in the use of techniques for remembering movements can be found.

Whitaker and Trumbo's (1976) study shows that verbal labels can be used to access stored distance information and that incoming distance information can be labeled quite consistently. Location information that specifies a position relative to the body midline can also be used to produce movements accurately. Shea (1977) used positions on a clock face to describe locations on a curvilinear track and found that reproduction of a labeled location was much more accurate than reproduction of an unlabeled condition. However, as the use of the label in production of a movement to the correct location was not tested, it is unclear whether the label allowed a correct movement to be made by a constructive process, or helped with the encoding of a criterion and its retrieval for reproduction.

Verbal labels that specify distance, position, or a number that results from counting while moving, can play a part in coding and retrieving movement information. They may do this by reducing uncertainty about the size of the criterion (Roy & Diewert, 1975), by allowing movement characteristics such as time to be controlled (Roy, 1978), or by allowing a position or distance to be specified so that movement information is not necessary to allow accurate production (Shea 1977). In other words, the number of available cues for reproduction are increased and isolated movements can be understood in terms of previous experience of movement of different types. An experiment by Minas (1977) in which subjects had to remember a sequence of actions, suggests that they did not, in fact, use verbal labels, or at least that coding was not in easily accessible verbal form.

Verbal labels are only one of the ways in which subjects can approach a movement memory task. Strategies such as the use of location, counting, or timing, for reproducing distance, may produce different levels of accuracy. Group differences in performance may obscure individual variation which could help us to understand movement codes as the active attempts of the subject to cope with the task demands, rather than as part of a passive perceptual process.

CONTEXT IN MEMORY FOR MOVEMENT

When we acquire a new piece of information we do so in a context and this may influence how we encode the material. For example, the word *bat* will be encoded differently as it occurs in a story about cricket rather than in a story about Dracula. When we come to retrieve the information later, cues from the context may help us to recall it. *Context* has a very wide meaning and in studies of verbal memory it has been used to describe the influence of the room in which a set of words was learned (Smith, 1979), the state of intoxication of the subject while they were learned (Eich, 1977), and the other words which were present at the time of learning (Thomson & Tulving, 1970). In general, it is studied because memory theorists want to know what it is which makes cues for retrieval effective or ineffective.

Studies of context in memory for movement have drawn quite heavily on the literature on memory for words. The notion of *encoding specificity*, which was used by Thomson and Tulving (1970) to mean that a cue will aid retrieval if it provides information which was processed during the encoding of the item to be remembered, has been used by Lee and Hirota (1980) in investigating the recall of linear movement. Thomson and Tulving (1970) found that if the word *cold* was learned in association with the word *ground* then providing *ground* as a cue for the recall of *cold* was very successful, while providing the cue *hot* did not help with the recall of *cold* although it is normally a very strong associate. Lee and Hirota use encoding specificity in a different way. They had subjects make criterion movements that were preselected or constrained and which were actively or passively generated, and then asked them to reproduce the movements either actively or passively. They argued that the method by which the criterion was produced is specific to the encoding of that movement and therefore that reproduction should be more accurate when input and output conditions were matched. They found that this was the case for constrained criterion movements.

The differences between the use of the term *encoding specificity* in these two studies are quite large and they have led Crocker (1982) to criticise Lee and Hirota for trying to transplant concepts from verbal to motor memory without due regard for the differences involved. In verbal memory the words to be remembered are presented at a particular time and in a particular place, but they are words which are in the subject's vocabulary already and which the subjects can produce easily. Differences in production do not count as errors. This means that the task is one which involves episodic rather than semantic, or general-knowledge, memory (Tulving 1972). The context operates by enabling subjects to produce a particular set of words out of the many which they know. In memory for linear movements the subject has to learn what the possible movements are, what they feel like, how to make them, how to discriminate them from each other, all at once, and the retrieval cues may operate on any of these aspects of the learning situation. When an active constrained movement is reproduced actively then the context for recall which operates when the movement is selected is the experimenter's instruction that the movement should be reproduced actively, and this was not available at encoding. The context that Lee and Hirota refer to can only operate during execution, so we have to understand what it is that is used to control the termination of a movement after it has been initiated. It may be that in this case differences in context are differences in matching incoming information in control of execution, rather than in selection and retrieval from memory.

Context has been used in a slightly different way by movement researchers interested in memory for patterns of movement which have been learned over trials. Shea and Morgan (1979) asked subjects to knock down barriers in a specified sequence in response to a light. There were several sequences to be learned and some subjects practised them in blocked trials while others learned them in random order. It was found that learning in a random order led to better retention than learning in blocked trials. This result is described as one in which contextual variety during learning has led to more information processing and therefore to better acquisition of the task. This has been confirmed by Lee and Magill (1983) who found that retention was better if subjects learned in a random order or if they learned in a specified order which meant that they tried a different pattern on each learning trial. Context here refers to predictability in the learning situation not to information available at encoding which is also present at retrieval. In Lee and Magill's (1983) study subjects who learned in a prescribed order were actually tested in a random order but this did not seem to affect their accuracy.

While the use of repeated trials and a pattern of movements make these studies different from STMM studies, their use of the term context makes them relevant here, if only because it helps us to see what such an umbrella term might be understood to mean in a particular situation. Learning in blocked trials means that subjects do not have to attend to as many asepcts of the task on each trial as they would if they were given a different movement on each trial, so they do not encode aspects of the task which would help in differentiating one movement from another. This means that there is less information available when the subjects are asked to recall and they make more errors. Context in practice is having an effect on how much of the input is processed in the first place, it is not explained by the presence or absence of specific recall cues.

Like interference, context is a wide concept which directs us to a dynamic rather than a static view of memory. We do not produce actions which are independent of what has gone before or what comes after, and our ability to recall or recognise movements will depend on how those movements have been dealt with when they were encoded. However, the two uses of context which we have discussed make it clear that we have to be quite specific in our description of what is happening at both encoding and retrieval if we are to understand how movements are remembered.

CONCLUSION

Remembering simple movements over a short duration was once thought to give information about kinaesthetic memory codes, which were abstracted from the subject's intention and any meaning the movement might have. It is now becoming clear that such kinaesthetic memory codes are altered by the presence of other perceptual input, by the subject's plans in organising the movement and by the strategies that subjects use when they actively encode movement. We can no longer say that kinaesthetic information is not codable, or that distance cannot be maintained in memory, although it is likely that location information is more accurately and easily dealt with than distance information.

When Ebbinghaus pioneered the use of the nonsense syllable, he intended that it should be used to give content-free information about the nature of verbal memory. The effects of repetition and interference were to be studied independently of meaning so that subjects did not bring different degrees of familiarity with words into the experimental situation. What they did bring however, was different abilities to make nonsense syllables meaningful; that is, different abilities to use strategies to remember them. The recognition of active constructive processes in encoding has led to advances in the understanding of verbal memory by concentrating attention on the encoding processes themselves, and the study of memory for movements is now undergoing a similar change.

It has been convenient to discuss movement to a remembered target in this chapter separately from considering the way movement is aimed at a physically present target in the preceding chapter. However, it is important to appreciate that accounts of short-term motor memory and accounts of movement execution share a view of movement representation in which both the sensory consequences of movement and the commands which are used to produce it are specified. The representation of sensory consequences is currently a matter for debate as theorists argue about the nature of the operations used in performance and whether or not memory for the operations can be activated and examined to provide internal representations of sensory consequences (Shea & Zimny, 1983). This debate directs us to look more carefully at what a person is trying to do when making a movement. Most movements are not meaningless, they are carried out in an action context and so they may be presented in memory at many levels.

This chapter has dealt with short-term memory and has not attempted to discuss memory for movement over the longer time periods encountered, for example, in everyday skills. The nature of the operations involved when movement is remembered in the context of a skill may be different because the movement has been practised and integrated with other movements. Issues of this kind have been left until the discussion of skill acquisition in Chapter 8.

In this chapter and in the preceding chapters an emphasis has been placed, not only on the representation of the motor commands to the

muscles, but also on sensory information that provides us with representations of our actions in relation to the environment. Feedback is
clearly a very important component in any account of movement control
and so in the next chapter we turn to a systematic consideration of
perceptual mechanisms that affect feedback processing. Discussion of
the relationships between the various sensory systems will point to the
particularly influential role of vision. This has implications, not only in
the provision of feedback, but also in organising, monitoring and updating central representations of action.

5

Perception and Action

Mary M. Smyth

INTRODUCTION

Making successful movements involves knowledge of the world and of one's position within it, so it is not possible to understand movement and action if perception is not considered too. In the 1960s the study of the control of skilled movement was known as sensory-motor or perceptual-motor skill but since the mid-1970s there has been a tendency for motor skill to become the focus of study. This emphasis on the output part of skill is due to a growth of interest in movement research and does not imply that skilled activity is independent of perceptual information. Perception, memory, decision making, and action cannot be studied all at once but this does not mean that they are not interrelated. These distinctions are imposed for purposes of study not because any one can best be understood in isolation.

In this chapter we will consider the types of information available to a person controlling and selecting movements. Perception informs us about our orientation to the world, our posture and balance, and this provides the framework within which voluntary movements are made. In controlling voluntary movements we use our perceptual systems to inform us of our relationship to objects in the world, and the relation

119

between the perceptual systems themselves is of considerable importance. Planning action that results in voluntary movement also requires perception. Many activities, such as playing a musical instrument, or even talking, require the use of a model of the pattern that we wish to produce in that the target of the action may be to reproduce what was seen or heard when it was performed by others. In addition, many skilled actions require decisions to be made about perceptual patterns so that the correct responses can be initiated. These three aspects of perception and action—balance and posture, relations between the senses, and the perception and recognition of form and pattern—make up the framework for the discussion of perception and action that follows.

TYPES OF PERCEPTUAL INPUT

The information available to the perceiving organism can be classified in many ways. The senses themselves are an obvious way of dividing up the information available from the world in terms of the type of energy that is received, but all the senses can register environmental events and inform us about their existence at a more abstract level than that of particular lights, sounds, or touches. We can know that something has occurred or changed, or even that it was repeated without needing to specify the sense involved. So, we can consider the senses, not simply as receptors for light or smell, but as different systems for picking up information about the same environmental events. If the same information is available in different ways we can refer to these ways as *modalities* (or sometimes *sense modalities*) to emphasize that the same object or event can be specified in a visual, auditory, tactile, olfactory, or gustatory mode. The interrelations between these will be discussed later.

Another way of classifying the types of perceptual information available goes beyond the traditional five senses and considers also receptors within the body that do not register environmental events. Since Sherrington (1906), the sense receptors have been divided into three classes—exteroception, proprioception, and interoception. *Exteroception* refers to vision, audition, touch, smell, and taste, which provide information about the environment. *Proprioception* has traditionally been understood as information from the movement of the body itself (from the Latin *proprius* meaning *own*), obtained via receptors in joints and muscles and skin and from the vestibular system of the inner ear. *Interoception* arises from the autonomic nervous system, for example, in the gastrointestinal tract. This classification, which appears to be made on the basis of receptors, is, as Gibson (1966) points out, not useful as a functional separation. The visual system not only provides information about the outside world but also about the movements of one's own body, and it may therefore be regarded as a proprioceptor. Lee (1978) has added to this by suggesting that perception of the movement of parts of the body, relative to the rest of the body, should be called proprioception, while perception of the movement of the body relative to the environment should be called exproprioception.

These terms seem somewhat clumsy but they make it clear that providing information about objects and events in the external world is only one function of the classical exteroceptors. Vision and audition have a primary use in the planning and guiding of activity. This may also be true to a limited extent for olfaction (as when one follows one's nose to the fish and chip shop), but it is not the case for taste. With vision we can perceive events in the environment, our movements, and the change in the relationship between our bodies and the environment that is brought about by our movements. Audition is important for orienting the body to events in the environment, for maintaining patterns of rhythmic output, and for providing information about our own movements when we speak or sing, in that what we hear can be used for ongoing control and for altering plans for future speaking and singing.

The classical proprioceptors are receptors in the muscles, tendons, joints, and skin, and the balance organs in the vestibule of the inner ear. They signal pressure, position, movement (velocity and acceleration), and force. The receptors in muscles, which are dealt with in detail in Chapter 2, have not always had a clear role in the conscious perception of movement because it has been argued that they do not provide information which reaches consciousness. However, it is now considered that, when necessary, all proprioceptive receptors can provide sensations (Roland, 1978). Because people are rarely exposed to passive movements of their limbs, most information from the articular proprioceptors is related to the execution of action, and is treated as feedback about the action as it is executed. We can also consider the proprioceptors as one modality in the perception of our own actions which we can feel as well as hear and see.

Some confusion in the terminology used for movement-related input is already apparent. This is common in the literature on movement action. If proprioception is a functional, not a structural, category, then it would be consistent to refer to visual proprioception and articular proprioception rather than vision and proprioception. This dichotomy is a clumsy one and we will tend to follow the traditional practice of using proprioception to refer to information from receptors in muscles, joints, the vestibular system, and in some cases, skin, rather than to the use made of the information by the organism. A further confusion arises from the use of the word kinaesthesis for the sensations of movement produced as movement occurs. Some writers use kinaesthetic and some use proprioceptive when they refer to movement information that is not auditory and not visual, but the meaning rarely differs. Gibson and Lee, who argue that if proprioception is a functional category then vision is proprioceptive, also refer to visual kinaesthesis as the sense of movement that can be provided by vision. We tend to call the information about the position and movement of the body that is available via joint, muscle, and cutaneous receptors *proprioception*, while *kinaesthesis* refers to sensing movement itself.

HOW MANY VISUAL SYSTEMS?

In classifying perceptual systems we can use the receptors themselves, or the way they function in relation to our perception of the environment and our own movements within it. The visual system falls into more than one functional grouping and this may reflect the existence of two structurally different visual systems. Trevarthen (1968) has argued that vision involves two parallel processes. One of these, *ambient vision,* is used for detecting space around the body, while the other, *focal vision,* examines detail in small areas of space. Focal vision is served by the fovea of the eye, its acuity is high and it is specialised for recognising objects, distinguishing detail, and for the control of fine movements. Ambient vision provides information about location and movement rather than identity, that is, about where objects are, rather than what they are.

Schneider (1969) provided evidence that there were two kinds of visual system in the hamster by destroying either the visual cortex of the brain or a midbrain structure called the superior colliculus. When the visual cortex was destroyed the hamster could orient its head and body in the direction of visual stimuli, but could not make any visual discriminations. When the superior colliculus was destroyed the pattern was reversed, and the hamster could discriminate well but could not orient.

This evidence suggests that there is not just a functional distinction between visual information used for orientation and localisation and that for identification and discrimination, but that there are two structurally distinct systems. The focal system has connections from the retina of the eye via the thalamus, to the visual cortex of the brain (see

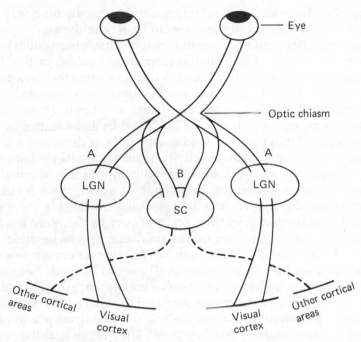

Figure 1. Human visual pathways. (A) Via lateral geniculate nucleus (LGN) in the thalamus to visual cortex in the occipital lobe. (B) Via superior colliculus (SC) in the midbrain to other cortical areas.

Figure 1). The second, phylogenetically older, system, which is the main system for the control of visually guided movements in simpler organisms, operates via the superior colliculus and other midbrain structures and may remain intact when the visual cortex is removed, at least in a rhesus monkey (Humphrey 1974).

Evidence for two visual systems in humans has come from patients who have suffered damage to the visual cortex or who have had half of it removed. These patients are blind in some areas of the visual field, and if damage extends to the whole visual cortex of the brain the patients are completely blind. However, patients with partial destruction of the visual cortex, who cannot report seeing a target in the affected part of the visual field, can point to it accurately and move their eyes in the correct direction, if they are asked to guess where the stimulus appeared (Weiskrantz, Warrington, Sanders, & Marshall, 1974). To some extent, what patients report depends on what question they are asked. If asked what they saw, they cannot report anything, but they can report being aware of something. A patient reported by Weiskrantz (1980) summed this up when he said "I had an impression that something was there. Where it was made a greater impression than what it was."

Weiskrantz (1980) reports cases in which residual vision could be used to make some pattern discrimination after considerable practice, but he concludes that it is more efficient as a detection system than as a pattern-vision system. There is some controversy over the explanation for residual vision, or *blindsight*. Campion, Latto, and Smith (1983) have argued that some of the data can be explained by light scatter from the blind visual field into the good field and by poor or degraded activity in the visual cortex rather than no activity at all. They believe that the two visual systems may not work independently in humans, although they may do so in other organisms. In general, however, there is considerable agreement that the second visual system is involved in the ability to make movements that orient the body or part of the body towards a stimulus in space, rather than in discrimination and recognition.

Some of the most important movements that orient us towards a stimulus in space are eye movements. These can be made because of a sudden movement in the environment or the presence of a flash of light, or they can be part of a structured search of the visual field. Didday and Arbib (1975) produced a model of the role of eye movements in perception that is based on two visual systems. They argue that the superior colliculus can be understood in terms of *distributed processing*, that is, there is no hierarchy of control with an executive neuron that responds to all the information on which a decision has to be made, but rather there is a network of units and it is the overall pattern of processing which leads to output (McCulloch and Pitts, 1943). Information in the superior colliculus is distributed spatially and the different regions compete so that only the most active region provides input to motor output networks. This means that eye movements can occur without any control from higher centres. However, the motor output that controls eye movements can be altered by spatially coded signals to the superior colliculus from the cortex if the eyes are to be moved to help resolve ambiguity in the visual field or to allow more attention to be paid to a particular component of the field. Thus, eye movements can occur because of direct input to the superior colliculus or because cortical areas are involved in active search.

Trevarthen (1968) believes that while focal vision is served by the foveal region of the retina, in which retinal cone cells are concentrated, ambient vision is served by the whole retina. However, if focal vision is occupied, the region of the retina that can provide ambient information is the periphery. Studies of subjects walking about while wearing two different, distorting prisms, one on each eye, have shown that subjects can fixate or "attend to" an object presented by one of the distorting prisms yet can use the other to control locomotion (Foley & McChesney, 1976). This suggests that the selection from the ambient and focal systems is independent. It is possible to select one type of input to attend to or to fixate, and another to guide orientation and locomotion.

The view that visual attention is tied to whatever is being fixated is a common one. We tend to assume that we are attending to something if we fixate it and that if we are not attending to something we cannot be responding to it. Blindsight patients make it clear that it is possible to respond to stimuli of which one cannot report, and in normal life information from the ambient system need not access awareness. In addition, some experimental studies suggest that it is possible to attend to stimuli that appear in areas of the visual field outside the area of fixation, (Posner 1980), so attention and fixation cannot be equated.

The research that Posner and his colleagues have carried out indicates that subjects are capable of attending to events that occur in the periphery and this echoes the statement made by Wundt in 1912, "If . . . we practice letting our attention wander over . . . different parts of the field of vision while keeping the same fixation point, it will soon be clear to us that the fixation-point of attention and the fixation-point of the field of vision are by no means identical" (p. 20). Nevertheless, in many cases a change of attention is associated with eye movements that maintain attended objects in focal vision. Some neurophysiological investigations of the role of the superior colliculus in monkey vision suggests that some layers in the superior colliculus are involved in both eye movements and attention shifts (Mohler & Wurtz, 1976).

Paillard, Jordan, and Brouchon (1981) suggest that there are two separate visual channels for positional and movement information. Motion can be inferred from two successive positions of the same object or limb, or it can be perceived directly. If movement in a limb takes place under conditions of stroboscopic illumination (regular flashes of light), direct perception of motion is not possible, but inferences can be made on the basis of sequential positions of the limb. Paillard et al. (1981) found that with stroboscopic illumination subjects who could use the whole of the visual field to obtain information about arm movement were less accurate in reaching but that accuracy was not decreased if only the centre of the visual field could be used, nor was it decreased if only the periphery could be used, provided movement was made to an object. They suggest that visual systems that perceive motion directly or infer it from position are both distributed across the whole visual field, but that in normal lighting conditions the direct perception of motion is inhibited in the centre of the retina while the positional system is inhibited in the

periphery. Under stroboscopic conditions, in which there is no possibility of direct perception of motion, the positional system can operate
in the periphery as well as in the centre.

The most common functional distinctions in the visual system are
between localisation and identification and between motion and position. These tend to be based on situations in which the individual perceiver is static and the display may or may not move. Even when the
movement being observed is that of the subject's own arm, the viewpoint is that of a stationary perceiver. However, when vision is available
for the control of movement in the world the observer may actually be
moving relative to objects and surfaces in the environment. Direct perception of the relative distances between the organism and the environment is possible if information can be derived from the variations over
time in the pattern of light at the eye, that is, in the optic-flow field
(Gibson 1966).

Optic flow is the pattern of motion of optic elements on the retina that
is caused by the relative motion of the environment and the organism,
and it can provide exproprioceptive information about the position and
overall movement of the organism relative to the environment. Optic
flow radiates from a single point, called the *focus of expansion*. This can be
seen easily when driving along a straight road because all the points in
the landscape seem to radiate from the point where the horizon crosses
the road. The pattern of optic flow is the same whether the environment
is moving past a stationary observer or whether the observer is moving
through the environment, but if another object is also moving through
the environment then the velocity, relative to the observer, will be different from that of the background, so the object and the background
will have different focii of expansion. The optic flow allows the observer
direct information about whether or not it is on a collision course with
another object, about time to contact, and about time to become adjacent. Bower (1974) has suggested that very young infants use optical
expansion to signify that an object is approaching them, and that they
can also use directional information to determine whether it will hit
them or pass by. A possible distinction in the types of use made of visual
information follows from the discussion of what Lee (1980) calls *exproprioception* and *exteroception*.

When visual information is used in planning and controlling action it
has to be used in different ways. Information about the relationship
between the person and the environment (exproprioception) may be in
terms of spatiotemporal information which does not specify the nature
of objects, and this information is of considerable importance in the
understanding of balance, locomotion, catching, hitting, and other

skilled activities in which relationship with the environment is of primary importance. There are also cases in which the initiation of skilled
activity depends on the perception of visual or auditory information
produced by other people or objects in the world (exteroception). Examples would include recognising and responding to particular patterns in
an industrial control panel, to a movement pattern presented by an
opponent in a sport, or to a series of sounds produced by other members
of a musical ensemble in which one is playing. Perceptual learning and
the recognition of pattern are important parts of the planning and initiation of action, although the links with movement are not direct. In the
most extreme case, we can argue that written or spoken language can be
an important part of the control of action, yet it may be perceived in
quite a different way from direct spatiotemporal relationships with the
environment.

Although there are some similarities between the division of perceptual information into that used for planning and that for controlling
action, and the two visual systems suggested by Trevarthen and others,
the division between perception for planning and perception for control
is one which concentrates on the uses made of visual information, not
on structural distinctions. The study of vision may require us to understand cognitively distinct visual systems which relate to the many levels
in which perceptual information is used in the selection, planning and
control of action.

ORIENTATION TO THE WORLD: BALANCE AND POSTURE

When we think about perception we rarely consider the perception of
the direction of gravity, yet maintaining an upright posture and keeping
balance are important for most of our activities. The changes in weight
distribution that make up balance are completely unnoticed unless
something goes wrong and balance is lost. Information about balance
does not come from any one sensory system. Gravity affects us in many
ways. It causes pressure on skin surfaces, the muscles have to resist
gravity in order to keep the body erect, and when a person is standing,
changes of balance affect not only the skin of the feet and muscles in the
lower leg but also the angle of the ankle joint.

Diseases of the inner ear can cause dizziness and loss of balance and it
is often not until such loss occurs that people realise that there are
balance organs in the inner ear. The inner ear contains the cochlea,

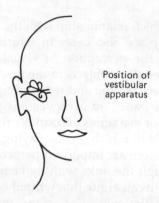

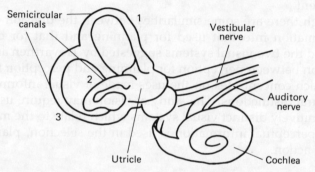

Figure 2. The two main components of the vestibular system, the utricle and the semicircular canals, are close to the cochlea which is part of the auditory system. The utricle provides information about linear acceleration while the semicircular canals signal rotational acceleration.

which is part of the auditory system, and the receptors of the vestibular system that provide information about balance and movement. The main components of the vestibular system (from *vestibule* of the inner ear), are the utricle and the semicircular canals, which provide information about gravity and about linear and rotational acceleration and deceleration in movements of the head (see Figure 2).

When spatial conditions are unusual the vestibular system may not provide appropriate information. The system is adapted to an active organism that does not move at constant velocity. Sitting in an aeroplane that is flying at constant speed will produce no sensations of motion because all the components of the vestibular system are moving at the same rate. Many of the aspects of vehicular transport that cause motion sickness involve the vestibular system, particularly when there is conflict between visual information about motion and the vestibular input. It can occur when reading in a moving car, when the visual field is reasonably stationary with respect to the head so movement is not conveyed visually, although the vestibular system is affected. This also occurs in enclosed cabins in moving vehicles, and the reverse effect occurs in fairground situations such as the haunted swing, when there is considerable visual information about movement but no corresponding vestibular input (Reason & Brand, 1975).

Vision has a stabilising effect on posture in many cases in which disease affects incoming proprioceptive information, and also for patients with vestibular lesions (Dichgans & Brandt, 1978). Considerable body sway is found in normal subjects standing with eyes closed and this can be up to 50% more than that found when the eyes are open. The amount of visual control of sway depends on the frequency of sway as high-frequency sway may be regulated by canal and proprioceptive input while low-frequency sway is affected more by utricle and visual information (Nashner, 1970). When a stationary observer is presented with a visual display that specifies that movement is occurring, both perceptual and postural effects are found. If the visual movement continues for some time an initial correct perception of visual motion is replaced by a sensation of self-motion, or vection, in the direction opposite to that of the seen motion. In addition, the subject will lean in the direction of the visual movement (Lestienne, Soechting, & Berthoz, 1977). If the seen movement is rotating at constant velocity it ceases to be perceived as self-motion after further exposure (Wong & Frost, 1978). When the visual motion stops a postural after effect occurs in which the subject leans in the direction opposite to the leaning that happened in relation to the moving display. Reason, Wagner, and Dewhurst (1981) argue that this after effect results from a realignment of the body upright during the exposure period so that normal visual information does not match with the felt position of the upright and compensation takes place in the opposite direction.

Very small visual movements can be used to alter body tilt. Lee and Lishman (1975) found that if the walls of a room were moved toward and away from a standing subject by as little as 6 mm the subject's forward and backward sway followed the movement of the room. Some of the most dramatic effects of vision on posture control are found in young infants who fall in the direction of the seen movement (see Figure 3). That is, the infants compensate for visual motion away from them, which normally means that they are swaying backwards, by swaying, and ultimately toppling, forward (Lee & Aronson, 1974). In the development of balance there is an early stage between 6 and 12 months that is not influenced by visual disturbance (Dichgans & Brandt, 1978), and

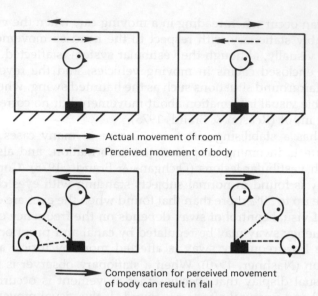

Figure 3. Moving room apparatus used by Lee and Aronson (1974) to demonstrate visual dominance of balance in young infants.

blind children have been reported to sit in a stable position at the same age as sighted children do (Adelson & Fraiberg, 1977), but at about 2 years of age there is increased dependence on vision that subsequently decreases until the adult stage when visual movement causes sway and tilt rather than a loss of balance.

Lee and Lishman (1975) argue that it takes time for the articular proprioceptive system to be calibrated correctly and that the normal child uses visual information about sway to control balance. They have also shown that adults learning a new stance, who are not receiving adequate information about posture from mechanoreceptors in the foot and ankle, will lose balance when exposed to visual movement. Although the joint and muscle receptors in the lower leg and the vestibular receptors all provide information about movement that is used to control balance, visual displacement, which indicates that the distance between the eyes and objects in the world is changing, is an important part of the control system.

Balance is important in locomotion as well as in standing still. Vision appears to play an important role here also—running over uneven ground is more difficult in the dark. While a considerable amount of the unevenness can be dealt with by the proprioceptive feedback loops in muscles (see Chapter 3), some anticipation of the nature of the ground allows changes to occur in the leg muscles before contact is made with the ground. Freedman, Wannstedt, and Herman (1976) have shown that muscle activity that will cushion the effect of stepping down from a height is initiated before contact with the ground and that this only occurs if subjects are allowed normal vision. Lee (1980) suggests that the timing of shock absorption in running over uneven ground is specified by visual information that gives time-to-contact information of the foot with the ground, and allows preparatory muscle activity to be initiated.

Knowing where we are in relation to gravity, and maintaining balance while standing, running, and walking are all served by many perceptual systems. Many of the movements that we find of interest assume normal balance and it sometimes seems that this does not require to be controlled. However, in these simple background activities it is clear that movement and perception cannot be separated and that the senses themselves interrelate and supplement each other in many ways.

PERCEPTION AND FEEDBACK

Feedback is the term most often used for perceptual information about our own actions. It is derived from the engineering- and information-based approach of the 1950s and it is defined in information terms. Feedback is information about the output of a system that can be used to alter that output, and most accounts of feedback refer to negative feedback, in which it is the difference between the actual output and the desired output that is used to inaugurate change.

The varied classificatory systems that are used to differentiate the sensory or perceptual systems, are reflected in the way in which feedback is labeled. In general, the term *efference* is used to refer to motor outflow while *afference* refers to information being fed back. Held (1965) extended this and referred to efference, *exafference* (or input which comes from outside), and *reafference* (or input which resulted from active movement) (see Figure 4). Following von Holst and Mittelstadt (1950) he argued that the afferent information from active and passive movement could be the same but only with active movement would the input be reafference, which could be compared with what was intended in order to correct calibration and coordination. The feedback systems that operate in muscle, and which make it unlikely that the afference is the same in active and passive movement, has been described in Chapter 2 and an account of the role of feedback in visually aimed movements was given in Chapter 3.

Feedback can be divided into that which is extrinsic to the activity

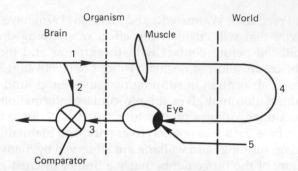

Figure 4. Held's labeling of feedback. Motor outflow from the brain (1—efference) is passed as a copy (2—efference copy) for comparison with incoming information (3—afference) which may be related to movement (4—re-afference) or independent of voluntary activity (5—ex-afference).

being performed, and that which is intrinsic to it. Extrinsic feedback is normally used for learning and may include comments from an experimenter or trainer (see Chapter 8). Intrinsic feedback derives from the execution of actions and occurs in the form of proprioceptive, visual, or auditory information about the nature of the actions and their consequences. This information may be used to alter ongoing action or to change the way in which future actions are implemented. In all cases, the use of the term feedback implies that there is an intended state or process that can be specified in terms of perceptual anticipations, and that it is possible for the action to produce input that is different from that which is expected.

The term exproprioceptive, which was discussed earlier, refers to information about the relationship between the body and the environment, which may be a result of body movement, or may be a result of movement in the environment. Visual information about the relationship between the body and the environment may operate as *feedforward*, in that it alters the way in which future movements are made, or it may be feedback, which alters the course of an ongoing movement. It is often difficult to decide what the role of perceptual information is in these circumstances, but the definition of feedback given above should make it clear that perception can only be feedback if it relates to an intended state, although the intention need not be a conscious one.

Relations among the Senses

Our senses do not often contradict each other. What objects in the environment look like, sound like, and feel like, is normally congruent and it would be hard to imagine why they should be otherwise. If we want to know which type of information is most important for the execution of a particular task, or whether the normal relationship between the senses is an unequal one, then we may have to alter the normal congruence. This has been done in many ways, some of which entail separating the source of two kinds of sensory input, and some of which systematically distort the input to one sensory system. A further approach is to consider how translations between different systems take place, how we know from looking at them that a cushion and a table will feel different to the touch, for example. This approach involves matching what is presented to one modality with something presented to another. We will consider each of the approaches in turn.

Visual Distortion and the Recalibration of Sensory Systems

The idea of distorting the input to one system has been popular since Stratton (1897) wore spectacles with lenses that turned the visual world upside down. Early workers such as Stratton and Kohler (1964) were very interested in the perceptual experiences that they had and which altered as they wore distorting spectacles for long periods. It should be emphasized, however, that distortions are distortions of relationships between the senses, not simply distortions of vision. If you wear distorting spectacles that displace the visual field 7 inches to the right you cannot *see* that this distortion exists until you make a movement, or look at your own feet, which feel and appear to be in different places, and then you realise that there is conflict between the senses.

The boundaries between perception and action in this area are not clear. If visual information is used in planning a movement and the movement when made does not achieve the goal set for it because the original visual information was wrong, then different ways of using vision to control action must be learned, or more reliance must be placed on the perceptual systems that are not distorted. That is, in order to interact correctly with the environment, someone who is wearing distorting spectacles has to alter the way in which movement is controlled. In addition to this, the perceptual relationship between different modalities may be altering over exposure to rearrangement, so that instead of seeing a limb in one place and feeling it in another, the experience returns to unity. The changes make up *adaptation* to visual distortion. Stratton found that after walking about wearing his inverting spectacles for some time, he was able to interact with objects in the world quite accurately. However, the question of whether the world looked normal

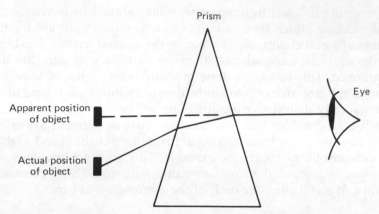

Figure 5. Optical displacement caused by a wedge prism. The apparent position of an object is the result of refraction left, or right, or up, or down, depending on the direction of the base of the prism.

was not one which he could easily answer because even when things seemed to look the right way up this was only the right way up as if his head was between his legs. The position where he felt his head to be was shifted so that the world could look upright.

The active element in adaptation to visual distortion, shown by Stratton when he walked about, has been put forward as the most important component by Held (1965). He suggests that if subjects wearing distorting prisms that displace the visual input several degrees to right or left (see Figure 5), are not allowed to see the results of an active movement they will not be able to compensate for the distortion and reach correctly. In Held's view the motor instructions sent out (efference) are matched with the visual information about the movement which comes back into the system (reafference) so that the intended goal can be compared with that which is actually reached in order to change the rules for the generation of the correct movement. The principle that active movement is necessary for the development of perception and action can also be applied to normal development because Held believes that a young animal needs to perceive the results of its active movement in order to develop effective visuomotor coordination.

Since the mid-60s many studies have found that adaptation can occur with active and passive movement (Welch, 1978). One important point seems to be that the felt position of the limb should be made important so that even with a passive movement there are two sources of information that conflict so that the conflict can be noticed and resolved. Adaptation will occur, for example, if the person wearing displacing prisms looks at his or her stationary arm but the arm is vibrated so that its felt position is a strong cue. (Adaptation is said to have occurred in an experiment if a subject makes pointing errors when the prisms are removed that are in the opposite direction to the prism displacement.) Similarly, adaptation will occur after passive movement if the movement has been across a patterned background, but if the background was homogenous no adaptation occurs (Melamed, Haley, and Gildow, 1973). The addition of error feedback also enhances adaptation (Welch & Rhoades, 1969) and the absence of kinaesthetic feedback in the actively moved limb prevents adaptation (Wallace & Garrett, 1973). It seems that it is the discrepancy between the felt and the seen position that is important in adaptation, not efference and reafference. That is, it is the amount of information available to the subject, in any form, which is the important factor in altering the way movement is controlled (Freedman, 1968).

Adaptation to a discrepancy between the felt and seen position of a limb occurs without visual distortion by prisms if subjects believe that discrepant information comes from the same object. Lackner (1977) did not allow his subjects to see their moving arm when it touched wooden pins, but allowed them to see pins which they assumed they were touching. The seen and felt pins were in fact displaced in space so that subjects received discrepant information. After exposure to this displacement, subjects altered the direction in which they pointed straight ahead, in the direction opposite to the displacement, that is, they showed an after effect (see Figure 6). Lackner found that active movement led to adaptation and a directional after effect but that passive movement did not. He argued that because the subjects could not see their hands they could not be using visual reafference and therefore that Held's account of the difference between active and passive movement was incomplete. That is, the subjects did not have a plan, make a movement, and discover it was wrong, and so correct the rules for generating movements. However, the active selection of movement increases the amount of information available from muscle spindles (see Chapter 2), and allows the discrepancy between seen and felt position to produce conflict that is resolved as felt and seen positions come together.

If a new relationship between two spatial senses can be learned fairly quickly, as is the case in adaptation studies, it is possible that the "normal" relationship is not itself a static one, but depends on continual relearning of the relationship between the senses. After prism adaptation the position in which an arm is felt to be is different from the felt position before adaptation, although the actual position may be the same. This means that the input from articular proprioception does not

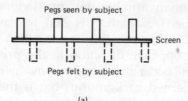

(a)

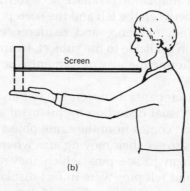

(b)

Figure 6. The experimental arrangement used by Lackner (1977) for studying adaptation to displaced vision. (a) Relative positions of posts for sight and touch, (b) Lateral view showing screen to prevent sight of hand.

specify a fixed spatial position for a limb but can be calibrated, or recalibrated, by vision. The recalibration of proprioceptive input has also been shown by Kenny and Craske (1981), who found that if subjects felt a touch on their forearm that was artificially made closer to the elbow than the actual position which they touched, they noticed the discrepancy at first but after repeated trials the two positions felt the same. In other words, the felt length of the arm was not fixed but could be induced to increase or decrease.

If calibration of the spatial senses is necessary for accurate control of spatial activity, the superiority of active movement in adaptation to distortion suggests that recalibration should also be active. Howarth (1978) has suggested that the warm up exercises carried out by athletes may help to recalibrate the senses and motor activity which have lost their fine tuning. Another possible contribution to recalibration comes from vision, which allows drift to be detected and corrected. Smyth and Marriott (1982) asked subjects to catch a ball while wearing a screen attached to the side of the head which prevented sight of the catching hand. The flight of the ball could be seen until within 250 msec of hand contact, when no correction could be made even if the hand could be seen. If the hand can be localised accurately without vision then catching perfor- mance should have been normal in this situation, but it was found that subjects made more errors when they could not see their catching hand, and that these errors related to their ability to place their hand accurately in the path of the ball. This suggests that peripheral vision may help to provide information that can be used to maintain accurate calibration of the spatial senses. Keeping one's eye on the ball does not necessarily mean that all the other sensory information necessary can be obtained from other input systems, or that vision is not necessary for maintaining accurate knowledge of the position of the body and limbs.

Vision and Hearing in Spatial Localisation

When we watch a ventriloquist with a dummy, the movements of the dummy's mouth are seen in one location and the sounds actually come from another, yet we perceive the sound of the words and the sight of the movements as coming from the same place. When subjects wear pseudophones that change the location of auditory information by 180 °, sounds are localised correctly when their sources are seen. Stratton, while wearing his inverting lenses, reported that the sounds of objects out of sight seemed to come from the opposite direction to where they had passed out of sight, but that when the source of the sound was in view the sound seemed to come from the object responsible for it. These examples suggest that if spatial information is available in two modal- ities the information in one modality is discarded in favour of the other, so that sounds seem to come from the visible location of the object producing the sound.

A more positive way of looking at ventriloquism effects is to consider that the senses normally work together so that perceived locations are those of unitary objects and events. Very young babies show visual orientation to a sound source, although it is not easy to find out at what age this first occurs. Wertheimer (1961) used soft clicks as the sound source and found that newborn babies made reflexive eye movements towards an off-centre click. Butterworth and Castillo (1976) could not repeat this result, although the clicks they used were louder than those used by Wertheimer and this may have had some effect on the babies' actions. Many developmental studies indicate that reliable responses cannot be obtained until babies are 4 or 5 months old (Flavell, 1977). Muir and Field (1979) investigated the sound-localisation abilities of babies two to seven days old and found that they turned their eyes to the side on which the sound of a rattle appeared, even when there was no seen movement. In adults, the interaction between the modalities of vision and audition has been shown by an aftereffect of the exposure to discrepant visual and spatial information (Radeau & Bertelson, 1974).

In general, however, localisation of sound is more accurate in the presence of vision (Jones 1975). Warren (1970) has argued that vision helps to organise auditory space, but Jones and Kabanoff (1975), who found that eye movements were necessary if vision was to help with auditory localisation, have suggested that it is memory for the direction of eye movements that facilitates such localisation. Shelton and Searle (1980) presented subjects with auditory targets that were outside the visual field and found that although the location of the targets could not be seen the availability of visual information had a strong effect on judgements in the horizontal plane. In addition, they altered the spatial and temporal relationships of the lights and the sounds and found support for the visual frame of reference argument when the lights came before the sound, and for the eye movement memory view when the light came after the sound. The presence of visual information helps in auditory localisation by providing a spatial framework and allowing eye movements which explore it.

Visual Dominance

When a light source and a sound source are moved apart in experimental situations, vision continues to provide the spatial framework and dominates over the auditory input. If the information about the location of a target is both felt and heard, or both felt and seen, the discrepancies between the positions is resolved in favour of one of the senses, then it may be possible to arrange them in a hierarchy of preference or dominance. Fisher (1962) found vision and proprioception to be dominant over audition, with some dominance of vision over proprioception, although this latter relationship was not complete. Hay and Pick (1966) used adaptive shifts in the arm marking the location of the source of a sound and found that yet again vision and proprioception both dominated audition and that vision dominated proprioception.

The dominance of vision over other sensory systems has been found in many situations. It is sometimes complete and sometimes only partial, a bias rather than a capture of the information presented by the second system. It has been found in tasks using the time to react to the onset of stimuli (Jordan, 1972), the offset of stimuli (Colavita & Weisberg, 1979), memory for pattern (Klein & Posner, 1974), prism rearrangment (Warren & Schmitt, 1978), prism distortion (Rock 1966), and the ability to retain one's balance (Lee & Aronson, 1974). When an object appears to be one shape and feels as if it is another, it is perceived as being the shape that is specified by vision. This extreme case is often called *visual capture* and has been demonstrated by Rock (1966) for objects that are seen as squares and felt as oblongs. They are recognised as squares. This finding is confirmed by Power and Graham (1976) who used experienced potters as subjects in the hope that they would have more tactile awareness and be more able to ignore the distorted visual input. The potters also believed that the shape was how it looked, not how it felt. This extreme of capture occurs even when the objects are well known and subjects are aware of the possibility of distortion. Power (1981) used a common coin (a 5-pence piece) that felt circular as it normally did, but was viewed via optic distortion that made it look oval (see Figure 7). Experienced psychologists reported that the coin felt oval and even congratulated the experimenter on the excellence of the technical services that had produced such a coin. However, in some cases, when there is extra information about visual distortion via sight of the hand, the dominance is partial and complete capture does not occur (Power, 1980).

Even when two types of perceptual input are not conflicting, there are some situations in which attending to one input prevents the use of the other. This is not surprising, but in some cases the modality that is attended to is not the one to which the subject was trying to attend, and in most cases the more powerful modality is vision. In a study of novice fencers and the time it took them to react to the movement of an opponent's foil, Jordan (1972) found that the time to react to the sight of the movement was longer than that to respond to the feel of the movement when subjects were blindfolded. If subjects were not blindfolded and could both feel and see the movement, they took longer to respond than they did when they could only feel, although the kinaesthetic information would have been an adequate basis for the responses. In other words, when the subjects were expecting the information to be visual they waited for it, even though the reaction would have been faster to the kinaesthetic input. Klein and Posner (1974) have confirmed this type of explanation of Jordan's result, by showing that subjects wait for the visual information if trials are presented in blocks so that they know that vision will be available, but do not wait if they do not know that vision will be provided.

When two modalities are presented with information at the same time and only one is attended to, the other input may not even reach the subject's awareness. As might be expected, the modality that is attended

Figure 7. Stimuli used in studies of visual capture of touch. The actual objects (a square of perspex and a coin) are drawn with a solid line and the visual image is shown as a dashed line. Subjects tend to report that these objects are rectangular and elliptical respectively, even though the coin is very familiar.

to is vision and Colavita (1974) showed that if subjects were expecting to have to react as quickly as possible to either a light or a tone and both the light and the tone were presented on some trials, subjects saw the light and responded to it, without being able to report hearing the tone at all. This occurs even when the subjects had previously matched the tone as being subjectively twice as intense as the light. Colavita (1974) argued that this dominance by vision was based on the hard-wiring of the auditory and visual systems. He suggested that the brief stimuli used in the experiment would evoke a reflex-orienting response that would involve the neural connections of the superior colliculus, which in turn has more direct connections with the visual system that with the auditory system, so that the orienting tendency favours the visual modality.

Evidence against this hard-wiring view is presented by Colavita and Weisberg (1979), who used the offset rather than the onset of a stimulus as the signal for the response. Turning off a stimulus that has been present does not lead to an orienting reflex, but it does lead to a very strong visual dominance effect if both the light and the tone are turned off at the same time. On 59 out of the 60 trials in which the light and tone were turned off at the same time, the subjects pressed the response key for the light going off, and were never aware that both stimuli had been removed at the same time. The one time the tone key was pressed the subject reported that it was an error. Colavita and Weisberg conclude that subjects attend to vision more than audition for such tasks and this is not a property of the physiological chracteristics of the two modalities, but appears to be a nonsensory, attentional mechanism.

If a light and a tone are presented either separately or together and the subject's task is to estimate the duration of the signal, the normal pattern of visual dominance does not occur. Walker and Scott (1981) asked subjects to estimate either the duration of presentation of a tone or a light, or both together. They found that the estimations were greater for the tone and for the tone plus the light than they were for the light alone. That is, when the visual cue was present with the auditory one, subjects behaved in the same way as they did when the auditory cue alone was present. Walker and Scott suggest that while vision is a spatial sense audition is primarily temporal, and differences in dominance relate to the nature of the task being performed rather than to fixed hierarchical relationships between input systems.

An attentional explanation for the dominance of vision over other sensory modalities in many situations has been put forward by Posner, Nissen, and Klein (1976). They believe that it takes longer to switch away from vision than it does from other modalities so the way to make sure that one picks up most of the relevant information is to give visual input priority and trust to a fast switch time to make use of other input. This attentional bias is considered to be nonsensory in that it is not always present to the same extent and can be affected by the strategies subjects use in an experimental task (Klein, 1977).

To say that subjects can use strategies in an experiment, does not always mean that they can decide to ignore visual information and only use auditory or kinaesthetic information. Warren and Schmitt (1978) used a visual-capture paradigm in which subjects looked at their hands through prisms that gave displaced visual information so that the hands looked as if they were further to one side than was actually the case. When subjects attended to vision they felt that the hand actually was in the position in which it looked to be. If subjects were told that the felt location and the seen location were not the same and that the visual information was to be ignored, they were not able to do this. Even when the effects of the prisms had been demonstrated and the subjects were told that they were paying too much attention to vision, they could not make an accurate judgement of where their hand was felt to be. However, Warren and Schmitt interspersed trials in which both visual and proprioceptive cues were available with a long series of trials in which only proprioceptive cues could be used, and in this context subjects were able to judge the felt position quite accurately even although contradictory visual information was present.

Just what constitutes a context in which people will allow another sense to override vision? This is not an easy question to answer. The potters whom Power and Graham (1976) investigated, could have been expected to have a long-term context, that is, a greater sensitivity to tactile and proprioceptive input. It is possible that potters are dependent on vision for the most important cues from their work, but they may not be aware of using visual input. It is often assumed that if we are not aware of using vision then we are not using it, but we have already seen that awareness and perception are not quite the same thing. We can use visual information to control locomotion without being aware of it, we may use it to position our limbs accurately (Smyth & Marriott, 1982), and Lee, Lishman and Thomson (1982) have shown that the run up to a long jump comes under visual control even though both coach and athlete may believe that this is not the case.

Vision informs us about objects and events in the external world, about our own movements, and the results of our own movements in the world. Surprisingly, it appears to give more potent information about our balance than the specialised balance organs in the inner ear, and the joint and skin receptors that signal pressure and sway. If an infant is attempting to stand, or a new stance is being learned, vision gives direct information about the movement of the body in relation to the world, and can be used to educate the other systems. Vision is the most informative of our spatial senses and we attend to it, not because it is difficult to switch to, but because we can be most efficient if we stay tuned to vision with fast switching times to other inputs. If we are not using perceptual input for spatial orientation then vision may not be the appropriate modality and may not dominate over other input.

Because attention to visual input cannot be prevented in some cases, even though it may not be needed and may lead to poorer performance, it is important to control the amount of visual information that is present when a task is being learned. While vision can give accurate spatial information that may allow a learner to understand what is required and to monitor movement in relation to this, performance may deteriorate if visual information that is present during learning is not normally available when the task is performed (Smyth, 1978). This issue is quite different from that of using films and demonstrations to help learners build up an understanding of what is required and where error has occurred, or training learners to use visual information that is available during the normal execution of a task (Lee, 1978). The instructor who realises that visual spatial information is often more important than that from any other modality must consider carefully when that information helps learning and when it does not.

SKILLED PERCEPTION

Perception and action relate at many levels; some are more obvious than others. The use of exteroceptive information about objects and events in the environment is important for the decision processes that result in action towards a goal. This means that selection has to be made from the large amount of information about the external world that is available to a perceiver at any one time, and the ability to recognise pattern appropriately is important for the control of action, although studies of pattern perception often do not seem to be directly relevant to movement.

Learning to perceive involves selecting from what is available although more than one selection may be possible at any time. The experienced bird watcher, for example, can perceive a red-backed sandpiper on the pebbles of the seashore, although the novice may find the camouflage effect of the bird's plumage against the pebbles is too successful. Skill in perception is widespread among adults. Judging a gymnastics routine or the quality of wine, using complex instrument displays to land an aeroplane or control an industrial process, and being able to tell who is conducting a performance of Beethoven's Fifth Symphony, are all example of such skill, but they seem to be limited to a few people. The perception of both written and spoken language may not seem skilled in the same way, but it is just as dependent on perceptual learning, although we may not remember much about the way that learning took place.

Perceptual learning is going on all the time as a person becomes able to detect and use the superordinate structure that permits grouping into larger units. Increased differentiation occurs as the perceiver comes to know what is relevant in any input so that preattentive processes allow attention to be directed to events and objects that have importance for the individual (Gibson, 1969).

Changes in organisation allow a one-syllable word to be read as quickly as one letter by someone who had learned to read, and the arrangement of the pieces on a chess board in the middle of a game to be remembered and reproduced as a pattern by a skilled player, while a novice tries to list the pieces. Many actions are performed in response to patterns that specify crucial aspects of environmental events and when the recognition of an object or event as being of a particular class is important, repeated experience allows identity to be recognised quickly.

The experimental paradigm known as *visual search* has been used to help us understand how people match stimulus patterns, how they identify them, and how they tell them apart. When a subject searches a page of letters for the target p all other letters are nontargets that may be detected as x or m before it can be decided that they are not p, or there may be only two classes used, p and not-p. If it is only necessary to detect the member of the positive set then the background may not be identified in any way. A match based on perceptual characteristics allows those items that match to be detected and recognised, but if a match does not occur, no further analysis of the nontarget item is necessary (Rabbitt, 1971).

Increasing perceptual skill makes it easier to identify target patterns, it also makes it more difficult to judge whether a pattern is almost correct or very far from the target, unless some attempt is made to maintain flexible categorisation systems during learning. A study by Henderson (1975) required skilled and unskilled darts players to say how accurate their throws were, in the absence of any visual information about accuracy. As one would expect, skilled players threw more accurately than unskilled players, and they knew when they were accurate even though they could not see where the dart hit the board. However, they seemed to have little information about very inaccurate throws. That is, skilled players could recognise accurate throws (the targets) but could not recognise the inaccurate ones (the background), except to say that they were not accurate. Perceptual judgments about the accuracy or quality of movement may be limited if all that can be done is to discriminate good from bad because these are the only categories available.

Selection in Perception

The problem of how people are able to select out some parts of a perceptual array and ignore others has often been dealt with as *selective attention*, although this includes other processes such as memory or response selection as well as perception. Since the 1950s many people have tried to find out how we rule out the material to which we do not want to attend, and this has sometimes been confused with the question of whether limitations on the amount we can attend to are automatically fixed or not. Selection and attention are important not only for perception, but for the study of action and for our understanding of how tasks facilitate or inhibit each other if they are performed together. These aspects of attention will be dealt with in Chapter 7.

One common method of investigating how subjects select one perceptual input in preference to another is the task known as *dichotic listening* in which subjects are required to repeat aloud (shadow) a stream of speech presented to one ear, and to ignore that presented to the other (Cherry, 1953). This can be done on a spatial basis, but if the content of the speech presented to the ears is switched, a spatial account of the process of selection would mean that the listener should carry on shadowing the new stream at the selected ear. Treisman (1960) found that after such a switch some of the material from the unselected ear was shadowed. This, and other effects related to the short-term storage of unattended items (e.g., MacKay, 1973), led to the view that the semantic content of speech was important for selection. An unpublished study by Simmonds and Darwin reported in Darwin (1976) suggests that if the intonation pattern of the speech presented to the selected ear was maintained even though the semantic content switched, there was no transfer of shadowing to the unselected ear. If it is the temporal pattern of speech, its intonation and rhythm, which is being selected, then the meaning that drives selection may be partly temporal patterning rather than simply semantic content.

The study of dichotic listening is not concerned with purely perceptual selection. The subjects have to make a response to one input while not responding to another, so some of the input has to be isolated from the control of responses. That is, one set of words must be decoupled from the control of vocal and other voluntary responses (Allport, 1980). If subjects do not have to shadow one message, but must simply detect targets, there is no decrease in efficiency if they have to detect targets in both streams of speech over that if they concentrate on one stream (Ostry, Moray & Marks, 1976). However, if subjects have to shadow one stream and respond to targets in both, they fail to detect targets in the message that is not being shadowed (Triesman & Geffen, 1967). So, in cases in which different aspects of the perceptual array are capable of controlling a required action, then selection between them means that only one input can activate responses that are within the domain of that action, while other inputs have to be prevented from doing so.

Neisser (1976) has argued that selection in perception is not a problem of deciding what should not be perceived but is a positive process inherent in the act of perceiving. In Neisser's account of perception appropriate schemas are actively and continuously tuned to the information that specifies an event that is extended over time. Irrelevant events present information but because no tuning occurs in response to them they remain unperceived. In selective-looking experiments (Neisser & Becklen, 1975), videotapes of two games are superimposed on the same television screen (see Figure 8). The subject's task is to follow one of the sources and to press a key every time a particular event, such as a ball throw, occurs. Adults can do this even when the two displays are very similar (Neisser, 1979). Unusual events in the game that is not being selected are rarely noticed and in general subjects do not seem to see the second game.

We do not normally need to distinguish one of two overlapping visual events so we do not need to use a specialised system to do this. If the flow within a scene can specify an event then different patterns of time and movement will not be perceived. When watching a football match it is possible to select patterns that relate to a team's overall plan for the game, or to watch one or two individual players. The ability to select the higher level of analysis depends on perceptual learning that allows an-

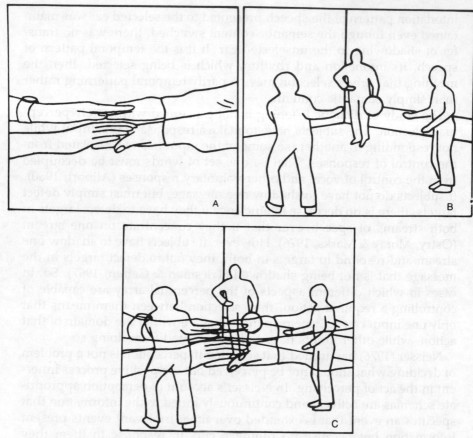

Figure 8. Outline of typical video images for the selective-looking experiment. (A) Handgame alone, (B) Ballgame alone, (C) Superimposed images. From "Selective looking: attending to visually specified events", by Neiser, U. and Becklen, R. (1975). *Cognitive Psychology*, *9*, 480–494.

ticipation of patterns in movement and timing but probably means that detailed information about the performance of individual players will not be picked up.

In order for selection to occur some preliminary analysis has to suggest what might be relevant and where it is. The early preattentive stage (Neisser, 1967) in vision has to allow us to separate possible objects and events, yet we cannot know it directly because it happens before selection. Kahneman and Henik (1981) have used a series of tasks to show that the spatial location of objects is an important part of such preattentive processing. They argue that this stage parses, or breaks up, the visual field into objects, or possible objects, so that selection can operate.

Position, colour, and size are some of the important components in preattentive processing, and information about possible groupings and how the array is structured allows selection to operate on objects rather than on the features available. A preattentive process that deals with possible objects, rather than features, can be used to initiate selective looking and listening that may subsequently be maintained by consistent spatial and temporal features of the objects or events selected.

PERCEPTUAL SCHEMAS

Perception is part of the relationship between a person and the environment, and as such, it is determined by both the needs and activities of the individual and by the information that is actually available. The way in which these two aspects of perception interrelate is important for understanding how perception is altered by experience and how it is dependent on the characteristics of the physical world.

A distinction made between *data driven* and *conceptually driven* processes in perception, reflects this dichotomy and emphasizes the links between attempts to understand perception in people and attempts to study machine intelligence. Data-driven processes are those in which no knowledge of the nature of the objects being perceived can be involved. These are often assumed to be useful only for a low level of perceptual analysis. However, in the work of Marr (1980), higher-level knowledge is not used to extract information from a visual array, and the grouping of features and the separation of figure from ground is achieved without the use of conceptually driven processes. Nevertheless, recognition of objects and events can be affected by experience or by the perceiver's emotions or intentions, and there are many cases in which the same input is recognised in different ways because it occurs in different contexts.

Conceptually driven processes can be conceived of as controlling the way in which information is used or as providing hypotheses that are tested against the input. When the same input can be interpreted in different ways higher-order knowledge provided by context or expectation may determine what is perceived. Handwriting presents many examples of this although it is possible that ambiguities of this sort are not common in the normal three-dimensional world (see Figure 9).

In many attempts to enable computers to think, solve problems, understand stories, or see objects, representations that organise knowledge into general classes and provide broad outlines of content have been used to add higher-order knowledge to that made available from data-driven processes. These representations have been called *frames*,

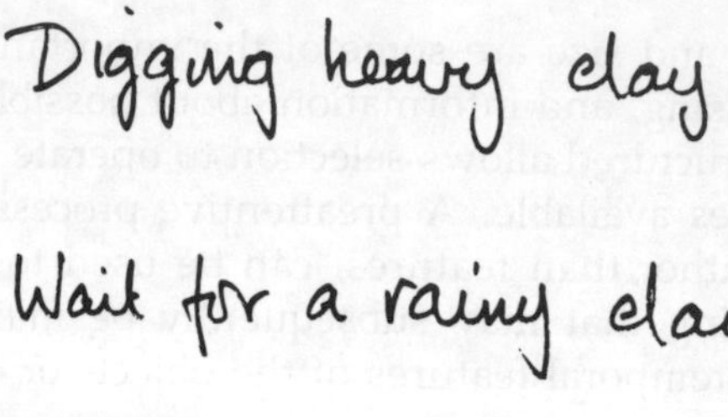

Digging heavy clay

Wait for a rainy day

Figure 9. The effect of context on perception. While the stimulus pattern for *clay* and *day* is the same, the context influences what is read.

scripts, and *schemas.* Minsky (1975) has proposed that a computer that is going to be able to recognise patterns will not be able to operate on the basis of input patterns at any one time. The system has to be ready for the new pattern with a frame or a hierarchy of frames that anticipates what the input will be and then searches for evidence to confirm this. The concept of schema can be understood in a very similar way and it is used extensively in the study of human memory and action.

The use of the word schema in this context owes a great deal to Bartlett (1932), who wrote that a person who is remembering something "has an over-mastering tendency simply to get a general impression of the whole, and on the basis of this, he constructs the possible detail". Bartlett had taken the concept of schema from Kant and Head and reinterpreted it as a "living . . . constantly developing . . . active organisation of past reactions or of past experiences". He was clearly putting forward a view of memory in which outlines are important, as are the rules for generating detail, although he did not specify how these operated.

Bartlett's (1932) description of how he selects and plays a tennis stroke is often quoted as a clear statement of some of the problems that have to be understood in the psychology of action. He wrote, "When I make the stroke I do not, as a matter of fact, produce something absolutely new, and I never merely repeat something old. The stroke is literally manufactured out of the living visual and postural 'schemata' of the moment and their interrelations" (p. 202). Again, the general nature of the response is remembered and the particular form in which it will be made is generated. Thus, one important strand in the history of this concept has been that of abstraction of general principles that are important for the memory of some material and the ability to re-create detail according to the context.

In perception we pick up on the "visual and postural schemata" of Bartlett and consider how our current perceptual input is related to what has gone before, and how we use anticipations based on previous input

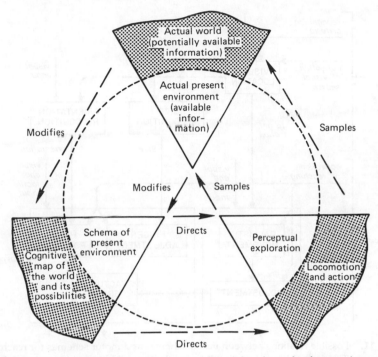

Figure 10. The cycle of perception embedded within the cycle of perception and action. From *Cognition and Reality*, by Neisser, U. (1976). San Francisco: Freeman. Reprinted with permission.

to direct our selection of relevant material from the perceptual array. Neisser (1976) uses schema to refer to the central cognitive structure in perception. He defines it as "that portion of the entire perceptual cycle which is internal to the perceiver, modifiable by experience, and somehow specific to what is being perceived" (p. 52). Neisser argues that perception is a cycle, not a chain of processes; anticipating schemas direct perceptual exploration of the environment, and information picked up from this exploration modifies the expectations of certain kinds of information so further exploration can be directed (see Figure 10). This perceptual cycle is embedded within a cycle of perception and action, shown in the outer layer of Figure 10.

Arbib (1981) uses the term *perceptual schema* to refer to a unit of internal knowledge of the world, which also corresponds to a domain of interaction, such as an object, a detail of an object, or even a part of a social interaction. He also equates schemas with *affordances* (Gibson, 1966), which are high-level descriptions of properties of the surfaces and substances of objects that are important for interaction with them. For Ar-

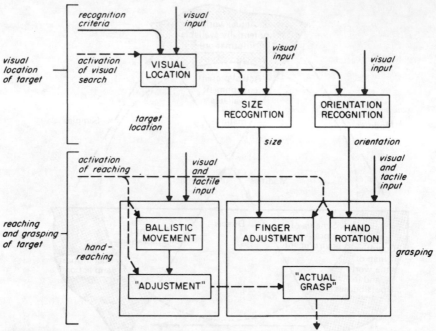

Figure 11. Possible relations between visual schemas and motor schemas for reaching and grasping. The dashed lines are activation signals, the solid lines are transfer of data. From "Interacting schemas in motor control", by Arbib, M. A. (1980). In Stelmach, G. E. and Requin, J., (Eds.) *Tutorials in Motor Behavior*. Amsterdam: North-Holland.

bib, perception of an object (or the activation of perceptual schemas) involves gaining access to motor schemas that are routines for interacting with objects. For example, visual information that relates to the recognition, location, and size and orientation of an object, may access schemas that control reaching for that object (see Figure 11). Different components of the visual information may relate to particular aspects of the control of reaching, such as finger adjustment and hand rotation. However, the accessing of motor schemas, or routines for interacting with objects does not have to lead to the execution of any of these routines. In this sense perception and action cannot be divided but the action is potential rather than actual. The actual course of action that results from the activation of perceptual schemas has to be planned and it is planning which links perceptual to motor schema, but the links between perception and action do not stop there. Arbib also believes that the motor schema has to update its representation of the object being controlled and therefore has to have a perceptual schema embedded within it. Both Arbib and Neisser emphasize the person continuously making, executing, and updating plans, in movement through a complex environment guided by an active information-seeking process.

Schemas can control perceptual activity by providing anticipations of temporally extended events and by directing search for relevant features. They operate on the information made available by the preattentive processes that detect features and group them into structures that are possible objects. The schemas are the general, abstracted knowledge structures that are built from our past experience with the world and help us to organise and understand our present experience of it. Increases in understanding of how we pick up information from the environment, how organisation principles operate preattentively, how structure is detected, and how experience leads to categorisation and differentiation, are helping us to understand how such schemas are developed and used.

CONCLUSION

It is not always easy to say which aspects of perception need to be treated in a chapter of their own, and which are a necessary part of other topics in the study of action. Even within traditional treatments of perception the literature on adaptation to prism rearrangement emphasizes the need to integrate any account of what a person sees or hears with some knowledge of the plans and actions that have produced the sights and sounds.

In this book our discussion of sensory information started with its treatment as feedback. Thus, in Chapter 2 we saw how the motor nervous system operates at a number of levels with the key to their coordination being feedback, beginning with the level of the spinal cord at which information from muscle receptors modulates contraction in that muscle. In Chapter 3, the importance of visual feedback was discussed in the context of improving the accuracy of aimed movements beyond the noise limitations of the motor system inherent in purely ballistic movement. However, in Chapter 4 our treatment of memory for movement led us to consider the strategic manipulation of sensory information and so, naturally into the discussion of perception and action in the present chapter. In subsequent chapters the contribution of sensory feedback to movement will not be forgotten. However, as evidenced in the next chapter on the sequencing of movement, the emphasis will shift from the detailed regulation of movement by feedback toward a discussion of relationships within complex sequences of activity between organised units of action. In this context an important role for vision and other perceptual systems is that of planning action, as well as monitoring and updating it. As we said at the beginning of the chapter, we can divide the activities of human beings for the purposes of study, and we may label the same processes in different ways at different times, but ultimately it must not be forgotten that perception and action are inextricably intertwined.

6

The Sequencing of Movements

Gerard van Galen
Alan M. Wing

INTRODUCTION

In Chapter 3 it was pointed out that movement of the hand to bring a cup of tea to the mouth is complex in the sense that it requires simultaneous control over several joints. However, a characteristic of many skills that is lacking in the cup of tea example is the sequencing of a number of logically separable components. In some skills it may merely be a matter of repeating a single component or a small number of components, perhaps with occasional minor modification. This might be an appropriate way of characterising the steps taken in walking over flat ground. In a large number of other activities our ability to sequence a number of separate movements each having different spatiotemporal characteristics is central. Examples of this range from the sequencing of finger movements in keyboard skills such as typing or playing the piano to activities that we carry out routinely every day such as dressing or making a cup of tea. These skills require a very specific ordering of movements, often in relation to objects in the environment.

One important concept in this area has been the motor program that has already been introduced in Chapter 3. Even a single movement

involves activity in many different muscles with some specific temporal
organisation and the process of organising the underlying commands to
the muscles can be called motor programming. In the present chapter
we are concerned with the way in which separate movements in a sequence become integrated into what appears as a smooth and coordinated flow of action. In this context the focus of interest addressed by
the concept of the motor program is comparatively high level; we are
concerned with the relations between successive movements rather than
the activity in individual muscles.

An important theme running through this chapter is that people impose structure on movement sequences they perform. Performance usually implies more than the stringing together or concatenation of the
individual components and the underlying structure of a sequence can
be investigated using either data on the timing of successive components or the patterns of errors people make in producing sequences.

FEEDBACK IN SEQUENCING MOVEMENTS

The origins of much of the present day research into the sequencing of
movements may be traced back to the work of Thorndike (1911). He
investigated the way cats learn extended sequences of lever-pressing
responses in order to open a box containing food. Thorndike's main
interests were in showing how the timing of reinforcement determines
the probability of successful learning and in demonstrating that ostensibly complex problem-solving behaviour can result from the temporal
contiguity of certain stimuli and the corresponding responses. Later,
Mowrer (1960) refined this stimulus–response contiguity principle as an
account of the learning of complex motor behaviour. He suggested that,
initially, successive movements are evoked as responses to external
stimuli. But, associated with each movement, there is proprioceptive
feedback from the preceding movement. As learning proceeds, temporal contiguity allows permanent memory traces to be set up in the
brain. Feedback from each successive response can then serve as a stimulus for the next response.

This view, that sequences of movements are produced on the basis of
a chain of feedback–response associations, is not now generally accepted. One of the most widely cited arguments against it was set out by
Lashley (1951). He pointed out that the processing of feedback must take
a finite amount of time. In the case of rapid skills like typing or speech,
where successive responses may be separated by less than 100 msec

there would simply not be enough time for selection of each successive response via a feedback pathway. Lashley proposed that rapid sequences of action are produced by a completely internalised specification of the commands required by the musculature, now commonly referred to as a *motor program*.

Another basis for objecting to the idea that feedback from the preceding response is required to elicit the following response comes from the study of individuals who lack proprioceptive feedback. Reference has already been made in Chapter 3 to Lashley's (1917) patient who, as a result of a gunshot wound, had no sensation in his lower limbs but was still able to control rhythmic alternation between flexion and extension. Other supportive data come from Rothwell, Traub, Day, Obeso, and Marsden's (1982) patient who had extensive proprioceptive losses in both upper and lower limbs resulting from degeneration of the peripheral neural pathways. Nevertheless, without vision this patient was able to tap the thumb repetitively, to touch the thumb to each finger in turn, or to move a finger in a complex spatial pattern.

Although Rothwell *et al.*'s patient was able to perform a wide variety of tasks in the laboratory it should be noted that he was moderately incapacitated in his performance of everyday activities as a result of his neurological condition. The difficulty caused by the lack of sensation was not in the short-term, moment-to-moment control of action, but rather in regulating activity over longer periods. In repetitive tapping, for example, the amplitude of the patient's movements became larger and larger. Indeed, Rothwell *et al.* noted that the patient's performance of any of the test tasks tended to deteriorate when he was asked to repeat them over a relatively long period (30 seconds or more). This suggests that, although feedback is not required for regulating the order or timing of each successive movement component, it is needed for general monitoring purposes such as checking on the overall accuracy of task performance.

A study by Wing (1977) of repetitive finger tapping in normal subjects assessed the role of auditory feedback in the timing of successive movements. Subjects made series of index finger movements bringing the index finger into contact with a touch plate. A short auditory pulse was provided to the subject at a constant, brief delay after each contact (see Figure 1). Once in each sequence the value of the auditory-feedback delay was perturbed, either by an increase of 20 or 50 msec or by a decrease of 10 msec. (None of the feedback delays were long enough to introduce a noticeable discrepancy between the proprioceptive and auditory feedback). If each successive response is triggered by feedback from the preceding response, then delaying feedback from one response

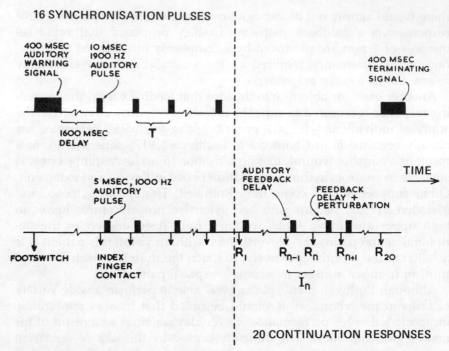

Figure 1. Perturbation of auditory feedback delay. From "Perturbations of auditory feedback delay and the timing of movement", by Wing, A. M. (1977). *Journal of Experimental Psychology: Human Perception and Performance*, 3, 175–186. Reprinted with permission.

should delay the initiation of the next response by the same amount. This turned out not to be the case; the delay in the response following perturbation of the feedback was smaller than would have been expected. In addition, at short interresponse intervals it was found that the effect of perturbation extended over more than the next response. Wing suggested that the auditory feedback was being used to monitor the accuracy of intervals being produced rather than as a trigger for each successive response.

PARAMETERS IN THE MOTOR PROGRAM

Because feedback from the periphery specific to the movement just completed is not required to stimulate the next movement in sequence, we are led to the idea that the sequencing or succession of movements is generated as part of a centrally organised motor program. A *motor pro-*

gram can be defined as a set of stored commands that ultimately indicate which muscles shall act at what time and with what intensity. In this section we first discuss a handwriting simulator designed by Vredenbregt and Koster (1971) which illustrates what is entailed in a motor program. Depending on the form the stored central commands take, the operation of a program may be made more versatile by allowing certain controlling values or parameters to be changed to suit the situation. This might mean, for example, that separate programs are not required for writing a particular letter smaller or larger than normal. We first show that the concept of continuously adjustable control parameters in motor programs receives some empirical support. In following sections, various studies are described that suggest that another important aspect of programs controlling movement sequences is their organisation in a set of superordinate levels.

Handwriting

In their simulation of handwriting Vredenbregt and Koster (1971) constructed a carriage that allowed free movement of a pen in up–down and left–right directions across a sheet of paper (see Figure 2). Two pairs of direct-current electric motors were used to produce movement in these two directions. By stepping up the applied voltage to one of the motors for varying amounts of time, pen strokes of different length were obtained. To obtain diagonal pen strokes two motors, one from each pair, were driven simultaneously. While the angle of the stroke could have been varied by modulating the voltage levels to each of the two motors (analogue control), instead Vredenbregt and Koster chose to switch the voltage between just two levels, off or on (binary control) and adjusted the times of onset and offset to each of the motors to achieve the desired effect. *Mechanical inertia* (resistance to changes in acceleration) and *viscosity* (resistance to changes in velocity) in the system meant that the abrupt transitions between the direction of the forces applied by the motor were smoothed out. This is clearly seen in the simulation of the letter *a* shown in Figure 3. The dynamics of the system were thus important in shaping the control provided by the sequence of voltage pulses; indeed, the simulation was only realistic insofar as system dynamics did the shaping. This corresponds to the fact that human-limb dynamics, which are determined by the physical properties of muscle and of the joint moved by the muscle, make a significant contribution to the form of voluntary movements. Allowance must be made for this contribution in the central commands to the muscles.

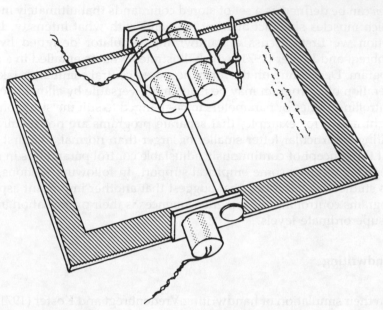

Figure 2. Mechanical simulation of handwriting. From "Analysis and synthesis of handwriting", by Vredenbregt, J., Koster, W. G. (1971). *Philips Technical Review, 32*, 73–78. Reprinted with permission.

In Vredenbregt and Koster's simulation, changes in the relative timing of the voltage pulses had an effect on the shape of the letter. If, halfway through the *a*, the time of application of the voltage to the motor that controlled upward movement was advanced, the eye of the loop became smaller. If the time of application was retarded, the loop of the *a* failed to close. In this way a series of progressive distortions of the letter *a* can be generated as shown at the bottom of Figure 3. If the simulation is taken as an account of the way people control handwriting, the effects of changes in relative timing could be taken as the basis of individual differences in writing style (though it does not account for how anyone develops a given style). But, for present purposes, the more interesting possibility is that unintended fluctuations in relative timing underlie the variability that is commonly seen within the writing of one individual. Why should errors in relative timing occur? One answer may be that, in people, time control is inherently "noisy". A biological timekeeper is likely to be variable and, in addition, even if the timing could be specified accurately within the CNS, it seems likely that neuromuscular transmission delays in effecting movement would introduce some temporal jitter.

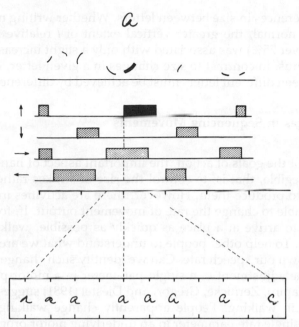

Figure 3. Timing control sequence for handwriting simulation. From "Analysis and synthesis of handwriting", by Vredenbregt, J., Koster, W. G. (1971). *Philips Technical Review*, 32, 73–78. Reprinted with permission.

In the simulation, if the intervals between the voltage pulses are increased, the size of the writing is increased. If there were no resistance to movement due to factors such as friction, the size increase would be in proportion to the increased length of the intervals. This raises the possibility that the way people adjust the size of handwriting is by scaling time. In cursive writing, size of writing varies as a function of the letter written. Thus, for example, in most people's writing the letters *e* and *l* are differentiated mainly on the basis of height, that is the vertical extent of the letter. The overall height of writing may also be adjusted, for example, to suit the line width of the paper being used. Wing (1980) asked subjects to write a series of words that included the letters *e* and *l* using either their normal-size handwriting or writing larger than normal. The timing of the successive up and down pen movements were recorded. It was found that, when subjects increased the size of their writing (by about 25%), there was a proportionate increase in the duration of each stroke. This supports the idea that there is a means of changing a rate parameter that can scale all the required time intervals at once, rather than a separate change being made to every interval specified in the underlying motor program. This does not appear to be the case for differences in size between letters. Whether writing normally or larger than normal, the greater vertical extent of *l* relative to *e* (a difference of over 75%) was associated with only a slight increase in stroke duration. Thus, in contrast to size changes in a given letter, differences in size between different letters must be achieved by differences in force.

Rate Changes in Sequencing Movements

In terms of the goals of action, the important aspect of handwriting is to make it legible, that is, to control the size of strokes rather than the time taken to produce them. However, there are activities in which we want to be able to change the rate of movement output. If, for example, our goal is to arrive at a place as quickly as possible, walking can be speeded up. To help other people to understand what we are saying we can slow down our speech rate. Can we identify such changes in output rate with the adjustment of a single parameter in a motor program? A study by Shapiro, Zernicke, Gregor, and Diestel (1981) suggests that this is the case in walking. People apparently change walking speed by adjusting a single rate parameter in an underlying motor program. Films were taken as subjects walked on a treadmill that could be set to run at various different speeds. The films were subsequently analysed to give the duration of each of four phases in the step cycle as shown in Figure 4. The period with the foot in contact with the ground (stance) is divided into two phases by the point at which the knee is maximally flexed. Two

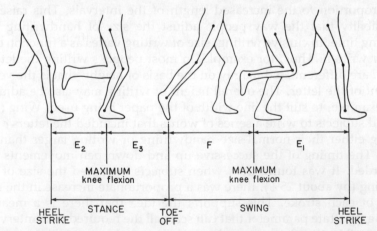

Figure 4. Phillipson step cycle showing subdivision into one flexion and three extension components.

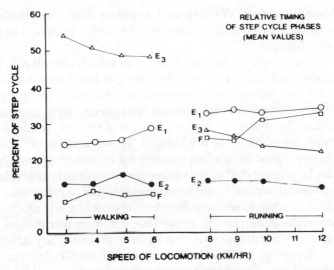

Figure 5. Duration of Phillipson step-cycle phases as a proportion of the total cycle duration at various rates of locomotion. From "Evidence for generalised motor programs using gait analysis", by Shapiro, D. C., Zernicke, R. F., Gregor, R. J., Diestel, J. D. (1981). *Journal of Motor Behavior*, *13*, 33–47. Reprintd with permission.

other phases are recognised in the period between the toe lifting off and returning to strike the ground (swing). The point of demarcation between the latter two phases is maximum knee flexion after the foot is lifted from the ground.

As the treadmill speed was increased from 3 to 6 km/h the total duration of the step cycle decreased from just over 1300 msec to 950 msec. This was the result of duration changes in all four phases of the step cycle, but the important point is that the contribution of each phase stayed in proportion, (see Figure 5). This result is consistent with an adjustable rate parameter in the motor program. It is as though the internal commands underlying walking are recorded on a tape that can be run past a playback head at various speeds.

The data of Shapiro *et al.* show that in going from walking to running (in running there is no period when the body is simultaneously supported by both legs) there is a qualitative change in the relative timing of the different phases. The transition between walking and running is not accomplished by a simple rate change; a program with a different organisation is required. Interestingly enough, as running speed increased from 8 to 12 km/h, Shapiro *et al.* found that step-cycle duration was constant at about 800 msec. This means that the changes in running speed were achieved by the scaling of the force developed in the propulsive phase of stance. Walking and running therefore demonstrate different ways of modulating parameters in a motor program to achieve performance changes.

Speech is an example of another activity in which output rate is often adjusted under voluntary control. However, it has been shown (Mac-Neilage, 1980) that changes in speech rate are not achieved by a uniform rescaling of the timing of movements in speech. Rate increases are achieved mainly by reduction of the duration of vowels, while the duration of consonants is relatively unchanged. These data are not consistent with simple rate adjustment of an underlying motor program. One way the data can be interpreted is that there are two different levels in the internal representation of speech movements for vowels and consonants. Speech rate increases may then be obtained by a uniform adjustment of vowel duration leaving consonant duration unchanged.

A parallel to the results for speech may be seen in a study of serial key pressing by Summers (1975). His task required subjects to press a sequence of nine keys. Once error-free performance was achieved, subjects were required to superimpose one of two different rhythms made up of long, 500-msec and short, 100-msec intervals. One group of subjects were given a long–long–short pattern the other a long–short–short pattern. After two training sessions with the rhythms, the subjects were told they were simply to reproduce the sequences as rapidly as possible without making errors in the order of the key presses. Summers was interested in the extent to which there would be transfer of the trained rhythm from paced to speeded performance conditions. The intervals produced by the subjects in the speeded condition are shown in Figure 6. In contrast to Shapiro *et al.*'s data on locomotion, neither of the conditions in Summers' study support the idea of a rate-adjustable motor program; the original rhythms are not scaled in the speeded condition. (It is unlikely that this lack of scaling can be attributed to a physical inability to make the short intervals any shorter. People are able to produce minimum intertap intervals of the order of 120 to 150 msec, considerably shorter than the minimum intervals observed by Summers).

Although there was no simple scaling of rate in Summers' data, in the case of the subjects trained on the long–long–short pattern there is an indication that the rhythmic structure is partly preserved in the speeded condition. This result could be considered a parallel of the case in speech production where the length of vowels, but not of consonants, decreased as the speech rate increased. Again we are led to the idea that, in the regulation of a sequence of movements, there is more than one level of representation of the elements.

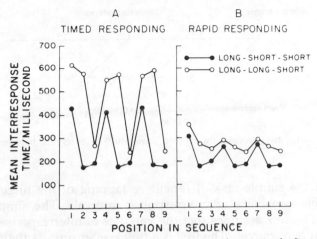

Figure 6. Changes in interresponse interval when performance of a finger sequencing task is speeded up. From "The role of timing in motor program representation", by Summers, J. J. (1975). *Journal of Motor Behavior*, 7, 229–241. Reprinted with permission.

LEVELS OF REPRESENTATION OF MOVEMENT SEQUENCES

A number of different approaches to the representation of levels of control in sequencing movement may be identified. The first two that we consider both involve time measures, either of simple repetitive movements with timing as the aspect of behaviour that the subject is expected to control or, of structured sequences in which the serial order of the movement elements is important. We then turn to studies of the nature of movement sequence representation based on order errors in execution of the sequences.

Timing of Repetitive Movement

An important characteristic of written music is the hierarchical nature of timing. Music is segmented by bars and beats within bars, and there can be further subdivision into quarter and eighth notes. These divisions make it likely that the production of musical rhythms would provide a fertile area for research into hierarchically organised processes underlying the sequencing of movement, and indeed, promising results have been obtained by Shaffer (1981) in the area of piano playing. However, in this section, we restrict discussion to the simpler task of tapping out interval sequences using one finger.

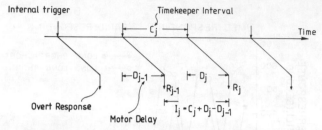

Figure 7. The two-process model for variability of intervals between repetitive responses.

Even in the simple task of repetitive tapping of the finger there is considerable variability of interresponse intervals. The simple model shown in Figure 7 assumes that the variance of interresponse intervals arises from two sources. The first is a timekeeper process that triggers a response at the required interval. The second source of variance is the motor delay that intervenes between the trigger and the recorded response. Assuming that the timekeeper intervals and response delays are independent, the interresponse interval variance is given by the sum of the timekeeper interval variance plus twice the motor delay variance. This simple two-process model predicts that successive interresponse intervals will be negatively correlated because chance variation in any given motor delay tends to induce changes of opposite sign in the interresponse intervals for which it is the boundary. That is, an interresponse interval longer than the average tends to be followed by one shorter than average more often than would be predicted purely by chance. Such negative correlation has been observed, for example, by Wing and Kristofferson (1973).

Using variability measures, Vorberg and Hambuch (1984) have developed an analytic procedure that can help determine whether a hierarchical structure underlies actively timed performance of sequences. Subjects (who were all musicians) were instructed to repeatedly tap out sequences of time intervals such as (525, 175, 350, 350) msec, the first four cycles in synchrony with a series of auditory presentations of the pattern, then for 16 cycles on their own. If performance of this task involved only a single timekeeping process, the timekeeper would have to be continually reset with progression through the sequence. An alternative to this single-timekeeper account is that timing is accomplished with the aid of several independent timekeepers capable of running simultaneously in hierarchic arrangements such as that shown in Figure 8. Now consider the variance of intervals defined between responses that are in corresponding positions in successive cycles—*the cycle vari-*

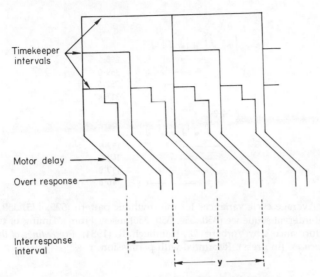

Figure 8. Hierarchical timing of rhythm.

ance. If it is assumed that all the timekeeper intervals and motor delays are statistically independent, the cycle variance for responses triggered by different levels of the hierarchy will be ordered according to the level. For example, consider the cyclic interval defined on the beat (X) and the off-beat cyclic interval (Y). Over the whole sequence their average will be the same, but the cycle variance of (Y) will be larger than that of (X). Both cyclic intervals receive the same contributions to their variance from the timekeeper at the highest level and from motor delay variance, however, (Y) has the additional variability due to the two intervals generated by the lower-level timekeeper. In general, hierarchical models predict an ordering of cycle variances whereas a serial model with one timekeeper switching between different intervals predicts equality of cycle variances. In hierarchical models, cyclic intervals bounded by responses triggered at the highest level of the hierarchy will have the smallest variance.

Vorberg and Hambuch's estimates of the cycle variances for various different temporal patterns led them to reject the serial model as a general account of timing. In the case of the (525, 175, 350, 350) msec pattern, for example, cycle variances of 299, 369, 352, and 317 msec^2 were observed (see Figure 9) and, statistically, these were significantly different. In this case the lowest of the cycle variances is associated with the response initiating the longest interval in the cycle and this presumably reflects a natural rhythmic tendency for that response to define a first beat in the bar. The differences in these cycle variances is thus evidence

Figure 9. Average cycle variances for the rhythmic pattern (525, 175, 350, 350) msec and the equal-interval sequence (350, 350, 350, 350) msec. From "Timing of two-handed rhythmic performance", by Vorberg, D., Hambuch, R. (1984). *Proceedings of the New York Academy of Sciences*, (in press). Reprinted with permission.

supporting an internal hierarchical structure to the timekeeping. In one trivial pattern that Vorberg and Hambuch studied, that of a simple pattern comprised of four equal intervals of 350 msec, no differences were observed between the cycle variances. In fact, the cycle-variance estimates for this equal interval case were all in the region of 140 msec^2, considerably less than the estimates for unequal interval patterns which were generally of the order of 300 msec^2, despite the same overall cycle duration of 1200 msec. It might therefore seem that there is some extra difficulty associated with hierarchical timing; but the real point is that, if an unequal interval pattern were attempted with serial timekeeping, performance might have been even more variable.

Timing of Structured Movement Sequences

The idea of using variance measures to test the nature of timing sequences of movements was also suggested earlier by Kozhevnikov and Chistovich (1965) in their analysis of speech control. They asked subjects to produce the same utterance on several occasions and then used the accoustic waveform to determine the timing of intervals between successive speech gestures. Because the variance of the overall duration of an utterance was less than the sum of the variances of the elements, they argued against a serial timing model of speech production in which each successive gesture is triggered by the occurrence of the preceding gesture. Instead they favoured a two-level account analogous to the one proposed by Wing and Kristofferson (1973) for repetitive tapping. A demonstration of the potential of this method may be seen in the work of Lackner and Levine (1975). Using a similar approach to Kozhevnikov and Chistovich they showed that subjects produced speech utterances with less relative variability in overall duration if what they had learned to say had syntactical, that is, grammatical, structure than if the same words were strung together randomly. Interestingly, a rhythm imposed on the random word strings significantly reduced the relative variability in overall duration. From this we may conclude that the timing accuracy of movement control is aided by imposed higher-level organisation.

Study of the timing of elements in movement sequences has not been limited to the inter-element times. The time taken to initiate sequences comprising series of differing movements is often used to explore organisational processes occurring prior to movement. In Chapter 3, in the case of simple aiming movements it will be recalled that difficulty of movement primarily affected the duration of the movement and not the RT. However, as suggested by the pioneering work of Henry and Rogers (1960), the complexity of a sequence of movements can have an affect on RT.

Klapp and Wyatt (1976) asked subjects to produce Morse code sequences comprising combinations of short (*dit*) and long (*dah*) key presses; *dit–dit, dit–dah, dah–dit, dah–dah*. On any given trial one of four lamps would light to indicate which pattern was required and the time to initiate the first key press was recorded. The largest effect on RT was due to the identity of the first element; reaction time was some 50 msec longer if the first element was the longer *dah* (see Table 1). The second element did not affect RT directly. However, the latency to initiate the first key press was shorter if the second element was the same as the first. Thus, for example, *dit–dit* was started quicker than *dit–dah*.

TABLE 1. RT in Milliseconds as a Function of the First and Second Elements in Two-Element Morse Code Sequences[a]

	Second response		
	dit	*dah*	Mean
First response			
dit	532	648	590
dah	689	597	643
Mean	611	623	

[a]Data from Klapp and Wyatt (1976).

At first sight these results might seem contradictory. On one hand, a long response in the initial position takes longer to prepare, on the other hand, a long response in the second position does not affect preparation. It is the relation between elements in the sequence that matters, thus, preparation takes less time if an element is repeated. To resolve this apparent contradiction, suppose the motor program has a hierarchical structure. At a low level the detail of each element in the sequence is spelled out; at this level a short response takes less time to organise than a long response. At a higher level, relations between elements are specified. It takes less time to prepare at this level if two elements are the same. There is one additional pertinent aspect of Klapp and Wyatt's data; as well as recording the time to initiate the first key press response, they also recorded the interval between successive key presses. Combining the data over both short and long first responses, it was found that this interresponse interval was some 40 msec longer if the second response was a *dah* than if it was a *dit*. This suggests that preparation at the lower level in the hierarchy was not completed until after the end of the first response, otherwise the effect of the length of the second response would have been seen on the initiation latency rather than on the interval between responses.

An extensive study of the sequencing of speech by Sternberg, Monsell, Knoll, and Wright (1978) supports the idea that preparation of the program proceeds during execution of the sequence. In one of their experiments subjects were trained to produce spoken utterances as fast as possible. On each trial a subject was presented with a list of one, two, three, or four words. After a fixed interval of 3.5 seconds, during which the subject was expected to prepare the production of the list, a signal to commence speaking was given. The reaction time from this signal to the onset of the utterance was recorded, together with the duration of the utterance. Sternberg *et al.* found a steady increase in RT with the number of items in the sequence, confirming the results of other experiments using letters and digits, (see Figure 10). The increase was about 10 msec for each additional word. Half of the word lists comprised one-syllable words, the other half consisted of two-syllable words. The two-syllable words were chosen to match the one-syllable words by having the same initial syllable, for example, cow and coward. Thus differences in RT would not be a reflection of any differences in the movements required at the beginning of the utterances. It may be seen that the slope did not depend on whether the list comprised one- or two-syllable words. However, there was an overall increase in reaction time for the two-syllable words of about 5 msec.

Sternberg *et al.* found a curvilinear relation between utterance dura-

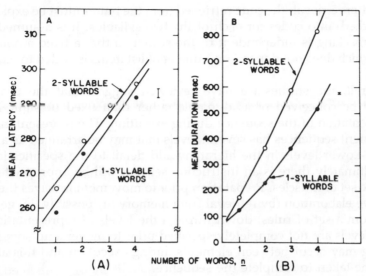

Figure 10. The effect of number of words on the latency (A) and duration (B) of utterances. From "The latency and duration of rapid movement sequences: Comparisons of speech and typewriting", by Sternberg, S., Monsell, S., Knoll, R. L., Wright, C. E. (1978). In Stelmach, G. E. (Ed.), *Information processing in motor control and learning*. London: Academic Press, Reprinted with permission.

tion and list length. Each additional word in the list slowed the overall rate of speaking by about 10 msec per word. This value is the same as that observed for the increase in RT with list length. This suggests that there is a process common to both the preparation and the execution of the sequences. Sternberg *et al.* theorised that preparation of an utterance means that a set of codes identifying the words in the utterance are placed, without ordering, in a temporary storage area they called a *response buffer*. On the command to start speaking, the first code is located by searching through the buffer in a serial fashion until it is found (a serial, self-terminating search). If there are more codes in the buffer, on average, it will take longer to find the first item. This model thus accounts for the linear increase in RT with list length.

Once speaking has been initiated, after the production of a word, it is assumed the next word is retrieved from the buffer by another self-terminating serial search. This causes a delay in the production of each successive list item that will depend on the list length. Thus, the total duration of the utterance, which is determined by the sum of the item durations and the delays between the items, will increase as a quadratic function of list length. In the case of a two-syllable word, it is assumed that, after retrieval, the code retrieved from the buffer must be expanded (unpacked) into codes for each of the two syllables. It is assumed that the unpacking is independent of the search so that a fixed amount of time which does not depend on number of list items is added to reaction time.

Overall, the studies we have reviewed suggest that the program should be conceived of as dynamic rather than fixed or static in its representation of the sequence during execution. The representation of movement sequences has several levels that may be arranged as a hierarchy. Lower levels in the hierarchy add detail to the specification so that ultimately there is an instruction set that will be appropriate to a specific set of muscles. Preparation prior to movement involves the progressive elaboration (by retrieval from memory or, possibly, by generation from a set of rules) down through the levels of representation. If some levels are not completely specified prior to movement, some processing may occur between elements during execution and this affects the time taken to complete the sequence.

ERRORS IN MOVEMENT SEQUENCES

So far we have discussed the sequencing of movement in terms of timing. In making inferences about the internal representation underlying the execution of sequences we have used the patterning of intervals between elements. The time to the first element, the RT, has been used in our discussion of preparatory processes occurring prior to movement. We now turn to the nature of errors that occur when sequences of movements are executed as these may also give clues about the internal representation of movement.

Serial Button-Pressing

A prototypical laboratory task for studying errors requires subjects to learn long series of button presses, with a different finger assigned to each button. The question asked is whether some finger transitions are more prone to error than others. Restle and Burnside (1972) looked at errors in learning long sequences of button presses such as (1234666662-323543). They found that errors during either learning or recall tended to occur at the boundaries of certain response groups within the sequence; for example, a 5 might appear between the 4 and 6 as an extension of the run (1234). Other response groups identified in this manner included trills, for example, (2323) and repetitions, for example, (66666). These groups of elementary response units simplify the description of the sequence at a higher level, although, in the final analysis the movements required do not change.

Povel and Collard (1982) trained subjects to produce rapid-button press sequences from memory. Different groups of subjects were given different cyclic permutations of the same basic pattern. Consider the sequences A (123234) and B (232341), where the numbers 1, 2, 3, 4 indicate a response should be made with the index, middle, ring, or little finger, respectively. If the sequences are produced repeatedly, there are no overall differences in the finger movements required. Nonetheless, Povel and Collard found different patterns of interresponse intervals in the two cases; in case A there was a long–short–short–long–short–short pattern whereas, with pattern B, alternation of long–short was seen. Apparently, subjects were segmenting the response streams differently. Sequence A lends itself to characterisation in terms of two runs (123) and (234). Representing the required finger-press movements in this way allows shorter times between finger presses within each run, but involves a certain amount of preparation that lengthens the time for the initial element of the run. A possible interpretation of the long–short pattern for sequence B is that subjects set up a structure based on three pairs (23), (23), (41). The important point to make here is that because both sequences required the same finger transitions the results show that the structure is not necessarily determined by the sequence of movements required. In this case it appears that subjects inserted different organisations into their movements based, perhaps, on their initial perception of the sequence.

Rosenbaum, Kenny and Derr (1983) developed an account of serial button pressing that attempts to draw data on errors and timing into one theoretical framework. In the experiment subjects were asked to memorize eight-item finger-press sequences involving the index and middle fingers of the left and right hand. When the subject felt comfortable performing the sequence from memory, a block of trials was run with each sequence to be performed as fast as possible six times without interruption. Each subject was tested a number of times on eight different sequences, constructed as shown in Table 2. As an example, the sequence (right index, left index, right index, left index, right middle, left middle, right middle, left middle) was produced by the left-most combination of choices. Rosenbaum *et al.* found reliable effects of position in the sequence on the interresponse intervals (see Figure 11). Perhaps the most noticeable effect is the division of the sequence into two

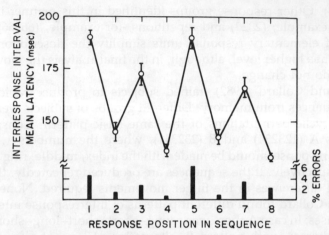

Figure 11. Patterning of interresponse intervals in the execution of a finger sequencing task. From "Hierarchical control of rapid movement sequences", by Rosenbaum, D. A., Kenny, S. B., Derr, M. D. (1983). *Journal of Experimental Psychology: Human Perception and Performance, 9,* 86–102. Reprinted with permission.

by the long latencies associated with responses 1 and 5. In addition, each half of the sequence is subdivided by the intermediate latencies at responses 3 and 7. The even numbered responses 2, 4, 6, and 8 are all short and, to a first approximation, equal.

Why, if subjects were only required to produce the sequences as rapidly as possibly, did this temporal patterning occur? Rosenbaum *et al.* argued that execution was based on a process analogous to the steps shown in Table 2 that were required to construct the sequences in the first place. As illustration consider the sequence listed earlier. Selection of the first element in the sequence requires a choice between hands at the higher level (right), between starting finger at the next level (index) and between a homologous or a nonhomologous transition at the lowest level (homologous). It is assumed that selection of the second element

TABLE 2. Selection of Elements in the Alternating Hand-Response Sequences Used by Rosenbaum *et al.* (1983)

Starting hand (every eight responses)	Right		Left	
Starting finger (every four responses)	Index	Middle	Index	Middle
Homologous/nonhomologous finger transition (every two responses)	H N	H N	H N	H N

only requires a decision to alternate the hand with the three levels in the table all held constant. Every second response, that is, at the first, third, fifth, etc, response, a homologous/nonhomologous decision must be made at the lowest level indicated in Table 2. Every fourth response, that is, at the beginning and middle of the sequence, a starting finger decision must be made in addition to the homologous/nonhomologous and alternation decisions. If it is assumed that a fixed amount of time is associated with each level of decision, a pattern of response intervals is predicted such that, for example, the interval between first and second responses will be shorter than the interval between the second and third responses. This model is qualitatively in agreement with the time intervals observed. Rosenbaum *et al.* also pointed out that, if there is a fixed probability of error associated with each decision point, there should be a larger probability of error at the third position in the sequence than at the second. The proportion of errors are plotted in the lower part of Figure 11, and indeed, a parallel with the latency data is seen.

Sternberg *et al.*'s account of their speech utterance data indicated that a significant amount of organisation occurs during execution of a sequence of movements. The Rosenbaum *et al.* account may be seen as presenting the extreme view that all processing occurs during execution. Not surprisingly, there are other possible perspectives on the Rosenbaum *et al.* results. For example, it is possible that the hierarchical decision process based on Table 2 is only an appropriate description of the way subjects learned the serial order of the sequence and of their timing during acquisition of the task. The timing observed when subjects were required to produce the learned sequence as rapidly as possible could have been due to the same effect as that reported in Summers (1975). It will be recalled that in his study the instruction to produce a sequence as quickly as possible left some of the original temporal pattern with which the sequence had been learned. The Rosenbaum *et al.* timing data may therefore have been a carry-over of the acquisition phase rather than a reflection of the processes underlying execution.

In our earlier discussion of rhythm we considered very simple repetitive movement tasks. However, in musical performance a major component of rhythm is stress, that is, variation in the intensity of notes due to alterations in the amplitude or force of the movements used to produce them. Stress patterns are also a prominent feature in many spoken languages. In analysing a corpus of errors in spoken German, MacKay (1971) noted that errors in which pairs of phonemes occurred with their order reversed, often involved a stressed element occurring before it was due. As an example MacKay cited the *b* in the stressed second syllable of "gebrauch" which, in one error, appeared early so that the word was spoken as "begrauch". An experiment that MacKay carried out using a button-pressing task indicates that this phenomenon, which he referred to as stress pre-entry, is not limited to speech. Subjects were trained to use the fingers of one hand to produce a sequence of button presses (5342) where 5 refers to the little finger and 2 to the index finger. Five different stress conditions were compared; a different finger was to be stressed or emphasized in four of them, and all fingers were to be equally stressed in the fifth. Each condition was run either at a comfortable rate (average of 119 msec per response) or at maximal rate (88 msec per response). The main finding was that when serial reversals occurred they usually involved the stressed element and typically it would occur one position early. A second finding was that serial reversals were more likely to occur at the faster response rate.

In discussing these observations MacKay suggested that initiating the output of successive components in a sequence of movements depends on an activation mechanism. He proposed that the elements of a sequence are represented in abstract form and in proper order in an output buffer. These elements prime or partially activate units that directly control particular movements. If the level of activation in a movement unit reaches some threshold, the corresponding behaviour occurs. He assumed that the ordered execution of a sequence results from a sweep of excitation passing over the elements in the buffer at some regulated rate. Summation of the excitation over a finite period by each of the movement units in turn brings each one up to threshold a finite time after onset of excitation. Using this model, MacKay accounted for stress pre-entry by supposing that intensity of movement, or stress, is marked by a higher level of initial priming. In consequence, when the triggering sweep of excitation arrives at a stressed element it will reach threshold in less time than when it reaches an unstressed element. If the sweep rate is fast enough, the stress unit may attain threshold before the preceding (unstressed) element.

The timing relationships between the sweep of excitation and the delay in threshold attainment in Mackay's model bear a formal resemblance to the timekeeper and the motor delay in the simple model of repetitive tapping described previously. In the tapping model we implicitly assumed that the ordering of the responses triggered by the timekeeper would be preserved at the periphery, but MacKay's model suggests that this may not always be the case. It can be shown that if there is a breakdown in ordering of responses, the correlation between successive interresponse intervals can drop from the negative values predicted by the tapping model down to zero (Wing, 1973). Breakdown in order is more likely to occur if, with a fixed amount of motor delay variability, the timekeeper intervals are progressively reduced, that is, if the response rate is increased. In MacKay's model, this is equivalent to an increase in the excitation sweep rate. Assuming that the time taken to attain threshold has some variability, we should therefore expect the increased likelihood of reversal that MacKay observed at the maximal rate of responding.

Typing

One difficulty in trying to study errors is that their frequency of occurrence in skilled performance is often very low so that collection of sufficient data can be laborious. However, in typing, which is after all just another key-pressing task, albeit a complex one, the use of keyboard entry into computers makes it easy to record very many key presses among which a reasonable number of errors may be expected. Rumelhart and Norman (1982) have taken a number of basic phenomena observed in skilled typewriting as constraints for a formal model of typing which they then tested by running it as a computer simulation. From their point of view perhaps the prime phenomenon was that high-speed films of typing showed that the fingers of the hands are in almost constant motion. The fingers start to move toward the target key before several preceding characters have been typed (Gentner, 1981). Viewing the film reminded them "of the movement of sea grass weaving in the waves, gracefully bending this way and that, all in motion at the same time" (Norman & Rumelhart, 1983, p. 47). This convinced them that typing could not be directed by a serial process in which each finger in turn makes a stroke and led them to favour instead a mechanism in which several fingers are guided simultaneously.

A second source of information that directed the development of their model was the nature of errors. One of the most common error categories in typing is transposition in which two adjacent letters are reversed (e.g., which → whihc). The large majority of such errors occur across hands, (Shaffer, 1976). This kind of error is easily generated if it is recognised that several fingers may simultaneously be moving in competition towards their individual target keys. The last class of information that Norman and Rumelhart drew on was the timing of keystrokes. As support for a model with distributed processing and with minimal central-feedback regulation they quoted the high speeds at which people are capable of typing. In normal skilled typing interkeystroke intervals of the order of 60 msec are not uncommon. Because the timing for a given keystroke depends heavily on the physical constraints presented

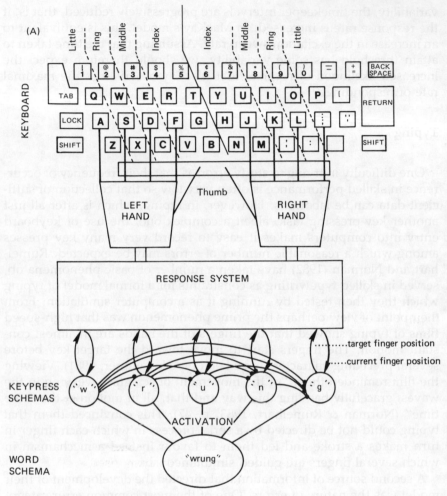

Figure 12. The activation triggered schema system applied to typing of the word *wrung*.

by the keyboard, the hand, and the context preceding the letter being typed, they argued that typing strokes are not triggered in serial fashion by a metronome-like timekeeper.

The model of typing that Norman and Rumelhart propose they call an activation-triggered schema system, (see Figure 12). They define a *schema* as an organized unit of knowledge which, when referring to output serves the the same function as a subroutine in a motor program. However, in justification of the new term, schemas are assumed to have a property not usually attributed to subroutines, namely, they interact with each other in determining motor output. The schema for a word to be typed (in the example, *wrung*), excites a set of lower-level, *child* keypress schemas that specify target positions for the individual letters *w, r, u, n, g*. These in turn act as *parent* schema and excite child schemas controlling actual finger, hand, and arm movements. In the model it is assumed that the activation level for each schema reflects the sum of the excitation or inhibition it receives as well as certain characteristics such as decay and random fluctuation or *noise* that one would expect in a memory system. While a schema receives excitation from its parent, *sibling* schema may interact with one another. In particular, Norman and Rumelhart introduce the inhibitory links shown among the keypress schemata in Figure 12 to ensure that the letters are typed in the correct order. When a key has been struck (and this is determined by fulfilling *trigger conditions*, namely, the finger being appropriately near to its target) the inhibition by the schema controlling that keypress is removed allowing the keypress schema for the next letter to rise to full activation. The keypress schemas for later letters are also partly released from inhibition and movement of the hands and fingers will begin to reflect their increasing influence.

Now consider the typing of the word *wrung*. Activations are pooled in the shared interest by the fingers of the left hand in moving to the top row to type *w* and *r* (see Figure 12). In the right hand a conflict occurs between the typing of *u* and *n* since both are typed by the right index finger and this results in a weakened movement towards the letter *u*. If a hand (or finger) has not been used for a while it will have more time to get into position for the next letter so that the *g* is typed with a small interstroke interval following the *n*.

Rumelhart and Norman (1982) have tested this model by giving it a text to type that they had also used with human subjects. Depending on their choice of details, such as the amount of noise in the activation levels, they observed that the model exhibited the same kinds of phenomena that we noted earlier for human subjects. The model may thus be taken as an explanation of the organisation of serial order in movement sequences. However, recent work by Grudin (1982) that focuses on the timing of typing errors has noted a discrepancy between human typing performance and that of the simulation. His conclusion is that the model's lack of explicit temporal regulation of keystrokes must be rethought even though Rumelhart and Norman originally saw this omission as a major virtue. Grudin carried out a detailed analysis of keystroke intervals associated with letter transposition. In Rumelhart and Norman's model keystrokes are in competition to occur as early as possible. Noise in the activation values of letter can occasionally lead to the wrong letter having the greatest activation and occurring first. Simulation times for the next keystroke are typically much shorter than normal keystrokes. However, Grudin's analysis showed that with human subjects timing is largely preserved in transpositions at least until the delay in the letter following the error. He therefore proposed that key striking, which Rumelhart and Norman had assumed to be the result of peripherally determined trigger conditions, is under the control of a central timing pattern that is sequence specific.

Slips of Action

To what extent do the theoretical ideas that we have been discussing apply to the real world? In studying the sequencing of movement, most researchers choose to work with tasks that can be carried out in the laboratory. To some extent this reflects the difficulty of transporting the sort of equipment needed for accurate measurement, particularly in cases where the timing of movement is of interest. However, most people do on occasion notice their own errors or slips of action. What they notice may not be fully representative of all errors made; it is likely that there is some selectivity in our perception of our own errors. Nonetheless, some interesting points do emerge from systematic study of the mistakes we make in everyday activities. Reason (1979) asked subjects to keep a diary of their slips of action noting the circumstances, what was intended, and what actually happened. An average of 12 errors per person was obtained over a 2-week period. He observed that actions deviating from the intended course are typically not fragments but intact sequences. Reason argued that the persistence of deviating actions, despite being unintended, supports the idea that there are units of action that can run off without conscious regulation. His view of the organisation of an action sequence is that a nested set of action units or subprograms is assembled in advance on the basis of a mental representation of the goal. He suggests the selection of subprograms may be biased by frequency of use or by recency; as a consequence intention may be diverted, for example, by a frequently used subprogram inappropriate to the current intention. As an example of such a capture error Reason cites a report from one of the diaries:

> I meant to get my car out, but as I passed through the back porch on the way to the garage I stopped to put on my wellington boots and gardening jacket as if to work in the garden.

In execution, it is assumed that each subprogram in the sequence runs autonomously without attention to feedback—behaviour is regulated in an open-loop manner. However, the transitions between subprograms depend on the recognition of completion of each unit which requires conscious attention to feedback and Reason calls this closed-loop control. The transition he calls the *critical decision point*. He argues that, no matter how well practised a skill is, there are critical decision points at which the closed-loop mode of control is necessary to ensure the intended outcome. The example of putting on the gardening boots may be viewed as a failure to check the outcome using feedback at a point where an initially common sequence of actions (going to the porch) can lead to two different outcomes and the route leading to the unintended outcome was selected. In between critical decision points, processing capacity is freed so that the central processor can carry out operations related to future aspects of the situation, or some other parallel mental activity not directly connected to performance of the current action.

When focal attention is engaged with some parallel mental activity, Reason suggests that only a short-lived record of the immediately preceding actions is retained in memory; this accounts for occasions on which people lose track of where they have arrived at in a sequence. These seem to be particularly likely to occur when there is an unanticipated interruption in a largely automated series of actions. A tea-making error illustrates this:

> Having filled the kettle and set it to boil, I automatically reached for the tea-caddy to spoon tea into the pot. Then I became aware that the caddy was empty, so I retrieved a fresh packet of tea from the cupboard, and emptied it into the caddy. But instead of resuming the tea-making sequence at the correct point, I shut the lid of the caddy and poured the now boiling water into an empty teapot.

On the basis of his analysis of slips of actions Reason suggests that, in execution, a program counter steps through the sequence of subprograms. The failure in the tea-making example occurred because the counter does not take acount of action content and there is no memory (or no check of memory) for the last few steps accomplished before taking the next step.

Although Reason favours a computer-program metaphor with a pointer stepping serially through the elements of action, Norman (1981) took the view that in the sequencing of action there is simultaneous

activation of all the constituent motor-memory elements, which he calls
schema. In line with his research on typing that we described in the
previous section, he proposed that serial order in execution is partly a
function of the activation level assigned to each schema as well as the
result of tests based on feedback that determine whether trigger conditions for performance of a schema have been met. Space does not allow
us to properly contrast the two approaches, but it is worth noting that
Norman's approach has many parallels with Reason in the way errors
are categorised. Perhaps the main difference is the importance Norman
attaches to memory decay (which he calls loss of activation) in the generation of errors. To quote Norman, "When the appropriate schemas . . .
are activated, some may lose activation as a result of the normal decay
and interference properties of primary memory". In his view such decay
underlies, for example, the common experience of arriving somewhere,
knowing that you came with some purpose, but not being able to remember what it was.

CONCLUSION

In this chapter a view of action has been developed that suggests that
motor output should not be viewed as continuously controlled but
rather as comprised of a stream of discrete, separable elements. The
problem, of course, is that movement sequences that we observe are
ostensibly one smooth flow as a result of the influence of the physical
system that is being driven and it is not a straightforward matter to
determine the psychological important elements in motor output.
Often it is a matter of letting the definition of the task suggest what may
be psychologically important components and then examine the data to
see whether they are consistent with the suggestion. This is probably a
fair characterisation of much of the research covered in this chapter.

We have reviewed a number of studies in which observations of time
relations between elements in movement sequences have suggested the
underlying organisation may be hierarchical. This view has received
some support from observations of the time taken to initiate movement
sequences as a function of relations between the elements in the sequence. The idea of the hierarchy is that the burden placed by the
sequencing of action on conscious, attention-demanding processing
should be reduced by the use of low-level subprograms or schemas to
produce certain units of action in automatic fashion. The issues of hier-

archic organisation and attention demands of movement are dealt with in subsequent chapters. The next chapter uses interactions between the simultaneous performance of two separate tasks to investigate processing demands of movement. Chapter 8 explores the possibility that hierarchical organisation underlies the development of automaticity in skill acquisition.

Doing Two Things at Once: Process Limitations and Interactions

Herbert Heuer
Alan M. Wing

INTRODUCTION

Casual observation suggests that people can carry out several different actions simultaneously. For example, consider some of the components of riding a bicycle. The legs drive the pedals round for propulsion, the arms may be used to turn the handlebars for steering (in combination with balance adjustments using the trunk), the hands may be used to ring the bell or to apply the brakes. In addition to all these activities, the rider is able to note objects in the vicinity and even to conduct a conversation with a companion.

However, some of these activities may affect the performance of others. Thus, in a congested urban area where appropriate reactions must be made as quickly as possible, most people would probably stop conversing and concentrate on incoming visual information. This example suggests that there is a limitation on our ability to maintain several different actions at once. In consequence, we must either select the more important or primary activities or run the risk of one (or more) of the activities being performed poorly. From one perspective, trying to do too many things at the same time means our ability to control any one of

THE PSYCHOLOGY OF HUMAN MOVEMENT

the activities may deteriorate. In this chapter, we develop this and an alternative view that considers interactions between specific components of two tasks rather than the simple global limit implied by "too many things at once". Thus, in this chapter we ask, what kinds of limitations exist in doing several things at once? Can we infer anything about the organisation of movement from the pattern of interactions in the performance of different combinations of tasks carried out simultaneously?

Some of the concepts that we introduce have been discussed by others under headings such as "the attention demands of movement". In providing an early definition of attention, James (1890) described attention as "the taking possession by the mind, in clear and vivid form of one out of what seems to be several possible objects or trains of thought. It implies withdrawal from some things in order to deal effectively with others" (p. 403–404). Much research still follows this phenomenological lead. For example, studies of selective attention are concerned with how people can filter out some (but not just any) information from the great variety of stimuli present in the environment at any point in time. In a sense, the question asked is what determines how information has access to consciousness and can thus be reported.

In this chapter we view the problem rather differently in considering the performance of several motor skills carried out at once. Here performance has a less-obvious relationship to conscious experience than do the verbal reports in, for example, experiments on selective attention. Conscious thought need not improve motor performance. This is nicely reflected in the rhyme about the millipede who was asked how he managed to coordinate his limbs in walking. He stopped to think of an answer, and from that time on he was unable to walk again. One of the aims of this chapter is to consider more indirect techniques that address the question of coordination of movements, hopefully in a manner less disruptive of performance!

EXPERIMENTAL METHODS

Investigators have used many different approaches to the assessment of interference in dual-task performance. An important distinction is between studies that employ two tasks of similar duration and studies in which one task is much shorter than the other. A second distinction is concerned with how the data obtained are analysed.

Type of Task

On a bicycle trip steering and pedaling must continue throughout whereas the bell might be used only once, if at all. Relative to propelling the bicycle along, the act of ringing the bell in response to someone walking in front of the bicycle is very brief. We first consider the combination of tasks that completely overlap in time, such as steering and pedaling in the bicycling example. Then we turn to combinations of tasks of unequal temporal extent.

Temporally Co-Extensive Tasks

By way of illustration, we take an experiment on dual-task performance reported by Schouten, Kalsbeek, and Leopold (1962). A serial choice-reaction time (RT) task was designated as the primary task. At fixed intervals one or the other of two tones was presented in a random sequence. In response subjects had to press a pedal with their right or left foot as fast as possible. This task was performed for three minutes. The intersignal interval was varied, and the shortest interval at which

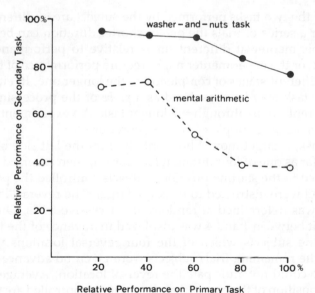

Figure 1. Changes in performance on manual assembly and mental arithmetic (secondary) tasks as a function of performance on a serial choice reaction time (primary) task. Data from Schouten *et al.* (1962).

subjects were able to respond making no more than two errors was determined. This interval was taken as defining the level of performance with 100% of the subject's effort devoted to this task.

The primary task was combined with various types of secondary tasks. The data shown in Figure 1 refer to (1) the application of washers and nuts to 8-mm bolts and (2) simple mental arithmetic (adding two digits). These tasks were also performed singly for 3 minutes to estimate the levels of performance with 100% effort allocated to each. In the combination of primary and secondary tasks the intersignal interval of the choice RT task was varied. As is evident from Figure 1, the performance in the secondary tasks declined when the signal rate of the primary task was increased. This demonstrates the basic interference observed in nearly all dual-task situations. Two points should be noted about this decline. First, it is steeper for the mental arithmetic task than for the washer-and-nuts task. Second, with low signal rates of the primary task and with the washer-and-nuts task as the secondary one there is hardly any interference at all.

Probe Tasks

Suppose the two tasks performed by the subject are of different durations. Over a series of trials the one of shorter duration can be initiated by the experimenter at different times relative to performance of the longer task, or the experimenter might require performance of the shorter task at different stages of completion of the longer one. In either case, the shorter task may be considered as a *probe* of the processing carried out at different points through the longer task. An experiment by Klein (1976) provides an example of such a procedure.

In one task, a target moved horizontally from the left side of a visual display as far as one of four different locations. It then reversed direction and returned to the starting position. Subjects controlled the position of a cursor and were instructed to track the target. The reversal location of the target was determined at random on successive trials. On half the trials a digit between 1 and 4 was displayed in advance of the trial. This informed the subjects which of the four reversal locations would be used. On the remaining trials subjects were given no advance information and so could not anticipate the reversal location. Average trajectories of the position of the cursor that the subjects controlled are shown in the upper part of Figure 2 for expected and unexpected reversals. Before the time of target reversal the trajectories follow the target track closely. Both trajectories diverge from the target after reversal, particularly in the case of unexpected reversals.

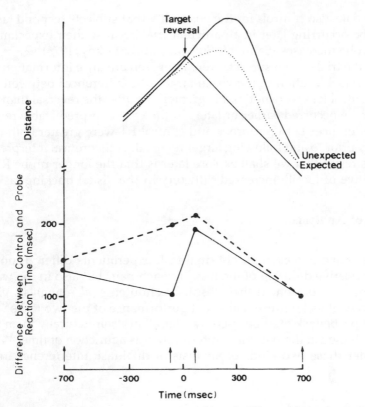

Figure 2. Tracking performance (upper graph) and difference between control and probe reaction time (lower graph) around the time at which the target reversed. The solid line shows the average data for trials on which the reversal was unexpected, the dotted line when the position of reversal was known in advance. Data from Klein (1976).

The second, shorter task was a choice RT procedure. Subjects had to use their free hand to indicate the pitch of an auditory tone presented occasionally 700 or 70 msec before or after the time of target reversal. Performance of this task was assessed by RT, and subjects were asked to make their choice as quickly as possible while minimizing the number of discrimination errors. The data are plotted in the lower half of Figure 2 as the amount by which the probe RTs exceeded RTs to tones presented at corresponding times when subjects simply watched the target. This procedure controls for any tendency on the part of the subjects to use changes in target motion to predict the time of occurrence of the probe. Such a strategy could otherwise have had effects on the probe RTs that would depend on the time of presentation of the probe. This treatment of the data also controls for the possibility that subjects respond faster to a probe occurring later in a particular trial because their expectancy for the probe increases (Salmoni, Sullivan, and Starkes, 1976).

On the trials when subjects were not given advance information about the reversal location of the visual target, the differences between probe and control RTs were noticeably greater just after the reversal than when the probe occurred earlier or later. In the case of a predictable reversal, the differences between probe and control RT were greater both immediately prior to and following target reversal. A theoretical interpretation of this result that we shall explore later is that the longer probe RTs are indicative of locally increased difficulty in the visual tracking task.

Type of Analysis

The above two examples of dual-task experiments differed, not only in the relative duration of the tasks in each pair, but also in the way the investigators presented their results. Schouten *et al.*'s analysis yielded relatively global representations of performance of the two tasks whereas the probe-task method used by Klein lent itself naturally to an analysis of change in the pattern of interference as a function of time. We now consider these two kinds of analysis of dual-task interference in more detail.

Global Performance Measures

In trying to do two things at once, a common experience is that if neither task is performed very well, giving priority to one task to obtain an improvement in its performance is achieved at the cost of some deterioration in performance of the other. If we plot performance on one task as a function of performance on the other we might see the hypothetical relation shown in Figure 3a. Note that the units along each axis are expressed relative to performance that would be achieved on that task alone. The line drawn indicates that if there is an improvement in the relative performance on task X, there will be an accompanying decline in the performance on task Y. This line intersects each axis at a level below that achieved in performance of that task alone indicating there is a concurrence cost (Navon & Gopher, 1979) associated with the introduction of a secondary task, even if that task is performed at a minimal level.

In other task combinations, it may sometimes be observed that

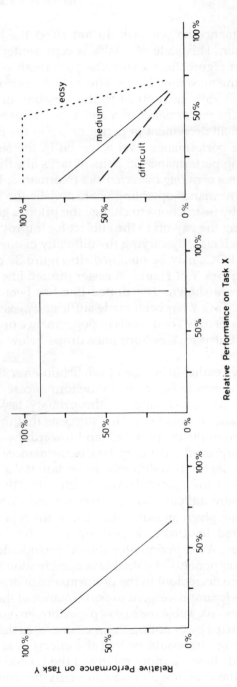

Figure 3. Examples of performance operating characteristics relating simultaneous performance on two separate tasks.

changes in performance on one task do not affect the level of performance on the other. This state of affairs is represented by the hypothetical function in Figure 3b. Varying the performance level in task Y from near 0 up to the maximum has no effect on the performance of task X which remains at 75%. In contrast to the situation in 3a there is no trade-off between the performance of X and Y in 3b. But again, each task is shown with a small decrement in performance in the dual-task situation relative to the performance level achieved in the single task case.

Functions relating performance on pairs of tasks like those of Figure 3 are called *performance operating characteristics* (Norman & Bobrow, 1975). Points along a performance operating characteristic (or POC for short) may be generated by instructions to change the priority given to the two tasks or by changing the pay-off to the subject for improving the level of performance on each task. By varying the difficulty of one or other of the tasks, a family of POCs may be obtained. In Figure 3c possible consequences of making task Y of Figure 3a easier (dotted line) or more difficult (dashed line) are shown. The dotted line has been drawn with a horizontal portion. Task Y has been made sufficiently easy that it may be combined with moderately good levels of performance on X before interference is demonstrated as Y performance drops below 100% with further improvement in X.

The results shown earlier in Figure 1 from Schouten *et al.*'s experiment show some resemblances to Figure 3c. In the former case, when subjects were faced with lower signal rates in the primary task, there was a decline in performance of that task. This suggests that there was a shift of priorities away from the primary task and toward the secondary task giving rise to the improved secondary-task performance. The difference between the curves for the two different secondary tasks may be understood as a parallel of the manipulation of difficulty, the mental-arithmetic task being more difficult than the washer-and-nuts task.

While we have not given an exhaustive list of the types of POCs that may be encountered in dual-task performance, the following point should now be clear. An experimenter should provide data on the performance of both components of a dual-task combination so that one can determine whether a decrement in the performance of one task is merely the result of a trade for improvement in performance of the other. Experimenters sometimes ask subjects to keep performance on one of the tasks constant, perhaps by denoting Y, for example, as the primary task. One reason for doing this would be that the effects of an experimental manipulation might show up more clearly in the secondary task X. But even in this case, the experimenter should verify the constancy of performance levels in Y.

Temporal Relations in Dual-Task Performance

In Klein's experiment the question asked about dual-task performance was not whether there was any interference per se. Instead, the issue of interest was whether interference changed over time, or to be more precise, whether particular phases of the visual-tracking task would be associated with reduced performance levels in the RT task. The elevation of the auditory RT just after unexpected reversals of the visual target may be taken as an indication of increased difficulty of the tracking task at that point.

A different approach may be taken to the analysis of temporal relations between the performance of two tasks. In some task combinations there may be no performance decrement, but the performance of the two tasks may not be independent. For example, the timing of responses under one task may be changed to fit in with the other task. If the timing changes simply involved postponement of responses in a probe task, a performance decrement would be manifested as a lengthening of probe RT. However, there is another possibility. The timing of the response in one task may be advanced on some trials and retarded on other trials. In a probe task the average RT might not change over different probe positions, but interference might be evidenced in a change in the distribution of times taken to respond to the probe. This could occur if production of the probe response were governed by some phase of the control of movement in the other task.

An example of an analysis of the relative phases of responding in dual-task performance is provided by McLeod (1977). The two tasks were compensatory tracking with a visual display and an auditory two-alternative choice RT task. In the tracking task, subjects held a lever to the right or left to impart a fixed acceleration of 10 cm/sec^2 to the right or 8 cm/sec^2 to the left to a cursor on a visual display. The instructions were to keep the cursor in the centre of the display. In the other task subjects responded to a series of auditory tones presented at intervals ranging from 1.5 to 2.5 seconds. In one condition a spoken response "high" or "low" was called for. In the other condition, subjects had to indicate the pitch of the tone using the nonpreferred hand to press one of two buttons.

McLeod analysed the data in terms of the probability of making a visual-tracking response relative to the time of each response made to the auditory stimulus. For a given sequence of intervals between visual-tracking responses he determined a theoretical function that should have been obtained if the times of visual-tracking responses were independent of the times of responding to the tones. This is shown as a

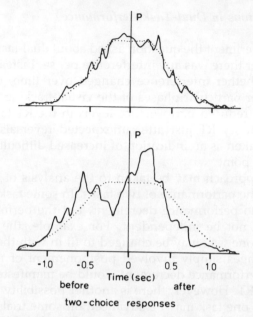

Figure 4. Probability of a tracking response as a function of the time before or after a vocal (upper graph) or manual (lower graph) choice response. From "A dual task response modality effect: Support for multiprocessor models of attention", by McLeod, P. (1977). *Quarterly Journal of Experimental Psychology*, 29, 651–667. Reprinted with permission.

dotted line in Figure 4, in the upper half for vocal responses to the tone and in the lower half for manual responses. Tracking performance was somewhat better in the vocal condition—the intervals between successive tracking responses were shorter—and this leads to a theoretical function with slightly narrower shoulders.

The solid lines in Figure 4 are the observed data. In the vocal condition, the observed distribution does not deviate significantly from the expected one. This is not the case in the manual condition. Visual-tracking responses made with the preferred hand are not independent of the time of response to the tone using the nonpreferred hand. Immediately before the response to the tone the probability of making a tracking response is less than would be expected under the hypothesis of independence. Tracking responses are sometimes withheld while the auditory probe stimulus is processed.

THEORETICAL APPROACHES TO DUAL-TASK PERFORMANCE

Many theoretical explanations of dual-task interference have been advanced. We treat three main classes in the following subsections. These classes are ordered according to their generality; that is, each one may be considered as a special case of the one that follows.

The Single-Channel Model

The origin of the single-channel model of dual-task performance lies in an observation first made by Craik in 1947 about the way people make tracking movements to a moving target in a single-task situation. Although the target moved continuously, Craik noted that his subjects only made corrections to track the target at certain points in time. He interpreted this form of correction as due to a central *intermittency*: At discrete intervals the subject notes the error in tracking and programmes and executes a corrective movement. During each correction period, the central decision processes are unable to act on new information. Thus, the ostensibly continuous activity is segmented into a sequence of discrete decisions and corrective movements.

This observation was followed up by Vince (1948) using an experimental paradigm in which the continuous movement of the target was replaced by a series of abrupt, steplike changes occurring at random intervals. She observed that movements in response to the steps were initiated more slowly when a step was closer to its predecessor. By loose analogy to the raised threshold that follows a nerve impulse, the term *psychological refractory period*, originally coined by Telford (1931), has come to refer to this lengthening in time taken to respond to the second of two closely spaced signals.

In developing the single-channel model of the psychological refractory period, Welford's (1967) fundamental assumption was that a central mechanism that translates a signal into action has a *limited processing capacity*. This restricts it to operate on one signal at a time. To protect the mechanism from interference between signals, a gate closes behind the first of a pair of signals. A signal arriving after the gate is closed must be held temporarily in store until the first signal is processed. In Welford's view, it is this holding or storage time that determines the lengthening of RT to the second signal. Moreover, he suggested the storage time persists beyond the response to the first signal because the single channel is occupied with feedback from the response.

The elements of Welford's model are represented in Figure 5. The reaction time to the first signal S_1 is denoted by RT_1. It is comprised of two parts: a perceptual component PT_1 and the duration of the decision that occupies the limited capacity channel, DT_1. The feedback delay associated with the first response is FT_1. The reaction time to the second signal RT_2 includes corresponding elements PT_2 and DT_2. But, in addi-

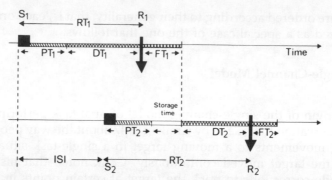

Figure 5. Fractionation of RT according to Welford's (1967) single channel model. RT_1 between stimulus S_1 and response R_1 is composed of perceptual and decision components PT_1, DT_1. RT_2 to the later-occurring S_2 has an additional storage-time component after PT_2 until the end of the feedback time FT_1 associated with R_1.

tion, there is the storage time following perceptual registration of the stimulus. Provided RT_1, FT_1, PT_2, and DT_2 do not change with the interval between S_1 and S_2, the RT to the second stimulus is directly related to the interstimulus interval. Each unit increase in the interstimulus interval reduces RT_2 by an identical amount until the interstimulus interval between S_1 and S_2 exceeds $RT_1 + FT_1 - PT_2$. This model thus predicts that a graph of RT_2 against the interstimulus interval should have a slope of -1 over a certain range of interstimulus intervals.

The prediction of the slope of -1 by this model is very important. The model provides a quantitative statement that may be tested directly. While earlier evidence appeared to support the model, more recent experiments suggest that it is inadequate as a general characterisation of dual-task performance. For example, Greenwald and Shulman (1973) found that the slopes relating RT_2 to interstimulus interval were not as steep as -1.

In Greenwald and Shulman's experiment, the task defined on S_1 required subjects to make a visual discrimination. The stimulus in each trial was selected either from the words "left" and "right" or from arrows pointing to the left and right. In either case a manual response to push a switch to the left or to the right was made. The task defined on S_2 required a vocal response to an auditory stimulus. Subjects had to respond to the spoken letters "A" or "B" by saying either "one" or "two" or by saying "A" or "B". When the second version of each task was combined there was no lengthening of RT_2 at all. Pushing a switch in response to the arrow and echoing the letters exactly did not show interference. The steepest slope was obtained with pushing a switch in response to the word "left" or "right" and saying "one" or "two" in response to "A" or "B". But even in this case the slope was not as steep as the predicted value of -1.

In response to this demonstrated inadequacy of Welford's single-channel model we now turn to a class of models that assumes that there can be simultaneous processing of both signals in double-stimulation experiments.

General Limited-Capacity Models

General limited-capacity models of dual-task performance, which have been extensively discussed by Kahneman (1973), are characterised by two basic assumptions. First, it is assumed that there is a single pool of processing resources underlying the performance of a task. These resources can be allocated to any number of tasks provided only that a limit L on the total allocation across tasks is not exceeded. Second, performance on any particular task is assumed to depend on the amount of resources allocated. Different tasks may have different relationships between performance and resources. Some examples of such hypothetical *performance-resource functions* are presented in Figure 6. The tasks X, Y, and Z shown in the figure differ in the amount of resources needed to obtain a particular performance level. For example, we say the demand of task Y is less than that of Z but greater than that of X. In addition, it will be noted that the performance-resource function for Z includes a horizontal portion. Beyond a certain level of performance adding further resources yields no further improvement. Research on motivation and performance has shown that high levels of effort or arousal can lead to declines in performance (for example, see Atkinson and Birch's, 1978, discussion of the inverted U-relation between arousal and performance). Thus, performance-resource functions may not all be monotonic increasing, a point not generally recognised in the literature.

The corollary of the two assumptions of general limited-capacity models is that the relative performance of tasks in combination depends on the proportion of resources allocated to each. This implies that different tasks performed together will not interfere with one another until the total of the resources required exceeds the available resource limit L (and then only if the tasks are not being carried out in a data-limited region). So, in the case of the refractory-period experiments, the slope of the function relating RT_2 to the interstimulus interval may lie anywhere in the range between 0 (the sum of the resources required by the two stimuli is less than L) and -1 (the resources required by S_1 alone sum to

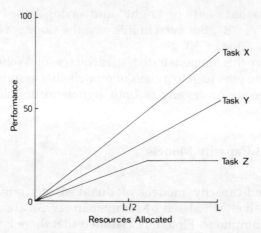

Figure 6. Examples of performance–resource functions for three different tasks.

L). Moreover, depending on the proportional allocation of resources to S_1 or S_2, interference effects (i.e., slowing of RT) might be seen in the response to S_1, the response to S_2, or in both.

General limited-capacity models also provide a basis for the interpretation of Klein's work that we described earlier. If the difficulty of a task such as visual tracking fluctuates over time it will draw resources from the general pool in varying degrees. The second task probes the amount of resources remaining. Poor performance (long RT) on the second task indicates few remaining resources, while a short RT indicates a good supply of resources in the pool. Klein's results indicate that the demand on the resource pool is heaviest shortly after a change in direction of the visual target whether the change is expected or unexpected. If the change is expected the demand is also elevated just prior to the direction change.

We now consider another study that used the probe technique to determine whether there is fluctuation in the resources demanded by a single movement of the arm to a target. In this experiment, which was reported by Ells in 1973, subjects made right-forearm movements of 30 ° about the elbow joint. These movements had to terminate in target areas of width 1.3 or 7.6 cm. In the probe task subjects indicated whether the pitch of a tone was high or low by making a choice response with the left hand. Probe signals were presented, one on each trial, at various positions during the movement and also at various times before and after the movement. A control condition showed that changes with time in expectancy for the probe had minimal effects on RT.

The arm movements made by the subjects were fast and, at least for

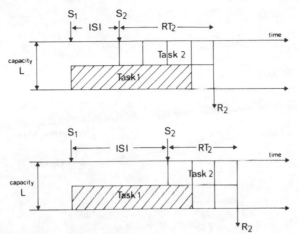

Figure 7. The effect of changes in overlap of the processing associated with two tasks on the RT of the later-occurring task. The integrated capacity over time (area in the figure) for each task is constant in both upper and lower halves of the figure.

the probe positions we consider below, the probe responses occurred after the end of the movement. This is important because it means that the appropriate index of spare capacity in the resource pool is the slope of the probe reaction time function, rather than its level. As McLeod (1980) pointed out, if the response to the probe occurs after the end of the primary task, as the probe stimulus is moved nearer the end of the primary task, the amount of temporal overlap between the tasks decreases. In terms of the general-capacity model there would thus be a reduction of RT even though the resource demand of the primary task remained constant (see Figure 7). The rate at which the RT decreases is an index of the proportion of capacity demanded by the primary task. A slope of $-\frac{1}{2}$ indicates a 50% capacity used by the primary task, -1 indicates 100% (as was assumed in Welford's model).

Ells' data on probe RT for the later probes are shown in Figure 8. They are shown as a function of the phase of the aiming movement. (From our point of view, it would have been better if the RT data had been plotted as a function of time. But, we assume that rescaling the results in terms of time would not materially alter their interpretation.) For the narrow target, the function decreases slowly after the first part of the movement and becomes steep later. In contrast to this increase in absolute value of slope, the absolute slope of the probe RT function decreases for movements to the wide target. The conclusion is therefore that the amount of capacity demanded increases for a movement aimed at a narrow target but decreases if the target is wide. Changing the target

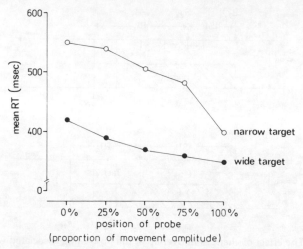

Figure 8. Probe RT as a function of the proportion of the primary-task movement completed where the primary task involved aiming at a wide or a narrow target. Data from Ells (1973).

width affects the pattern of demand for resources as a function of time in addition to the overall demand level (as reflected by the overall steeper slope of the function in the narrow target condition). One reason for this may be that visual guidance which draws heavily on resources is more critical in bringing the arm to a stop within a narrow target.

There are a number of arguments against general limited-capacity models. First, they may be criticised for their lack of heuristic value. For example, they don't explain *why* the resource demands change in Ells' and Klein's experiments. Nor do they predict that in the choice-response task that McLeod combined with tracking, there would be the different patterning of responses for the auditory and vocal conditions. The type of explanation that we would like in each case would be one formulated in terms of the particular processes involved in each task. And this is not provided in sufficient detail by general limited-capacity models.

A second line of argument that is based on experimental evidence may be used against general limited-capacity models. Suppose there are two separate tasks; one calls for a response to the letters A or B, the other for a response to the digits 1 or 2. In each case the measure of performance is RT. Now consider a paradigm in which simultaneous responses are required. If interference, as measured by slowing of RT, is greater with the combination A + 1 than with A + 2, it would imply that more resources are demanded in responding to stimulus 1. Then, ac-

TABLE 1. RTs for All Combinations of First and Second Signals[a]

		First stimulus			
		Red square	Green square		
Second stimulus (inside square)	5	763	850	First finger	Second response (right hand)
	+	858	790	Second finger	
		First finger	Second finger		
		First response (left hand)			

[a] In milliseconds. Data from Wakelin, 1967.

cording to general limited-capacity models, in the combination B + 1 interference should also be greater than in the case of B + 2.

An experiment by Wakelin (1967) shows that this prediction of general limited-capacity models is not necessarily supported. In a double stimulation experiment on the refractory period, he used a red or green square as the first stimulus. The second stimulus appeared inside the square and was the digit 5 or the symbol +. The response to the first stimulus was made with the left hand, to the second stimulus with the right hand, in each case using the first two fingers. Table 1 gives the RTs for the different stimulus pairs (averaged over three different interstimulus intervals of 0, 250, and 500 msec). With the red square as the first stimulus (first column in the table), the RT to the second stimulus was 95 msec longer if it was a + than if it was the digit 5. But with a green square as the first stimulus (second column), the reverse was true; the reaction time to the + was 60 msec shorter than to the digit 5. A similar pattern of interference was also seen in the RTs to the first stimulus. What determines RT in this situation appears to be the relation between responses. RTs are faster (though still slower than under single-task conditions) if corresponding fingers of the left and right hand are involved.

General limited-capacity models require that the ordering of secondary-task performance be the same whatever the primary task. Wakelin's results violate this requirement. If task 1 interferes more with task A than does task 2, but task 2 interferes more with task B than does task 1, one is lead to contradictory conclusions about the relative capacity demands of task 1 and 2. This pattern of results, of which other examples may be found in the work of North cited by Navon and Gopher (1979), can only be explained if it is assumed that there is something specific about each task combination.

Structural Interference Models

Structural interference models assume that the interference between two tasks depends on the degree to which the tasks make demands on one or more of the same underlying processes or structures. Dual-task performance depends on the specific composition of each of the tasks studied in combination. If one task requires structures (A, B, F) and another task (C, D, F) interference will be observed in simultaneous performance because (F) is a structure required by both tasks; that is, there is partial overlap in the *composition* of the resources demanded by the two tasks.

Structural interference models may be formulated as extensions of general limited-capacity models. Thus, Navon and Gopher (1979) assume that there are several different pools of resources each with its own capacity limit. The amount of interference between two tasks performed simultaneously depends on the overlap of their respective demands for resources and the extent to which their joint demand on any given resource pool is in excess of capacity.

From the viewpoint of the general limited-capacity model discussed in the last section, the absence of performance decrements in a dual-task situation is taken to imply an abundant supply of resources. If instead, we assume there are multiple pools of resources, the further possibility exists that the two tasks demand none of the same resources. Their respective resource demand compositions may not overlap. For example, one task may require (A, B, E), the other (C, D, F). In such cases, resource supplies that might be freed on completion of one task would be irrelevant to performance of the other. On the other hand, the presence of interference indicates at least some overlap, and in an admittedly somewhat superficial way the amount of interference may be taken as an indicator of the amount of overlap in resources demanded.

We now return to reconsider the interpretation of the experiment by Ells discussed earlier. How is the interpretation affected if the data are viewed from a structural interference perspective? The main change is that the capacity demands inferred from the probe RT functions are no longer taken as characteristic of the movement studied but as characteristic of the specific task combination. The tracking task places demands on a set of resources, which are also demanded by the manual probe task, and the tracking task demands manifest certain fluctuations in the course of the movement. With this perspective it is less surprising that McLeod (1980) obtained different probe RT functions for manual and vocal probe responses. But one might ask how manual and vocal responses differ in the composition of the resources each demands and what this implies for the resource demands of the movement task.

The problems posed by structural interference models are very different from those of general limited-capacity models. Questions are asked about which processes or structures are involved in motor performance, and these are traced by appropriate secondary tasks. Dual-task methodology thus becomes a means to analyse the nature of processes or structures involved in the control of movements.

In adopting the structural interference approach some investigators have concerned themselves with the anatomical substrate and have attempted to define structures in terms of parts of the CNS. This is done in the model of functional cerebral space by Kinsbourne and Hicks (1978) and more specifically by Friedman and Campbell Polson (1981). Friedman and Campbell Polson consider each cerebral hemisphere as a separate resource pool. Therefore, interference between different tasks should vary depending on whether they demand resources from different or identical hemispheres. Other investigators have focused their attention on function without reference to the anatomical basis. They have defined resource pools in terms of different cognitive functions such as encoding, retention, response selection, or imagery. These functions are purely conceptual in the sense that their anatomical basis remains unspecified. In principle it is possible that some of these functions are achieved by one and the same part of the brain.

In the next two sections we consider studies that combine cognitive tasks with motor tasks and that throw some light on the resource composition of the motor tasks. These studies base their analysis on global performance measures. They are concerned with what one might call *high-level structural interference.*

In the third section we turn to several kinds of interference that might be described as *low-level structural interference.* Although the terms used here suggest a dichotomy, the difference between high- and low-level interference is best seen as a continuum because interference could occur at any level of the CNS or even as a result of skeletomuscular interactions when responding. The most trivial form of low-level interference results from the fact that a certain limb can only be in one position at a time. Less-trivial forms may be evidenced from the interdependence of movements with both arms. The studies reviewed are concerned with interference between simultaneous movements, and they typically analyse not only global performance measures but the temporal relations between movements in some detail. Thus, our somewhat pragmatic criterion used to classify interference as high level or low level is based on whether a motor task is combined with a cognitive task or with another motor task.

THE USE OF DUAL-TASK METHODOLOGY IN THE
ANALYSIS OF MOVEMENT CONTROL

Cognitive Functions and Movement Execution

The first way to analyse high-level structural interference is in terms of cognitive functioning. Johnston, Greenberg, Fisher, and Martin (1970) performed some experiments in which a compensatory visual-tracking task was combined with a series of tasks that involved memorization of verbal material. Each of the memory tasks was chosen to emphasize selectively different cognitive processes. In the first, subjects remembered those nouns that belonged to a particular category from a series of nouns presented auditorily. This *encoding* task was carried out at various difficulty levels by varying the rate of presentation of the words or the intensity level of the words relative to background noise. In a *retention* task subjects had to remember a list of nouns throughout the tracking task. The words were presented prior to tracking and recall of the words was only required after the tracking task was finished. The difficulty of this task was varied by changing the number of words to be remembered. The third task consisted of *recall* of a previously learned list of words during the tracking task. Variation of difficulty was achieved by imposing various degrees of constraint on the order of recall; free, serial, backward serial, and alphabetic were used.

Each of these secondary tasks caused decrements in the visual-tracking task that were a function of task difficulty. But, the most interesting finding was a consistent ordering of the amount of interference over the different secondary tasks. This ordering remained unchanged whether the maximal amounts of interference with the most difficult versions of each task or whether the average amounts across the various levels of difficulty were considered. There was least interference with retention, somewhat more with encoding, but the largest decrement in tracking performance was observed with recall. Johnston *et al.* had also run a control condition in which relatively little interference with tracking occurred when subjects simply had to count aloud. Thus, the maximal interference associated with the recall condition was probably associated with processes involved in the selection of responses rather than in their production.

The results of Johnston *et al.* were confirmed by Trumbo and Milone (1971) who used a similar design. Their subjects had to learn a sequence of stimulus lights or auditorily presented numbers, remember the sequence and reproduce it, either verbally or by pressing keys. Each of the three phases, learning, retention, and recall, was combined with pursuit tracking. Again, interference was largest during the recall phase, second largest during encoding and smallest during retention.

Strictly speaking, we are not really justified in assuming that the interference seen in these experiments is structural in nature rather than just a reflection of a general limited-capacity effect. To make this distinction we need to find a different task from tracking which, combined with the various secondary tasks, gives no indication of interference associated with response selection but which, for example, shows interference associated with retention or encoding. This would be a clear indication of different resource compositions of the two primary tasks and incompatible with a general limited-capacity interpretation. But to our knowledge no such data are available. A structural interpretation of the results, therefore, is justified only if one accepts the validity of the structural interference concept in general, even if it is not proved for each specific set of data.

A complete set of data is available on the involvement of imagery in tracking. Baddeley and his associates (1975, 1980) showed that learning tasks that involve imagery interfere with tracking. The use of imagery was varied by instruction to the subjects to use different types of mnemonics or by the nature of the material to be learned. This material could either be sentences that described the positions of numbers in an imagined configuration of squares or syntactically identical sentences that had no spatial reference. Interference with a continuous pursuit-tracking task was observed only with the learning tasks that involved imagery. In contrast, with a light-intensity discrimination task imagery tasks interfered less than rote-learning tasks. And a similar result using simple RT instead of accuracy of light discrimination was reported by Griffith and Johnston (1973). These results clearly indicate a structural interference mechanism. One may therefore conclude that in tracking, a spatial system is involved that is closely related to the one used in mental imagery.

These results on imagery fit nicely with results from a study based on individual differences. Fleishman and Rich (1963) found that subjects who did well on a spatial orientation test also performed better on a bimanual tracking task. Interestingly enough, this correlation was only observed in the early stages of training on the tracking task. This suggests that the interference between tracking and tasks requiring imagery might also decline as subjects become more proficient at tracking. This topic is developed further in the chapter on skill acquisition.

Hemispheric Sharing of Cognitive and Motor Activities

A second way to analyze high-level structural interference is in terms of anatomically defined structures, specifically in terms of cerebral hemispheres. It is known that each arm is controlled mainly by the contralateral cerebral hemisphere. In addition, each hemisphere is specialized for processing certain types of material, the left hemisphere for verbal processing, the right hemisphere for visuospatial processing. This knowledge allows some a priori predictions about structural interference between certain types of cognitive tasks and movements with the left or right arm. Processing verbal material and moving the right arm should draw on common resource pools of the left hemisphere, while processing visuospatial material and moving the left arm both involve primarily the right hemisphere. Therefore, in these task combinations, more interference should be observed than with simultaneously processing verbal material and moving the left arm or moving the right arm while processing visuospatial material.

These predictions were nicely confirmed in a series of experiments by McFarland and Ashton. As an example we take a study in which repetitive button pressing was combined with a running memory task (McFarland & Ashton, 1978). Subjects made rapid alternating movements between two buttons that were located either 6 or 12 cm apart, using their right or left hand. Performance was measured in terms of response rate and variability. In the memory task subjects were presented with a series of visual stimuli and, for each stimulus, had to indicate whether or not they had seen that stimulus earlier in the series. Two types of stimuli were used, printed words and pictures of people's faces. Performance was assessed by the proportion of correct responses.

Considering the response rates for both distances of the buttons McFarland and Ashton found only unilateral interference. In line with expectations, the verbal memory task caused a performance decrement only in the right hand as compared to single-task performance, while performance of the left hand deteriorated only in combination with the visuospatial memory task. Complementing these results, performance in the verbal memory task was worse when it was combined with right-hand movements as compared to performance without a second task and the visuospatial memory task suffered when it was combined with movements of the left hand.

The general pattern of results reported by McFarland and Ashton has been found in a number of experiments using various motor tasks, although most experiments examine only the asymmetric interference caused by speaking or other kinds of verbal performance. Thus, there is considerable evidence in favor of the predictions outlined at the beginning of this subsection, which are based on a structural interference model and some independent a priori knowledge about the anatomical structures involved in certain tasks.

The results described so far based on dual-task methodology have simply been in line with knowledge arising from other sources. This, of course, corroborates the validity of structural interference models. We now go a step further. The assumption that hand movements are controlled mainly by the contralateral cerebral hemisphere is based on the anatomical connections of the efferent tracts. But planning and executing movements involves more than just sending motor commands from the brain to the muscles. For example, before the start of even a simple movement there is a slowly rising negative potential called the *Bereitschafts* or *readiness* potential which is widely spread over the cortex (e.g., Deecke, Grozinger, & Kornhuber, 1976). Thus, processes involved in the planning of movement, at least, do not appear to be restricted to the contralateral hemisphere.

In principle, it should be possible to examine the relative involvement of both hemispheres in different motor tasks that differ in certain aspects by means of the dual-task technique. This means going beyond our present knowledge about the cerebral localisation of different processes of motor control. The problem is how to localise such processes that are not located in the contralateral hemisphere but which are located in the left or right hemisphere independent of the hand used. Research of this kind is still in a very preliminary stage, and there are only some hypotheses that are not yet strongly corroborated. For example, Summers and Sharp (1979) suggest that the sequencing of finger movements is mainly an achievement of the left hemisphere.

Simultaneous Movements

In this subsection we turn to low-level structural interference. As an example consider McLeod's analysis of temporal relations in dual-task performance described earlier. Subjects had to use one hand for a visual-tracking task at the same time as discriminating the pitch of auditory tones. McLeod reported that tracking performance was poorer in the dual-task situation than when it was carried out alone. And when the auditory task required a vocal response this tracking decrement was less than if the nonpreferred hand was used. But, McLeod's significant observation was that, when responses for the tasks were both manual, there was a strong dependence in the times at which they were emitted. In contrast, vocal-choice responses and manual-tracking responses were produced as two separate, temporally independent streams. This suggests that in the performance of pairs of tasks requiring manual responses a significant limitation is the need to coordinate motor output. This coordination is presumably at a relatively late stage, beyond the point at which the processing of the stimulus information for the two tasks could involve separate processing pathways.

What is the nature of the limitations in coordinating responses with both hands? Apparently, such responses are somehow coupled, and this coupling is such that in McLeod's experiment the fast response to the auditory signal delays the tracking response which would otherwise have occurred at that time. The coupling of movements with both hands is somewhat complex, and we shall discuss it in more detail before returning to McLeod's results.

First consider a set of results obtained by Kelso, Southard, and Goodman (1979). When people made rapid movements with the hands to separate targets following an auditory "go" signal, the initiation and termination of the two movements was, on average, roughly simultaneous. This was true even though the targets were widely disparate in difficulty—one target was further away from the starting point and narrower than the other—and, in a single-hand control condition, the MT to the narrow target was longer than to the wide target. Typical movement trajectories for the left and right hand in the bimanual condition are plotted in Figure 9a. Moreover, although the hands moved at different speeds to different points in space, the times to peak acceleration and deceleration were almost identical in the two hands (see Figure 9b). However, it should be noted that, in contrast to the similarity in timing of simultaneous movements, the peak values of the acceleration become more dissimilar than they would have been when made as isolated movements. This is a necessary consequence of the similarity in timing, given the different task demands.

Kelso et al. argued that such simultaneity of action was an outcome of organising muscles into functional groups or coordinative structures that can be controlled as units. In the present case the coordinative structure is supposed to involve the active muscles of both arms. The operation of such a coordinative structure is viewed as being governed by parameters of two types. One is defined in terms of a certain relationship in the timing of activity in the arm muscles. The other specifies absolute level of muscle activity which is modulated for each arm, given the constraints set by the common timing. In other words, the grouping of muscles in functional units applies to some parameters of control but

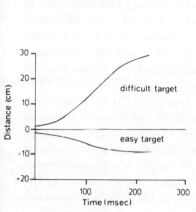
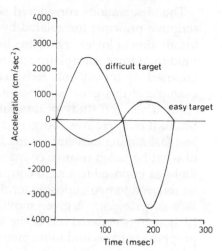

Figure 9. Position-time and acceleration-time curves for simultaneous movements of the left and right hands to an easy and a difficult target. From "On the coordination of two-handed movements", by Kelso, J. A. S., Southard, D. L., Goodman, D. (1979). *Journal of Experimental Psychology: Human Perception and Performance, 5*, 229–238. Reprinted with permission.

not to others. (One might wonder whether the concept of coordinative structures is necessary at all to explain these data. With simpler words one might state that *temporal control* is a single process for both arms, while *force control* is achieved for each arm separately, but adjusted to the common timing.)

Schmidt, Zelaznik, Hawkins, Frank, and Quinn (1979) have discussed a conceptually related model for two-handed movements in which each hand goes to a different target. They suggested that a central motor program provides a framework for the movements. But, before this general pattern of movement can be executed on a particular trial, parameters for the movement must be specified. They argued that certain common properties of the two-handed movements (e.g., the MT) are the result of parameters with the same value applied to both hands. Other properties of the movements (e.g., the movement distances) result from parameters with different values for each hand.

Schmidt *et al.* observed that the times at which the two hands arrived at the endpoints of the bilateral aiming movements were strongly and positively correlated. This they attributed to a common source of variability in the selection of timing parameters. In contrast, they found the between-hand correlation of distance errors was essentially zero. This is consistent with the view that variability introduced in selecting parameters governing the degree of muscle activity is specific to each arm.

The observations considered so far are consistent with a general descriptive principle formulated by von Holst (1939). From studies of the locomotion of lower organisms he concluded that timing control is more rigid than force control; forces are more easily adjusted to the demands imposed on movement. Kelso *et al.*'s observations are thus one more example of this general principle. Von Holst took a somewhat broader approach to the study of interlimb interactions than did Kelso *et al.* or Schmidt *et al.* He was concerned with a larger class of movements than just fast aiming movements made with the two arms. In his discussion of what he called relative coordination (a more or less loose coupling of limbs as opposed to a rigid coupling observed in absolute coordination) he referred to two opposing tendencies which he called *Magneteffekt* and *Beharrungstendenz*. A given movement will retain its own characteristics (Beharrungstendenz) but at the same time tends to assume some of the properties of a second movement performed simultaneously (Magneteffekt).

In a summary report, Gunkel (1962) gives some examples of relative coordination in humans. In one case subjects had to move their forearms forward and backward with different frequencies. Figure 10a, b shows unidirectional effects. In Figure 10a the slow rhythm is superimposed on the fast one, and in Figure 10b the fast rhythm shows an amplitude modulation in phase with the slow one. Figure 10c gives an example of essentially alternating performance. While the fast rhythm is performed the other movement is stopped. But each time the other hand is moved this intrudes into the fast rhythm. Gunkel reported some further observations without presenting detailed data. For example, the legs exhibit more of a tendency to close coupling than do the hands, which is reasonable in view of our everyday usage of these limbs. And in right-handed people she observed less coupling when the right hand had to perform the fast rhythm, whereas in left-handed people this was reversed in most cases.

In Figure 10 the two curves for both limbs are plotted as mirror images of each other. That is, an upward deflection in one trace designates a forward movement and in the other trace a backward movement. The superposition of Figure 10a is said to be phase-shifted by 180°. The conclusion is that this is the preferred phase relationship between movements of these two limbs (*Koaktionslage* in von Holst's terms). A phase shift of 180° is the one we use when walking: While one arm swings forward, the other arm swings backward. But this is not always the preferred relationship. Cohen (1971) studied simultaneous flexions and extensions of both wrists at rates of 2 to 4 cycles per second. There was a clear preference for symmetrical movements, that is, for simultaneous

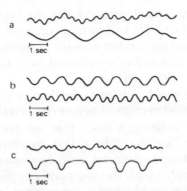

Figure 10. Examples of relative coordination between simultaneous arm movements observed by Gunkel (1962). In each part, upward deflection in the upper trace indicates a forward movement of the arm, upward deflection in the lower trace indicates a backward movement.

activity in the corresponding muscles of each arm (homologous activity). With homologous activity the correlation between the two continuous movements was larger than with nonhomologous activity. Sometimes subjects even shifted from performing instructed asymmetrical (nonhomologous) movements to symmetrical (homologous) ones. A shift in the reverse direction from homologous to nonhomologous movement was never observed.

In view of the symmetrical anatomy of our bodies the homologous coupling observed by Cohen (1971) appears quite natural. But apparently other factors also help determine the preferred phase relationship. These have to do with the common use of the limbs or with certain nervous structures which are particularly suited to handle coordination problems in biologically important skills such as locomotion.

The crosscoupling of both arms causes limitations in their independent use. In situations where we are able to perform two movements simultaneously these limitations appear primarily as an intrusion of temporal aspects of one movement in the other. But these limitations can result in an inability to perform two simultaneous movements as well. An example is the alternating performance shown in Figure 10c. Another example is described by Cohen (1970). Cohen asked his subjects to perform alternating flexions and extensions with one wrist. With the other wrist the subjects had to perform a single movement in response to an auditory signal. The effects of the single movement on the alternating movement were somewhat variable. Sometimes the alternating movement stopped at one of the reversal points and restarted after the single response was executed. The continuation of the alternating movement was not in phase with the movements that had occurred just before the interruption. On other occasions the cycle of the alternating movement in which the single movement occurred was not lengthened but shortened. This was most often a result of premature reversal of the hand performing the alternating movement to bring it into phase with the single movement of the other hand.

We are now in a position to return to the data of McLeod considered at the beginning of this subsection. There exist certain relationships between movements of both arms such that we are unable to perform them simultaneously, for example a fast movement during certain phases of an alternating movement with the other hand. Such relationships are incompatible with the temporal coupling. This appears to have been the situation in McLeod's experiment, which shows some obvious similarity to Cohen's study. In both cases responding with one hand—alternating or tracking movements—was often delayed until after the end of the single fast movement with the other hand.

There is one further type of interaction between responses that should be considered before concluding this section: Temporal dependence between responses may be observed because one effector has mechanical consequences on body posture which are compensated by the other effector. In a study by Cordo and Nashner (1982) subjects were instructed to pull a hand-held lever when they heard an auditory signal. The subjects wore surface EMG electrodes over the gastrocnemius muscles in the calf of the leg and the biceps in the upper arm. In one condition they stood normally during each trial; in another they leaned against a padded crossbrace at shoulder height. In the supported condition it was found that biceps EMG onset occurred, on the average, 130 msec after auditory tone onset. No clear burst of EMG activity associated with the tone was seen in the gastrocnemius muscle. However, in the unsupported condition, the pull on the handle by the subject required postural support by the gastrocnemius (and also the hamstrings in the thigh) to stop the subject from falling forward. The average gastrocnemius EMG onset occurred 111 msec after the auditory tone prior to the biceps EMG. In this condition the biceps EMG was significantly slowed to 155 msec.

Thus, in one sense, the postural response could be said to interfere with the speed of the handle pulling. But, clearly, the slowing of the biceps' response is better considered as functionally useful because it prevents the subject from falling. This viewpoint is reinforced by Cordo and Nashner's observation that when the postural response in the gastrocnemius is slowed (by having the subject stand on a slowly tilting platform), there is slowing of the biceps response to a similar degree.

LEVELS OF INTERFERENCE

In this chapter our aim has been to understand the nature of constraints on doing several things at once. In doing so, we have avoided questions about conscious experience of our own activity, that is about attention in the everyday meaning of the word. Instead we have outlined a broader framework for treating the interactions that occur between the performance of several different tasks that are carried out simultaneously. The basic notion of this framework is that of structural interference.

The structural interference approach we adopt allows us to study which processes or structures are involved in motor tasks. Whenever two tasks involve common processes or structures, interference should be observed. These common processes or structures can obviously be located at different levels of the nervous system. Somewhat pragmatically we have distinguished between high-level and low-level structural interference. A last point we need to discuss is whether these two forms of interference need different theories or can be explained by a single theory.

It has already been mentioned that studies of high-level interference generally use global performance measures while studies of low-level interference consider in more detail the temporal (or other) relationships between the simultaneous activities. Consider now a structural theory like that of Navon and Gopher (1979), which is basically a theory of differentiated limited capacity. Can such a theory handle the data on lower-level structural interference?

The obvious answer to this question is no. Any theory that is based on a theoretical construct, such as resources, that is linked to better or worse performance, can only handle global performance measures. At best a fitting in of responses might be explained. One could assume that responses in both tasks make high demands on a common resource pool. From this one would expect that while one response is executed another response will have to wait until the first response is finished and more resources are available. But theories like that of Navon and Gopher seem to be irrelevant for the explanation of, for example, the phenomena of relative coordination. Here theories are needed which do not only treat better or worse performance but the details of interactions, for example, the different changes of timing and forces when two aiming movements are performed simultaneously instead of singly.

Thus, at present, different types of theories appear necessary for high-level and low-level structural interference. The first type is generally discussed under the heading of attention, the latter type under the heading of coordination. One might ask whether this is so because the bases of the observed phenomena are different or because the data obtained differ. Our suggestion is that the second answer is the correct one.

Consider the high-level interference between imagery and movement. In the experiments described previously global performance measures were used, and a multiple-resource pools theory seemed fully adequate to explain the results obtained. But now consider an experiment of Johnson (1982). In this experiment a simple aiming movement had to be performed and reproduced after a short interval. Interpolated between these movements there was another movement with a different length. Such interpolated movements typically introduce a bias in the reproduction of the first movement. If the interpolated movement is shorter, the reproduction tends to be too short, if it is larger, the reproduction is too long. Johnson showed that this result also obtains when the interpolated movement is not really performed but only imagined.

What we have here is a high-level interference between imagery and memory for a movement that is not simply described in terms of better or worse performance. This result can thus hardly be explained by a multiple-resource pools theory, but instead a theory is required similar to those needed for low-level interference. Certain aspects of one task intrude into the performance of the other task—in this case it is the movement distance. Such effects are, therefore, not bound to low-level interference, but they may be observed in high-level interference as well, provided both tasks may be described in the same way, for example, in terms of movement trajectories or end positions. Such a common reference system is lacking in most studies of high-level structural interference. In the case of imagery and movements, space may be used as a common reference system, in most other task combinations only time remains.

Such considerations might suggest that low-level and high-level structural interference are not basically different phenomena. The difference in theories is only a result of the different kinds of data, and in situations where high-level interference can be described in the same way as low-level interference, multiple-resource pools theories are no longer adequate. Instead, theories would have to explain more specific kinds of interference between simultaneously performed activities.

CONCLUSION

In this chapter we have developed a view of the limitations in human perceptual-motor performance that assumes any given task draws on a number of distinct processes or resources. When two tasks must be carried out simultaneously a decline in overall performance levels should not necessarily be expected. Interference only occurs when both tasks draw on a single resource beyond its capacity. The resulting pattern of deficits is then characteristic of the particular tasks and of that limiting resource. In dual-task performance, where there is no decline in global measures of performance, it is important to appreciate that there may be some temporal accommodation between the tasks to facilitate equitable sharing of resources.

The structural composition of a task should not be conceived of as rigidly fixed. There may be a number of distinct ways in which a task might be performed, each one with different demands on resources. Moreover, in the acquisition of skill at a task, the processes underlying performance may evolve to make fewer demands on resources. The freed capacity might then be utilised for improved performance of other tasks. These kinds of issues are taken up in the next chapter on skill acquisition. One common observation of the development of skill is that the movements seem to require less attention and that the ability to do more than one thing at a time is increased. This can be termed automatisation. The changes that occur as skill develops include changes in the organisation of a sequence of movements and in the role of feedback. These changes may lead to automatisation because there is less demand on central resources or because there is more efficient use of separate lower-level structures that do not require central resources.

The Acquisition of Skill

Peter Johnson

INTRODUCTION

A common way of determining the essence of skill is to describe the performance of a task by well-practised people and contrast it with the performance of people who have had less practice. Reason (1977) quoted from Arnold Bennett's novel *Clayhanger* in which differences in the skill of typesetting are eloquently described. Most noticeable in Bennett's account was that the unskilled apprentice composed a line of type "with his feet, his shoulders, his mouth, his eyebrows, with all his body except his hands" while the expert used only his right hand which could scarcely be followed in its twinklings (Bennett, 1910, p. 114). For Bennett, skill was characterised by economy and speed. Bartlett (1958) in discussing skill provides a classic description of a skilled cricketer that emphasises effortlessness. Economy of effort can also be seen in the activity in muscles as skilled movement develops. Kamon and Gormley (1968) have described the activity in muscles of the back, arms and legs of skilled gymnasts and novices during performance of the single-knee circle mount on the horizontal bar. They found that bursts of muscle activity were much shorter in the trained gymnast (see Figure 1) and that

THE PSYCHOLOGY OF HUMAN MOVEMENT

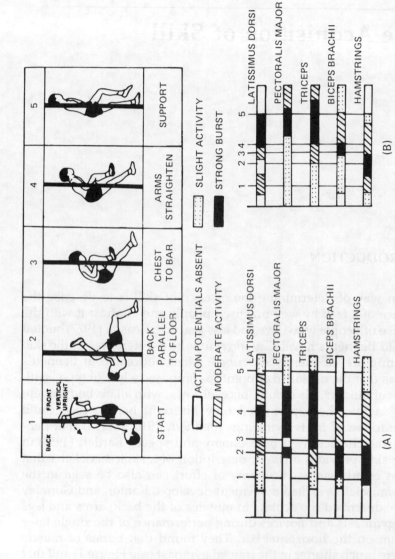

Figure 1. Economy of muscle activity in the skilled performer. The relative amount of activity in muscles of the arm, leg, and back contributing to the single knee circle mount are shown for early stages of training (A) and the skilled gymnast (B). The numbers refer to the five phases of the movement illustrated at the top of the figure. From Kamon, E. and Gormley, J. (1968). *Ergonomics, 11,* 345–357. Reprinted with permission.

periods of greatest activity were organised in a more sequential, coordinated fashion. The movements actually required less expenditure of muscular effort for the gymnasts than for the novices.

Shaffer (1981), in contrasting skilled and unskilled piano playing, describes the skilled performance as being faster, more fluent, expressive, and creative. A systematic technique for using verbal descriptions of movement behaviour to describe and classify actions has been developed by Hallberg (1976). In his study groups of subjects were shown video tapes containing 30-picture sequences of approximately four minutes each. The pictures included gripping, lifting, and balancing movements in walking, sitting, and standing positions (and transitions between these positions). Fifteen judges were asked to pick which of 79 listed adjectives best described the picture sequences. By means of a statistical technique known as cluster analysis, Hallberg obtained a quantitative assessment of movements with *stiffness, pace,* and *ease* as some of the main dimensions of motor behaviour. One way in which skill in a particular task might be characterised would be to take subjects with varying amounts of training and have performances rated along these dimensions. We would expect, for instance, skilled dart throwers' movements would be rated as lower in terms of stiffness and higher in terms of ease and pace than the movements of unpractised players.

Often, skill is characterised in terms of the speed of performance. Thus, Crossman (1959) gave a quantitative picture of skill development in the industrial process of cigar manufacture by plotting the number of cigars produced per unit of time by a given operator as a function of the number of cigars produced, (see Figure 2). An impressive feature of these data is the way that performance improves over a very long time period, in this case 2 years. As a corollary of the data shown in Figure 2, Crossman found that the distributions of times taken to complete one cycle of an industrial assembly task are different for novice and expert operators. In general, the average cycle time for an expert is less than that of a novice. However, this is not due to an overall speeding up of all cycle times. Instead, the proportion of short cycle times relative to very long ones increases so that the distribution becomes more positively skewed with practice (see Figure 3). Similar data have been obtained by Long, Nimmo-Smith, and Whitefield (1983) for the interresponse times of typists. The skilled person makes fewer very slow responses and more fast responses. These findings show improvements in performance can be seen over very long time periods. In the remainder of this chapter the emphasis will be less on the description of changes in performance, whether qualitative or quantitative, and more on trying to gain an understanding of the processes that underlie the acquisition of skill.

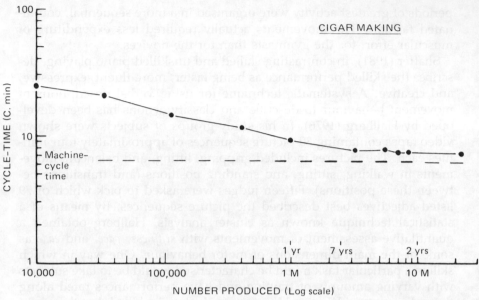

Figure 2. Reduction in operator time in producing cigars as a function of practice. From "A theory of the acquisition of speed-skill", by Crossman, E. R. F. W. (1959). *Ergonomics*, 2, 153–166. Reprinted with permission.

STAGES IN SKILL ACQUISITION

A widely held view of skill acquisition is that there are qualitative changes in the way a task is performed. An influential description of different stages of skill acquisition incorporating this idea is that of Fitts (1964). Three phases of skill acquisition, a cognitive phase, an associative phase, and an autonomous phase are recognised. In the initial cognitive phase, a decision framework or logic for performing the task is set up. According to Fitts, one feature of this phase is that subjects tend to verbalise each part of the task that they are attempting. Words appear to be used in helping recall what has to be done as a kind of framework for behaviour. Verbal reports at this stage represent detailed descriptions of the decision processes and performance strategies that are being attempted. Shea and Zimny (1983) trained subjects to make different movement sequences in response to a red or a green signal light and to provide verbal reports of their strategies. They found that in random presentation of trials subjects reported more comparisons between response patterns whereas those who practised in blocked trial conditions reported fewer attempts to distinguish the patterns. The blocked condi-

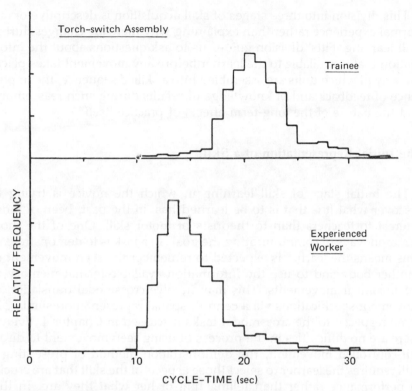

Figure 3. Changes in the distribution of cycle times with skill. From "A theory of the acquisition of speed-skill", by Crossman, E. R. F. W. (1959). *Ergonomics*, 2, 153–166. Reprinted with permission.

tions led to poorer retention which Shea and Zimny attributed to the differences in the level of processing carried out by the subjects.

In the associative phase, component parts of the skill are tried out and an appropriate set of elementary units of action is assembled. At this stage the provision of knowledge of results is important if associations are to be formed between the components of the skill. During this stage new patterns of action begin to emerge. Fitts viewed the final, autonomous stage in the acquisition of a skill as the automatisation of component processes in the skill as the degree of cognitive control is minimised. The autonomous phase is marked by the loss of the ability to provide a verbal description of the task. It may even be the case that verbalisation of a highly developed skill may interfere with performance. Taking a general limited-capacity view of attention (see Chapter 7), a reduction in the attention demanded by the skilled task means that there is an improved ability to carry out other tasks at the same time.

This division into three stages of skill acquisition is descriptive of our normal experience rather than explaining why there are changes during skill learning. Fitts' division guides us to ask questions about the information that is available to the learner before any movement takes place, the way in which units are assembled into a skilled sequence, the importance of feedback and of knowledge of results during such reassembly, and the nature of the long-term effects of practice itself.

The Initial Representation of a Skill

The initial stage of skill learning in which the novice is trying to discover what it is that is to be learned has, in the past, been of more interest to teachers than to theorists of motor skill. One of the most common ways of communicating the goals of a task is to demonstrate it. This means the learner is expected to remember the seen movement of another body and to use the information available in that memory to create similar movements. This may involve crossmodal translation of movement specifications via a central, spatial representation similar, in some respects, to the crossmodal tasks discussed in Chapter 4. Even if there are no difficulties in the process of using seen movement to direct self-controlled movement, the demonstration method of presenting a skill requires the learner to select those aspects of the skill that are crucial to performance rather than telling him or her what they are. In this respect, teaching a perceptual motor skill is not unlike learning mathematics. The teacher has to have an adequate picture of the learner's current state of knowledge so that any new material can be presented in a way that can be understood within the existing knowledge structure.

Newell (1981) has suggested that there are other ways in which movements can be represented to learners in addition to visual demonstration. These include relevant sounds, particularly when timing or rhythmic performance is involved and this may mean that a rhythm template is made available against which the produced movement can be compared. Keele (1973) describes the Suzuki method of violin teaching in which the young child is exposed to the sound of a piece of music over and over again before attempting to play it. The child is encouraged to see the goal of violin playing as making music, not practising movements for their own sake. An auditory representation of a particular goal may be matched to the auditory feedback associated with the movements actually made so that progress can be monitored by the learner from an early stage. In other situations a model of correct performance may only be developed as learning takes place, in which case the learner will be very dependent on other people for monitoring of performance until late in acquisition of the skill.

It is possible to provide learners with a model for a task by guiding them through an initial presentation. This can be done by moving the learner passively through the movements or by providing feedback so that it is impossible to make a mistake. Guidance has been studied as a learning aid over successive trials rather than as an initial presentation of the task (Annett, 1969). In general it has not been found to be as useful as other forms of training, possibly because motivation is low when subjects cannot make mistakes during practice. Nevertheless, as a means of presenting a task, guidance may still serve a useful purpose.

Assembling a Skill from Elementary Units

A central idea in Fitts' view of skill is that any skill is comprised of a number of elementary procedural units or short, fixed sequences of operations. He took as an analogy the use of subroutines in computer programming. A subroutine provides a limited, fixed set of operations on one or more variables. It may be used by main programs that have very varied purposes. For instance, a subroutine to print out letters or numbers on a line printer is likely to be used by most computer programs. In the analogy it is assumed that a skill is compiled from a number of basic units of action. Different programs may call on different sets of subroutines. There may be a hierarchy in which one subroutine, when it is active, calls lower subroutines, and so on. In much the same way, it is assumed that different skills involve the assembly of different combinations of elementary units of action. However, some skills may have several elementary units in common. These skills will presumably resemble one another to a greater extent than skills with very few or no common elements. Suppose the same people tend to perform well in two tasks (A, B) but people performing well in these two tasks do not do well in (C). This would indicate that (A, B) have a greater number of elements in common than (A, C) or (B, C). We should then expect that a particular individual who has mastered activity A should learn B more rapidly than C, given that there are more elements in common between (A, B) than (A, C). We should then say that there had been positive transfer of training between (A, B).

Transfer of training is important to those who teach and learn skills but it is also important in helping us to understand how motor control is organised. In a hierarchy of control the units at the lowest level are specific to particular groups of muscles and cannot be used interchangeably. This means that the instructions appropriate to one limb may not be appropriate to another so that transfer across the limbs will not occur. At a higher level, we can consider a general or equivalence class of actions (Glencross, 1980) in which common or general features of actions are represented but these features are independent of the actual units, namely, individual movements, and may be used in a variety of situations to achieve specific goals. Evidence for such a level of representation can be found in studies of bilateral transfer or transfer between muscle groups in such tasks as handwriting, positioning movements and rhythmic tapping. While spatial and temporal components of movement can be transferred across different muscle groups or limbs, the ability to transfer force or velocity may be limited or absent. Suppose that while driving a car one were to try braking with the left foot. For smooth slowing of the car, this involves applying a steadily increasing force to the brake pedal, a skill learned by drivers at an early stage with the right foot. However, the result of braking with the left foot is likely to be a sudden abrupt halt of the car and this suggests that the unit controlling force parameters is at too low a level to permit transfer across limbs.

Reason (1979) also adopted a computer-programming metaphor in his account of slips of action and this has been described in Chapter 6. He suggested that many errors are associated with points in the program at which there is more than one possible ensuing course of action. He called these critical decision points and suggested that at these points a feedback mode of control (closed-loop) should be used that relies on conscious attention. He argued that at other times action may be governed by pre-arranged instruction sequences (subroutines) that run off independently of feedback. When control is delegated to a subordinate program, Reason used the term *open-loop control* and assumed that at these times central-processing capacity or attention is freed to allow mental activity independent of the current action. He stated that both modes of control will be present at all phases of motor learning. Even in the very early stages of skill acquisition, the novice is assumed to have in his repertoire some preformed units of action that are relevant to the task and that allow a degree of open-loop control. The assumption is that, with practice, the learner will need to resort to the closed-loop mode of control less and less and, ultimately, only at a few critical decision points.

Developing Automatisation

Automatisation of performance is considered to be the last stage in the development of skill. An experiment by Frith and Lang (1978) shows

how predictability is a key element in automatisation of the performance
of a task. Subjects were required to move a joy-stick control to keep a
cursor superimposed on a target that moved under computer control on
a visual display. Both the target and cursor could move in horizontal and
vertical directions on the display. However, the movement of the target
in the horizontal direction was programmed independently of movement in the vertical direction. Subjects performed the task in two 5-
minute sessions separated by a 10-minute rest period. Two separate
groups of subjects were run in two different conditions. In Condition I,
the movement of the target was essentially unpredictable in both horizontal and vertical directions. In Condition II, the vertical component
was identical to Condition I, but the horizontal component was a simple
sine wave that repeated every 2 seconds and was therefore highly
predictable.

The performance of subjects was assessed by determining the mean
average distance of the cursor from the target. The performance of subjects in Condition I showed no improvement either within or between
sessions. The results for Condition II are summarised in Figure 4. In the
first 5-minute session there is an improvement in the tracking of the
predictable horizontal component but not of the unpredictable vertical
component. Between the two sessions there was an improvement in the
performance of both vertical and horizontal components of the task.
Frith and Lang concluded that the improvements in performance were
accomplished by subjects first building an internal representation of the
more predictable component. This allowed tracking of the horizontal

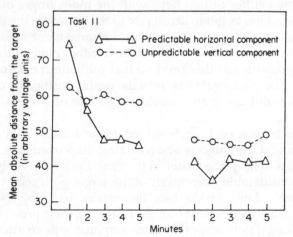

Figure 4. Improvement in horizontal and vertical components of tracking with practice. From "Learning and reminiscence as a function of target predictability in a two-
dimensional tracking test", by Frith, D. C., Lang, R. J. (1978). *Quarterly Journal of Experimental Psychology, 31*, 103–109. Reprinted with permission.

component to become more automatic so permitting a greater proportion of attentional capacity and hence more effort to be put into coping with the less predictable vertical component.

This account of the automatisation process relates to a distinction made by Poulton (1957) between two classes of skill which he called *closed* and *open* skills. The adjectives open and closed in this context do not refer to the control loops involved in movement. Poulton used the qualifier closed to refer to those skills that can be carried out without reference to the environment. These he contrasted with open skills that require adaptation of movement to events in the environment. Poulton based this distinction largely on the notion of predictability within the environment and closed skills referred to a highly predictable environment while open skills referred to an unstable, unpredictable environment. Skills such as gymnastics, bowling, and golf might be classified as closed skills while basketball, tennis, or football would be considered open skills. However, the point to make here is that novices acquiring a particular skill may not be aware of the predictability in the environment whereas the skilled performer has built up an internal model of the predictability. Skilled performers can thus better anticipate environmental demands and select better responses accordingly. This, in turn, reduces the need to monitor feedback since the outcome of actions will be more predictable.

Pew (1966) investigated the development of organisational structure in a simple target-control task. The basic task consisted of maintaining the position of a target in the centre of a visual display. To do this the subject pressed either of two keys with the index finger of each hand. One key caused the target to accelerate to the left while the other caused it to accelerate to the right. This control arrangement made the target position unstable and liable to accelerate to either edge of the screen. In fact the equipment was designed so that optimum performance (maximising the time the target is kept in the centre position) would only be achieved by maintaining an infinitely high rate of alternation between the two keys.

Five subjects took part, each subject for at least 24 1-hour sessions. Over this period all subjects showed clear improvements in the time they managed to keep the target in the centre position. Early in training there was considerable movement of the target with relatively long intervals between key presses (see Figures 5a, b). Subjects apparently waited for visual feedback about the results of their previous response before initiating a new response. Each response was an attempt to compensate for the inadequacies of the previous one. By the end of training, two contrasting strategies predominated in the performance of the task.

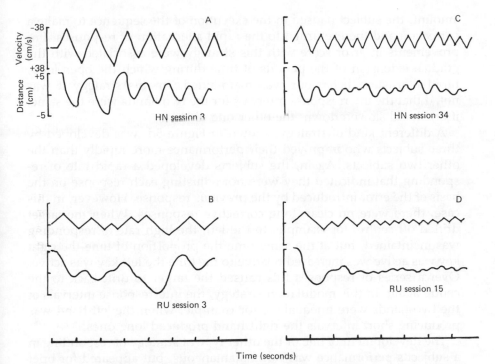

Time (seconds)

Figure 5. Performance traces for the acceleration control task. Two subjects whose data early and late in practice are shown in (A), (C) and (B), (D) develop different forms of control later in practice identified as open-loop mode (C) and modulation mode (D). The lower record of each pair presents the displacement of the target which the subject was trying to keep centred on the oscilloscope screen. The upper trace indicates the instantaneous velocity of the target; periods of linear increase or decrease in velocity represent the duration of operation of each key. From "Acquisition of hierarchical control over the temporal organization of a skill", by Pew, R. W. (1966). *Journal of Experimental Psychology, 71,* 764–771.

These are illustrated in Figure 5c, d. In both cases the mean interresponse time was reduced by nearly 50% from early to late in training. In Figure 5c, d it appears that the subjects generated responses at a rate more rapid than could be controlled had each one been organized and executed as a response to perceived error. In addition a distinct temporal patterning of responses developed that was consistent with the formation of sequences of individual responses into larger units.

In the strategy illustrated in 5c and used by two of the subjects, a series of rapid alternating responses was made in the course of which there was a gradual overall drift in the mean position of the target. After a certain time, or, more likely, after the drift had reached a certain amount, the subject paused in the execution of the sequence to make a correction and then returned to the rapid alternation of responses. Improvements in error score with this strategy were associated with the gradual extension of the periods of time during which the open-loop, rapid-alternation behaviour was maintained. In this strategy it was noted that the interresponse intervals for the two hands were the same; if one hand slowed down, the other one did also.

A different kind of strategy, shown in Figure 5d, was developed by three subjects who improved their performance more rapidly than the other two subjects. Again, the subjects developed a rapid rate of responding that indicated they were not adjusting each response on the basis of the error introduced by the previous response. However, in this case, there were no clear, long corrective responses. When the target drifted off centre, for example, to the left, the high rate of responding was maintained, but at the same time the proportion of time the right key was active was increased relative to the time the left key was active. Over a series of responses this caused the target to drift back to the centre again. In this modulation strategy, the interresponse intervals of the two hands were unequal so, for example, when the left hand was producing short intervals the right hand produced long ones.

The development of one or the other type of strategy of responding in a subject's performance was not instantaneous, but appeared for brief periods in a trial and then disappeared. However, as training progressed, these periods became more frequent. On the basis of this, Pew suggested that as skill developed, there is a transition from strict closed-loop control to open-loop control with highly automatised action sequences and only occasional executive monitoring. Early in practice, feedback is used to construct the next response while after a given amount of practice, the subject does not need to construct the next response on the basis of feedback, instead feedback is used simply to check that the subject's internal representation of the task is adequate and that the correct predictions about what the next response should be were reached.

THEORETICAL ACCOUNTS OF
THE LEARNING PROCESS

The issues of control, automaticity, and stages of skill acquisition that have been raised so far can be better understood within a framework of learning. There are several competing theoretical positions, each of which contributes to our understanding, but each of which also raises questions that have yet to be answered.

Adams' Theory

A closed-loop model of motor learning has been developed by Adams (1971, 1976) in which movements are initiated by a memory trace and controlled by a reference mechanism known as a perceptual trace that is developed from external knowledge of results about the earlier outcomes for a particular movement. Annett (1969) drew a distinction between information available to the subject about his or her performance from within the task (intrinsic feedback) and information not contained within the task but supplied by an external agent (extrinsic feedback). In Adams' model these appear as feedback and knowledge of results, respectively. Adams claims that skill learning involves the acquisition of a reference mechanism (perceptual trace) that contains information or intrinsic feedback from previous responses with which to compare feedback from the current movement. Some kind of comparator mechanism is needed to evaluate the perceptual trace with respect to incoming feedback, although this is not described by Adams. The perceptual trace is built up as a function of the amount of exposure to the various sources of feedback in a situation; proprioceptive, visual, and auditory information can all contribute to the development of the perceptual trace. When learning is advanced, few errors are made because the perceptual trace is composed of feedback traces from a large number of movements which are correct or almost correct. Adams suggests that, at this stage, error can be detected purely on the basis of kinaesthetic feedback without visual input or knowledge of results. That is, he views the perceptual trace as a motor image, similar in some ways to a visual image in memory.

The notion of a motor image suggests that a movement is converted to a kinaesthetic or proprioceptive image and this may be misleading. Johnson (1982) has shown that images of linear-positioning movements are based on a spatial rather than a visual or motor representation. This implies that the perceptual trace is neither motor nor visual but is based on a higher level of abstraction of the task parameters, which in the case of the linear positioning task are spatial, (i.e., concerning position, direction and extent of movement). Consequently, the effects of experience through practising a movement are not simply to form an exact copy of the resultant feedback, but to construct a representation of higher-level, more abstract, parameters of the task. This suggests that feedback from a particular source, such as vision, may not be required for comparison with the perceptual trace. In an earlier experiment by Johnson (1980) it was shown that, while changing the type of feedback available from visual and kinaesthetic to kinaesthetic alone brought about a deterioration in accuracy on a linear-positioning task, performance was by no means reduced to the level it had been in the early learning trials. The notion of a modality-specific perceptual trace should be replaced by one of an amodal, or abstract representation of the task requirements.

While the perceptual trace represents how the task was executed, knowledge of results is a means of evaluating the adequacy of performance. It might be thought that knowledge of results in Adams's model is related to the verbal stage of learning in Fitts' model because a common means of providing knowledge of results is by verbal comments. Training instructors can, for example, tell the trainee that the tennis stroke was too hard or that the angle of the chisel on the lathe was too low. However, it is inappropriate to consider that knowledge of results should always be verbal. In many cases, the provision of a videotaped record along with a demonstration of correct task performance is more useful. The extent to which all aspects of a task can be verbalised is largely unknown and, in any case, is likely to vary from task to task. Indeed, it would be useful to know what are the relationships between verbalisation of task parameters and level of skill. It has generally been assumed (by Fitts and others) that there is a close relationship between verbal reports and conscious control. This stems from early conceptions that regarded cognition as being only concerned with conscious processes; hence, Fitts' cognition phase of skill acquisition is characterised by conscious control with the capability of making verbal reports. However, it is unlikely that asking trainee typists what they are doing would elicit comments on their timing of keystrokes even though changes in interkeystroke interval are most pronounced early in practice.

A number of criticisms of Adams's theory have been put forward. One criticism is that for every movement, there is assumed to be a separate memory trace. Given the enormous variety of movements that can be performed this assumption would seem to pose a very great burden on storage capacity and on retrieval processes. Another problem is that of novelty; performance of a task is never an exact replica of an earlier performance, but rather appears to be constructed anew (Bartlett, 1932). These difficulties are addressed by schema theories of skill acquisition which assume generative processes rather than fixed memory traces underlie the execution of skilled movements.

Schema Theory

Schmidt (1975, 1976) suggested that, on the basis of a representation of the goal and as a result of knowledge of results over trials we develop recall schema that can generate an appropriate motor program at the time it is needed. Proprioceptive information arising from movement leads to development of a recognition schema that can assist in guiding movement by generating the expected feedback consequences of movement. With respect to learning, the utility of both the recall schema and of the recognition schema is assumed to increase with the amount and variability of previous practice trials. Thus, a direct prediction of the schema theory is that performance on one type of movement will be more readily transferred to a different movement (still within the same general class of movements) following increased practice and variability of the original task.

More details of the schema theory may be found in Chapter 5, but, in general, empirical tests have confirmed Schmidt's view that variability of practice improves learning. As an example consider a study of children learning to throw bean bags at a target on the floor by Carson and Wiegand (1979). Children practised the task over 100 trials using either the same bean bag on every trial or else using a bag selected on each trial from one of four bags of different weight. After practice it was found that the group given variability of training with the bags of different weights were significantly more accurate using a bean bag of a novel weight than were the children only exposed to a bean bag of a single weight. From the theory we should say a better schema had been formed as a consequence of exposure to varied conditions of practice. What is particularly interesting is that, given a new task of tossing a ball of wool at a target on a wall, performance of the group given variability of practice was again better. The improved schema facilitated transfer to the new skill.

Other experimental support for the schema view of skill acquisition comes from positioning tasks. Newell and Shapiro (1976) trained subjects to move to different locations and then tested their recall for a novel movement, which was within the range on which they had been trained, but which had not previously been produced by subjects. Comparisons of subjects' errors with those of other subjects who did not experience variable training favoured the variable practice group (see Figure 6).

These kinds of results may be considered examples of transfer of training. The point here, however, is that the schema theory is being proposed as an underlying process to explain the transfer phenomena.

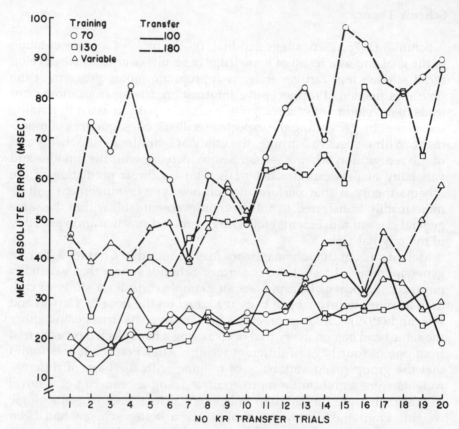

Figure 6. Variability of practice. Subjects learned to move a lever a fixed distance in a stated time. In one group the time was 70 msec, in a second group it was 130 msec, a third group (varied practice) trained on half the trials at each of the times. The subjects given varied practice performed with less error on a movement that had to be made with a duration of 180 msec, outside the original range of times. From Newall, K. M. and Shapiro, D. C. (1976). *Journal of Motor Behavior, 8,* 223–243. Reprinted with permission.

What schema theory in its present form fails to do is specify the mechanisms by which positive or negative transfer effects occur. Until some mechanisms have been specified, the constraints of the system and, more importantly, the practical implications of how actions will be affected by transfer cannot be predicted.

COORDINATIVE STRUCTURES AND TRANSFER

An alternative view of how skill is acquired has been put forward by Turvey (1977) and deals with the development of functional units in which different groups of muscles can be coordinated. Such a unit can be called a *coordinative structure*. A coordinative structure for handwriting might involve muscle groups in the arm, wrist, and fingers. Muscle groups brought together in a coordinative structure need not be anatomically related; a musician is often required to use fingers of both hands as one functional unit. Turvey suggests that a coordinative structure involves both a *structural prescription* that determines which muscles groups are being used, and a *metrical prescription* which determines the ratio of activity in the various muscle groups. Newell (1981) suggested that transfer might occur across metrical prescriptions within a given structural prescription. Negative transfer is assumed to occur between two tasks because similar muscle groups are activated in each case (the structural prescription is the same) but the ratio of activity between the muscle groups (the metrical prescription) is changed.

The view of skill that deals with the development of coordinative structures is different from the hierarchical models presented so far. Hierarchical models are marked by the passing of control to lower levels with increased practice. In learning to drive a car, for example, at first a gear change might require the whole of our conscious control simply to move the gear lever. Consequently, while we are executing one action, the rest of our driving comes to a complete stop. Later on, when the driver has become more skilled, gear changes are carried out automatically. Indeed, all the actions of driving can, at times, appear to be carried out without our conscious awareness; the experience of having reached the office without being aware of driving from home is not uncommon.

A hierarchy allows the control of minor subunits of action to be passed down to lower command centres. The office manager passes the responsibility of collecting the mail to the office junior, while retaining control of the signing of outgoing mail. This kind of *top-down* model for movement control places considerable reliance on the higher-level executive control structures because they must possess the necessary commands to initiate the lower structures. One advantage of such a structure is that higher-level control need not be involved in the execution details of the lowest levels.

Turvey and his associates (Turvey, 1977; Kugler, Kelso, & Turvey, 1980) pointed out that a hierarchical control system does not explain how the hierarchy came to be formed or even how a particular unit comes to be organised under the control of one executive. A particular collective or subunit may be prescribed prior to the motor act or it might be formed at the time of the action. Some plan is required to prescribe which muscles operate together. In addition, a given command will have different outcomes under different environmental conditions and the motor system could be expected to produce errors if a plan were imposed from a higher level of organisation in which the current state of the lower systems was not specified. Some adaptive behaviour is possible if the resultant feedback can be compared with the initial instruction specifications but, unfortunately, feedback is reactive. If the act is carried out and then checked, the information will relate to conditions that no longer exist. Moreover, feedback does not specify how the motor commands should be corrected.

In place of such systems of organisation, Turvey suggests a *coalition* between action, perception, and the provisions and demands of the environment. Coordinative structures or particular patterns of muscle activity are *tuned* by the environment to accommodate successful action. Tuning is the way in which coordinative structures are able to take advantage of context and information about the body, the environment and the interaction between the two. It is this tuning that alters as a function of practice and about which Turvey has little to say. According to Turvey (1977), higher units exert control over lower units by altering two kinds of control parameters; those of the units themselves and those of the pathways by which units may interact.

Gallistel (1980) has pointed out that babies spend a great amount of time repeatedly practising the same action. The feedback from this practice may play an important role in the tuning referred to by Turvey, that is, in adjusting the parameters of the neural circuitry to make the action smoother and more accurate. In a sense, this practice develops and optimises the control parameters responsible for the coordination of action. Optimization is the process whereby the values of a number of different parameters are adjusted simultaneously to find the best combination in terms of some desired end-goal or movement outcome. This process in adults may well be the same thing as the automatisation of lower units or subroutines. Fowler and Turvey (1978) describe how a particular coordinative structure comes to be formed in order to solve the problem of controlling a large number of degrees of freedom by a single control structure. The skilled actor is able to optimise the values of the task-relevant parameters of movement whilst the novice must first search out the organisational constraints of the task.

PRACTICE

A key feature of skill acquisition is the effect of practice and rehearsal. As a general rule, skill in performance increases as a direct function of the amount of practice. While practice may not make for perfection, it usually brings about performance improvement and, as mentioned previously, this improvement can continue for a very long time. Snoddy (1926) found that subjects' performance at mirror tracing of visual images improved as a positive function of practice. In general it is found that the logarithm of the time taken to perform a task plotted against the logarithm of the number of trials produces a straight line; this relationship is known as the *log–log linear law* or *power law* of practice. Crossman (1959) put forward a mathematical model to explain this law in which it is assumed that improvement occurs because subjects become more efficient at selecting methods of performing. Each method is selected on a probabilistic basis and it is the probabilities that change as a function of experience. Recently, Newell and Rosenbloom (1981) rediscovered this power law of practice and found that it holds, not just for improvements in the time to complete a task, but also for the number of errors that occur. Furthermore, the law holds for all kinds of learning including perceptual motor tasks, perceptual tasks (such as visual search), verbal tasks, and problem-solving tasks.

As a possible explanation of this improvement in performance over time, Newell and Rosenbloom hypothesise that subjects acquire and organise environmental knowledge by forming and storing structured collections, or chunks, of the elements of a task. This chunking hypothesis was originally outlined in a paper by Miller (1956). Chunking may be defined as the formation of meaningful groups at either an input, storage or output stage of psychological processing. The consequence of chunking is to reduce the processing load of the task because there is less to do per unit of time. In a classic study of Morse code operators by Bryan and Harter (1897) it was found that the skill of receiving Morse code was marked by changes in perceptual organisation. In the early stages operators were coding in terms of single letters, but by the end of their training, they were operating at the level of words or phrases. Bryan and Harter suggested that the same was also true of their production of Morse code. In the process of acquiring these skills, the operators formed input and output chunks which enabled them to process larger amounts of information in the same space of time. The novice spells out each word into letters and then into the Morse equivalent before producing the appropriate key presses. The trained operator has automatised the translation process such that whole words can be constructed directly as a series of key presses. A higher-level dictionary of Morse code signals has been created that avoids spelling out each word into letters and thence into the Morse code equivalents.

So, one of the main functions of practice may be to alter the organisation of elements of the task by allowing the creation of chunks of information and this may apply to perceptual motor skills as well as to other activities. However, changes in tuning also occur with practice of a perceptual motor skill and these involve the translation process between stored organised units and the motor output system. In the account of motor control proposed by Gallistel (1980), it is suggested that tuning may involve the ability to translate body-space representations necessary for understanding a skill in overall terms, into neuromuscular space so that the action is *known* neuromuscularly. It is assumed that this process becomes more efficient with practice.

Knowledge of Results and Feedback

Information about performance that is available to the learner, either during or after the performance, has been of considerable interest to theorists accounting for skill acquisition and it is also a topic of practical importance for both teacher and learner. Knowledge of results of performance is information related to the achievement of the goal of the performance sequence. It can be either positive or negative, it can be delivered as part of the subgoal structure of the task rather than at the end, it may be subjective or objective, and it may motivate the performer as well as providing information. The uses of knowledge of results will vary as tasks vary. The teacher may also have to adjust knowledge of results for individual learners as their knowledge of both the goal to be achieved and of the methods of achieving it may develop differently. In general, knowledge of results cannot escape being task bound although there may be some uses which are relatively independent of any task situation.

Feedback during performance has a different history from knowledge of results. While knowledge of results is derived from behaviourist accounts of learning, feedback stems from control systems engineering and was introduced into psychological accounts of perceptual motor skill by Craik (1947). Feedback is information about current performance that is picked up as performance proceeds. Pew (1974) suggested that in the transition from closed to open-loop control that comes with practice, the functional role of feedback changes. Early in practice, feedback is used to construct each successive movement. Later, feedback is used simply to check that the subject's internal representation of the task is adequate so that the prediction about what successive movements should be are valid. Thus, the function of feedback in the early stages of skill acquisition is to construct an appropriate response pattern, while in later stages, it serves to check the adequacy of an internal representation of the task.

Management of Practice

The issues raised in the views of skill acquisition presented above have implications for the management of practice. In principle practice can be thought of as a continuum of procedures with overt practice at one extreme and covert or mental practice at the other. Overt practice has been widely researched by psychologists interested in training (Holding, 1965; Annett, 1971). A major focus of these investigations has been how much practice should be given and how it should be spaced. As a general rule, massed practice is found to be less efficient than spaced practice. In an investigation of the learning of Morse code Bray (1948) reported that performance was the same for a group of subjects given 4 hours of practice in a session and another group who received 7 hours. Thus, the 3 extra hours were completely ineffective. It would have been far better if there had been a break halfway through the longer practice session. Long practice sessions can also be broken up by varying the topic. One way to create variety is to break up the skill to be acquired into components and practise these separately, perhaps embedded in other tasks. However, there is a disadvantage to learning a skill by parts rather than as a whole—the learner may have difficulty integrating the elements.

In teaching a skill, instructors are often concerned with the extent to which good performance on a particular skill will help in the acquisition of good performance on another skill. If the original skill contains many of the subskills required by the new skill then learning will be enhanced. This we discussed as *transfer of training*. We pointed out that one skill may interfere with performance on another task. If previously learned skills do interfere with the new skill to be learned, then the instructor will be faced with a certain amount of *untraining*, that is inhibition of prior skills, before training on the new skill can proceed. It should be noted that there is evidence to suggest that when two skilled activities follow a similar path but then at some point diverge, there is a high chance of the two becoming confused so that an inappropriate routine or procedure ensues. These are probably points that will need special attention in training.

Generalisation of a skill over a variety of contexts is likely to be an explicit goal of training; it is unlikely that all eventualities can be anticipated and specifically practised. The essence of Schmidt's view of skill learning is that we set up general rules (schema) that allow us to generate movements that will be appropriate for any particular eventuality. As mentioned in the discussion of schema theory, variability of practice is a desirable feature in a training programme since it will result in the establishment of a more general or abstract code which will also be more resistent to interference or decay. An additional bonus in making use of variety in the learning context is that it is likely to help with the breaking up or spacing of practice as discussed above.

Last, but by no means least in the points to be remembered in the management of practice, is the importance of information about the outcome of performance. Current practice in this area involves the use of video. The use of video and film loops has been to provide analysis of both skilled performance and unskilled attempts. The two different roles of this medium are to provide a template of a perfect response or to provide a form of feedback for the learner. In providing a template, the belief is that this will lead to the formulation of a more accurate model of the actions while providing a record of the learner's failures may offer an additional form of feedback. However, at present there has been insufficient research to distinguish whether or not visual aids are better related to perceptual modelling of the task and its environment or the responses and their consequences. It is highly probable that such functions are likely to vary with different tasks and environmental contingencies.

The use of film and videotaping can be described as giving knowledge of performance rather than knowledge of results (Gentile, 1972). For skills in which the environment is relatively predictable (Poulton's closed skills) the learner's task at a comparatively late stage in practice may be to develop consistency over trials and it is at this stage that video feedback is most useful (Rothstein & Arnold, 1976). Newell and Walter (1981) have argued that at this stage in the learning of a closed skill a videotape may not provide kinematic feedback, such as displacement, velocity, or acceleration values of movement, and that detailed kinetic feedback, such as, impulse or force, is also likely to be unavailable. They suggest that there may be situations in which direct presentation of either the kinematic information, which describes the time course of movement through space, or the kinetic information, which describes the forces exerted over time, could be useful to the learner. However, this may only be the case when very high levels of competence have been reached.

Mental Practice

The concept of mental or covert practice is, perhaps not surprisingly, better defined in the area of verbal learning than in motor skills. The studies of Tulving and Donaldson (1975) lead to two classes of covert rehearsal being suggested for verbal material; *maintenance* and *elaborative rehearsal*. Maintenance rehearsal is supposed to enable items to be kept in some memory store to prevent decay. Elaborative rehearsal extends a memory trace by activating say an associative network that integrates new information with existing memory traces and so embellishes the memory trace.

In motor skills mental practice involves asking subjects to spend a prescribed period of time thinking about or imagining the actions being performed. The majority of experiments indicate that mental practice is better than no practice but not as effective as actual practice. If the methods used by experimenters to conduct a mental practice session are examined, it is apparent that task-relevant features or cues are often available to subjects during mental practice. In only a few experiments were no cues present at all. In some, visual cues, such as the apparatus itself or feedback lights, were present, in other cases the experimenters provided verbal instructions about the goal and procedures of the task, which were either written or spoken to the subject. On analysing the effects of these various types of cues, it appears that visual cues are by far the most efficient aids to mental practice. That is, in those cases where visual cues were present, mental practice consistently produces improvements compared to control subjects receiving no practice. This suggests that mental practice involves a visual process. One of the most common instructions to subjects during mental practice is to imagine that they are in the task environment performing the task itself. Richardson (1967a,b) suggests that visual imagery is a likely process operating in mental practice.

In a series of experiments investigating the effect of imagery instructions on performance, Johnson (1982) instructed subjects to imagine making movements along a linear track to a particular point. He found that once subjects had learned to move the slide to a criterion point along the track, instructions to imagine moving to a new point on the same track resulted in a biasing of the subjects' subsequent recall of the learned criterion movement towards the imagined point. This bias was equal in size to that produced by subjects who actually made an interpolated movement to this point (see Figure 7). Furthermore, instructions to imagine moving to the criterion point, after a number of actual movement learning trials, resulted in less error than a control group who counted backwards after the actual movement learning trials. It was evident that the variability in individual subjects' responses was much lower in the imagery conditions than in the actual movement and counting backwards control conditions. This suggests that imagery of movements involves a perceptual memory system rather than a system specif-

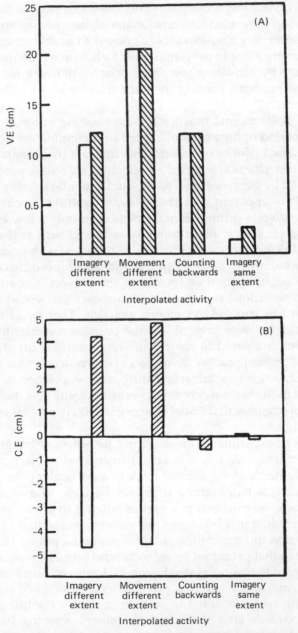

Figure 7. Comparison of the effects of a real and imaged interpolated movements on VE and CE of motor recall. From "The functional equivalence of imagery and movement", by Johnson, P., (1982). *Quarterly Journal of Experimental Psychology, 34A*, 349–365. Reprinted with permission.

ic to motor output. Another experiment showed that the bias produced by imagery could be suppressed only by a concurrent visual–spatial task and not by motor tasks, which further supports a visual–spatial basis for mental practice.

The implications of this for the practice and rehearsal of actions are still to be investigated. However, one might suggest that, if it is the spatial aspects of motor control which can be covertly rehearsed rather than the temporal or force parameters, then any cues such as visual aids, written instructions, or auditory signals which highlight the spatial aspects of a task will be most helpful during covert rehearsal periods. Furthermore, incorrect or irrelevant spatial cues could produce negative interference or biasing effects if they occur during covert rehearsal periods. In terms of the cost-effectiveness of training procedures, normally any procedure that allows the trainee to practise the task successfully without actually doing the job is cheaper. Given this rather general rule of thumb, training procedures may be designed which make use of covert practice to rehearse the spatial parameters within the task. It then becomes necessary to analyse, perhaps by task analysis, the various control parameters within a particular task. One possibility which makes use of the independence of spatial control parameters is that subjects might be given feedback of the force and temporal aspects of the task by means of actual practice while covertly rehearsing the spatial aspects of the task by imagery.

CONCLUSION

The course of skill acquisition is earmarked by a series of changes in which different strategies of performing are evident. These different styles have been described as a series of stages by Fitts who was also influential in advancing the hierarchical view of the organisation of skills. Changes both in perceptual and in motor aspects of skills appear to be important in accounting for skilled performance. Motor organisation is concerned with the construction of a number of structures brought together to produce appropriate responses. Perceptual organisation is concerned with developing appropriate models which will permit the performer to anticipate the appropriate response and its effects. One of the main effects of mental practice may be the result of development of a mental model.

Feedback in skilled and unskilled performance is not an all or nothing feature, instead, its function changes through the course of skill acquisition. Early in training, feedback, in various forms, is used to construct an adequate representation of what constitutes a good performance. The skilled performer uses feedback to check that the actions are appropriate and are being executed correctly. In some cases, a failure to make appropriate or sufficient checks can result in slips of action. This appears to be most important at branching points where one course of action is common to two different tasks, since it is here that slips of actions are most likely to occur.

The result of achieving skill in any task is an ability to perform the task in an autonomous, effortless, and fluent manner. As a consequence some processing capacity of the performer is freed, perhaps to devote to activity independent of the primary task or possibly allowing increased attention for monitoring other aspects of the task situation.

In the next chapter we also deal with the acquisition of skill, but we do so in the context of human development where it is necessary to take account of both maturation and experience. This means that we have to consider possible relationships between changes in the way the nervous system is organised, changes due to practice and interaction with the environment, and changes due to the development of the overall cognitive system of the child.

9

The Development
of Movement Control

Laurette Hay

INTRODUCTION

From conception, through birth, until the teens, human beings show continual anatomical changes that we call growth. These are obvious increases in body size and weight. Height is commonly used as an index of growth of the skeletal structure. There are also increases in volume and weight of the individual body organs including, of course, the brain.

At birth, the brain weighs about 300–350 g and it increases to 1250–1500 g in adults. Most of this growth occurs during the first year, when the weight increases from 350 g to about 1000 g. It is generally accepted that the complete population of neurons is already present at birth. A large part of the postnatal growth of the brain is ascribed to increases in the length of individual neurons and their dendrites, and to the myelination of the axons. Postmortem examinations have enabled researchers to follow myelogenesis at the various levels of the nervous system. For example, in the pyramidal tract the cross-sectional area of neurons at the bulbar level measures 5.4 mm² at 11 postnatal months, which is three times the area at birth (1.9 mm²) (Yakovlev, 1962). In the next section we consider the pattern of myelination in more detail. At this stage it suffices to note that although neural conduction can occur in unmyelinated fibres, it is more efficient and rapid once myelination has occurred.

As the child grows there are increases in muscle strength related to changes in muscle-fibre composition. Although there is no increase in the number of muscular fibres in a given muscle after birth, muscles become wider and longer because of the increase in size of the muscle fibres themselves. The growth in width and length of the fibres is due to an increase in the number and length of the myofibrils, which are the contractile units of the muscular fibre. However, more significant than increases in muscle strength are the changes in the patterns of movement employed by the newborn child. At birth, the neonate exhibits various stereotyped movement sequences in response to different stimuli. These sequences are largely automatic and involuntary and are termed *reflexes*. They are, however, more organized than the simple, monosynaptic reflexes discussed in Chapter 3 on the physiology of movement. Most of them can be classified according to their functional significance. The reflexes reveal innate patterns of sensorimotor coordination in the nervous system. Some of them are functional before birth, others unfold in an ordered sequence with the neonate's development to the extent that they can be used as a diagnostic tool in the neurological evaluation of babies.

With the emergence of voluntary patterns of movement clearly directed toward the achievement of goals, the reflex patterns disappear. An issue that we shall discuss later is the relation between reflex and voluntary movements in the development of motor control. Are they, for example, antagonistic or quite independent?

The main focus of this chapter will be to consider the significance of changes with age in voluntary movement control. What are the implications of improvements in the performance of certain tasks with age for our theories of motor control in adults?

MYELINATION

Maturation of the human CNS in terms of myelination takes place in a fixed sequence that depends partly on the anatomical level and partly on the function of the neural pathways. On one hand, the sequence of myelination begins in the phylogenetically older structures; the areas myelinated later in the maturational sequence tend to be those that are phylogenetically newer. Thus, subcortical systems are myelinated be-

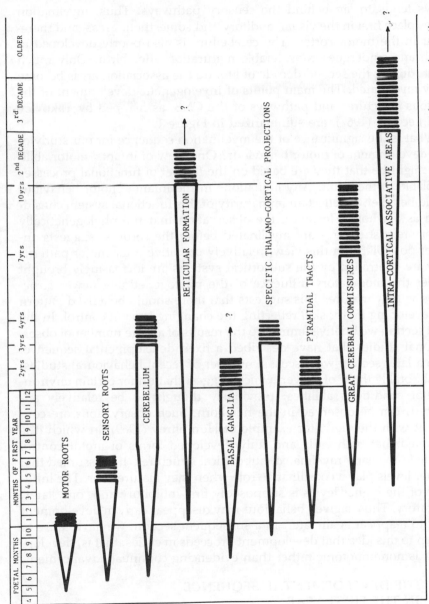

Figure 1. The myelination of neurons in the CNS as a function of age; the vertical stripes indicate the approximate time of completion of myelination. From "The myelogenetic cycles of regional maturation of the brain", by Yakovlev, P. I., Lecours, A. R. (1967). In Minkowski, A. (Ed.), *Regional development of the brain in early life*. Oxford: Blackwell. Adapted with permission.

fore cortical pathways. On the other hand, myelination of motor pathways tends to lag behind the sensory pathways. Thus, myelination takes place first in the visual, auditory and somesthetic areas, and thereafter in the motor cortex. The cerebellum is also poorly developed at birth and undergoes considerable maturation after birth. Only much later, during the second decade of life, do the association areas become fully myelinated. The main points of myelogenetic development of the various structures and pathways of the CNS, as mapped by Yakovlev and Lecours (1967), are summarized in Figure 1.

What is the significance of the myelination sequence for our study of the development of motor behaviour? One view of infants' motor abilities might be that they are based on the full set of functional processes available to the adult. Any limitations in the infant's motor behaviour could be taken to reflect an immaturity of this functional system considered as a whole. However, the observation that the phylogenetically older brain structures are myelinated before the cortices, suggests another possibility. In this view, relatively primitive early motor patterns that are controlled by the subcortical systems are increasingly brought under the modulatory influence of the phylogenetically newer structures as they mature. This suggests that there should be a fixed pattern of developing motor skill reflecting the changing level of control. In the next section we briefly summarize the results of a large number of observational studies that have described a fixed developmental sequence.

In a later section we discuss a number of recent behavioural studies, most notably those of Bower, which suggest that under certain environmental conditions abilities, previously thought to be relatively advanced, can be observed in the newborn. Such observations are consistent with the view, for example of Humphrey (1969), in which it is assumed that both early and fully developed forms of motor control reside in the early myelinated, subcortical structures. It is assumed that higher levels play a coordinative role when they mature later. The influence of the higher levels is supposedly first inhibitory and, only later, excitatory. Thus, a given behaviour may disappear early in development only to reappear again later. In a subsequent section, we have cause to return to this idea that development proceeds in cycles, that is, development is nonmonotonic rather than evidencing continual advancement.

THE DEVELOPMENTAL SEQUENCE
IN THE FIRST YEAR

Main Stages

The commonly recognised stages in the development of motor activity during the first year of life are summarized in Table 1. In this table

TABLE 1. Development of Motor Behaviour during the First Year of Life[a]

Age (months)	Motor control	Age (months)	Motor control
Birth		6	Lifts head up in supine position
	When supine head sideways predominates		Assists when pulled up by the hands
	Momentarily lifts head up when prone		Rolls from supine to prone position
	Reacts with mass motor activity to stimulation		When prone maintains head and chest up
	Hands kept fisted		Enjoys bouncing
			Partially supports weight in standing position
			Grasps palmarwise
2	When supine, holds head predominantly in midline	8	Accomplishes hand-knee position, begins to crawl
	When prone, holds head up		Begins to sit without support
	When held erect, head slightly wobbly		When supported attempts to stand briefly
	Range of movements in shoulder joints increased		Uses radial palmar grasp predominantly
	Keeps hands loosely fisted or opened		
	Holds a toy for a short time		
	Generalized motor reaction is diminished		Crawls with considerable skill
			Pulls up to standing position
			Pokes objects with index finger
4	Sits with support holding head steady	10	Begins to use pincer grasp
	Moves fingers, scratches		
	Reaches for a toy and grasps it		
	Moves extremities independently		
	Muscle tone is of normal quality		
			Walks if led
			May stand momentarily alone
			Quite skillful in pincer grasping
		12	Slowly releases cube into cup

[a]Adapted from Dekaban (1970).

significant advances in voluntary motor control are charted. The development proceeds according to two well-established principles (Gesell, 1946); the *cephalocaudal principle,* which states that there is progressive mastery starting with the muscles in the neck, followed by the arms, trunk, and legs successively, and the *proximodistal principle,* in which motor control progresses from the axis of the body to the peripheral muscles, that is, from the trunk to the limbs.

Associated with these increasing motor abilities are changes in muscle tone. At birth, muscle tone is characterised by a low level in the axial muscles and a high level in the limbs. The normal pattern of development is for the axial muscles to show increases of tone, which is probably important in allowing the infant to maintain postures against the influence of gravity. Tone in the distal muscles progressively decreases.

The newborn infant exhibits a variety of specific reflex reactions to different types of stimuli. Some of these involve several parts of the body while others are more local to the point of stimulation. Table 2 lists and describes some of these reflexes. They are called primitive reflexes because they are functional before or just after birth, and also because they are a distinctive feature of this early stage in development. The general trend is for the disappearance or attenuation, that is, reduction of amplitude, of most of these primitive reflexes during the first year of life. Some other reflexes do not disappear and may be elicited in adults, such as the palpebral reflex, which is a blink response to a sudden tactile, visual, or auditory stimulation.

The main postural and locomotor stages, which are directly related to the development of axial muscle tone, are the progressive righting of the head and trunk, and then the upright standing position which leads to assisted and later independent walking, after the end of the first year. These activities are anticipated in the neonate by certain reflexes, such as the supporting reflex for standing or the stepping reflex for walking behaviour. Nevertheless, the change from automatic, reflex-patterned behaviour to voluntary behaviour is based on construction of motor programs that are not limited to the distinct fragments of behaviour that constitute primitive reflexes. The main improvement in these new motor programs is the ability they confer on the infant to anticipate and thus to react more rapidly to external perturbations.

The disappearance of the primitive reflexes is consistent with the previously noted increasing myelination of the cerebral cortex at a time when the subcortical areas are already well myelinated. A lower level, more primitive reflex organization of motor behaviour is inhibited under the emerging influence of the cerebral cortex. The cortex is subsequently able to initiate and regulate activity of lower levels in a coordinated

TABLE 2. Suppression of Primitive Reflexes during the First Year of Life[a]

Age (months)	Specific reflex reactions[b]	Age (months)	Specific reflex reactions	Age (months)	Specific reflex reactions
Birth	Tonic neck reflexes Moro reaction Sucking reflex Rooting reflex Tongue retrusion reflex Hand grasping reaction Supporting reaction Stepping reflex Indefinite plantar extensor Reciprocal kick reaction Auropalpebral reflex Vertical suspension, head up: the legs are flexed Vertical suspension, head down: hips slightly flexed	4	Vertical suspension head down: hips still slightly flexed Moro and tonic neck reflexes either absent or in a rudimentary form Sucking reflex Stepping reaction Reciprocal kick reaction Indefinite plantar extensor Vertical suspension head down: legs almost straight Vertical suspension head up: legs mainly extended	8	Well developed "falling and rising" reaction Vertical suspension head up: keeps legs straight Vertical suspension head down: extends arms to the floor, spine hyperextended Sucking reflex Indefinite plantar extensor Reciprocal kicking reaction disappears
2	Moro reaction, tonic neck reflexes, hand grasp reflex and tongue retrusion reflex gradually disappear Still present are Sucking reflex Rooting reflex Reciprocal kick reaction Stepping reflex Indefinite plantar extensor Vertical suspension head up: legs still slightly flexed	6	Sucking reflex Stepping reaction "Rising and falling" reaction Vertical suspension head up: legs straight Vertical suspension head down: extends arms to the floor, spine hyperextended Sucking reflex Indefinite plantar extensor	10	Permanent type of "falling and rising" reaction Landau reaction is demonstrated for the first time Vertical suspension head down: extends arms to the floor
				12	Sucking reflex Indefinite plantar extensor Sucking reflex becomes less pronounced Plantar response is predominantly flexor The Landau reaction is well developed Head down suspension: extends hands to the floor

[a] Adapted from Dekaban (1970).

[b] *Tonic-neck reflex:* turning the head right or left produces an extension of the arm of the same side and a flexion of the arm of the opposite arm. *Moro reaction:* Startle reaction to an intensive stimulation (loud noise, sudden loss of head support) which involves throwing both arms away from the body with the fingers spread, followed by bringing them back together, often accompanied by extension and adduction of the legs. *Rooting reflex:* Touching the infant's face produces head movements bringing his mouth into contact with the source of stimulation. *Tongue retrusion reflex:* Pushing out solid food when placed on the anterior part of the mouth. *Hand grasping reaction:* A pressure on the palm produces a closing of the fingers. *Supporting reaction:* Extension of the legs elicited by a pressure on the sole of the feet. *Stepping reflex:* Stepping movements which occur when the infant is held upright with his feet in contact with a surface (walking reflex). *Indefinite plantar extensor:* Fanning and extension of the toes elicited by stimulation of the sole of the foot (Babinski reflex). *Reciprocal kick reaction:* Pedaling movements with simultaneous flexion and extension of both legs. *Landau reaction:* When the infant is supported by the examiner's hand in prone position, he holds up his head and bends up his spine, with complete extension of the thighs.

fashion. This viewpoint helps explain why a reflex can disappear only to ultimately reappear in a voluntary form, as is the case in the stepping reflex. The cortical connections that are made first are inhibitory. This results in disappearance of the behaviour until excitatory connections, allowing complete cortical control, are established.

Primitive Reflex Patterns and Voluntary Activity

The above view, of an intimate link between early primitive reflexes and voluntary motor behaviour, is not accepted by all writers. McDonnell (1979), for example, has even suggested that voluntary movement has a completely separate neurological basis from reflex movement. He argued this on the grounds that if one considers lateralisation of activity, up to 12 weeks of age the left hand is more often moved and is better oriented toward a visual stimulus than is the right hand. This is the opposite of the dominance pattern seen with neonate reflexes. Observations on later evolution of laterality in relation to the emergence and development of visually guided reaching during the second half of the first year, led McDonnell to hypothesise that this new behaviour is distinct from reflexes, and, instead, is on a continuum with earlier non-reflexive, instrumental behaviour. An idea that can be seen as related to McDonnell's view is that at any stage voluntary movement in the newborn would be smoother and more coordinated if it were not for the intrusive or competitive nature of the well-established reflexive behaviour. This notion is developed in a later section of this chapter which discusses liberated motor behaviour.

A more generally accepted view is that of Piaget. For Piaget (1952), the point of departure is the set of innate reflexes functioning at birth. Early on, the operation of reflexes brings the organism into contact with the environment which leads to progressive modification of innate activity. This interaction is described in two complementary processes: assimilation and accommodation. The term *assimilation* refers to the stimulus ensemble that sets the activity in motion and to which the activity is directed. Integration of any stimulating object into activity is related to a tendency to repeat the activity, which is another feature of assimilation. *Accommodation* is defined as the modification of the reflex as a result of contact with the external world. This modification first involves consolidation of the reflex by repetition (without which it would simply drop out of the repertoire). Second, it involves increasing efficiency of reflex activity, and finally, coordination between reflexes. An illustrative example is provided by the sucking reflex that is initially only elicited passively by lip stimulation but which gives way to active exploration for the mother's breast. The interplay between the processes of assimilation and accommodation determines the course of development and continues until a state of equilibrium is attained.

From the piagetian viewpoint, exercising a reflex prevents its disappearance and in addition encourages the later development of a corresponding voluntary behaviour. Supporting evidence comes from experiments on training of the stepping reflex by André-Thomas and Dargassies (1952) and is confirmed by Zelazo, Zelazo, and Kolb (1972). While it is widely accepted that reflexes can be trained, through reinforcement procedures, the behavioural significance of this is still a subject of debate. Zelazo (1983), for example, considers his findings consistent with the view that, with practice, newborn stepping progresses from a reflexive to an instrumental response, which implies that the task itself is intrinsically a rewarding experience. Increased stepping involves a higher level of control and forms the basis for independent walking. Thus, he considers the disappearance of reflexive stepping a consequence of child-rearing practices that limit opportunities for exercise, rather than an effect of maturation in which there is increasing inhibition of lower centres by the cortex. Nevertheless, experimental and crosscultural studies indicate that despite prolonged practice there appears to be a maturational limit to the onset of independent walking. Zelazo suggests that the constraint is cognitive in origin and supports this by noting the emergence of a number of specific cognitive abilities and resulting motivational changes during the period when independent walking appears.

This cognitive interpretation of the development of locomotion has been challenged by Thelen (1983) on the basis of her studies of spontaneous kicking in infants, which she considers in many respects similar to the stepping reflex. She argued that, in spite of an important cognitive transition at the end of the first year of life, cognitive requirements are not necessary to explain the onset of walking, which is mostly the province of mechanisms phylogenetically more primitive than the human cerebral cortex. She proposed that development of locomotion requires partly unknown biodynamic changes interacting with a subcortical neural substrate. A detailed experimental analysis of kicking showed that muscle strength may not develop synchronously with increasing muscle mass. She suggested that this may limit or abolish behavioural expression of a reflex at times of rapid physical growth and in situations involving strength. So the retention of the stepping reflex with practice may be simply a compensatory effect of physical training, which could be produced either with experimental exercise or with natural child-rearing practices as shown in crosscultural studies. Thelen provided additional support to her alternative interpretation. First, she mentioned experimental evidence that contradicts the association of stepping with pleasurable feelings in the neonate. Second, she reported experiments in which kicks were actually used as operants in instrumental conditioning, for example, infants learned to use kicks to control an overhead mobile. But in such cases it took only few minutes to establish conditioning, revealed by significant increases over baseline kick rates. The increases in step rate in Zelazo's training experiments occurred over many weeks and this, she argued, is more consistent with a gradual increase in strength than with an immediately established conditioning in the operant task. As a conclusion, she emphasized the gradual rather than the discontinuous nature of locomotor development. There is a continuity between the early stepping reflex and later independent walking, which involves integration of subcortical pattern-generating centres with the neural substrate for control of posture and balance. In addition, there are important changes in body proportions, bone, and muscle strength.

Environmental Influences

The importance of the role of the environment in determining the development of visuomotor abilities has been demonstrated by White (1970). He studied visuomotor development in babies exposed to various experimental manipulations of their environment. His work reflects the same kind of interest as the now classic studies of Held and Hein on the effects of sensorimotor deprivation in baby cats and monkeys (Hein & Held, 1967). White showed that the rate at which visuomotor coordination develops can be significantly retarded or accelerated depending on whether the individual is exposed to an impoverished or an enriched sensory environment. He conducted his experiments on infants reared in an institution that provided a relatively poor sensory and motor environment (the infants were laid in supine position most of the time, in homogenous visual surroundings). Rearing conditions were varied in a number of ways. Figure 2 contrasts the development of reaching in a control group with that for a group exposed to enrichment conditions specifically designed to hasten visual discovery of the hands. In the enriched group two attractive pacifiers were placed on each side of the crib until day 68. This group was then given improved mobility and brighter visual surroundings. The results show the plasticity of several components of sensorimotor development, that is, there is a dependence on environmental conditions. Among the prerequisites for the

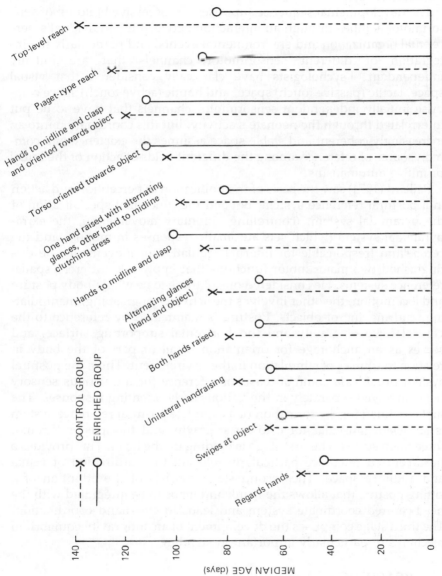

Figure 2. The effect of environmental conditions on the median age of first occurrence of a variety of responses related to reaching. Data redrawn from White (1970).

CONTROL GROUP

ENRICHED GROUP

Top-level reach

Piaget-type reach

Hands to midline and clasp and oriented towards object

Torso oriented towards object

One hand raised with alternating glances, other hand to midline clutching dress

Hands to midline and clasp

Alternating glances (hand and object)

Both hands raised

Unilateral handraising

Swipes at object

Regards hands

MEDIAN AGE (days)

140 120 100 80 60 40 20 0

normal developmental sequence, watching the hand occupies a place that appears to be critical. It leads to a developmental sequence which we describe later.

The developmental sequence supposes a progressive build up of sensorimotor abilities through an interaction between the individual's perceptual organization and environmental events, and particularly the integration of different sensorimotor channels that are initially independent. Psychologists have classically considered that visual space, tactile (passive touch) space, and haptic (active touch) space comprise initially independent sensorimotor channels that have to be put interrelated through the neonate's activity. But this coordination into an increasingly coherent and stable space assumes the existence of a common source of reference among the different fields of action of the initial primitive automatisms.

Paillard (1974) saw the basis of the unification of perception and action in a postural reference system. Beyond the functional specialization of the pyramidal system, (controlling voluntary movements), the extrapyramidal system (which sets automatic responses in motion) and the cerebellum (responsible for internal regulation of movement), he distinguished two major motor functions that imply two different spatial reference systems. He considered one of these to be whole-body posture and locomotion, the other involves the activities of grasping, manipulating, and moving of objects. Posture is maintained by reference to the vertical force of gravity and the horizontal supporting surface, and serves as an anchorage for orientation of all or part of the body in relation to sources of stimulation in the environment. Thus, the postural system provides a common basis of reference for the various sensory fields involved separately in the various early orienting responses. The first condition for the formation of a complete postural reference system is sufficient muscular force to resist gravity and this passes through three main stages. The first stage is holding up the head. This provides a head-centred reference particularly relevant to coordination of visual and auditory space. The second stage consists of the adoption of a sitting posture that allows the trunk and limbs to be integrated with the head-centred coordinate system and leads to eye–hand coordination. The third stage comprises the development of an antigravity equilibrium mechanism, particularly important in standing.

REACHING

Up to this point we have attempted to review development of all kinds of motor behaviour in the first year of life. Our approach was mainly descriptive. We are now going to focus our attention on a particular skill, but a very common one—reaching for objects in the environment. By studying the development of this skill in detail, we hope to probe the development of information processing. Why have we selected reaching as a model for the development in other abilities? Phylogenetically, prehensile capability in primates and in humans may be considered as one of the most characteristic developments of this branch. Moreover, as Koupernik (1954) indicated, there is a higher correlation between prehension and oriented development than between, for example, walking and development. Finally, during the first months of life, interactions between the infant and its environment mainly involve the hand.

In its fully developed form, reaching behaviour is comprised of several components, as suggested by Paillard and Beaubaton (1978). In their analysis the first component is visual capture of the object by a saccadic movement of the eye to bring the image on the fovea. At this time information is available about the object's spatial position that will be needed in the selection of direction and distance of movement of the hand toward the object. With the image on the fovea, the second component involves visual analysis leading to perceptual identification of the object and consequent elaboration of a plan of action. Anticipatory adaptation to the object's physical characteristics, such as size, shape, and weight, can then be translated into an appropriate posture for the hand and fingers. Manual capture of the object that we may identify as a third component can now take place. This is comprised of ballistic transport of the hand toward the object according to a predetermined trajectory with terminal adjustments relative to the object guided by visual feedback. The fourth and last component in Paillard and Beaubaton's analysis is manipulation of the object. It begins with tactile contact in a form determined by the anticipatory hand posture. This is followed by carrying out the intended action with the object for which vision may be required to varying degrees.

Although it isn't easy to find an unequivocal statement in the literature on the development of reaching, most authors agree that babies achieve true, voluntary reaching at about 5 months. Before this, reflex reactions are seen that may include, separately, the components of reaching. Even though the development is not complete at 5 months (other changes will ultimately occur), this age is considered the completion of a first important developmental cycle. The main lines of the development of the neonate's visuomotor reactions in the presence of an object are summarized in Table 3, on the basis of the studies of McGraw (1941) and White, Castle, and Held (1964).

TABLE 3. Main Lines of Visuomotor Infants' Reactions in the Presence of an Object

Age (months)	Visuomotor reactions to object
Birth	no focussing, no clear patterning of objects tactually elicited grasp
1	tonic neck reflex position poor focussing, no attention to object, jerky ocular pursuit focussing, attentional reactions to object, continuous ocular pursuit shifts in activity during object fixation
2	decrease of tonic neck reflex in intensity swiping with hand fisted tactually elicited grasp continues frequent fixation of the hand decrease of tonic neck reflex in frequency focussing nearly at an adult like level abrupt decrease in activity when object is presented hand raising toward object with alternative glances
3	disappearance of tonic neck reflex sustained hand regard bilateral hand activity, hands clasped over the midline and occasionally glanced at hands clasped over the midline under visual control predominance of bilateral responses disappearance of tactually elicited grasp

4	bilateral responses with alternate glances
	occasional "Piaget type reach" (one hand raising toward object
	   with alternate glances from hand to object)
	
	"Piaget type reach" with anticipatory grasp
	emergence of top level reaching (rapid approach of the hand with
	   anticipatory opening)

5	disappearance of "Piaget type reach" predominance of top level reaching

White described the development of reaching as follows. From birth, an innate eye–head component allows the infant to localize and track objects with the head and eyes. This is separate from a tactile–manual component evidenced in the grasp reflex. At 2 to 3 months, development of visual perception encourages infants to attend to environmental objects particularly their own hands that they contemplate at length. This visual capture of the hand upsets the initial isolation of the two components and is closely followed by the appearance of a form of reaching, *swiping*. This implies a new capacity for localization that coordinates the eye–head movements with those of the arm. However, at this stage, grasping is governed exclusively by tactile stimulation without visual control. The more advanced form of reaching that then follows (hand approach with alternate glances between object and hand) indicates a matching of the eye–head and hand–object visuomotor systems.

In the following stage (3–4 months), the co-occurrence of reciprocal grasping of the hands in the midline, which is important in developing tactile–motor sensibility, and direct vision of the movements establishes coordination between vision and touch that then becomes centred on interactions with objects (4–5 months). Finally, the infant succeeds in integrating various patterns of response coordinating them via intersection at the object to which they are applied all together. The alternate glances between hand and object combined with a direct approach followed by slow grasp of the object reflects integration of the eye–hand and eye–object visuomotor systems with the tactile motor system of the hand. At this time there are beginnings of visually directed grasp. The end of this stage consists of complete integration of anticipatory grasp into a rapid and direct reach from a point outside the visual field.

Liberated Voluntary Motor Activity

Although the above description suggests that the neonate is incapable of coordinated reaching, recent research by Bower (1974) has shown that the newborn can make reaching responses with capture of an object. However, this surprising observation requires very specific conditions: the baby must be wide awake but, most important, it must be either seated or held in an upright position to allow movements of head and arms that are otherwise inhibited if the baby lies on its back. Under these conditions Bower observed an average of 13 reaches per minute, al-

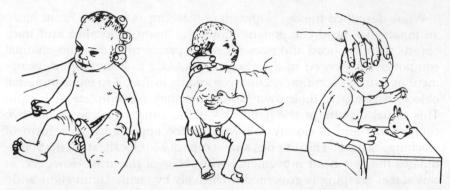

Figure 3. Manipulation of neonate posture to obtain "liberated" motor activity. From *Evaluation neurologique du nouveau-né et du nourrisson*, by Amiel-Tison, C., Grenier, A. (1980). Paris: Masson. Adapted with permission.

though in more recent studies (Di Franco, Muir, & Dodwell, 1978) much lower rates were observed.

Bower's observations were corroborated in an interesting study by Amiel-Tison and Grenier (1980). They presented evidence for a previously undocumented form of motor behaviour in the neonate and in infants of less than 2 months. They termed it *liberated motor behaviour* because it emerged once involuntary activity associated with reflexes (particularly those associated with head position) had been inhibited. This inhibition was obtained in a progressive manner following a number of subtle manoeuvres, including three main phases (represented in Figure 3), the essential one being to hold the newborn in a sitting position with a hand on the back of the neck, and then on the top of the skull, in order to stabilize the head in a suitable position. Once positioned like this, the typical primitive obligatory movement patterns gradually disappeared, and a new distribution of muscle tone appeared. At the same time spontaneous movements appeared slower and more coordinated, rather like those of older children. The existence of more gentle and coordinated movements than the abrupt activity seen in babies a little older and the interruption of the gentler movements by stereotyped reflexes has also been remarked on by other authors (Trevarthen, Hubley, & Sheeran, 1975).

An important characteristic of these early reaching responses is that they seem to be oriented toward the object rather than being simple extension reactions without a goal. In an experiment in which an object (an orange foam rubber sphere, 35 mm in diameter, placed at 190 mm from the infant) was presented to neonates at one of five different positions (at the median line, 30 ° or 60 ° to the left or right of centre), Bower, Broughton, and Moore (1970a) observed that 40% of reaches touched the object and another 30% came within 5 ° (15 mm) of the object.

In a more recent paper, Ruff and Halton (1978) observed lower degrees of success in reaching. They also found lower rates of responding than reported by Bower. Ruff and Halton concluded that contact with an object by the infant was a matter of chance. A method inspired by signal detection theory was proposed by McDonnell (1979) in an attempt to resolve this discrepancy in findings. The method consisted of establishing the distribution of hand positions when presented with a stimulus, as if it were background noise. Then, after the stimulus has been moved through some angle, a new distribution of hand positions was determined and treated as if it were signal plus background noise. A test of statistical significance was then performed to show whether the arm movements were oriented to the target. This method has the advantage of not setting arbitrary criteria for saying whether the hand is near the target. It also eliminates the contribution of individual differences in the starting position of the hand or in the general level of activity. McDonnell's results tended to support Bower's position, but emphasised the need for greater rigour in measurement.

Anticipation of Movement Consequences

Bower (1970a) attempted to show that the early reaching reaction includes an expectation for the sensory consequences of contact with the object. The importance of this is that it would, even more than the movement direction, differentiate between reaching and simple, unaimed arm extension as a reaction to the presence of the object. Bower exposed newborn babies to a virtual image of an object so that stimulus-directed movements could not make physical contact. The infants showed greater frustration (as measured by the number of consecutive cries) with movements to virtual images than to real objects, supporting the idea that there is tactile expectancy associated with the movement.

Another point recorded by Bower is that reaching movements were usually unimanual, and some of them were made with an anticipatory grasp that could indicate that the infants were taking account of object size. This anticipation involved both an opening and partial closing of the hand entirely in advance of contact with the object. This postural

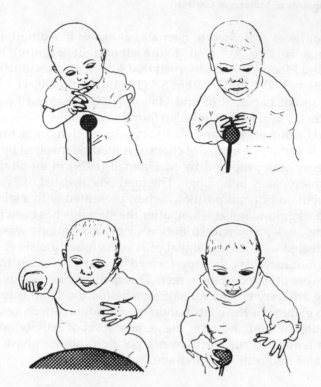

Figure 4. Examples of responses in the presence of an object. From "Visually preadapted constituents of manipulatory action", by Bruner, J. S., Koslowski, B. (1972). *Perception*, 1, 3–14. Adapted with permission.

anticipation stands in strong contrast to the initial stereotyped closing movements triggered by the tactile stimulus of placing an object in the hand of the newborn.

Other characteristics of early responses to objects have been studied, but usually in infants slightly older than 2 months. A study by Bruner and Koslowski (1972) was devoted to showing that responses to an object seem to take some account of size. During the experiment, the infant was seated in an upright position and presented with a ball of either small (30 mm) diameter or large (250 mm) diameter. The responses were filmed and divided into two broad categories. Some of them are represented in Figure 4. The results showed that small objects more frequently elicited responses adapted (in terms of the degree of opening and shaping of the hands) to the prehensible object, such as, proximal activity in the midline and hovering near the object, grasping, and adduction to the midline. In contrast, large objects more frequently

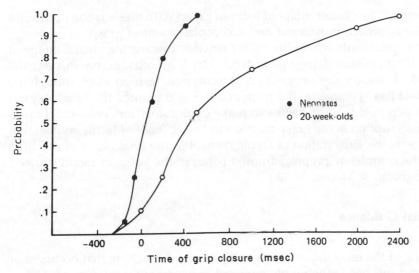

Figure 5. Closing of grip relative to time of arrival of the hand at an object. From *Development in infancy*, by Bower, T. G. R. (1974). San Francisco: Freeman. Reprinted with permission.

elicited responses appropriate to an object that could be touched but not held, such as, swiping or breaking away from midline activity of the hand. It thus appears that infants' responses are organized on the basis of visual information about object size and prehensibility.

The set of data that we have just reviewed leads to the idea that early reaching movements of the neonate can be relatively elaborate, taking account of various types of information obtained through the visual system. Indeed, much of this research was originally motivated by the desire to demonstrate that even early on the infant has a good visual appreciation of the environment despite having had little physical experience by which touch could have "educated" vision.

By about 5 months reaching has become more accurate and is not restricted to particular postural conditions as shown by Bower (1974). Bower also noted that by this age there is a change in the temporal relation between the approach movement and grasping of the object. Closing of the grip after arrival of the hand at the object occurs later in the 5-month-old than in the neonate. As shown in Figure 5 the median latency for the 5-month-old is 450 msec after contact whereas in the neonate it is zero msec. Thus, there is a change from an anticipation of grasp that is accurate in the sense that it coincides exactly with arrival at the object, to a better-adapted form of grasp with dissociation of the end of the approach movement and accomplishment of grasp.

In experiments where the infant reaches toward the virtual image of an object another change is evidenced by 5 months. Before this age the hand closes on the image in a stereotyped fashion even though no contact has been made. But from about 5 or 6 months the hand stays in the open position and begins to make exploratory movements. There is an interruption of the grasp reaction in the absence of tactile contact that suggests the substitution of tactile control in the final phase of reaching for the completely preprogrammed reach of the younger infant (Bower, Broughton, & Moore, 1970b).

Visual Guidance

One of the most important developments in reaching that occurs at or around this age is the involvement of concurrent visual control. This is evidenced by the fact that when a reaching movement misses the object it can be corrected during the movement. The hand, instead of being withdrawn before returning toward the object, moves onto a correct course thus reducing, under visual control, the distance between it and the object. Wishart, Bower, and Dunkeld (1978) showed that up to 5 months there is no difference in the probability that an initial attempt at reaching at an object is successful in darkness or with the light on. However, at 7 months, the probability of success is significantly higher if the light is on so the arm can be seen (Figure 6).

Visual guidance during movement allows increased precision so that reaching for the object will more often be successful, even if the motor programme for the ballistic movement is faulty or if some external factor causes the ballistic movement to be misdirected. One way of inducing a faulty ballistic movement is to make the subject wear prismatic goggles that laterally displace the apparent position of the object relative to the body. This trick was used by McDonnell (1975) to differentiate between visually guided movements and movements triggered ballistically on the basis of visual information in infants between the ages of 4 and 10 months. Overall, he observed that the accuracy of reaching was little affected by wearing prisms, even in the youngest infants. In addition, the analysis allowed McDonnell to distinguish several forms of trajectory correction, indicating an improvement in the precision of visual guidance over the period studied. But on the basis of the change with age in the percentage difference between the conditions with and without prisms, it seems that visual guidance reaches a peak at 7 months. After

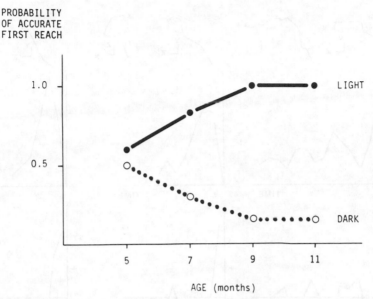

PROBABILITY
OF ACCURATE
FIRST REACH

Figure 6. The accuracy of reaching for an object in the light or dark as a function of age. Data from Wishart *et al.* (1978).

this age failures become more numerous under the prism conditions than under normal conditions. This peak in visual guidance at 7 months has been corroborated by further studies of McDonnell and Abraham (1981) on prism adaptation in infants of 5 through 10 months.

McDonnell (1979) proposed that there is a relation between the evolution of visual guidance and shifts in reaching documented by Halverson (1931) between the ages of 4 and 12 months. Three main changes were found in approach trajectories reflecting a proximodistal segmentation, that is, a progressive involvement of the joints of the arm in approaching the object. First, with the shoulder alone (sweeping); second, with the shoulder and partly the elbow (parabolic); and last, with all the joints of the arm together (straight). McDonnell suggested the coincidence in time of occurrence of visual guidance and the parabolic approach at 7 months are functionally related, the latter reflecting ongoing corrections in trajectory path. Furthermore, he suggested that the earlier sweeping movements of the arm (4–5 months) reflected an immature ballistic approach, whereas the subsequent straight approach (9 months) was based on a return to an improved ballistic transport component.

Particularly detailed studies of the transport component of the reaching movements of infants between the ages of 3 and 8 months have been carried out by von Hofsten (1979, 1980). He examined each reaching

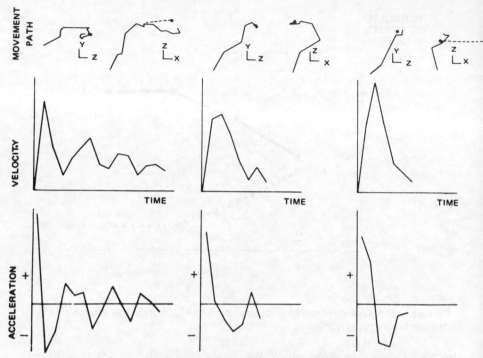

Figure 7. Subcomponents in movement: velocity and acceleration profiles for three different movements showing decreasing number of movement elements. From "Development of visually directed reaching: The approach phase", by Hofsten, C. von. (1979). *Journal of Human Movement Studies, 5,* 160–178. Reprinted with permission.

movement to determine whether submovements, each consisting of a period of acceleration followed by deceleration, could be identified in the approach to the target. Figure 7 shows three different reaching movements comprising four, two, and one such submovements or steps. Von Hofsten found that the average number of submovements in each reaching movement declined with age. In the younger babies the steps were all of similar duration but later on the duration of the first step, as a proportion of the total movement, increased (see Figure 8A). Concomitant with the increase in relative duration of the first step, this step accounted for an increasing proportion of the distance covered by the reaching movement (see Figure 8B). It was also noted that the first step was increasingly the step with the greatest acceleration.

One interpretation of von Hofsten's results is that over this period of months the children come to depend more on a preplanned, ballistic mode of control in approaching the object. The question is why do the younger children not use the large first step with subsequent smaller

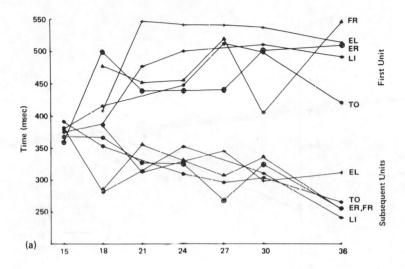

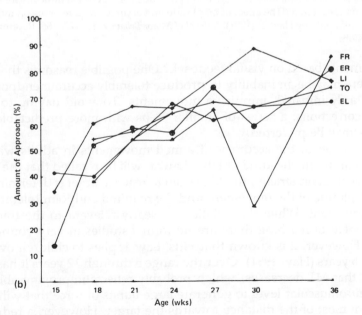

Figure 8. (a) Duration of first and later movement elements as a function of age. (b) Proportion of movement completed in the first movement element as a function of age. From ''Development of visually directed-reaching: The approach phase'', by Hofsten, C. von. (1979). *Journal of Human Movement Studies, 5,* 160–178. Reprinted with permission.

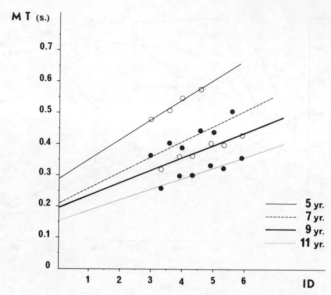

Figure 9. Movement time as a function of the index of movement difficulty for children of various ages. From "The effect of amplitude and accuracy requirements on movement time in children", by Hay, L. (1981). *Journal of Motor Behavior*, 13, 177–186. Reprinted with permission.

movements based on visual feedback? One possible reason is that early on there may be an inability to produce tolerably accurate endpoints to voluntarily initiated, impulsive movements. To avoid having to make large corrections, a series of smaller steps with more predictable endpoints may be preferred.

In Chapter 3, the accuracy of aimed movements in adults was discussed under the heading of Fitts' Law. It will be recalled that the speed of movement or, strictly, the MT taken to reach a target is determined by the amplitude of the movement and the required endpoint tolerance for the movement. While this relation is clearly relevant to the transport component of reaching there are no formal studies in very young children. However, it is known that Fitts' Law applies to children over the age of 5 years (Hay, 1981). Over the range 5 through 12 years it has been found that MT decreases, which probably reflects improving ability at the neuromuscular level to generate large bursts of force that will carry the arm most of the distance towards the target. However, a reduction with age in the slope of the function is also noted sometimes (see Figure 9). One interpretation of this reduction in slope is that not only are the movements of older children more rapid, but they are also made more accurately for any given distance. Suppose we assume (see Chapter 3) that movement control in the Fitts' task consists of a large ballistic initial movement with subsequent correction or corrections based on visual feedback. It is interesting to speculate that even beyond the age of 5 years, children's motor control is still improving as a result of reducing variability in the large initial impulsive component.

Our discussion of the development of reaching has taken us from a consideration of the temporal coordination of hand grasp and arm transport to a quite general analysis of the accuracy of aimed movements. To close this section we return to the relation between hand grasp and transport in reaching as recently studied by Wing and Fraser (1982). These authors had the opportunity to take film records of reaching movements of a 13-year-old girl who had worn an artificial, mechanically operated hand since the age of 2 years. Although reaching with her artificial (left) hand was slower than with her natural (right) hand the interesting finding was that there were certain similarities between the hands in the formation of grasp during approach to the object (see Figure 10).

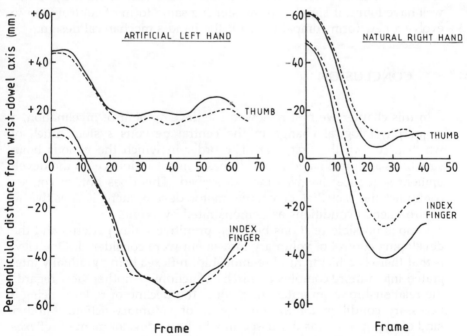

Figure 10. Position of the thumb and index finger relative to the line of approach to an object for the natural versus artificial hand. From "The contribution of the thumb to reaching movements", by Wing, A. M. and Fraser, C. (1983). *Quarterly Journal of Experimental Psychology, 35A,* 297–309. Reprinted with permission.

The figure shows that approximately two-thirds of the way through reaching movements, the index finger begins to move inward (relative to an axis between the wrist and the object being approached). However, the thumb is relatively stable. In the artificial hand, the mechanical design of the hand was such that the observed stability of the thumb could only be achieved by an awkward movement of the arm. Why, then, did the girl stabilize the thumbs? Wing and Fraser suggest that visual feedback for guidance of the hand toward the object in reaching is most simply provided by a point on the hand near the object, in this case the thumb. So it simplifies visual-feedback processing if the thumb is stabilised relative to the line the hand (or the wrist) takes in approaching the object.

The interesting issue from the point of view of development is how the girl arrived at this mode of control of the artificial hand, a mode that worked against the simplest way of operating the hand (given the mechanical design)? One possibility is that the stability of the thumb on the natural right hand in approaching the object was fully developed by the second year of life. When fitted with the artificial left hand the girl may well have found it simpler to transfer the same form of control than to evolve a new form compatible with the hand's mechanical design.

CONCLUSION

In this chapter we first reviewed the development of myelination, a major physiological change in the central nervous system much of which occurs in the first year. The order in which the various brain structures are myelinated probably has a major influence on the development sequence that was then described. This does not, of course, contradict the fact that perceptual-motor development is sensitive to environmental conditions as demonstrated by White.

Various possible relations between primitive reflex patterns and the developing control of voluntary movement were considered. One view is that there is a hierarchical relationship, reflexes being gradually integrated into a more complex hierarchy of actions. Another view regards the relationship as an antagonistic one, the decline of reflexes being a necessary condition for the emergence of voluntary action. Another kind of hypothesis was discussed in which the development of reflexes and of voluntary actions are considered quite distinct processes with independent origin and evolution. Despite this divergence of views of the relationship, the attenuation of reflex-patterned activity implies an increasing psychological differentiation between the subject and sources of stimulation and confers an increase in freedom of action (the subject can react or not react). This transition also implies an increase in the subject's capacity to modulate actions according to their sensory consequences. It is accompanied by a perceptual unification for the subject, in the sense that there is an integration of information over the different sensory-motor channels involved in primitive activity.

Another source of evidence about the relationship between primitive reflexes and voluntary control of movement is the study of damage to higher levels in the CNS. In the next chapter several of the consequences of brain damage are discussed. One of these, spasticity, is often thought of as comprising an abnormal balance of reflex and voluntary control. Other disorders that are considered relate to the planning and execution of movement as discussed in earlier chapters.

10

Disorders of Movement

Alan M. Wing

INTRODUCTION

The discussion of the physiology of movement control in Chapter 2 introduced some of the major motor structures of the brain including the cerebral motor cortex, the basal ganglia, and the cerebellum. In this chapter we explore the contribution of these CNS structures to motor control by considering some of consequences of their being damaged. Much of the research in this area has aimed at providing evidence that a particular structure is involved in a particular function. Often there are extensive debates in the literature about what the functionally important pathways between different brain structures are. These are of course interesting issues. However, from the psychological point of view there is a second issue that is at least as important. Can the various movement disorders be interpreted within the theoretical framework for movement control that has been developed from studies of normal subjects? In studying normal movement control in the other chapters of this book, the idea has been introduced that control of movement involves various functionally distinct processes. These include processes involved in preparation for movement, on the one hand, and in the execution of movement, on the other. Included in the first category are processes for

269

THE PSYCHOLOGY OF HUMAN MOVEMENT

the construction of motor programs specifying which effectors will be used, with what level of activity, and with what timing. Execution processes determine the running of the program and, for example, the allocation of attention to feedback. One of the goals of this chapter is to consider damage to the CNS in terms of the selective deficits they may produce in the control of movement and to determine whether these deficits may be identified with different functional processes. In this respect, the present chapter represents the application of many of the theoretical ideas developed earlier in this book.

PATHOLOGICAL CHANGES IN THE CNS

In cases of impaired movement control associated with diseases of the CNS the immediate cause of impairment is a lesion. In a clinical context a lesion refers to any kind of failure in neural function. The purpose of this section is to provide some insight into the nature of CNS lesions, and in the next we briefly note some of the clinical procedures used to help identify the site of a lesion in the CNS. For a more complete treatment of these topics the reader should refer to a recent neurology text such as that by Adams and Victor (1981).

Lesions in the nervous system that result in impaired movement can arise in a number of ways. The most common of these is some kind of failure in the brain's blood supply, a cerebral vascular accident (CVA). The term *stroke* is used for the sudden onset of neurological symptoms resulting from disruption of the vascular system in the CNS. More than any other organ of the body, the brain is critically dependent on an adequate supply of oxygenated blood, which it receives through a complex arterial network. A stroke may occur anywhere in the vascular supply to the CNS including the cerebral cortex, cerebellum, midbrain, brainstem, and spinal cord. Depending on which part of the brain's vascular system malfunctions, different sets of symptoms arise. The study of the effects of stroke has proved one of the more instructive approaches to the analysis of human brain function. Certainly, cases of stroke comprise a major part of the neuropsychological literature.

There are two main classes of stroke; occlusive and haemorrhagic. The more common is the *occlusive stroke* in which there is a loss of blood supply affecting a substantial number of neurons. The most common cause is an embolism, which may be a blood clot or other plug brought through the blood and forced into a smaller blood vessel where it obstructs circulation. The area of CNS tissue left without blood supply, which may comprise *white matter* (myelinated axons) or *grey matter* (cell bodies, dendrites, unmyelinated axons), undergoes neuronal degeneration and is called an *infarct*. At the level of the individual neuron, if the cell body loses its blood supply, the entire neuron degenerates. If blood fails to reach the region through which the axon passes, the axon but not the cell body will degenerate. In the CNS, although there may be a degree of regeneration of an axon from its parent cell body, the original synaptic connections are not remade.

The middle cerebral artery is particularly susceptible to occlusion. This artery includes in its supply territory grey matter of the central motor and sensory strips, the temporal and parietal cortex, the thalamus, and basal ganglia as well as white matter of, for example, the important efferent and afferent pathways of the internal capsule (see Figure 1). Depending on which branch or branches of the middle cerebral artery are affected by an occlusion, the resulting infarct may produce paralysis as a result of involvement of the precentral motor strip of the cortex or the efferent pathways in the internal capsule. Such lesions are often termed *upper-motoneuron lesions* as a contrast to lesions involving neurons synapsing with the muscle, or the lower motoneuron. There are also quite likely to be sensory deficits due to involvement of the immediately adjacent sensory strip in the cortex or the afferent pathways in the internal capsule.

In a *haemorrhagic stroke* there is bleeding from a ruptured blood vessel, commonly as a result of high blood pressure. If the bleeding is into CNS tissue (intracerebral haematoma) the blood forms a roughly circular mass that disrupts the tissue. As bleeding continues, adjacent brain tissue is displaced and compressed and this impairs neuronal function. In the case of a smaller haemmorhage where the patient survives, there may eventually be considerable restitution of function as the blood that escaped is resorbed. This is because, unlike infarction, the tissue is not destroyed but pushed aside. Common sites for haemorrhage resulting from high blood pressure are the penetrating branches of the middle cerebral artery which will affect the putamen and the adjacent internal capsule.

In many cases it is now possible to get a direct picture of the site of a lesion in the CNS using an x-ray technique known as computerised axial tomography, or CT scan. The CT scan provides a picture of the varying density levels through thin layers or slices of the skull and brain, tilted at a slight angle from the horizontal (see Figure 2).

In a scan such as the one shown in Figure 3A, dark areas represent regions of relatively low density, light areas represent relatively high density. Thus, the bone of the skull, for example, shows up as near

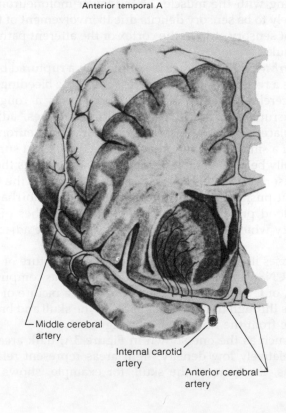

AREA FOR CONTRAVERSION
OF EYES AND HEAD

Rolandic A

MOTOR   SENSORY

BROCA'S AREA

HIP
TRUNK
ARM
HANDS
FINGERS
THUMB
FACE
LIPS
TONGUE
MOUTH

Anterior parietal A

Posterior
parietal A

Prerolandic A

Angular A

Superior
division of
middle
cerebral A

VISUAL
CORTEX

Lateral
orbito-frontal A

CENTRAL SPEECH
AREA

Inferior division of
middle cerebral A

Posterior temporal A

Middle cerebral stem

AUDITORY AREA

Temporal polar A

Anterior temporal A

Middle cerebral
artery

Internal carotid
artery

Anterior cerebral
artery

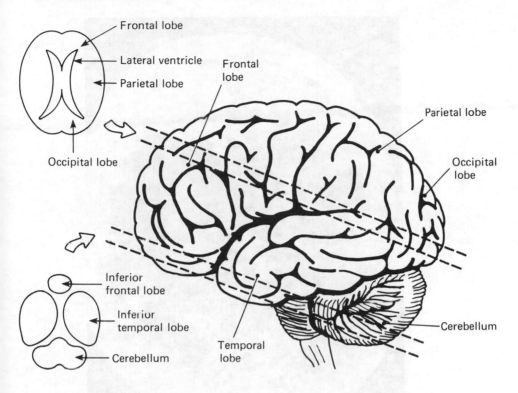

Figure 2. Lateral view of the cerebrum and cerebellum showing the orientation of the CT scan and cross-sectional diagrams showing the resultant slice imaged.

white because it is much more dense than the tissue of the CNS. The ventricles containing cerebrospinal fluid, which is very similar to water in density, show up darker than the more dense CNS tissue that surrounds them. A week or two after an occlusive stroke, infarcted CNS tissue, which is of lower density than healthy tissue, shows up on the CT scan as a darker area. In Figure 3A an infarct may be seen on and near the convoluted surface of the cortex on the right side of the brain in the region of the motor and sensory strips. As a result of this infarct the patient lost sensory and motor function on one side of the body. Because the major afferent and efferent pathways between the cerebral cortex and the spinal cord cross from one side to the other, this patient's deficits were on the left side of the body.

Figure 1. Distribution of the middle cerebral artery including the subcortical structures.

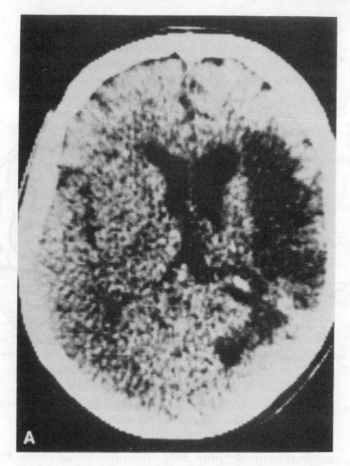

Figure 3. Imaging an infarct with CT and PET scans. (A) CT scan of a patient 4 weeks poststroke showing decreased attenuation in the region served by the right middle cerbral artery indicating an infarct. (B) PET scan in the same patient showing decreased regional cerebral bloodflow within area of infarct but also in the right caudate and thalamus (arrowed). From "Visual evoked potentials and position emission tomographic mapping of regional cerebral blood flow and cerebral metabolism: Can the neuronal potential generators be visualized?", by Celesia, G. G., Polcyn, R. D., Holden, J. E., Nickles, R. J., Gatley, J. S., and Koeppe, R. A. (1982). *Electroencephalography and Clinical Neurophysiology, 54*, 243–256. Reprinted with permission.

When normal functioning ceases in one part of the brain, it might be expected that there would be changes in the activity of other brain structures connecting with the infarcted area. This is strikingly illustrated in Figure 3B. This shows a picture of the metabolic activity of a similar slice of brain to that in Figure 3A obtained by a new technique

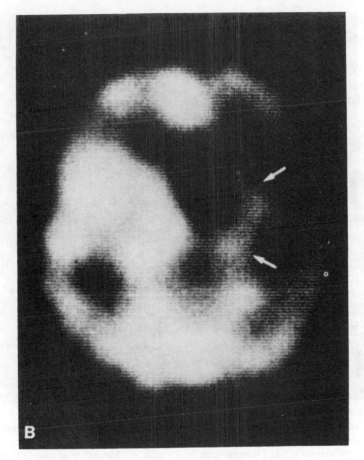

Figure 3. (*Continued*)

called positron emission tomography, or PET scan. The lighter areas indicate brain structures that are metabolically more active. While the infarcted area shows up with no discernable activity, that is, dark, it is particularly interesting to note that the area just to the right of the ventricles including the intact thalamus and caudate nucleus also show up dark relative to the corresponding areas on the other side of the brain. These right-sided subcortical structures have projections to and from the infarcted right cortex. Because these no longer serve any useful function, the metabolic activity of the right side subcortical structures is depressed relative to those on the left.

Strokes usually affect a clearly delimited area on one side or other of the brain. Other types of lesions can involve sets of neurons that are not

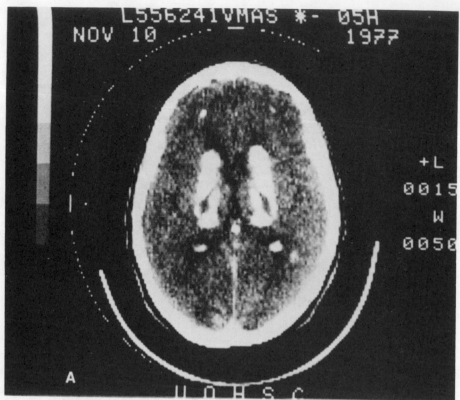

Figure 4.   CT scan of patient with hyperparathyroidism showing dense calcification in (A) the basal ganglia and thalamus, (B) the dentate nuclei of the cerebellum. From "Intra-cranial calcification in hyperparathyroidism associated with gait apraxia and parkin-sonism", by Margolin, D., Hammerstad, J., Orwoll, E., McClung, M., and Calhoun, D. (1980). *Neurology, 30,* 1005–1007. Reprinted with permission.

restricted to one lateralised region. Examples of such lesions affecting the basal ganglia include Parkinson's disease (involving the substantia nigra) and Huntington's chorea (the caudate nuclei). A case study of a metabolic disorder that resulted in an interesting CT scan, is described by Margolin *et al.* (1980). As a result of overactivity of the parathyroid glands there were bilateral accumulations of calcium in the basal ganglia and the dentate nuclei of the cerebellum. This calcification shows up on the CT scan as areas of hyperdensity and clearly outlines these structures (see Figure 4).

CLINICAL ASSESSMENT OF MOVEMENT

Despite the advent of the CT scan, the clinician's examination of the patient still plays an important role in identifying the site and extent of a

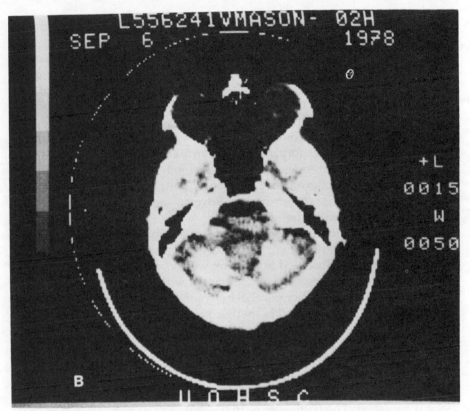

Figure 4. (*Continued*)

lesion in the CNS. A full neurological examination includes an assessment of many psychological functions such as general alertness and mental orientation, sensation and perception, memory, comprehension, and production of language. In this chapter attention is restricted to some of the consequences of lesions in those areas of the brain directly concerned with control of movement. The motor portion of the neurological exam may be conveniently divided into two: tests involving movement produced or elicited by the clinician's actions, and observations of the patient's own movements. This division corresponds roughly to the clinician's distinction between signs and symptoms of disorder.

Movement Elicited by the Clinician

Perhaps the most familiar of the neurological tests is the reflex elicited by a brisk tap of the skin immediately above a muscle tendon using a reflex hammer. Called the *deep-tendon reflex* by clinicians, the normal response to the resulting brief stretch of the muscle connected to the tendon is a rapid, but relatively weak, contraction. It will be recalled from Chapter 2, that the stretch reflex is mediated by the excitatory effect of muscle spindles on the alpha motoneurons that cause the muscle to contract. The *gain* of the deep-tendon reflex is the strength of the contraction for a given tap force. The gain is regulated by descending pathways from the contralateral motor cortex. Lesions in these pathways, that is, upper-motoneuron lesions typically caused by a stroke, result in a reduced sensory threshold and an elevated response to a given stimulus so that the gains of the tendon reflexes are elevated. The amplitudes of the reflexes are larger than normal and the muscles are said to be *hyperreflexive* (*hyper* means above normal; later we will also use the prefix *hypo* meaning below normal).

From the previous chapter it will be recalled that in the newborn the motor area of the cerebral cortex matures relatively late. Strong deep-tendon reflexes are observed in the first weeks of life which thus appear as a parallel to the hyperreflexia associated with upper-motoneuron lesions in the adult. A further parallel between the immature CNS and the effects of lesions in the adult is seen in primitive reflex patterns such as the grasp reflex elicited by tactile stimulation of the palm of the hand. Damage to the cortex resulting from a stroke can lead to the release of these primitive reflex patterns. For example, stroking the palm of an adult's hand does not normally elicit grasping, but this may be observed in a patient who has extensive cortical damage, particularly if the frontal lobe is damaged. The pattern of partial restoration of motor function that can occur following hemiplegia (Twitchell, 1951) has certain resemblances to the developmental sequence. This has been used as a basis for a physiotherapy programme advocated by Brunnstrom (1970). She argued the therapist's role is to lead the patient through the developmental sequence.

Another test employed by the clinician is based on passive manipulation of a limb about a joint. Normally, there is a slight feeling of resistance to movement resulting from activity in the muscle that is stretched, even though the patient is supposedly relaxed. This resistance is referred to as *tone* and it reflects the operation of the spinal and long-loop reflexes discussed in Chapter 2. In the case of damage to pathways originating in the motor cortex contralateral to the side of the body being tested there is usually increased resistance to passive stretch that is called *hypertonia*. This hypertonia has a characteristic quality often described as being like the opening of a clasp knife. Initially resistance to stretch is high, but if the clinician continues to move the limb, there will be a sudden drop in resistance (see Figure 5).

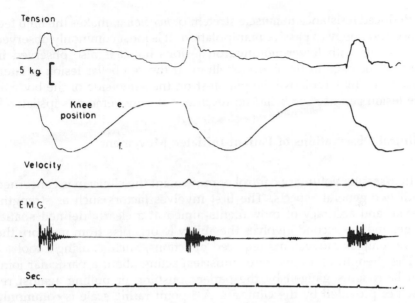

Figure 5. The spastic stretch reflex. The velocity of knee flexion as the knee was passively flexed from full extension to 90° of flexion is shown. An indication of tension developed in the passively stretched quadriceps muscle was provided by the force exerted by the examiner on a transducer at the ankle. The EMG developed in the muscle is shown on the bottom trace. From "The quadriceps stretch reflex in human spasticity", by Burke, D., Gillies, J. D., and Lance, J. W. (1970). *Journal of Neurology, Neurosurgery and Psychiatry, 33,* 216–233. Reprinted with permission.

By looking at the integrated EMG over a range of velocities of passive movement, Burke, Gillies, and Lance (1970) showed that the excitation of the clasp knife stretch reflex increases with velocity. This form of hypertonicity is termed *spasticity*. Usually, spasticity is more marked in the extensors of the leg and in the flexors of the arm, that is, in the muscles that allow movements to be made in the presence of gravity— the antigravity muscles. Spasticity is associated with elevated deep-tendon reflexes and impaired muscle strength.

An example of a different form of hypertonia is *rigidity*, which often occurs in Parkinson's disease. It differs from spasticity in several respects. First, the increased resistance to passive movement affects flexors and extensors equally and, usually, both sides of the body are affected. Second, the hypertonia is steady and yielding throughout the range of movement. The analogy drawn here is usually with the plastic quality of bending a lead pipe, in contrast to the abrupt drop in resistance of a clasp knife. Third, the hypertonia in Parkinson's disease is not velocity dependent (Meyer & Adorjani, 1980).

Reduced resistance to muscle stretch, or *hypotonia,* makes the limb feel loose and floppy to passive manipulation. It is most commonly observed in patients with lower-motoneuron lesions but it is also observed in cases of damage to the neocerebellum. If the cerebellar lesion is lateralised, the hypotonia will be manifest on the same side of the body as the lesion because cerebellar representation of movement is ipsilateral.

Clinical Observations of Patient-Initiated Movement

In assessing voluntary control of movement the clinician is concerned with two general aspects. The first involves factors such as strength, speed, and accuracy of movements aimed at a clearly defined spatial target and the second involves the ability to organise from memory the more complex movements required in actions, such as using a tool.

The strength of a muscle (or muscles) acting about a particular joint can be roughly gauged by the patient pushing or pulling against resistance provided by the clinician. A 5-point rating scale is commonly used to describe performance (see Table 1). A reduction in strength on one side of the body can be an indication of damage in the pyramidal tract pathways originating in the contralateral motor cortex. A clinician will thus be very attentive to any asymmetries in strength. Complete loss of muscle power on one side of the body is called *hemiplegia,* while the term *hemiparesis* is used if there is weakness rather than complete paralysis. Paralysis of both sides of the body is commonly a result of a lesion at some level of the spinal cord, which will usually result in sensory loss also. If the lesion is low down the cord, the lower half of the body will be paralysed and the term *paraplegia* is used. *Tetraplegia* or *quadriplegia* refer to paralysis of all four limbs; this occurs with high-level spinal cord lesions.

The speed and accuracy of movement is usually assessed in movements requiring control over a group of spatially distributed muscles. For example, in examining upper-limb control a procedure known as the finger–nose test is commonly employed. In this test, which may be

TABLE 1. MRC Scale of Muscle Power

0. No contraction
1. Trace of contraction
2. Full movement with gravity eliminated
3. Full movement against gravity
4. Active movement against gravity and resistance
5. Normal power

considered a field version of the Fitts' tapping task described in Chapter 3, the patient alternately touches his or her own nose and then the clinician's finger held some distance away. By moving the target finger about and requiring the patient to track the changing target positions, the clinician can also look at eye–hand coordination and the ability to implement corrections to movement. In this task both the speed of movement and the accuracy of the movement at its endpoint are assessed. In Parkinson's disease, for example, movement of either arm is likely to be slowed down, but the patient with a lesion in the cerebellum does not typically move slowly; on the contrary, it is characteristic for the hand (ipsilateral to the lesion) to overshoot the position of a target in space. Referred to as *past-pointing* by clinicians, it means that, for example, in the finger–nose test the cerebellar patient may bump his or her own nose, in some cases quite forcibly.

Cerebellar patients often manifest large oscillations at right angles to the line of approach as the hand closes in on the target. This uncontrolled oscillation in position of a limb as it is moved towards a spatially defined target is termed *intention tremor*. It is considered part of a failure of voluntary movement coordination termed *cerebellar ataxia*. Intention tremor is quite different from a tremor often seen in cases of Parkinson's disease that predominates when the patient's limb is stationary (though not completely relaxed). The latter tremor is usually referred to as *resting tremor*. Figure 6 shows muscle activity alternating between the flexor and extensor of a parkinsonian patient's stationary arm. When a voluntary contraction is initiated, there is suppression of the antagonist activity, the periodic firing of the agonist becomes continuous and the movement is made smoothly.

Having considered movement to a spatial target we now turn to consider how the clinician assesses a patient's organisation of more complex, goal-directed activity. Patients with certain left-hemisphere lesions may exhibit difficulty in producing purposeful actions that is not attributable to paralysis, muscular weakness, or to disturbances of comprehension. This is termed *apraxia* and a commonly used clinical test is to ask the patients to show how they would carry out a familiar gesture such as waving goodbye. Alternatively, the patient might be asked to mime the use of a tool such as a saw. If the patient fails to follow the verbal command, the test can be made somewhat easier by asking the patient to imitate the clinician or by presenting the patient with the object or tool. Another test that is often carried out by clinicians in the assessment of apraxia is imitation of a sequence of gestures or postures, for example, of the hand. Although a patient who is not severely apraxic may be able to produce each item in isolation, the order or even the form of the components may be changed when the patient attempts to copy

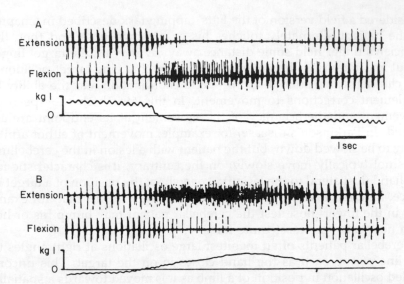

Figure 6. Parkinsonian tremor disappears during voluntary movement of the index finger into flexion (A) or extension (B). EMG activity shown from extensor indicis and flexor indicis. From "Pathophysiology of parkinsonian tremor," by Rondot, P. and Bathien, N. (1978). In Desmedt, J. E. (Ed.), *Physiological tremor, pathological tremors and clonus.* Basel: Karger. Reprinted with permission.

the standard provided by the clinician. Figure 7 shows a sequence of hand postures that patients with apraxia might find difficult even though they would have no difficulty in producing each component in isolation.

EMPIRICAL STUDIES OF MOTOR DISORDERS

In the previous section we have discussed how, on the basis of the pattern of signs and symptoms observed in a patient, a clinician approaches the question of where there is damage in the CNS. We now

Figure 7. Assessment of apraxia; sequencing of hand postures through fist on edge, open palm on edge, open palm down.

interpret various aspects of the different types of movement disorder from a functional viewpoint. We draw on studies of patients with upper-motoneuron lesions, lesions of the basal ganglia, and lesions of the cerebellum. However, even if it were possible, the aim is not to give a complete picture of each disorder. Instead, examples have been selected to illustrate some of the consequences of different types of disruption in the organisation and execution of movement. We begin with a consideration of factors affecting simple aiming movements and progress toward issues that relate to higher-level, conscious factors in movement control.

Execution: Agonist–Antagonist Relations

As we have already said, the muscles of patients with upper-motoneuron damage are typically hyperreflexive. If a muscle is overresponsive to passive stretch it is quite conceivable that reaction to stretch imposed by the action of another muscle during active movement could limit the effectiveness of that other muscle's activity in moving a limb towards a desired target. However, McLellan (1977) has shown that in spastic patients there is a dissociation between hyperreflexivity in passive movement and the coactivation that occurs in antagonist muscles in voluntary movement. In an assessment of a drug that reduces stretch-reflex activity at the spinal level, McLellan observed the effects of changes in plasma concentration of the drug on passive and active movements of the lower limb. Figure 8 shows that the drug reduced the quadriceps' (a knee extensor) response to passive stretch but not the degree of co-contraction in alternating voluntary flexion and extension of the knee. This result indicates that, although hyperreflexivity is associated with hemiplegia, it is not the underlying cause of the loss of voluntary movement.

Sahrmann and Norton (1977) asked spastic patients to repeatedly flex and extend the elbow to the maximum as rapidly as possible. They found that the time to perform 10 such movements was positively correlated with the degree of spasticity of the biceps and brachioradialis (i.e., with the sensitivity to stretch of these elbow flexor muscles). However, Sahrmann and Norton noted that the co-contraction observed during the rapid alternating movements was of a form that again indicated it was not triggered by exaggerated stretch reflexes. Instead of an exaggeration of activity in the antagonist muscle in phase with the movement, there was a persistence of flexor activity into the extension phase of the movement. The patients' difficulty was in reversing the direction

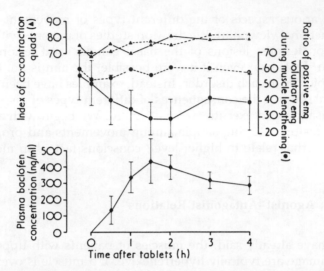

Figure 8. Mean data from six patients showing time course of changes in quadriceps co-contraction during voluntary movements (triangles), quadriceps response to congruent passive stretch (circles), and plasma baclofen concentration after an oral dose of baclofen (continuous line) and placebo (broken line, 4 patients only). From "Co-contraction and stretch reflexes in spasticity during treatment with baclofen", by McLellan, D. L. (1977). *Journal of Neurology, Neurosurgery and Psychiatry, 40,* 30–38. Reprinted with permission.

of movement, that is, switching the roles of the agonist and antagonist muscles. This study also indicates that loss of voluntary movement in spastic patients is not a simple consequence of the elevated-stretch reflex; the motor disorder in upper-motoneuron lesions involves some kind of difficulty in the selection of muscles.

From reciprocal action of muscles in a sequence of alternating movements, we now turn to a series of studies of the selection and relative timing of reciprocal muscles in single, unidirectional aiming movements that were carried out by Hallet and his colleagues (1975a,b). In their paradigm subjects watched an oscilloscope screen that represented elbow angle by the position of a horizontal line alongside a horizontal target line. At random intervals after the beginning of a trial, the target line would jump to a new vertical position and the subject was required to match this as rapidly as possible by flexing the elbow. The amount of elbow flexion needed to do this was always the same and subjects were given plenty of practice so that the movement could be made automatically in open-loop fashion. In an initial study with normal subjects Hallet *et al.* (1975a) confirmed Wachholder and Altenburger's (1926) finding of a triphasic pattern of EMG activity. First, the biceps as agonist are

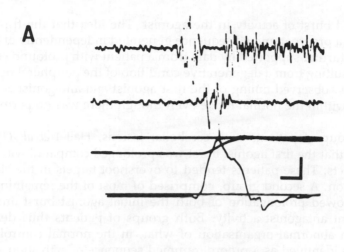

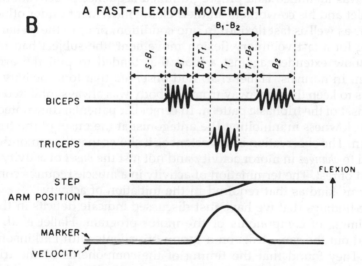

Figure 9. EMG activity in biceps and triceps during fast flexion of the elbow. (A) is a photographic record of a single trial; the six oscillographic traces (vertical and horizontal calibration bar .5 mv, 50 ms) are diagrammatically represented in (B). From "EMG analysis of stereotyped voluntary movements in man", by Hallet, M., Shahani, B. T., and Young, R. R. (1975). *Journal of Neurology, Neurosurgery, and Psychiatry, 38*, 1154–1162. Reprinted with permission.

activated, then the triceps as antagonist, then the agonist biceps fires again (see Figure 9). They found that if the load that the subject works against is unexpectedly increased, the timing of the first two components is unchanged. The first adjustment to the pattern only comes in the second burst of activity in the agonist. The idea that the triphasic pattern is a preprogrammed sequence generated independently of feedback was further supported by data from a patient with profound sensory loss resulting from a degenerative condition of the peripheral nerves. Hallet *et al.* observed timing of the first agonist and antagonist activity that was within the normal range even though there was no peripheral feedback.

In a group of patients with cerebellar lesions, Hallet *et al.* (1975b) observed that the first agonist burst was prolonged compared with normal subjects. These patients tended to overshoot targets in the clinical examination. A second group, comprised of most of the remaining patients, showed prolongation of both the initial agonist burst and the subsequent antagonist activity. Both groups of patients thus demonstrated an abnormal organisation of what, in the normal control subjects, was identified as a preprogrammed sequence of activation.

Hallet and his co-workers studied elbow movement under other conditions as well as fast flexion. In one condition, prior to the visual signal calling for a fast voluntary flexion movement, the subject had to keep the elbow extended against a load that tended to pull the arm into flexion. In normals, Hallet *et al.* had observed that tonic activity in the triceps to keep the arm away from the body was always inhibited before the onset of the triphasic pattern. In cerebellar patients, they noted there was a slowness in inhibiting the antagonist at the onset of the triphasic pattern. The observation is important as it shows that the motor deficit is linked to *changes* in motor activity and not just the *onset* of activity after a period of rest. The termination of activity in a muscle requires control of the same kind as that required in the initiation of activity.

The findings that we have just discussed indicate deficits in the relative timing of components of the motor program. Hallet *et al.* (1977) carried out the same tests on a group of patients with Parkinson's disease. They found that the timing of the components of the triphasic EMG pattern in parkinsonian patients was within the normal range. Moreover, they observed that in parkinsonian patients, a movement made in the opposite direction to an initial load was normal in the sense that the antagonist inhibition was completed by the time of agonist onset. Thus, the lesions in the basal ganglia associated with Parkinson's disease do not affect timing in the motor program.

A feature of the bradykinetic symptoms (slowness of voluntary movement) in Parkinson's disease is that patients fail to increase the velocity of movement for movements of larger amplitude (Flowers, 1976). Hallet *et al.*'s result indicates that this failure should not be attributed to errors in the timing of reciprocal activity in the agonist and antagonist. In a further study of parkinsonian movement, Hallet and Khoshbin (1980) employed a task that required the patients to move the arm to targets at various distances from the starting point. A failure to increase the level of EMG for larger amplitude movements was observed, although the timing was within normal limits (It is interesting to note the clinical observation that given a sudden demand with sufficient arousal value, a patient with Parkinson's disease can sometimes overcome the bradykinesia. A patient might, for example, stand a reasonable chance of catching an object abruptly thrown towards him). Hallet and Khoshbin concluded that the basal ganglia and the cerebellum are involved in two different aspects of preprogrammed movement. A timing component is determined by the cerebellum while the basal ganglia are responsible for an activational or energising component of programming.

Preparation: Movement Latency Data

In the preceding section we have seen evidence of abnormalities in the earliest preprogrammed components of simple rapid movements in various patient groups. The question might then be raised as to whether the timing and activation differences seen in the patients arise as a result of failures of programming prior to movement, or if a correct motor program is constructed and failure occurs in its execution? From the discussion in Chapters 3 and 6 of the use of RT as an index of preparation processes that take place prior to movement, it seems worthwhile to consider whether some patient groups exhibit long latencies in the initiation of movement.

Nakamura and Taniguchi (1977) have reported simple RT measures of finger extension in a group of patients with residual hemiparesis associated with upper-motoneuron lesions following stroke. In addition to recording the overt behavioural response, EMG records were taken to identify the time of onset of the muscle activity. They were thus able to present data on the time between the reaction signal and the onset of EMG (premotor time) separately from the time from EMG onset to overt movement of the finger away from the response key. Their results showed that the time from onset of muscle activity to the overt movement was greater on the affected side. However, the interesting feature of their data is that there was no difference between the two arms in the slowing of the premotor time between the reaction signal and EMG onset. This demonstrates that slowness of movement onset in the involved arm of these patients is not a problem of selection of the appropriate muscle, but rather it reflects difficulty in recruiting sufficient motor units to effect movement.

As long ago as 1925, Wilson reported that the average RT of patients with Parkinson's disease is 30% slower than normal controls. More recently, Angel, Alston, and Higgins (1970) showed that the time taken to make a visually based correction and reverse the direction of a movement is slowed in parkinsonian patients. The amount of the slowing is of the same order as the slowing in the initiation of a movement. The deficit thus applies both to the initiation of movement from rest and to altering activity. Evarts, Teravainen, and Calne (1981) asked whether parkinsonian slowness of initiation reflects difficulty in response selection. They argued that if this is the case, the difference in RT between a parkinsonian patient in a choice task should be greater than in a simple RT task. In the latter, subjects can prepare the required response in advance and trigger the movement on receipt of the signal to move. In the case of the choice task, the required response cannot be selected in advance because it is not known until the time the reaction signal is presented. Evarts *et al.* found that parkinsonian patients, though slower in initiating wrist rotation movements than normals, were not additionally slow in choice relative to simple RT.

In a recent study, Bloxham, Mindel, and Frith (1984) confirmed a suggestion in the data of Evarts *et al.* that parkinsonian patients are actually differentially slowed on simple reaction time. In Bloxham *et al.*'s experimental design, simple and choice RT trials were interleaved. On all trials a signal to extend either the left or the right index finger was preceded by a warning signal. The intersignal interval was either 250 or 2000 msec; the subject did not know which it would be in advance. On choice trials the warning signal provided no information as to which finger movement would be called for by the reaction signal. On the simple RT trials, the warning signal precued the subject on whether to move the left or right finger. Figure 10 summarises their results. A bigger difference between parkinsonian patients and normal controls is seen in simple RT than in choice RT. Nonetheless, it will be noted that the parkinsonian patients' simple RTs do speed up with the longer intersignal interval. It therefore appears that they do indeed prepare the movement in some way, but they are either slower in preparing it or it is less easily triggered at a given point in time. These results complement Hallett's conclusions based on the EMG studies described in the previous section; the basal ganglia appear to play a role in the activation of movement.

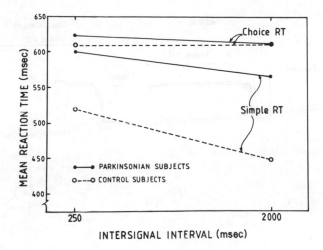

Figure 10. Simple and choice RT at two interstimulus intervals in parkinsonian patients and normal controls. Data from Bloxham, Mindel, and Frith (1984).

Feedback

In Chapter 6 it was noted that movement sequences can be executed despite profound sensory deficits. One example cited was that of Rothwell *et al.*'s (1982) patient who, despite severe sensory losses due to peripheral nerve lesions, was able to touch each finger in sequence using the thumb. This observation was taken as support for the concept of a motor program capable of directing a sequence of movements without the contribution of peripheral feedback. It is also worth noting that Rothwell *et al.*'s patient showed a normal triphasic activation pattern of the agonist and antagonist confirming Hallet *et al.* (1975a). However, this patient did experience difficulty in the maintenance of muscle tension. Holding an object, for example, required continual visual monitoring otherwise it would be dropped. This can be appreciated when data from a task in which the patient was asked to maintain constant force or position are examined (see Figure 11).

Proprioceptive disturbances often occur in association with motor disorder resulting from a stroke because of the common blood supply to the anatomically adjacent pathways and cortical areas subserving motor and sensory function. In cases of CNS lesions that give rise to distortion of sensory input rather than loss of input it may be considerably harder to discount inaccurate information than to substitute for lack of informa-

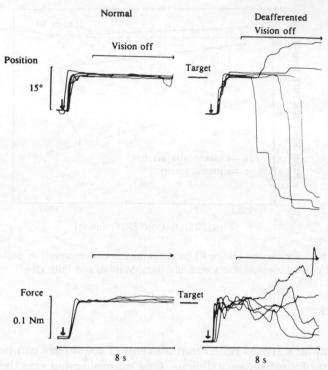

Figure 11. Maintenance of position and force with and without vision by deafferented man. From "Manual motor performance in a deafferented man", by Rothwell, I. C., Traub, M. M., Day, B. L., Obeso, J. A., Thomas, P. K., and Marsden, C. D., (1982). *Brain, 105*, 515–542. Reprinted with permission.

tion. Faced with proprioceptive disturbances, patients must depend much more heavily on vision to correct errors relative to a desired position for the limb. Such processing of visual feedback may be rather slow, compounding any difficulties introduced by the slowing of motor output.

In a disorder known as *visuomotor ataxia* patients can exhibit what appears to be a failure in relating visual perception to action. Rondot, DeRecondo, and Ribadeau Dumas (1977) described this condition in patients who had had surgery of the right cerebral cortex in an area between the parietal and occipital lobes. After the operation these patients tended to neglect the left side of the body and left visual space. This syndrome of *spatial neglect* ameliorated with time. However, it was noted that the patients were still left with a difficulty in reaching for objects in the left visual field despite being able to use vision to correctly identify the object. Often the reaching movement, although in the right general direction, would fall short of the object. Rondot *et al.* demonstrated that the problem was not in the organisation and execution of movement per se. On command patients were, for example, able to touch their right hand with the left without the aid of vision. Their deficit thus appears to involve monitoring of the consequences of action and making appropriate corrections if a discrepancy between the position of the hand and the target is detected

Holmes (1939) observed that in cerebellar ataxia, compound movements requiring simultaneous coordination among several joints are likely to be carried out in decomposed fashion with movements of the various joints carried out sequentially rather than simultaneously. His example was that to bring the hand to touch the nose from a starting point above and in front of the nose, a cerebellar patient will first lower the arm at the shoulder and then use elbow flexion rather than doing the two together. It is possible that this represents a conscious strategy on the part of the patients to overcome inaccuracy in the programming of movement. (Such programming errors were noted in Hallet *et al.*'s 1975b study of rapid elbow flexion; on a number of occasions, their cerebellar patients made an inappropriate movement at the more proximal shoulder joint.) Given inaccuracy in coordinating movements over two separate joints, coupled with errors in the programming of muscle activity around one joint it seems reasonable to suppose a patient may resort to special strategies in guiding movement. It may be that if one limb segment is moved at a time there is a better chance of visual monitoring of the consequences of moving that segment up to a point where it may be fixed at a given position so that the consequences of moving the next segment may then be attended to. Luria (1963) stressed that in the case of loss of automatic movement routines associated with lower levels of control, the patient can substitute higher-level cognitive processes to aid action. This view is consistent with that of Holmes who considered the recovery of motor control often seen following cerebellar lesions to be the result of substitution of conscious cortical control for automatic cerebellar mechanisms. As support for this idea Holmes observed that cerebellar ataxia increases if a patient's attention is diverted from the movement being performed.

CONSCIOUS REPRESENTATION OF GOAL-DIRECTED ACTION

We have just considered the role of conscious mechanisms in compensating for the loss of lower level, automatic motor processes. We now turn to a discussion of apraxia and what might be called the loss of conscious representation of actions despite preservation of lower-level automatic processes subserving, for example, simple aimed movements.

It will be recalled that apraxia is a term used to describe difficulties in carrying out actions to command that are not attributable to weakness or to failures of comprehension. In a study of a large number of brain-damaged patients, Liepmann (1905) reported a high incidence of apraxia involving the left hand in subjects with a deficit in language production causing nonfluent speech and also hemiplegia of the right side of the body. (Because the right side was paralysed, it would not have been possible to determine whether there was apraxia of the right hand.) This he termed *sympathetic apraxia*. Although less common, apraxia of the left hand was also found in patients with a right-sided hemiplegia but no speech problems. Liepmann noted that patients with a left-sided hemiplegia were not apraxic with the right arm. These observations have been confirmed in more recent studies, for example, Kimura and Archibald, (1974). The implication is that some part, or parts, of the left cerebral cortex other than the motor strip contralateral to the hemiplegic right side is normally involved in the organisation of goal-directed movement. The fact that apraxia is frequently, but not invariably, associated with language deficits suggests these areas are anatomically close to, but distinct from, the areas subserving language production.

In presenting a neuropsychological account of the disorder, Liepmann (1908) subsequently made a theoretical distinction between two types of apraxia, *ideomotor* and *ideational*. He assumed that actions are represented in the left parietal region of the cortex by memory traces. He supposed these action-memory traces are anatomically separate from elements in the precentral motor area that are responsible for ennervation of the particular muscles required by the action. (Note that Liepmann did not ascribe a role to subcortical structures in the preparation of movement.) Figure 12, based on the theoretically similar ideas of Heilman, Rothi, and Valenstein (1982) provides a schematic representation.

In ideational apraxia, Liepmann assumed that the concept of the nature of an action (the idea) would be lost if a cortical lesion included the left parietal region because the action-memory traces would be destroyed. Taking this proposal one step further, Heilman *et al.* hypothesised that the action-memory traces are also important in perceiving and interpreting actions performed by other people. In support of this view, Heilman *et al.* noted that patients with postcentral lesions of the cerebral cortex that included the left-parietal area were more impaired in the recognition of mimed action than were patients with left precentral lesions.

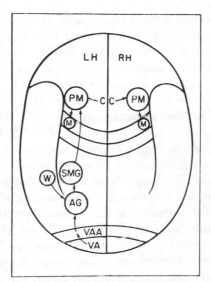

Figure 12. Hypothesised cortical centres and pathways for the control of praxis; VA, visual area; VAA, visual association area; AG, angular gyrus; W, Wernicke's area; SMG, supramarginal gyrus; PM, premotor area; M, motor area; CC, corpus callosum. From "Two forms of ideomotor apraxia", by Heilman, K. M., Rothi, L. J., and Valenstein, E. (1982). *Neurology* (NY), *32*, 342–346. Reprinted with permission.

It is commonly observed that apractic patients do better demonstrating the use of an object with the object in the hand than if they are asked to mime its use. Part of the reason for this may be that the object provides some constraint on movement. For example, it obviates a commonly reported error made by apraxic patients in miming, namely, the use of part of the body as the implement. But perhaps equally important is the possibility that the object helps evoke the action-memory trace as suggested, for example, by DeRenzi, Faglioni, and Sorgato (1982). The object may serve as a proprioceptive cue for retrieving the information from memory. Clinical descriptions of apraxia suggest that context in general and not just the object itself may assist in evoking the correct action. An apractic patient may use a hammer very effectively in knocking a hook into the wall when asked to hang a picture even though unable to demonstrate the use of a hammer in a test situation.

Although we have been discussing apraxia in terms of memory for actions, it should be noted that patients suffering from apraxia do not necessarily have impaired memory for other types of information. Conversely, there have been cases of patients with severe amnesia who, nevertheless, did not suffer from apraxia and were able to perform everyday activities. For example, Milner (1962) described a patient who had surgical lesions of the hippocampus to alleviate intractable epilepsy.

After the operation this patient was unable to retain factual information but, nevertheless, was able to carry out in a competent manner the activities of daily living. Moreover, he was able to acquire new skills and showed improved performance on various tasks carried out in the psychological laboratory over a number of days. He was able to retain procedural information for how to perform the tasks, even though he was unaware that he had performed the task the day before.

In ideomotor apraxia, Liepmann supposed that the action-memory traces in the left parietal region become isolated or disconnected from precentral motor execution areas of either hemisphere. He proposed that the organisation of actions carried out with the left hand is exercised via the pathways of the corpus callosum to the right hemisphere motor area. This leads to the prediction that a lesion restricted to the corpus callosum could produce an apraxia limited to the left side. Data from a study of patients treated for intractable epilepsy by lesioning this pathway between the two hemispheres (Gazzaniga, Bogen, & Sperry, 1967) do not fully accord with this prediction based on Liepmann's model. Following callosal section, patients did exhibit some degree of left-sided apraxia to verbal command but they were able to carry out the act if it was demonstrated by the clinician. This suggests that there was a disconnection between language input and motor-planning processes rather than between planning and execution centres. However, in defence of Liepmann's position, it should be noted that patients who have had a long history of epilepsy may have an atypical distribution of function over the cerebral cortex. It is conceivable that, in these patients, there was bilateral representation of the action-memory traces prior to the sectioning of the corpus callosum by the neurosurgeon. This would account for the fact that the surgery had relatively minor effects on actions carried out with the left hand.

More recently, Watson and Heilman (1983) have described a patient with an infarct involving the anterior portion of the corpus callosum whose deficits did accord with Liepmann's view. The patient was a 43-year-old, right-handed woman. As a result of the CVA there was some weakness of the legs but upper-limb strength and tone remained normal. While voluntary function of the right hand remained normal, she was completely unable to demonstrate the use of objects with the left, either by pantomime or with the object in the hand. After several weeks, there was improvement in left-hand function such that the intent of actions performed to command became recognisable. However, she made spatiotemporal movement errors even with the object in her hand. One example cited involved hammering; with a hammer in the hand she made a few slow, large-amplitude swings to-and-fro but not in an up-

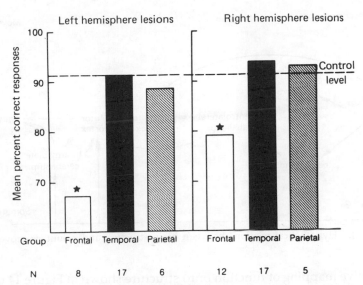

Figure 13. Summary of Kolb and Milner's results for facial series copying. From *Fundamentals of Human Neuropsychology*, by Kolb, B. and Whishaw, I. Q. (1980). San Francisco: Freeman. Reprinted with permission.

and-down direction. This patient's deficits are thus in accordance with Liepmann's view.

Kolb and Milner (cited in Kolb & Whishaw, 1980) have explored the reproduction of facial movement sequences in patients with damage to various diferent cortical areas. They observed that patients with damage to the precentral area of the left cerebral cortex made the most errors in reproducing the sequences. In contrast, patients with lesions of the left parietal area did not have undue difficulty (see Figure 13). This indicates a difference in the roles of left parietal and left precentral cortex in the organisation of movement. One possible interpretation of this finding is that each action-memory trace (residing in the parietal lobe) only specifies a single unit of action. A sequence requiring several units may be the product of a functionally (and anatomically) distinct preparatory process such as that discussed in Chapter 6 in accounting for the effects of sequence length on RT.

CONCLUSION

We are now in a position to sketch a general account of the organisation of action in interpreting the results of CNS lesions, amplifying the

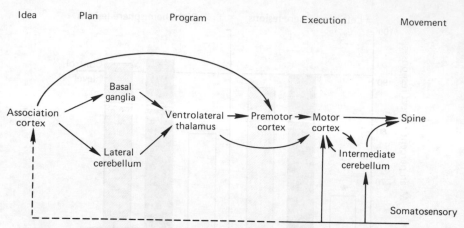

Idea   Plan   Program   Execution   Movement

Figure 14. Hypothetical relations between brain structure and voluntary movement control.

speculative mapping of function onto structure shown in Figure 14 originally proposed by Allen and Tsukuhara (1974). As our starting point we assume there exists a particular goal calling for action. This might, for example, arise out of a social context prompting some gesture, or it might perhaps have been stimulated by a verbal request to carry out an action. The left parietal region of the cerebral cortex appears to be involved in determining the means of achieving the goal by the specification of an action using a stored set of action-memory traces. It seems likely that movement is represented in these traces in general spatial terms that are not specific to the particular set of effectors that will actually be used. Although the individual action-memory traces involve the left parietal region, it seems the construction of the movement sequence involves a separate process in the left-frontal cerebral cortex. The relative timing of agonist and antagonist muscle activity in a motor program involves the cerebellum. Intensive aspects of the program depend on the basal ganglia. Damage to the motor cortex and/or the corticospinal pathways can upset both the agonist–antagonist relations and the recruitment of activity. As movement takes place, if proprioceptive feedback pathways depending on the intact cerebellum and sensory-motor cortex are lost, there is heavy dependence on vision, and on conscious mechanisms for the regulation of movement.

Afterword

Mary M. Smyth
Alan M. Wing

This book has been about human movement and action. The movements studied have ranged in complexity from maintainance of the position of the thumb against external forces to visually guided movement of the hand and arm in reaching for an object in space, from the repetitive tapping of a single finger to the simultaneous activity of fingers of both hands in typing. We have seen contrasts between the slow, effortful attempts of the learner and the fluency and ease of highly skilled, automatic performance, between the restricted-movement repertoire associated with the immature or the damaged CNS and the variety of coordinated movement to be seen in the normal adult.

In the course of the book we have encountered all sorts of ingenious methods for describing and analysing movement after it is completed, as it proceeds and even, one is tempted to say in the case of RT, before it occurs. In some cases, the technology of measurement can seem quite out of proportion to the complexity of the movement being studied while in other cases the use of simple observations can deceive one into thinking the underlying ideas are also simple. Despite this great diversity, and despite the differing backgrounds of the contributors, as editors of this volume we do see an underlying common ground, one that ties in closely with the information-processing approach found in cognitive psychology. In this approach it is assumed that behaviour, or in

297

our case, movement, should be understood as the result of the operation of a set of underlying processes each having a distinct function. These processes may be said to provide representations of the world about us and of the movements that we may employ to act on the environment. In the context of trying to understand goal-directed movement we have attempted to show that control of the movements that we make devolves upon many different processing levels. When people become skilled, they do more than just string together the requisite movements; skill implies that there is an underlying conceptual organisation motivated by an intention to achieve an explicit goal and that there are a number of alternative sets of movements that could be used to attain the goal. In this book we have used the term action to refer to higher levels of organisation than those involved in producing individual movements, but we have also wanted to trace the links between the intention to achieve a goal and the actual movements by which the action plan is instantiated.

Consider the case of handwriting. It is clearly a skill that can be described at various levels ranging from the initial organization of ideas to be communicated, the generation of grammatical structure, the selection of words to convey meaning, the determination of letter sequences, through the appropriate placement of individual pen strokes on the page. Processes that control, for example, finger movements in creating a single letter will be rather different from the processes involved in the selection of the upper-case form of a letter that occurs in the initial position of a sentence. It thus seems reasonable to hypothesise that underlying the production of handwriting, there is a series of different representations or codes for the material to be written (Ellis, 1982). With various levels of representation, it is interesting to speculate how transformations between the codes are achieved. In some cases it may be a matter of accessing a large memory, rather like looking up a word in a dictionary. In other cases the code may be generated on the basis of applying a set of rules, perhaps like determining the spelling of a novel word by known regularities in the relation between word sounds and letter sequence. Activity at different levels of representation must be coordinated. It would seem important, for example, that creative thought processes should not get too far ahead of the relatively slow production of letters. One possible method for communication between different levels is via an external feedback loop. Visual feedback might, for example, be important in inserting movements of the hand across the page at orthographically acceptable locations, typically between words. Thus, in studying handwriting, and the various other skills treated in this book, the issues considered are often part of the wider study of cognitive processes.

In this book the concept of *hierarchy* has often been used in referring to the relations between different levels of control. Although dictionaries define hierarchy in terms merely of a grading of organisation, some writers (e.g., Turvey, Shaw, & Mace, 1978) have taken issue with the application of hierarchy in characterising the control of movement, basing their criticism on a more constrained meaning, namely, that interactions between processes in a hierarchy can only occur in one direction: from higher to lower levels. In such a strict definition there is no communication between processes at the same level nor is there input to a given level from lower levels.

When applying the concept of hierarchy to action, the analogy is sometimes drawn with managerial organisation in a business. There, hierarchical structure means that the managing director issues instructions to a number of under-managers such as the production manager or sales manager. These managers, in turn, control people working at lower levels, such as the factory foremen or the salespeople and so on down to the workers on the shop floor. With progression down through the levels of management there is increasing specialisation of function and the roles become much more restricted. The idea of this structure is that those at top managerial levels need not be concerned with the details, for example, of the day-to-day running of the salesroom. Nonetheless, it would clearly be inappropriate for the managing director to have no lines of communication from lower levels. And it would be a poor organisation if managers at the same level with different responsibilities did not interact. The essence of the hierarchy in management is that it indicates a line of responsibility, it shows who will normally decide on the goals of the system as a whole. It is certainly not intended as defining barriers to communication. With this analogy in mind it is therefore understandable that when we use the term in the context of control of movement the intention is to indicate dominance relations existing between processes. We do not usually intend to rule out the possibility of semi-independent operation by processes lower in the hierarchy.

Throughout this book we have tended to avoid extended theoretical arguments such as that involving the concept of hierarchies. Such disputes do exist and often they centre around the differences between a cognitive or information-processing approach and the approach of Turvey and his associates based on the work of Gibson and the Russian physiologist Bernstein. In Gibson's ecological perception the emphasis is on the active organism in a three-dimensional world with which it has a dynamic relationship. This approach has produced interesting research into the perception of the changes in relationship between environment and organism, of which the work of Lee (1978) on visual control of movement is an excellent example. This work was dealt with at some length in the chapter on perception and action because it is central to the argument that movement and action are part of a cycle of processing and not independently packaged output units. In that chapter, as in others, the somewhat eclectic approach was adopted of treating studies from any theoretical perspective that would help us to understand movement and action. Such eclecticism is explicitly rejected by ecological theorists (Michaels & Carello, 1981) who argue that one framework or the other must be correct.

In perception, information-processing accounts have often dealt with the perception of written language. Because this provides a two-dimensional input, it may be that an ecological approach that emphasises three dimensions is not appropriate (Fowler, 1981). It seems unlikely that systems that evolved to deal with a three-dimensional world are not also used in two-dimensional contexts, so some kind of rapprochement of the two views may be inevitable. At the moment we can say that different approaches deal with different types of situations and that each may have a contribution to make. The situation is not quite so clear in the debate over ecological and information-processing approaches to studying the control of movement and action, partly because the ecological approach has not yet produced much data in proportion to its theories. While recognising the importance of seeing action occur in an environmental context, we feel that the explanations given for reaching or running should not be different in principle from those given for playing a musical instrument or for writing a letter and therefore we have maintained a representational view, although this is qualified in some places.

The ecological view of how movement is controlled is based on the work of Bernstein as well as Gibson. Bernstein (1967) emphasised the kinematic aspects of movements, the physical context in which movements occur, and the forces that operate on a body in addition to the muscular forces that are provided by the body. Bernstein was interested in how the many degrees of freedom of the body are regulated so that movements can be produced in many different contexts and out of this concern came the concept of coordinative structure, which stresses the relative autonomy of organised subsystems. This concept was discussed in the chapters on dual-task performance and skill acquisition, but quite briefly because, as yet, we only have outline sketches of what coordinative structures might be and how they may develop. One of the main functions of a theory of coordinative structures is to remove the need for hierarchical organisation within the nervous system and to allow for minimal involvement by higher-level processes in the direction of organised units at lower levels. Again, it seems likely that there will be some reconciliation between the two views, particularly if we are to describe nonecological tasks such as handwriting, in which the idea of levels of representation seems quite powerful.

The debate between cognitive and ecological approaches to movement and action is presented in introductory form in a collection of chapters by proponents of the different views edited by Kelso (1982). A more difficult presentation of the ecological view may be found in Kelso (1981). For the more cognitively oriented reader, we hope that the chapters in this book will encourage further reading, both on action and on the links between action and the rest of cognition. The study of how humans interact with their environment involves many different disciplines and points of view. We have tried to reflect some of these throughout the book, but any book is necessarily selective. The study of action is developing rapidly and new integrations and perspectives are likely to appear at any time. We hope that our introduction will enable many students to find, and then to follow-up on, their own interest in this expanding and exciting area.

Glossary

Absolute error (AE)—average of the unsigned deviations of movement endpoints with respect to a target.

Active movement—movement initiated by the subject.

Afference—conduction of information from sensory receptors to the brain, incoming sensory information. The term *reafference* is used to refer to sensory information arising from active movement.

Agonist—muscle primarily responsible for movement in a given direction.

Antagonist—muscle acting to oppose movement in a particular direction.

Apraxia—deficits in the production of purposeful movement sequences or gestures that are not attributable to muscle weakness.

Ataxia—movement that is irregular and uncoordinated.

Ballistic movement—fast movement running its course without amendment once initiated.

Bradykinesia—slowness of movement execution.

Central nervous system (CNS)—the brain and spinal cord; the peripheral nervous system includes the sensory and motor nerves, the sensory receptors and the muscles.

Constant error (CE)—average of the (signed) deviations of movement endpoints with respect to a target.

Closed loop control—where action is controlled with respect to feedback about the previous consequences of action.

Contralateral—referring to the opposite side of the body; thus, each cerebral hemisphere exerts a contralateral influence.

Corollary discharge—information arising from movement commands that suppresses the effects of the sensory consequences of the movement.

Dystonia—strictly, abnormal muscle tone, but often used to refer to postural abnormalities.

Efference—conduction of information from the brain to the muscles, outgoing motor commands.

Electromyography (EMG)—the study of the electrical activity of the muscles.

Extensor—muscle whose action is to increase the angle of a joint.

Exteroception—perception of visual or auditory information of objects in the environment.

Feedback—information about the output of a system that is used in combination with some reference to alter the output of the system. The term *negative feedback* is used to indicate the information results in action that will reduce and eventually eliminate the feedback.

Flexor—muscle that acts to reduce the angle of a joint.

Hemiplegia—complete loss of muscle function over one side of the body. (*Paraplegia*—paralysis of both lower limbs. *Quadriplegia*—paralysis affecting all four limbs and the trunk, also called tetraplegia).

Hierarchy—a hierarchical system is one in which there is a consistent ordering of dominance relations among the constituent processes.

Ipsilateral—referring to the same side of the body; thus, each cerebellar hemisphere exerts an ipsilateral influence.

Isometric contraction—muscle contraction that develops force without change of muscle length.

Isotonic—contraction of muscle that results in muscle length changes (and, therefore, movement).

Kinaesthesis—the sensation of movement of the body parts.

Knowledge of results (KR)—information about the outcome of an action that is usually externally mediated.

Locomotion—transport of the body; includes walking and running.

Motoneuron—neuron carrying nerve impulses to the muscle. The term *lower motoneuron* refers to neurons running from the spinal cord to the muscle. The term *upper motoneuron* is used to refer to neurons running from the cerebral motor cortex to the spine.

Motor constancy—the phenomenon in which the same outcome can be achieved by more than one set of movements; the term *motor equivalence* is also used.

Motor program—the internal representation of movement, sometimes used to refer to the direct precursors in the central nervous sytem of muscle activity.

Motor unit—the motoneuron plus the muscle fibres it innervates.

Movement time (MT)—the time taken to complete a movement after the onset of movement terminating reaction time.

Open loop control—where action is controlled without reference to feedback.

Parameter—a quantity that can vary and whose value is descriptive of movement or of factors controlling movement.

Paresis—weakness of musculature usually used in context of central nervous system origin.

Passive movement—movement of the subject by an external agent.

Posture—maintenance of relative position of parts of the body against external influences including gravity.

Proprioception—information about position and movement of body parts available via joint, muscle, and cutaneous receptors.

Reaction time (RT)—the time interval between a signal to act and the onset of movement. If the subject has prior knowledge of the movement required the term used is *simple reaction time*. If the information about the required movement is contained within the signal to act, the term *choice reaction time* is used.

Recruitment—the selection of an appropriate number of motor units to provide graded force.

Reflex—a rapid, involuntary response resulting from sensory stimulation.

Schema—a unit of memory that represents, for example, an action in terms of rules required to generate the movement.

Spasticity—hyperactivity of the "antigravity" muscle groups (leg extensors, arm flexors) usually showing abrupt drop on continued passive movement, often associated with paresis.

Synergy—functional grouping of muscles that act as a single unit.

Transfer of training—change in performance level on one task resulting from performance of a second task.

Tremor—involuntary, periodic movement about a joint or joints; it is considered pathological if the frequency is low or the amplitude large.

Tone (tonus)—constant slight tension characteristic of healthy muscle recognized by the resistance experienced when the limbs are moved or displaced passively.

Variable error (VE)—the reciprocal of the consistency of movement; the square root of the variance of movement endpoints around the mean endpoint position.

References

Adams, J. A. (1971). A closed loop theory of motor learning, *Journal of Motor Behavior, 3*, 111–149.

Adams, J. A. (1976). Issues for a closed loop theory of motor learning. In Stelmach, G. E. (Ed.), *Motor control: Issues and trends*. London: Academic Press.

Adams, J. A. (1978). Theoretical issues for knowledge of results. In Stelmach, G. E. (Ed.), *Information processing in motor learning and control*. New York: Academic Press.

Adams, R. D., & Victor, M. (1981). *Principles of neurology* (2nd ed.). New York: McGraw Hill.

Adelson, E., & Fraiberg, S. (1977). Gross motor development. In Fraiberg, S. (Ed.), *Insights from the blind*. New York: Basic Books.

Alderson, G. J. K., Sully, D. J., & Sully, H. G. (1974). An operational analysis of a one-handed catching task using high speed photography. *Journal of Motor Behavior, 6*, 217–226.

Allen, G. I., & Tsukuhara, N. (1974). Cerebrocerebellar communication systems. *Physiological Review, 54*, 957–1006.

Allport, D. A. (1980). Attention and performance. In Claxton, G. (Ed.), *Cognitive psychology: New directions*. London: Routledge and Kegan Paul.

Amiel-Tison, C., & Grenier, A. (1980). *Evaluation neurologique du nouveau-ne et du nourrisson*. Paris: Masson.

Andre-Thomas, X., & Saint-Anne-Dargassies, S. (1952). *Etudes neurologiques sur le nouveau-né et le jeune nourrisson*. Paris: Masson.

Angel, R. W., Alston, W., & Higgins, J. R. (1970). Control of movement in Parkinson's disease, *Brain, 93*, 1–14.

Annett, J. (1969). *Feedback and human behaviour*. Harmondsworth: Penguin.

Annett, J. (1971). Acquisition of skill, *British Medical Bulletin, 27*, 266–271.

Annett, J., Golby, C. W., & Kay, H. (1958). The measurement of elements in an assembly task: The information output of the human motor system, *Quarterly Journal of Experimental Psychology, 10*, 1–11.

Anson, J. G. (1982). Memory drum theory: Alternative tests and explanations for the complexity effects on simple reaction time, *Journal of Motor Behavior, 14*, 228–246.

Arbib, M. A. (1972). *The metaphorical brain: An introduction to cybernetics as artificial intelligence and brain theory.* New York: Wiley.

Arbib, M. (1980). Interacting schemas for motor control. In Stelmach, G. E. & Requin, J. (Eds.), *Tutorials in motor behavior.* Amsterdam: North Holland.

Arbib, M. A. (1981). Perceptual structures and distributed motor control. In Brooks, V. B., (Ed.), *Handbook of physiology, Section 1, The nervous system, Volume II, Motor Control, Part 2.* Bethesda, MD: American Physiological Society.

Arshavsky, Y. I., Berkinblit, M. B., Gel'fand, J. M., Orlovsky, G. N., & Fukson, O. I. (1972a). Activity of the neurones of the ventral spinocerebellar tract during locomotion, *Biophysics, 17,* 926–935.

Arshavsky, Y. I., Berkinblit, M. B., Gel'fand, J. M., Orlovsky, G. N., & Fukson, O. I. (1972b). Recordings of the neurones of the dorsal spinocerebellar tract during evoked locomotion, *Brain Research, 43,* 272–275.

Asanuma, H., & Sakata, H. (1967). Functional organization of a cortical efferent system examined with focal depth stimulation in cat, *Journal of Neurophysiology, 30,* 35–54.

Asatryan, D. G., & Fel'dman, A. G. (1965). Functional tuning of the nervous system with control of movement or maintenance of a steady posture, I, *Biophysics, 10,* 925–935.

Atkinson, J. W., & Birch, D. (1978). *An introduction to motivation.* New York: Van Nostrand.

Baddeley, A. D., Grant, S., Wight, E., & Thomson, N. (1975). Imagery and visual working memory. In Rabbitt, P. M. A., & Dornic, S. (Eds.), *Attention and performance V.* New York: Academic Press.

Baddeley, A. D., & Lieberman, K. (1980). Spatial working memory. In Nickerson, R. S. (Ed.), *Attention and performance VIII.* Hillsdale, NJ: Erlbaum.

Bairstow, P. M., & Lazzlo, J. I. (1979). Perception of size of movement patterns. *Journal of Motor Behavior, 11,* 167–168.

Bartlett, F. C. (1932). *Remembering.* Cambridge: Cambridge University Press.

Bartlett, F. C. (1958). *Thinking: An experimental and social study.* London: Allen and Unwin.

Beggs, W. D. A., & Howarth, C. I. (1972). The accuracy of aiming at a target: Some further evidence for a theory of intermittent control, *Acta Psychologica, 36,* 171–177.

Benesh, R., & Benesh, J. (1977). *Recording dance: The birth of choreology.* London: Souvenir.

Bennett, A. (1910). *Clayhanger.* Harmondsworth: Penguin.

Bernstein, N. A. (1967). *The coordination and regulation of movement.* London: Pergamon Press.

Bilodeau, E. A., & Bilodeau, I. McD. (Eds.). (1969). *Principles of Skill Acquisition.* New York: Academic Press.

Bizzi, E. (1980). Central and peripheral mechanisms in motor control. In Stelmach, G. E., & Requin, J. (Eds.), *Tutorials in motor behavior.* Amsterdam: North-Holland.

Bizzi, E., Accornero, N., Chapple, W., & Hogan, N. (1982). Arm trajectory formation in monkeys, *Experimental Brain Research, 46,* 139–143.

Bizzi, E., Polit, A., & Morasso, P. (1976). Mechanisms underlying achievement of final head position, *Journal of Neurophysiology, 39,* 435–444.

Bloxham, C. A., Mindel, T. A., & Frith, C. D. (1984). Initiation and execution of predictable and unpredictable movements in Parkinson's disease, *Brain, 107,* 371–384.

Bower, T. G. R. (1974). *Development in infancy.* San Francisco: Freeman.

Bower, T. G. R., Broughton, J. M., & Moore, M. K. (1970a). Demonstration of intention in the reaching behaviour of neonate humans, *Nature, 228,* 679–681.

Bower, T. G. R., Broughton, J. M., & Moore, M. K. (1970b). The coordination of visual and tactual inputs in infants, *Perception and Psychophysics, 8,* 51–53.

Bray, C. W. (1948). *Psychology and military proficiency.* Princeton, NJ: Princeton University Press.

Broadbent, D. E. (1977). Levels, hierarchies and locus of control, *Quarterly Journal of Experimental Psychology, 29*, 181–201.

Brooks, V. B. (1979). Motor programs revisited. In Talbott, R. E., & Humphrey, D. R. (Eds.), *Posture and movement*. New York: Raven Press.

Brown, J. S., & Slater-Hammel, A. T. (1949). discrete movements in the horizontal plane as a function of their length and direction, *Journal of Experimental Psychology, 39*, 84–95.

Brown, T. G. (1911). The intrinsic factors in the act of progression in the mammal, *Proceedings of the Royal Society, London: B, 84*, 308–319.

Bruner, J. S., & Koslowski, B. (1972). Visually preadapted constituents of manipulatory action, *Perception, 1*, 3–14.

Brunnstrom, S. (1970). *Movement therapy in hemiplegia: A neurophysiologic approach*. New York: Harper & Row.

Bryan, W. L., & Harter, N. (1897). Studies in the physiology and psychology of the telegraphic language, *Psychological Review, 4*, 27–53.

Bryant, P. E., Jones, P., Claxton, V., & Perkins, G. M. (1972). Recognition of shapes across modalities by infants, *Nature, 240*, 303–304.

Bucy, P. C, Keplinger, J. E., & Sequeira, E. B. (1964). Destruction of the pyramidal tract in man, *Journal of Neurosurgery, 21*, 385–398.

Burke, D., Gillies, J. D., & Lance, J. W. (1970). The quadriceps stretch reflex in human spasticity, *Journal of Neurology, Neurosurgery and Psychiatry, 33*, 216–233.

Butterworth, G., & Castillo, M. (1976). Co-ordination of auditory and visual space in newborn human infants, *Perception, 5*, 155–160.

Campion, J., Latto, R., & Smith, Y. M. (1983). Is blindsight an effect of scattered light, spared cortex and near threshold vision?, *Behavioral and Brain Sciences, 6*, 423–486.

Carlton, L. G. (1978). Retention characteristics of movement rate information, *Journal of Motor Behavior, 10*, 105–112.

Carlton, L. G. (1980). Movement control characteristics of aiming responses. *Ergonomics, 23*, 1019–1032.

Carlton, L. G. (1981). Processing visual feedback information for movement control, *Journal of Experimental Psychology: Human Perception and Performance, 7*, 1019–1030.

Carson, L. M., & Wiegand, R. L. (1979). Motor schema formation and retention in young children: A test of Schmidt's schema theory, *Journal of Motor Behavior, 11*, 247–251.

Celesia, G. G. Polcyn, R. D., Holden, J. E., Nickles, R. J., Gatley, J. S., & Koeppe, R. A. (1982). Visual evoked potentials and positron emission tomographic mapping of regional cerebral blood flow and cerebral metabolism: Can the neuronal potential generators be visualized?, *Electroencephalography and Clinical Neurophysiology, 54*, 243–256.

Chernikoff, R., & Taylor, F. V. (1952). Reaction time to kinaesthetic stimulation resulting from sudden arm displacement. *Journal of Experimental Psychology, 43*, 1–8.

Cherry, E. C. (1953). Some experiments on the recognition of speech with one and two ears, *Journal of the Acoustical Society of America, 25*, 975–979.

Christina, R. W. (1970). Minimum visual feedback processing time for amendment of an incorrect movement, *Perceptual and Motor Skills, 31*, 991–994.

Cohen, L. (1970). Interaction between limbs during bimanual voluntary activity. *Brain, 93*, 259–272.

Cohen, L. (1971). Synchronous bimanual movements performed by homologous and non-homologous muscles, *Perceptual and Motor Skills, 32*, 639–644.

Colavita, F. B. (1974). Human sensory dominance. *Perception and Psychophysics, 16*, 409–412.

Colavita, F. B., & Weisberg, D. (1979). A further investigation of visual dominance, *Perception and Psychophysics, 25,* 345–347.

Connolly, K. J., & Jones, B. (1970). A developmental study of afferent-reafferent integration, *British Journal of Psychology, 61,* 259–266.

Cooke, J. D. (1980). The organization of simple, skilled movements. In Stelmach, G. E., & Requin, J. (Eds.), *Tutorials in motor behavior.* Amsterdam: North-Holland.

Cordo, P. J., & Nashner, L. M. (1982). Properties of postural adjustments associated with rapid arm movements, *Journal of Neurophysiology, 47,* 287–302.

Craik, K. J. W. (1947). Theory of the human operator in control systems. I. The operator as an engineering system, *British Journal of Psychology, 38,* 56–61.

Crocker, P. R. E. (1982). Encoding specificity in short term memory for movement information: A comment on Lee and Hirota (1980), *Journal of Motor Behavior, 14,* 81–85.

Crossman, E. R. F. W. (1959). A theory of the acquisition of speed-skill. *Ergonomics, 2,* 153–166.

Crossman, E. R. F. W., & Goodeve, P. J. (1963). Feedback control of hand-movement and Fitts' Law, Published in *Quarterly Journal of Experimental Psychology,* (1983) *35A,* 251–278.

Dale, H. H., Feldberg, W., & Vogt, M. (1936). Release of acetylcholine at voluntary motor nerve endings. *Journal of Physiology* (London), *86,* 353–380.

Darwin, C. J. (1976). The perception of speech. In Carterette, E. C., & Friedman, M. P. (Eds.), *Handbook of perception* (Vol 7). New York: Academic Press.

Davenport, R. K., & Rogers, C. M. (1970). Intermodal equivalence of stimuli in apes, *Science, 168,* 279–280.

Deecke, L., Grozinger, B., & Kornhuber, H. H. (1976). Voluntary finger movement in man: Cerebral potentials and theory, *Biological Cybernetics, 23,* 99–119.

Dekaban, A. (1970). *Neurology of early childhood.* Baltimore: Williams & Wilkins.

DeLong, M. R. (1974). Motor functions of the basal ganglia. In Schmitt, F. O., & Worden, F. G. (Eds.), *Neurosciences, Third Study Program.* Cambridge, MA: MIT Press.

DeRenzi, E., Faglioni, P., & Sorgato, P. (1982). Modality-specific and supramodal mechanisms of apraxia, *Brain, 105,* 301–312.

Dichgans, J., & Brandt, T. (1978). Visual-vestibular interaction: Effects on self-motion perception and postural control. In Held, R., Leibowitz, H. W., & Teuber, H. L. (Eds.), *Handbook of sensory physiology: Perception.* New York: Springer-Verlag.

Didday, R. L., & Arbib, M. A. (1975). Eye movements and visual perception: A "two-visual system" model, *International Journal of Man-Machine Studies, 7,* 547–569.

Diewert, G. L. (1975). Retention and coding in motor short-term memory: A comparison of storage codes for distance and location information, *Journal of Motor Behavior, 7,* 183–190.

Di Franco, D., Muir, D., & Dodwell, P. (1978). Reaching in very young infants. *Perception, 7,* 385–392.

Eccles, J. C. (1957). *The physiology of nerve cells.* Baltimore: Johns Hopkins Press.

Eich, J. E. (1977). State-dependent retrieval of information in human episodic memory. In Birnbaum, I. M., & Parker, E. S. (Eds.), *Alcohol and human memory.* Hillsdale, NJ: Erlbaum.

Ellis, A. W. (1982). Spelling and writing (and reading and speaking). In Ellis, A. W. (Ed), *Normality and pathology in cognitive functions.* London: Academic Press.

Ells, J. G. (1973). Analysis of temporal and attentional aspects of movement control, *Journal of Experimental Psychology, 99,* 10–21.

Eshkol, N., & Wachman, A. (1958). *Movement notation.* London: Weidenfeld and Nicolson.

Evans, S. H. (1967). A brief statement of schema theory, *Psychonomic Science, 8,* 87–88.

Evarts, E. V. (1968). Relation of pyramidal tract activity to force exerted during voluntary movement, *Journal of Neurophysiology, 31,* 14–27.

Evarts, E. V. (1973). Motor cortex reflexes associated with learned movements. *Science, 179,* 501–503.

Evarts, E. V., & Tanji, J. (1976). Reflex and intended responses in motor cortex pyramidal tract neurons of monkey, *Journal of Neurophysiology, 39,* 1069–1108.

Evarts, E. V., Teravainen, H. T., & Calne, D. B. (1981). Reaction time in Parkinson's Disease, *Brain, 104,* 167–186.

Ferrier, D. (1886). *The functions of the brain.* London: Smith, Elder.

Festinger, L., & Canon, L. K. (1965). Information about spatial location based on knowledge about efference, *Psychological Review, 72,* 373–384.

Fisher, G. H. (1962). Resolution of spatial conflict, *Bulletin of the British Psychological Society, 46,* 3A.

Fitts, P. M. (1954). The information capacity of the human motor system in controlling the amplitude of movement, *Journal of Experimental Psychology, 47,* 381–391.

Fitts, P. M. (1964). Perceptual-motor skill learning. In Melton, A. W. (Ed.), *Categories of human learning.* New York: Academic Press.

Fitts, P. M., & Peterson, J. R. (1964). Information capacity of discrete motor responses, *Journal of Experimental Psychology, 67,* 103–112.

Flavell, J. H. (1977). *Cognitive development.* Englewood Cliffs, NJ: Prentice-Hall.

Fleishman, E. A., & Rich, S. (1963). Role of kinesthetic and spatial-visual abilities in perceptual motor learning, *Journal of Experimental Psychology, 66,* 6–11.

Flowers K. (1976). Visual "closed-loop" and "open-loop" characteristics of voluntary movements in patients with Parkinsonism and intention tremor, *Brain, 99,* 269–310.

Foley, J. E., & McChesney, J. (1976). The selective utilization of information in the optic array, *Psychological Research, 38,* 251–265.

Fowler, C. A. (1981). Some aspects of language perception by eye: the beginning reader. In Tzeng, O. J. L. & Singer, H. (Eds.), *Perception of print: Reading research in experimental psychology.* Hillsdale, NJ: Erlbaum.

Fowler, C. A., & Turvey, M. T. (1978). Skill acquisition: An event approach with special reference to searching for the optimum of a function of several variables. In Stelmach, G. E. (Ed.), *Information processing in motor control and learning.* New York: Academic Press.

Fowler, S. C., & Notterman, J. M. (1975). An observed short-term memory effect for isometric force emission, *Perception and Psychophysics, 17,* 393–397.

Freedman, S. J. (1968). On the mechanisms of perceptual compensation. In Freedman, S. J. (Ed.), *The neuropsychology of spatially oriented behavior.* Homewood, IL: Dorsey Press.

Freedman, W., Wannstedt, G., & Herman, R. (1976). EMG patterns and forces developed during step-down, *American Journal of Physical Medicine, 55,* 275–290.

Friedman, A., & Campbell Polson, M. (1981). Hemispheres as independent resource systems: Limited-capacity processing and cerebral specialization, *Journal of Experimental Psychology: Human Perception and Performance, 7,* 1031–1058.

Frith, C. D., & Lang, R. J. (1978). Learning and reminiscence as a function of target predictability in a two-dimensional tracking task, *Quarterly Journal of Experimental Psychology, 31,* 103–109.

Fritsch, G., & Hitzig, E. (1870). "Über die elektrische Erregbarkeit des Grosshirns. In G. v. Bonin (Ed.), *Some papers on the cerebral cortex.* Springfield, IL: Thomas, 1960.

Fuchs, A. F., & Kornhuber, H. H. (1969). Extraocular muscle afferents to the cerebellum of the cat, *Journal of Physiology, 200,* 713–722.

Gallistel, C. R. (1980). *The organization of action: A new synthesis.* Hillsdale, NJ: Erlbaum.

Gazzaniga, M. S., Bogen, J. E., & Sperry, R. W. (1967). Dyspraxia following division of the cerebral commisures, *Archives of Neurology, 16,* 606–612.

Gentile, A. M. (1972). A working model of skill acquisition with application to teaching, *Quest, 17,* 3–23.

Gentile, A. M. (1974). Research in short-term motor memory: Methodological mire. In Wade, M. G., & Martens, R. (Eds.), *Psychology of motor behavior and sport.* Urbana, IL: Human kinetics.

Gentner, D. R. (1981). *Skilled finger movements in typing.* Technical Report CHIP104, La Jolla, CA: University of California, San Diego, Center for Human Information Processing.

Gesell, A. (1946). The ontogenesis of infant behavior. In Carmichael, L. (Ed.), *Manual of child psychology.* New York: Wiley & Sons.

Gibb, C. B. (1965). Probability learning in step-input tracking, *British Journal of Psychology, 56,* 233–242.

Gibson, E. J. (1969). *Principles of perceptual learning and development.* New York: Appleton-Century-Crofts.

Gibson, J. J. (1966). *The senses considered as perceptual systems.* Boston: Houghton Mifflin.

Glencross, D. J. (1973). The effects of changes in direction, load, and amplitude of movement on gradation of effort, *Journal of Motor Behavior, 5,* 207–216.

Glencross, D. J. (1975). The effects of changes in task conditions on the temporal organization of a repetitive speed skill, *Ergonomics, 18,* 17–28.

Glencross, D. J. (1977) Control of skilled movements, *Psychological Bulletin, 84,* 14–29.

Glencross, D. J. (1980). Levels and strategies of response organisation. In Stelmach, G. E., & Requin, J. (Eds.), *Tutorials in Motor Behavior.* New York: North-Holland.

Glencross, D. J., & Oldfield, S. R. (1975). The use of ischemic nerve block procedures in the investigation of the sensory control of movements, *Biological Psychology, 2,* 227–236.

Golam, I., Wolgin, D. L., & Teitelbaum, P. (1979). A proposed natural geometry of recovery from akinesia in the lateral hypothalamic rat, *Brain Research, 164,* 237–267.

Greenwald, A. G., & Shulman, H. G. (1973). On doing two things at once. II. Elimination of the psychological refractory period, *Journal of Experimental Psychology, 101,* 70–76.

Griffith, D., & Johnston, W. (1973). An information-processing analysis of visual imagery, *Journal of Experimental Psychology, 100,* 141–146.

Grillner, S. (1975). Locomotion in vertebrates: central mechanisms and reflex interaction, *Physiological Review, 55,* 247–304.

Grillner, S., & Shik, M. L. (1973). On the descending control of the lumbosacral spinal cord from the "mesencephalic locomotor region", *Acta Psychologica Scandinavia, 87,* 320–333.

Grudin, J. T. (1982). *Central control of timing in skilled typing.* Technical Report ONR 8202. La Jolla, CA: University of California, San Diego, Center for Human Information Processing.

Gundry, J. (1975). The use of location and distance in reproducing different amplitudes of movement, *Journal of Motor Behavior, 7,* 91–100.

Gunkel, M. (1962). Über relative Koordination bei willkürlichen menschlichen Gliederbewegungen, *Pflügers Archiv für die gesamte Physiologie, 275,* 472–477.

Hagman, J. D. (1978). Specific-cue effects of interpolated movements on distance and location retention in short-term motor memory, *Memory and Cognition, 6,* 432–437.

Hallberg, G. (1976). A system for the description and classification of movement behaviour, *Ergonomics, 19,* 727–739.

Hallett, M., Shahani, B. T., & Young, R. R. (1975a). EMG analysis of stereotyped voluntary movements in man, *Journal of Neurology, Neurosurgery, and Psychiatry, 38,* 1154–1162.

Hallett, M., Shahani, B. T., & Young, R. R. (1975b). EMG analysis of patients with cerebellar deficits, *Journal of Neurology, Neurosurgery, and Psychiatry, 38,* 1163–1169.

Hallett, M., Shahani, B. T., & Young, R. R. (1977). Analysis of stereotyped voluntary movements at the elbow in patients with Parkinson's disease, *Journal of Neurology, Neurosurgery, and Psychiatry, 40,* 1129–1135.

Hallett, M., & Khoshbin, S. (1980). A physiological mechanism of bradykinesia. *Brain, 103,* 301–314.

Halverson, H. M. (1931). An experimental study of prehension in infants by means of systematic cinema records, *Genetic Psychology Monographs, 10,* 110–286.

Harvey, N., & Greer, K. (1982). Force and stiffness: Further considerations. *Brain and Behavioural Sciences, 5,* 547–548.

Hay, J. C., & Pick, H. L. (1966). Visual and proprioceptive adaptation to optical displacement of the visual stimulus, *Journal of Experimental Psychology, 71,* 150–158.

Hay, L. (1981). The effect of amplitude and accuracy requirements on movement time in children, *Journal of Motor Behavior, 13,* 177–186.

Heilman, K. M., Rothi, L. J., & Valenstein, E. (1982). Two forms of ideomotor apraxia, *Neurology* (NY), *32,* 342–346.

Hein, A., & Held, R. (1967). Dissociation of the visual placing response into elicited and guided components, *Science, 158,* 390–392.

Held, R. (1965). Plasticity in sensory motor systems, *Scientific American, 213,* 84–94.

Helmholtz, H. von. (1866). *Handbuch der physiologischen Optik* (Vol. 3). Leipzig: Voss.

Henderson, S. E. (1975). Predicting the accuracy of a throw without visual feedback, *Journal of Human Movement Studies, 1,* 183–189.

Henry, F. M. (1952). Independence of reaction and movement times and equivalence of sensory motivators of faster response, *Research Quarterly, 23,* 43–53.

Henry, F. M. (1974). Constant and variable performance errors within a group of individuals, *Journal of Motor Behavior, 6,* 149–154.

Henry, F. M. (1980). Use of simple reaction time in motor programming studies: A reply to Klapp, Wyatt and Lingo, *Journal of Motor Behavior, 12,* 163–168.

Henry, F. M., & Rogers, D. E. (1960). Increased response latency for complicated movements and a "memory drum" theory of neuromotor reaction, *Research Quarterly, 31,* 448–458.

Hermelin, B., & O'Connor, N. (1975). Location and distance estimates by blind and sighted children, *Quarterly Journal of Experimental Psychology, 27,* 295–300.

Hick, W. E. (1949). Reaction time for the amendment of a response, *Quarterly Journal of Experimental Psychology, 1,* 175–179.

Higgins, J. R., & Angel, R. W. (1970). Correction of tracking errors without sensory feedback, *Journal of Experimental Psychology, 84,* 412–416.

Hofsten, C. von. (1979). Development of visually directed reaching: The approach phase, *Journal of Human Movement Studies, 5,* 160–178.

Hofsten, C. von. (1980). Predictive reaching for moving objects by human infants, *Journal of Experimental Child Psychology, 30,* 369–382.

Holding, D. H. (1965). *Principles of training.* London: Pergamon Press.

Holmes, G. (1922). Clinical symptoms of cerebellar disease and their interpretation. The Croonian lectures, *Lancet; 1,* 1177–1182, 1231–1237; *2,* 59–65, 111–115.

Holmes, G. (1939). The cerebellum of man, *Brain, 62,* 1–30.

Holst, E. von (1939). Die relative Koordination als Phänomen und als Methode zentralnervöser Funktionsanalyse, *Ergebnisse der Physiologie, 42,* 228–306.

Holst, E. von, & Mittelstadt, H. (1950). Das Reafferenzprinzip. *Naturwissenschaften, 37,* 464–476.

Howarth, C. I. (1978). Strategies in the control of movement. In Underwood, G. (Ed.), *Strategies of information processing*. London: Academic Press.

Howarth, C. I. & Beggs, W. D. A. (1981). Discrete movements. In Holding, D. H. (Ed.), *Human skills*. New York: Wiley.

Howarth, C. I., Beggs, W. D. A., & Bowden, J. M. (1971). The relationship between speed and accuracy of movement aimed at a target, *Acta Psychologica, 35*, 207–218.

Hubbard, A. W., & Seng, C. N. (1954). Visual movements of batters, *Research Quarterly, 25*, 42–57.

Humphrey, D. R. (1972). Relating motor cortex spike trains to measures of motor performance, *Brain Research, 40*, 7–18.

Humphrey, N. K. (1974). Vision in a monkey without striate cortex: A case study, *Perception, 3*, 241–255.

Humphrey, T. (1969). Postnatal repetition of human prenatal activity sequences with some suggestions of their neuroanatomy basis. In Robinson, R. J. (Ed.), *Brain and early behavior*. New York: Academic Press.

James, W. (1890). *The principles of psychology*. New York: Holt.

Johnson, P. (1980). The relative weightings of visual and non-visual coding in a simple motor learning task, *Journal of Motor Behavior, 12*, 281–291.

Johnson, P. (1982). The functional equivalence of imagery and movement, *Quarterly Journal of Experimental Psychology, 34A*, 349–365.

Johnston, W. A., Greenberg, S. N., Fisher, R. P., & Martin, D. W. (1970). Divided attention: A vehicle for monitoring memory processes, *Journal of Experimental Psychology, 83*, 164–171.

Jones, B. (1974a). The role of central monitoring of efference in short-term memory for movements, *Journal of Experimental Psychology, 102*, 37–43.

Jones, B. (1974b). Is proprioception important for skilled performance?, *Journal of Motor Behavior, 6*, 33–45.

Jones, B. (1975). Visual facilitation of auditory localization in schoolchildren: A signal detection analysis. *Perception and Psychophysics, 17*, 217–220.

Jones, B., & Kabanoff, B. (1975). Eye movements in auditory space perception, *Perception and Psychophysics, 17*, 241–245.

Jordan, T. C. (1972). Characteristics of visual and proprioceptive response times in the learning of a motor skill, *Quarterly Journal of Experimental Psychology, 24*, 536–543.

Kahneman, D. (1973). *Attention and effort*. Englewood Cliffs, NJ: Prentice-Hall.

Kahneman, D., & Henik, A. (1981). Perceptual organisation and attention In Kubovy, M. & Pomerantz, J. R. (Eds.), *Perceptual organization*. Hillsdale, NJ: Erlbaum.

Kamon, E., & Gormley, J. (1968). Muscular activity pattern for skilled performance and during learning of a horizontal bar exercise, *Ergonomics, 11*, 345–357.

Keele, S. W. (1968). Movement control in skilled motor performance, *Psychological Bulletin, 70*, 387–402.

Keele, S. W. (1973). *Attention and human performance* Pacific Palisades, CA: Goodyear.

Keele, S. W. (1981). Behavioral analysis of movement. In Brooks, V. B. (Ed.), *Handbook of Physiology, Section 1, The Nervous System, Volume II, Motor Control, Part 2*. Bethesda, MD: American Physiological Society.

Keele, S. W., & Ells, J. G. (1972). Memory characteristics of kinesthetic information, *Journal of Motor Behavior, 4*, 127–134.

Keele, S. W., & Posner, M. I. (1968). Processing visual feedback in rapid movements, *Journal of Experimental Psychology, 77*, 155–158.

Keele, S. W., & Summers, J. J. (1976). The structure of motor programs. In Stelmach, G. E. (Ed.), *Motor control: Issues and trends*. London: Academic press.

Kelso, J. A. S. (1977a). Planning and efferent components in the coding of movement, *Journal of Motor Behavior*, 9, 33–47.

Kelso, J. A. S. (1977b). Motor control mechanisms underlying human movement reproduction, *Journal of Experimental Psychology: Human Perception and Performance*, 3, 529–543.

Kelso, J. A. S. (1981). Contrasting perspectives in order and regulation of movement. In Long, J. & Baddeley, A. (Eds.), *Attention and performance IX*. Hillsdale, NJ: Erlbaum.

Kelso, J. A. S. (Ed.) (1982). *Human motor behavior*. Hillsdale, NJ: Erlbaum.

Kelso, J. A. S., & Frekany, G. A. (1978). Coding processes in preselected and constrained movements: Effects of vision, *Acta Psychologica*, 42, 145–161.

Kelso, J. A. S., & Holt, K. G. (1980). Exploring a vibratory systems analysis of human movement production, *Journal of Neurophysiology*, 43, 1183–1196.

Kelso, J. A. S., Southard, D. L., & Goodman, D. (1979). On the coordination of two-handed movements, *Journal of Experimental Psychology: Human Perception and Performance*, 5, 229–238.

Kelso, J. A. S., & Wallace, S. A. (1978). Conscious mechanisms in movement. In Stelmach, G. E. (Ed.), *Information processing in motor control and learning*. New York: Academic press.

Kenny, F. T., & Craske, B. (1981). The kinaesthetic fusion effect: Perceptual elimination of spatial discordance in kinaesthetic modality, *Perception and Psychophysics*, 30, 211–216.

Kerr, B. A. (1978). Task factors that influence selection and preparation for voluntary movements. In Stelmach, G. E. (Ed.), *Information processing in motor control and learning*. London: Academic Press.

Kimura, D., & Archibald, Y. (1974). Motor functions of the left hemisphere, *Brain*, 97, 337–350.

Kinsbourne, M., & Hicks, R. E. (1978). Functional cerebral space: A model of overflow, transfer and interference effects in human performance: A tutorial review. In Requin, J. (Ed.), *Attention and performance VII*. Hillsdale, NJ: Erlbaum.

Klapp, S. T. (1975). Feedback versus motor programming in the control of aimed movements, *Journal of Experimental Psychology: Human Perception and Performance*, 104, 147–153.

Klapp, S. T. (1980). The memory drum theory after twenty years: Comments on Henry's note, *Journal of Motor Behavior*, 12, 169–171.

Klapp, S. T., & Erwin, I. (1976). Relation between programming time and duration of the response being programmed, *Journal of Experimental Psychology: Human Perception and Performance*, 2, 591–598.

Klapp, S. T., & Wyatt, E. P. (1976). Motor programming within a sequence of responses, *Journal of Motor Behavior*, 8, 19–26.

Klein, R. M. (1976). Attention and movement. In Stelmach, G. E. (Ed.), *Motor control: Issues and trends*. New York: Academic Press.

Klein, R. M. (1977). Attention and visual dominance: A chronometric analysis, *Journal of Experimental Psychology: Human Perception and Performance*, 3, 365–378.

Klein, R. M., & Posner, M. I. (1974). Attention to visual and kinaesthetic components of skills, *Brain Research*, 71, 401–411.

Knust, A. (1979). *A dictionary of kinetography Laban (Labanotation)*. Plymouth, England: MacDonald and Evans.

Kohler, I. (1964). The formation and transformation of the perceptual world. *Psychological Issues*, 3, 1–173.

Kolb, B., & Whishaw, I. Q. (1980). *Fundamentals of human neuropsychology*. San Francisco: Freeman.

Kornhuber, H. H. (1971). Motor functions of cerebellum and basal ganglia: The cerebellocortical saccadic (ballistic) clock, the cerebellonuclear hold regulator, and the basal ganglia ramp (voluntary speed smooth movement) generator, *Kybernetic, 8,* 157–162.

Koupernik, C. (1954). *Le développement psycho-moteur du premier age.* Paris: Presses Universitaires de France.

Kozhevnikov, V. A., & Chistovich, L. A. (1965). *Speech: Articulation and perception.* (Report No. 30543.) Washington, D.C.: U.S. Department of Commerce, Joint Publication Research Services.

Kugler, P. N. K, Kelso, J. A. S., & Turvey, M. T. (1980). On the concept of coordinative structures as dissipative structures: I Theoretical lines of convergence. In Stelmach, G. E., & Requin, J. (Eds.), *Tutorials in motor behavior.* Amsterdam: North Holland.

Laabs, G. J. (1973). Retention characteristics of different reproduction cues in motor short-term memory, *Journal of Experimental Psychology, 100,* 168–177.

Laabs, G. J. (1974). The effect of interpolated motor activity on short-term retention of movement distance and end-location, *Journal of Motor Behavior, 6,* 279–288.

Laabs, G. J., & Simmons, R. W. (1981). Motor memory. In Holding, D. (Ed.), *Human skills.* New York: Wiley.

Lackner, J. R. (1977). Adaptation to visual and proprioceptive rearrangement: Origin of the differential effectiveness of active and passive movements, *Perception and Psychophysics, 21,* 55–59.

Lackner, J. R., & Levine, K. B. (1975). Speech production: Evidence for syntactically and phonologically determined units, *Perception and Psychophysics, 17,* 107–113.

Langolf, G. D., Chaffin, D. B., & Foulke, J. A. (1976). An investigation of Fitts' Law using a wide range of movement amplitudes, *Journal of Motor Behavior, 8,* 113–128.

Lashley, K. S. (1917). The accuracy of movement in the absence of excitation from the moving organ, *American Journal of Physiology, 43,* 169–194.

Lashley, K. S. (1951). The problem of serial order in behavior. In Jeffress, L. A. (Ed.), *Cerebral mechanisms in behavior.* New York: Wiley.

Laszlo, J. I. (1967). Training of fast tapping with reduction of kinesthetic, tactile, visual and auditory sensations, *Quarterly Journal of Experimental Psychology, 19,* 344–349.

Laszlo, J. I., & Ward, G. R. (1978). Vision, proprioception and corollary discharge in a movement recall test, *Acta Psychologica, 42,* 477–493.

Lee, D. N. (1978). The functions of vision. In Pick, H. L., & Saltzman, E. (Eds.), *Modes of perceiving and processing information.* Hillsdale, NJ: Erlbaum.

Lee, D. N. (1980). Visuo-motor coordination in space-time. In Stelmach, G. E., & Requin, J. (Eds.), *Tutorials in motor behaviour.* Amsterdam: North-Holland.

Lee, D. N., & Aronson, E. (1974). Visual proprioceptive control of standing in human infants, *Perception and Psychophysics, 15,* 529–532.

Lee, D. N., & Lishman, J. R. (1975). Visual proprioceptive control of stance. *Journal of Human Movement Studies, 1,* 87–95.

Lee, D. N., Lishman, J. R., & Thomson, J. A. (1982). Regulation of gait in long jumping, *Journal of Experimental Psychology: Human Perception and Performance, 8,* 448–459.

Lee, R. G., & Tatton, W. G. (1978). Long loop reflexes in man: Clinical applications. In Desmedt, J. E. (Ed.), *Cerebral motor control in man: Long loop mechanisms. Progress in clinical neurophysiology,* (vol 4). Basel: Karger.

Lee, T. A., & Hirota, T. T. (1980). Encoding specificity principle in motor short term memory for movement extent, *Journal of Motor Behavior, 12,* 63–67.

Lee, T. A., & Magill, R. A. (1983). The locus of contextual interference in motor skill acquisition, *Journal of Experimental Psychology: Human Learning and Memory, 9,* 730–747.

Lestienne, F., Soechting, J., & Berthoz, A. (1977). Postural readjustments induced by linear motion of visual scenes, *Experimental Brain Research, 28*, 363–384.

Liepmann, H. (1905). Die linke Hemisphäre und das Handeln, *Münchener Medicinischer Wochenschrift, 49*, 2375–2378.

Liepmann, H. (1908). *Drei Aufsätze aus dem Apraxiegebiet.* Berlin: Karger.

Llinas, R. R. (1981). Electrophysiology of the cerebellar networks. In Brooks, V. B. (Ed.), *Handbook of Physiology, Section 1, The Nervous System, Volume II, Motor Control, Part 2.* Bethesda, MD: American Physiological Society.

Long, J., Nimmo-Smith, I., & Whitefield, A. (1983). Skilled typing: A characterisation based on the distribution of times between responses. In Cooper, W. E. (Ed.), *Cognitive aspects of skilled typewriting.* New York: Springer-Verlag.

Luria, A. R. (1963). *Restoration of function after brain injury.* Oxford: Pergamon.

MacKay, D. G. (1971). Stress pre-entry in motor systems, *American Journal of Psychology, 84*, 35–51.

MacKay, D. G. (1973). Aspects of the theory of comprehension, memory and attention, *Quarterly Journal of Experimental Psychology, 25*, 22–40.

MacNeilage, P. F. (1980). Distinctive properties of speech motor control. In Stelmach, G. E., & Requin, J. (Eds.), *Tutorials in motor behavior.* Amsterdam: North-Holland.

Margolin, D., Hammerstad, J., Orwoll, E., McClung, M., & Calhoun, D. (1980). Intracranial calcification in hyperparathyroidism associated with gait apraxia and parkinsonism, *Neurology, 30*, 1005–1007.

Marr, D. (1980). Visual information processing: The structure and creation of visual representations, *Philosophical Transactions of the Royal Society, B290*, 199–218.

Marsden, C. D., Merton, P. A., Morton, H. B., & Adam, J. (1978). The effect of lesions of the central nervous system on long-latency stretch reflexes in the human thumb. In Desmedt, J. E. (Ed.), *Cerebral motor control in man: Long loop mechanisms. Progress in clinical neurophysiology,* (Vol 4). Basel: Karger.

Marsden, C. D., Merton, P. A., & Morton, H. B. (1972). Servo action in human voluntary movement, *Nature, 238*, 140–143.

Marsden, C. D., Merton, P. A., & Morton, H. B. (1976). Servo action in the human thumb, *Journal of Physiology, 257*, 1–44.

Marteniuk, R. G. (1977). Motor short-term memory measures as a function of methodology, *Journal of Motor Behavior, 9*, 247–250.

Marteniuk, R. G., & Rodney, M. (1979). Modality and retention effects in intra- and cross-modal judgments of kinesthetic and visual information, *British Journal of Psychology, 70*, 405–412.

Matthews, P. B. C. (1972). *Mammalian muscle receptors and their central actions.* Baltimore: Williams & Williams.

Mauritz, K. H., Dichgans, J., & Hufschmidt, A. (1979). Quantitative analysis of stance in late cortical cerebellar atrophy of the anterior lobe and other forms of cerebellar ataxia, *Brain, 102*, 461–482.

McCulloch, W. S. (1945). A heterarchy of values determined by the topology of nervous nets, *Bulletin of Mathematical Biophysics, 7*, 89–93.

McCulloch, W. S., & Pitts, W. H. (1943). A logical calculus of the ideas imminent in nervous activity, *Bulletin of Mathematical Biophysics, 5*, 115–133.

McDonnell, P. M. (1975). The development of visually guided reaching, *Perception and Psychophysics, 18*, 181–185.

McDonnell, P. M. (1979). Patterns of eye-hand coordination in the first year of life, *Canadian Journal of Psychology, 33*, 253–267.

McDonnell, P. M., & Abraham, W. C. (1981). A longitudinal study of prism adaptation in infants from six to nine months of age, *Child Development, 52*, 463–469.

McFarland, K., & Ashton, R. (1978). The lateralized effects of concurrent cognitive and motor performance, *Perception and Psychophysics, 23*, 344–349.

McGraw, M. B. (1941). Neural maturation as exemplified in the reaching-prehensile behavior of the human infant, *The Journal of Psychology, 11*, 127–141.

McLellan, D. L. (1977). Co-contraction and stretch reflexes in spasticity during treatment with baclofen, *Journal of Neurology, Neurosurgery and Psychiatry, 40*, 30–38.

McLeod, P. (1977). A dual task response modality effect: Support for multiprocessor models of attention, *Quarterly Journal of Experimental Psychology, 29*, 651–667.

McLeod, P. (1980). What can probe RT tell us about the attentional demands of movement? In Stelmach, G. E., & Requin, J. (Eds.), *Tutorials in motor behavior.* Amsterdam: North-Holland.

Melamed, L. E., Haley, M., & Gildow, J. W. (1973). Effect of external target presence on visual adaptation with active and passive movement, *Journal of Experimental Psychology, 98*, 125–130.

Meyer, D. E., Smith, J. E. K., & Wright, C. E. (1982). Models for the speed and accuracy of aimed limb movements, *Psychological Review, 89*, 449–482.

Meyer, M., & Adorjani, C. (1980). Tonic stretch reflex for quantification of pathological muscle tone. In Feldman, R. G., Young, R. R., & Koella, W. P. (Eds.), *Spasticity: Disordered motor control.* Chicago: Year Book Medical Publishers.

Michaels, C. F. & Carello, C. (1981). *Direct perception.* Englewood Cliffs, NJ: Prentice-Hall.

Millar, S. (1975a). Effects of input conditions on intramodal and cross-modal visual and kinesthetic matches by children, *Journal of Experimental Child Psychology, 19*, 63–78.

Millar, S. (1975b). Spatial memory by blind and sighted children, *British Journal of Psychology, 66*, 449–459.

Miller, G. A. (1956). The magic number seven plus or minus two: Some limits on our capacity for processing information, *Psychological Review, 63*, 81–97.

Miller, R. B. (1953). *Handbook of training and equipment design.* WADC Technical Report, 53–136.

Milner, B. (1962). Les troubles de la memoire accompagnent des lesions hippocampiques bilaterales. In *Physiologie de l'Hippocampie.* Paris: Centre Nationale de al Recherche Scientifique.

Minas, S. (1977). Memory coding for movement, *Perceptual and Motor Skills, 45*, 787–790.

Minsky, M. (1975). A framework for representing knowledge. In Winston, P. H. (Ed.), *The psychology of computer vision.* New York: McGraw-Hill.

Mohler, C. W., & Wurtz, R. (1976). Organisation of monkey superior colliculus: Intermediate layer cells discharging before eye movements, *Journal of Neurophysiology, 39*, 722–724.

Mowrer, O. H. (1960). *Learning theory and behavior.* New York: Wiley.

Muir, D., & Field, J. (1979). Newborn infants orient to sounds, *Child Development, 50*, 431–436.

Muybridge, E. (1899). *Animals in motion.* London: Chapman and Hall.

Nakamura, R., & Taniguchi, R. (1977). Reaction time in patients with cerebral hemiparesis, *Neuropsychologia, 15*, 845–848.

Nashner, L. M. (1970). *Sensory feedback in human posture control.* M.I.T. Reports, MVT–70–3.

Nashner, L. M. (1976). Adapting reflexes controlling the human posture, *Experimental Brain Research, 26*, 59–72.

Navon, D., & Gopher, D. (1979). On the economy of the human processing system, *Psychological Review, 86*, 214–255.

Neisser, U. (1967). *Cognitive psychology.* New York: Appleton-Century-Crofts.

Neisser, U. (1976). *Cognition and reality.* San Francisco: Freeman.

Neisser, U. (1979). The control of information pick-up in selective looking. In Pick, A. D. (Ed.), *Perception and its development: A tribute to Eleanor J. Gibson*. Hillsdale, NJ: Erlbaum.

Neisser, U., & Becklen, R. (1975). Selective looking: Attending to visually specified events, *Cognitive Psychology, 7*, 480–494.

Newell, A., & Rosenbloom, P. S. (1981). Mechanisms of skill acquisition and the law of practice. In Anderson, J. R. (Ed.), *Cognitive skills and their acquisition*. Hillsdale, NJ: Erlbaum.

Newell, K. M. (1981). Skill learning. In Holding, D. H. (Ed.), *Human skills*. New York: Wiley.

Newell, K. M., Carlton, L. G., & Carlton, M. J. (1982). The relationship of impulse to response timing error, *Journal of Motor Behavior, 14*, 24–45.

Newell, K. M., Carlton, L. G., Carlton, M. J., & Halbert, J. A. (1980). Velocity as a factor in movement timing accuracy, *Journal of Motor Behavior, 12*, 47–56.

Newell, K. M., & Shapiro, D. C. (1976). Variability of practice and transfer of training: Some evidence towards a schema view of motor learning, *Journal of Motor Behavior, 8*, 233–243.

Newell, K. M., Shapiro, D. C., & Carlton, M. J. (1979). Coordinating visual and kinesthetic memory codes, *British Journal of Psychology, 70*, 87–96.

Newell, K. M., & Walter, C. B. (1981). Kinematic and kinetic parameters of information feedback in motor skill acquisition, *Journal of Human Movement Studies, 7*, 235–254.

Nichols, T. R., & Houk, J. C. (1976). The improvement in linearity and the regulation of stiffness that results from the actions of the stretch reflex, *Journal of Neurophysiology, 39*, 119–142.

Norman, D. A. (1981). Categorization of action slips, *Psychological Review, 88*, 1–15.

Norman, D. A., & Bobrow, D. G. (1975). On data-limited and resource-limited processes, *Cognitive Psychology, 7*, 44–64.

Norman, D. A., & Rumelhart, D. E. (1983). Studies of typing from the LNR research group. In Cooper, W. E. (Ed.), *Cognitive aspects of skilled typewriting*. New York: Springer Verlag.

Ostry, D., Moray, N., & Marks, G. (1976). Attention, practice and semantic targets. *Journal of Experimental Psychology: Human Perception and Performance, 2*, 326–336.

Paillard, J. (1974). Le traitement des informations spatiales. In *De l'espace corporel a l'espace écologique*. Symposium de l'Association de Psychologie Scientifique de Langue Francaise (Bruxelles, 1972). Paris: Presses Universitaires de France.

Paillard, J., & Beaubaton, D. (1978). De la coordination visuo-motrice a l'organisation de la saisie manuelle. In Hecaen, H., & Jeannerod, M. (Eds.), *Du contrôle moteur à l'organisation du geste*. Paris: Masson.

Paillard, J., Jordan, P., & Brouchon, M. (1981). Visual motion cues in prismatic adaptation: Evidence of two separate and additive processes, *Acta Psychologica, 48*, 253–270.

Patrick, J. (1981). Mode of execution of movement and characteristics of motor short-term memory, *Acta Psychologica, 47*, 117–127.

Penfield, W., & Rasmussen, T. (1950). *The cerebral cortex of man: A clinical study of localization of function*. New York: MacMillan.

Pepper, R. L., & Herman, L. M. (1970). Decay and interference effects in short-term retention of a discrete motor act, *Journal of Experimental Psychology Monograph, 83*, 2..

Pew, R. W. (1966). Acquisition of hierarchical control over the temporal organization of a skill, *Journal of Experimental Psychology, 71*, 764–771.

Pew, R. W. (1974). Human perceptual-motor performance. In Kantowitz, B. H. (Ed.),

Human information processing: Tutorials in performance and cognition. Hillsdale, NJ: Erlbaum.

Piaget, J. (1952). *The origins of intelligence in children.* New York: International Universities Press.

Posner, M. I. (1967). Characteristics of visual and kinesthetic memory codes, *Journal of Experimental Psychology, 75*, 103–107.

Posner, M. I. (1980). The orienting of attention, *Quarterly Journal of Experimental Psychology, 32*, 3–25.

Posner, M. I., Nissen, M. J., & Klein, R. M. (1976). Visual dominance: An information-processing account of its origins and significance, *Psychological Review, 83*, 157–171.

Poulton, E. C. (1957). On prediction in skilled movements, *Psychological Bulletin, 80*, 113–121.

Poulton, E. C. (1981). Human manual control. In Brooks, V. B. (Ed.), *Handbook of physiology, section 1, the nervous system, volume II, motor control, part 2.* Bethesda, MD: American Physiological Society.

Povel, D. J., & Collard, R. (1982). Structural factors in patterned finger tapping, *Acta Psychologica, 52*, 107–125.

Power, R. P. (1980). The dominance of touch by vision: Sometimes incomplete, *Perception, 9*, 457–466.

Power, R. P. (1981). The dominance of touch by vision: Occurs with familiar objects, *Perception, 10*, 29–33.

Power, R. P., & Graham, A. (1976). Dominance of touch by vision: Generalization of the hypothesis to a tactually experienced population, *Perception, 5*, 161–166.

Rabbitt, P. M. A. (1966). Error correction time without external error signals, *Nature, 212*, 438.

Rabbitt, P. M. A. (1971). Times for analyzing stimuli and related responses, *British Medical Bulletin, 27*, 259–265.

Rabbitt, P. M. A. (1981). Sequential reactions. In Holding D. H. (Ed.), *Human Skills.* New York: Wiley.

Radeau, M., & Bertelson, P. (1974). The after-effects of ventriloquism, *Quarterly Journal of Experimental Psychology, 26*, 63–71.

Reason, J. T. (1977). Skill and error in everyday life. In Howe, M. J. A. (Ed.), *Adult learning.* Chichester: Wiley.

Reason, J. T. (1979). Actions not as planned. In Underwood, G., & Stevens, R. (Eds.), *Aspects of consciousness.* London: Academic Press.

Reason, J. T., & Brand, J. J. (1975). *Motion sickness.* London: Academic Press.

Reason, J. T., Wagner, H., & Dewhurst, D. (1981). A visually driven postural after-effect, *Acta Psychologica, 48*, 241–251.

Restle, F., & Burnside, B. L. (1972). Tracking of serial patterns, *Journal of Experimental Psychology, 95*, 299–307.

Richardson, A. (1967a). Mental practice: A review and discussion. Part 1., *Research Quarterly, 38*, 95–107.

Richardson, A. (1967b). Mental practice: A review and discussion. Part 2., *Research Quarterly, 38*, 263–273.

Rock, I. (1966). *The nature of perceptual adaptation.* New York: Basic Books.

Roland, P. E. (1978). Sensory feedback to the cerebral cortex during voluntary movement in man, *Behavioural and Brain Sciences, 1*, 129–171.

Rondot, P., De Recondo, J., & Ribadeau Dumas, J. L. (1977). Visuomotor ataxia, *Brain, 100*, 355–376.

Rondot, P., & Bathien, N. (1978). Pathophysiology of parkinsonian tremor. In Desmedt, J. E. (Ed.), *Physiological tremor, pathological tremors and clonus*. Basel: Karger.

Rosenbaum, D. A. (1977). Selective adaptation of "command neurons" in the human motor system, *Neuropsychologia, 15*, 81–92.

Rosenbaum, D. A. (1980). Human movement initiation: Specification of arm, direction, and extent, *Journal of Experimental Psychology: General, 109*, 444–474.

Rosenbaum, D. A., Kenny, S. B., & Derr, M. A. (1983). Hierarchical control of rapid movement sequences, *Journal of Experimental Psychology: Human Perception and Performance, 9*, 86–102.

Rosenbaum, D. A., & Patashnik, O. (1980). A mental clock setting process revealed by reaction times. In Stelmach, G. E., & Requin, J. (Eds.), *Tutorials in motor behavior*. Amsterdam: North-Holland.

Rothstein, A. L., & Arnold, R. K. (1976). Bridging the gap: Applications of research on videotape feedback and bowling. *Motor skills: Theory and Practice, 1*, 35–62.

Rothwell, J. C., Traub, M. M., Day, B. L., Obeso, J. A., Thomas, P. K., & Marsden, C. D. (1982). Manual motor performance in a deafferented man, *Brain, 105*, 515–542.

Roy, E. A. (1977). Spatial cues in memory for movement, *Journal of Motor Behavior, 9*, 151–156.

Roy, E. A. (1978). Role of preselection in memory for movement extent, *Journal of Experimental Psychology: Human Learning and Memory, 4*, 397–405.

Roy, E. A., & Diewert, G. L. (1975). Encoding of kinesthetic extent information, *Perception and Psychophysics, 17*, 559–564.

Roy, E. A., & Diewert, G. L. (1978). The coding of movement extent information, *Journal of Human Movement Studies, 4*, 94–101.

Rudel, R. G., & Teuber, H. L. (1964). Pattern recognition within and across modalities in normal and brain-injured children, *Neuropsychologia, 2*, 1–18.

Ruff, H., & Halton, A. (1978). Is there directed reaching in the human neonate? *Developmental Psychology, 14*, 425–426.

Rumelhart, D. E., & Norman, D. A. (1982). Simulating a skilled typist: A study of skilled cognitive-motor performance, *Cognitive Science, 6*, 1–36.

Sahrmann, S. A., & Norton, B. J. (1977). The relationship of voluntary movement to spasticity in the upper motor neuron syndrome, *Annals of Neurology, 2*, 460–465.

Salmoni, A. W., & Sullivan, S. J. (1976). The intersensory integration of vision and kinesthesis for distance and location cues, *Journal of Human Movement Studies, 2*, 225–232.

Salmoni, A. W., Sullivan, S. J., & Starkes, J. L. (1976). The attention demands of movement: A critique of the probe technique, *Journal of Motor Behavior, 8*, 161–169.

Schmidt, R. A. (1969). Movement time as a determiner of timing accuracy, *Journal of Experimental Psychology, 79*, 43–47.

Schmidt, R. A. (1975). A schema theory of discrete motor skill learning. *Psychological Review, 82*, 225–260.

Schmidt, R. A. (1976). The schema as a solution to some persistent problems in motor learning theory. In Stelmach G. E. (Ed.), *Motor control: Issues and trends*. London: Academic Press.

Schmidt, R. A., & Gordon, G. B. (1977). Errors in motor responding, "rapid" corrections, and false anticipations, *Journal of Motor Behavior, 9*, 101–112.

Schmidt, R. A., & McCabe, J. F. (1976). Motor program utilization over extended practice, *Journal of Human Movement Studies, 2*, 239–247.

Schmidt, R. A., & McGown, C. (1980). Terminal accuracy of unexpectedly loaded rapid movements: Evidence for a mass-spring mechanism in programming, *Journal of Motor Behavior, 12*, 149–161.

Schmidt, R. A., Zelaznik, H. N., & Frank, J. S. (1978). Sources of inaccuracy in rapid movement. In Stelmach, G. E. (Ed.), *Information processing in motor control and learning.* London: Academic Press.

Schmidt, R. A., Zelaznik, H. N., Hawkins, B., Frank, J. S., & Quinn, J. T., Jr. (1979). Motor-output variability: A theory for the accuracy of rapid motor acts, *Psychological Review, 86*, 415–451.

Schneider, G. E. (1969). Two visual systems, *Science, 163*, 895–902.

Schouten, J. F., Kalsbeek, J. W. H., & Leopold, F. F. (1962). On the evaluation of perceptual and mental load, *Ergonomics, 5*, 251–260.

Schutz, R. W. (1977). Absolute, constant and variable error: Problems and solutions. In Mood, D. (Ed.), *Proceedings of the Colorado Measurement Conference.* Boulder, CO: University of Colorado.

Schutz, R. W., & Roy, E. A. (1973). Absolute error: The devil in disguise, *Journal of Motor Behavior, 5*, 141–153.

Seashore, H., & Bavelas, A. (1941). The functioning of knowledge of results in Thorndike's line-drawing experiment, *Psychological Review, 48*, 155–164.

Shaffer, L. H. (1976). Intention and performance, *Psychological Review, 83*, 375–393.

Shaffer, L. H. (1981). Performances of Chopin, Bach and Bartok: Studies in motor programming, *Cognitive Psychology, 13*, 327–376.

Shapiro, D. C., Zernicke, R. F., Gregor, R. J., & Diestel, J. D. (1981). Evidence for generalized motor programs using gait pattern analysis, *Journal of Motor Behavior, 13*, 33–47.

Sharp, R. H., & Whiting, H. T. A. (1974). Exposure and occluded duration effects in a ball-catching skill, *Journal of Motor Behavior, 6*, 139–147.

Sharp, R. H., & Whiting, H. T. A. (1975). Information-processing and eye movement behavior in a ball-catching skill, *Journal of Human Movement Studies, 1*, 124–131.

Shea, J. B. (1977). Effects of labelling on motor short-term memory, *Journal of Experimental Psychology: Human Learning and Memory, 3*, 92–99.

Shea, J. B., & Morgan, R. L. (1979). Contextual interference effects on the acquisition, retention and transfer of a motor skill, *Journal of Experimental Psychology: Human Learning and Memory, 5*, 179–187.

Shea, J. B., & Zimny, S. T. (1983). Context effects in memory and learning movement information. In Magill, R. A. (Ed.), *Memory and control of action.* Amsterdam: North Holland.

Shelton, B. R., & Searle, C. L. (1980). The influence of vision on the absolute identification of sound-source position, *Perception and Psychophysics, 28*, 589–596.

Sheridan, M. R. (1979). A reappraisal of Fitts' Law, *Journal of Motor Behavior, 11*, 179–188.

Sheridan, M. R. (1981). Response programming and reaction time, *Journal of Motor Behavior, 13*, 161–176.

Sheridan, M. R. (1984). Response programming, response production, and fractionated reaction time, *Psychological Research, 46*, 33–47.

Sherrington, C. S. (1906). *The integrative action of the nervous system.* New Haven, CT: Yale Univ Press.

Shik, M. L, Severin, F. V., & Orlovsky, G. N. (1966). Control of walking and running by means of electrical stimulation of the mid-brain, *Bifizika, 11*, 659–666.

Skoglund, S. (1973). Joint reception and kinaesthesis. In Iggo, A. (Ed.), *Handbook of sensory physiology: Somatosensory system* (Vol. 2). Berlin & New York: Springer Verlag.

Smith, S. M. (1979). Remembering in and out of context, *Journal of Experimental Psychology: Human Learning and Memory, 5*, 460–471.

Smith, W. M., & Bowen, K. F. (1980). The effects of delayed and displaced visual feedback on motor control, *Journal of Motor Behavior, 12*, 91–101.

Smyth, M. M. (1978). Attention to visual feedback in motor learning, *Journal of Motor Behavior, 10*, 185–190.

Smyth, M. M. (1980). Visual bias in guided and preselected movements, *Acta Psychologica, 44*, 1–19.

Smyth, M. M., & Marriott, A. M. (1982). Vision and proprioception in simple catching, *Journal of Motor Behavior, 14*, 143–152.

Snoddy, G. S. (1926). Learning and stability, *Journal of Applied Psychology, 10*, 1–36.

Stein, R. B. (1982). What muscle variable(s) does the nervous system control in limb movements?, *Behavioural and Brain Sciences, 5*, 535–541.

Stelmach, G. E., Kelso, J. A. S., & Wallace, S. A. (1975). Preselection in short-term motor memory, *Journal of Experimental Psychology: Human Learning and Memory, 1*, 745–755.

Sternberg, S., Monsell, S., Knoll, R. L., & Wright, C. E. (1978). The latency and duration of rapid movement sequences. Comparisons of speech and typewriting. In Stelmach, G. E. (Ed.), *Information processing in motor control and learning*. London: Academic Press.

Stratton, G. M. (1897). Some preliminary experiments in vision without inversion of the retinal in age, *Psychological Review, 4*, 182–187, 341–360, 363–481.

Summers, J. J. (1975). The role of timing in motor program representation, *Journal of Motor Behavior, 7*, 229–241.

Summers, J. J., Levey, A. J., & Wrigley, W. J. (1981). The role of planning and efference in the recall of location and distance cues in short-term motor memory, *Journal of Motor Behavior, 13*, 65–76.

Summers, J. J., & Sharp, C. A. (1979). Bilateral effects of concurrent verbal and spatial rehearsal on complex motor sequencing, *Neuropsychologia, 17*, 331–343.

Telford, C. W. (1931). The refractory phase of voluntary and associative responses, *Journal of Experimental Psychology, 14*, 1–36.

Teuber, H. L. (1974). Key problems in the programming of movements, *Brain Research, 71*, 533–568.

Thach, W. T. (1970). Discharge of cerebellar neurons related to two maintained postures and two prompt movements (II), *Journal of Neurophysiology, 33*, 537–547.

Thach, W. T. (1978). Correlation of neural discharge with pattern and force of muscular activity, joint position, and direction of the intended movement in motor cortex and cerebellum, *Journal of Neurophysiology, 41*, 654–676.

Thelen, E. (1983). Learning to walk is still an "old" problem: A reply to Zelazo (1983). *Journal of Motor Behavior, 15*, 139–161.

Thomson, D. M., & Tulving, E. (1970). Associative encoding and retrieval: Weak and strong cues, *Journal of Experimental Psychology, 6*, 255–262.

Thorndike, E. L. (1911). *Animal intelligence*. New York: MacMillan.

Treisman, A. M. (1960). Contextual cues in selective listening, *Quarterly Journal of Experimental Psychology, 12*, 242–248.

Treisman, A. M., & Geffen, G. (1967). Selective attention: Performance or response?, *Quarterly Journal of Experimental Psychology, 19*, 1–17.

Trevarthen, C. B. (1968). Two mechanisms of vision in primates, *Psychologische Forschung, 31*, 299–337.

Trevarthen, C., Hubley, P., & Sheeran, L. (1975). Les activités innées du nourrisson, *La Recherche, 6*, 447–458.

Trumbo, D., & Milone, F. (1971). Primary task performance as a function of encoding, retention and recall in a secondary task, *Journal of Experimental Psychology, 91*, 273–279.

Tulving, E. (1972). Episodic and semantic memory. In Tulving, E., & Donaldson, W. (Eds.), *Organization of memory*. New York: Academic Press.

Tulving, E., & Donaldson, W. (Eds.). (1972). *Organization of memory*. New York: Academic Press.

Turvey, M. T. (1977). Preliminaries to a theory of action with reference to vision. In Shaw, R., & Bransford, J. (Eds.), *Perceiving, Acting and Knowing: Toward an ecological Psychology*. Hillsdale, New Jersey: Erlbaum.

Turvey, M. T., Shaw, R. E., & Mace, W. (1978). Issues in the theory of action: degrees of freedom, coordinative structures and coalitions. In Requin, J. (Ed), *Attention and Performance VII*. Hillsdale, NJ: Erlbaum.

Turvey, M. T., Fitch, H. L., & Tuller, B. (1982). The Bernstein perspective: I. The problem of degrees of freedom and context-conditioned variability. In Kelso, J. A. S. (Ed.), *Human motor behavior: An introduction*. Hillsdale, N.J.: Erlbaum.

Twitchell, T. E. (1951). The restoration of motor function following hemiplegia in man, *Brain, 74*, 443–480.

Tyldesley, D. A., & Whiting, H. T. A. (1975). Operational timing, *Journal of Human Movement Studies, 1*, 172–177.

Vallbo, A. B. (1971). Muscle spindle response at the onset of isometric voluntary contractions in man. Time difference between fusimotor and skeltomotor effects, *Journal of Physiology, 218*, 405–431.

Vilis, T. J, Hore, J, Meyer-Lohman, J, & Brooks, V. B. (1976). Dual nature of the precentral responses to limb perturbations revealed by cerebellar cooling, *Brain Research, 117*, 336–340.

Vince, M. A. (1948). The intermittency of control movements and the psychological refractory period, *British Journal of Psychology, 38*, 149–157.

Vince, M. A. (1949). Rapid response sequences and the psychological refractory period, *British Journal of Psychology, 40*, 23–40; *Naturwissenschaften, 37*, 464–476.

Vorberg, D., & Hambuch, R. (1984). Timing of two-handed rhythmic performance. *Proceedings of the New York Academy of Sciences* (in press)

Vredenbregt, J., & Koster, W. G. (1971). Analysis and synthesis of handwriting, *Philips Technical Review, 32*, 73–78.

Wachholder, K., & Altenburger, H. (1926). Beitrage zur Physiologie der willkurlichen Bewegung. 10. Enzelbewegungen, *Pflugers archiv die Gesamte Physiologie des Menschen und der Tiere, 214*, 642–661.

Wakelin, D. R. (1967). The role of the response in psychological refractoriness, *Acta Psychologica, 40*, 163–175.

Walker, J. T., & Scott, K. J. (1981). Auditory-visual conflicts in the perceived duration of lights, tones and gaps, *Journal of Experimental Psychology: Human Perception and Performance, 7*, 1327–1339.

Wallace, B., & Garrett, J. B. (1973). Reduced felt arm sensation effects on visual adaptation, *Perception and Psychophysics, 14*, 597–600.

Wallace, S. A. (1977). The coding of location: A test of the target hypothesis, *Journal of Motor Behavior, 9*, 157–159.

Walsh, W. D., Russell, D. G., Imanaka, K., & James, B. (1979). Memory for constrained and preselected movement location and distance: Effects of starting position and length, *Journal of Motor Behavior, 11*, 201–214.

Warren, D. H. (1970). Intermodality interactions in spatial localisation, *Cognitive Psychology, 1*, 114–133.

Warren, D. H., & Schmitt, T. L. (1978). On the plasticity of visual-proprioceptive bias effects, *Journal of Experimental Psychology: Human Perception and Performance, 4*, 302–310.

Watson, R. T., & Heilman, K. M. (1983). Callosal apraxia, *Brain*, *106*, 391–403.

Weiskrantz, L. (1980). Varieties of residual experience, *Quarterly Journal of Experimental Psychology*, *32*, 365–386.

Weiskrantz, L., Warrington, E. K., Sanders, M. D., & Marshall, J. (1974), Visual capacity in the hemianopic field following a restricted cortical ablation, *Brain*, *97*, 709–728.

Welch, R. B. (1978). *Perceptual modification: Adapting to altered sensory environments.* New York: Academic Press.

Welch, R. B., & Rhoades, R. W. (1969). The manipulation of informational feedback and its effects upon prism adaptation, *Canadian Journal of Psychology*, *23*, 415–428.

Welford, A. T. (1967). Single-channel operation in the brain, *Acta Psychologica*, *27*, 5–22.

Welford, A. T. (1968). *Fundamentals of skill.* London: Methuen.

Welford, A. T. (1980). The single-channel hypothesis. In Welford, A. T. (Ed.), *Reaction times.* London: Academic Press.

Wertheimer, M. (1961). Psychomotor co-ordination of auditory-visual space at birth, *Science*, *134*, 1692.

Whitaker, L. A., & Trumbo, D. (1976). Scaling estimates of amplitude for movements without visual guidance, *Journal of Motor Behavior*, *8*, 75–82.

White, B. L. (1970). Experience and the development of motor mechanisms in infancy. In Connolly, K. (Ed.), *Mechanisms of motor skill development.* New York: Academic Press.

White, B. L., Castle, P., & Held, R. (1964). Observations on the development of visually directed reaching, *Child Development*, *35*, 349–364.

Whiting, H. T. A. (1980). Dimensions of control in motor learning. In Stelmach, G. E., & Requin, J. (Eds.), *Tutorials in motor behavior.* Amsterdam: North-Holland.

Wilson, D. M. (1961). The central nervous control of flight in a locust, *Journal of Experimental Biology*, *38*, 471–490.

Wilson, S. A. K. (1925). Some disorders of mobility and muscle tone with special reference to the corpus striatum, *Lancet*, *2*, 1, 53, 169, 215, 268.

Wing, A. M. (1973). *The timing of interresponse intervals by human subjects.* Unpublished Ph.D. thesis. Hamilton, Ontario: McMaster University.

Wing, A. M. (1977). Perturbations of auditory feedback delay and the timing of movement, *Journal of Experimental Psychology: Human Perception and Performance*, *3*, 175–186.

Wing, A. M. (1980). The height of handwriting, *Acta Psychologica*, *46*, 141–151.

Wing, A. M., & Fraser, C. (1983). The contribution of the thumb to reaching movements, *Quarterly Journal of Experimental Psychology*, *35A*, 297–309.

Wing, A. M., & Kristofferson, A. B. (1973). The timing of interresponse intervals, *Perception and Psychophysics*, *13*, 455–460.

Wishart, J. G., Bower, T. G. R., & Dunkeld, J. (1978). Reaching in the dark. *Perception*, *7*, 507–512.

Wong, S. C. P., & Frost, B. J. (1978). Subjective motion and acceleration induced by the movement of the observers' entire visual field, *Perception and Psychophysics*, *24*, 115–120.

Woodworth, R. S. (1899). The accuracy of voluntary movement, *Psychological Review Monograph Supplements*, *3*, No. 3.

Woodworth, R. S. (1938). *Experimental psychology.* New York: Holt.

Wundt, W. (1912). *An introduction to psychology.* London: George Allen.

Yakovlev, P. I. (1962). Morphological criteria of growth and maturation of the nervous system in man, *Association for Research in Neurons and Mental Diseases. Research Publications*, *39*, 3–46.

Yakovlev, P. I., & Lecours, A. R. (1967). The myelogenetic cycles of reginal maturation of the brain. In Minkowski, A. (Ed.), *Regional development of the brain in early life.* Oxford: Blackwell.

Yarbus, A. L. (1967). *Eye movements and vision.* New York: Plenum Press.

Zelazo, P. R. (1983). The development of walking: New findings and old assumptions, *Journal of Motor Behavior, 15,* 99–137.

Zelazo, P. R., Zelazo, N. A., & Kolb, S. (1972). "Walking" in the newborn, *Science, 176,* 314–315.

Author Index

327

Subject Index